Honolulu

HAWAII IS

20°

MERCATOR PROJECTION

SCALE

MILES

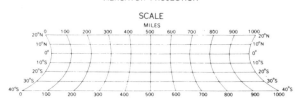

| 20°N | 0 | 100 | 200 | 300 | 400 | 500 | 600 | 700 | 800 | 900 | 1000 | 20°N |

hington
anning

Christmas

0°

vis

. Malden

Starbuck

eva

Vostok .   . Caroline

Nukuhiva

Hiva Oa   MARQUESAS IS

Tahuata

Flint

T U A M O T U   A R C H I P E L A G O

Borabora

Raiatea   Papeete

Napuka

tutaki   SOCIETY IS   Tahiti

Mauke

20°

arotonga

AUSTRAL IS

Tubuai

Hereheretue

Mangareva

Pitcairn

Rapa .

140°

The Changing Pacific

H. E. Maude

The
Changing
Pacific

ESSAYS IN HONOUR OF

H. E. Maude

EDITED BY NIEL GUNSON

1978

Melbourne
OXFORD UNIVERSITY PRESS
OXFORD   WELLINGTON   NEW YORK

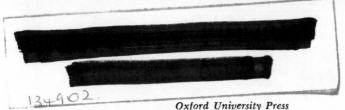

134902

Oxford University Press

OXFORD LONDON GLASGOW
NEW YORK TORONTO MELBOURNE WELLINGTON
IBADAN NAIROBI DAR ES SALAAM LUSAKA CAPE TOWN
KUALA LUMPUR SINGAPORE JAKARTA HONG KONG TOKYO
DELHI BOMBAY CALCUTTA MADRAS KARACHI

This book is published with the assistance of
a special fund administered by the Department
of Pacific and Southeast Asian History of the
Australian National University.

© *Oxford University Press 1978*

First published 1978

NATIONAL LIBRARY OF AUSTRALIA CATALOGUING IN
PUBLICATION DATA

The changing Pacific.
Index.
Bibliography.
ISBN 0 19 550518 2.

*1. Oceanica—Social conditions—Addresses, essays,
lectures. I. Gunson, Walter Niel, ed.*

301.299

PRINTED IN AUSTRALIA BY BROWN PRIOR ANDERSON PTY LTD
PUBLISHED BY OXFORD UNIVERSITY PRESS, 7 BOWEN CRESCENT
MELBOURNE

Contents

Illustrations

ABBREVIATIONS

A.A.	*American Anthropologist,* Menasha, Wisconsin
A.B.C.F.M.	American Board of Commissioners for Foreign Missions, Boston
A.N.U.	The Australian National University, Canberra
H.&F.R.	*Home and Foreign Record of the Presbyterian Church of the Lower Provinces of British North America,* Halifax
H.R.A.	*Historical Records of Australia*
J.P.H.	*The Journal of Pacific History,* Canberra
J.P.S.	*Journal of the Polynesian Society,* Wellington
L.M.S.	London Missionary Society; L.M.S. archives, now Archives of the Council for World Mission, in the Library, School of Oriental and African Studies, University of London
M.L.	Mitchell Library, Sydney
M.R.	*The Missionary Register of the Presbyterian Church of Nova Scotia,* Halifax
N.L.	National Library of Australia, Canberra
N.M.	*The Nautical Magazine and Naval Chronicle,* Glasgow
P.I.M.	*Pacific Islands Monthly,* Sydney
R.P.M.	*The Reformed Presbyterian Magazine,* Edinburgh, formerly (until 1854) *The Scottish Presbyterian,* Glasgow
S.P.C.	South Pacific Commission

Introduction

Twenty years ago Harry Maude joined the Department of Pacific History at the Australian National University. I am now the only member of the Department as it then was who was present when he arrived, and I look back fondly to the intellectual stimulation of Harry's joining us. As a post-graduate student with little practical experience of the Pacific Islands I learnt much of Pacific peoples and places from listening to the exchange of anecdotes and memorabilia between Professor J. W. (Jim) Davidson, R. P. (Dick) Gilson and Harry. It seemed that there was not a figure of consequence in the Pacific Islands, either islander or expatriate, whom they did not know personally, and I was flattered that they assumed I was equally knowledgeable when all too often I had to brief myself surreptitiously. Later, when I made my first field trip to the Gilbert and Ellice Islands in 1957, I felt I knew Harry and his wife, Honor, much better through the many appreciative references to their residence in those islands by my local hosts and informants.

Harry Maude soon became an institution in the Department. Though self-effacing and almost elusive he quickly became a focal person for all scholars working in the field of Pacific studies—not only historians but also anthropologists, prehistorians, demographers, geographers and political scientists sought him out for bibliographical information, leads for their own work, and general advice. His extensive library, now housed in the Barr Smith Library, University of Adelaide, was placed at the disposal of all his visitors and he shared his material generously. Perhaps too generously, for many of Harry's ideas and thoughtful advances have appeared in the papers and books of other scholars, usually with his blessing, but sometimes without acknowledgement — and his work has even been plagiarized. Not that Harry has seemed to mind since he always conveyed the impression that he was only interested in the advance of knowledge, not in how the information was made available. Much of his time, particularly after returning home from the University, was spent in answering his extensive circle of correspondents on islands subjects. Many of the contributors to this book have valued this correspondence as being vital to their own research.

In at least three ways outside his specific research interests Harry Maude has made a significant contribution to the discipline of Pacific history. First, in the field of publications and publicizing Pacific history he has been the initiator of many schemes to inform the world at large and the islanders themselves of their historical-cultural heritage. Over many years Harry has been in-

volved with South Pacific Commission and U.N.E.S.C.O. programmes to foster vernacular literature. At the Australian National
University he was largely responsible for initiating the Pacific
History series of monographs and together with Jim Davidson he
founded and edited *The Journal of Pacific History,* doing most of
the promotion work himself and taking general responsibility for
the manuscripts and publications sections of the *Journal.* The
features which he initiated have been highly valued by librarians
and researchers alike.

Second, he has been a pioneer in the field of bibliographical
promotion and manuscript collection. Through his encouragement
several valuable bibliographies such as Philip Snow's *Bibliography
of Fiji, Tonga and Rotuma* have been published, and the Pacific
Manuscripts Bureau, managed by Robert Langdon at the Australian National University, was his brain-child.

Third, and perhaps more important than these visible achievements, has been Harry Maude's influence at an academic level.
Although his own academic background was eminently respectable
Harry appeared sometimes to be a little unsure of his identity in
academia. Although made to feel at home in Davidson's informal
community of scholars, he retained a healthy independence from
the preoccupations and display savantry endemic in the closed
walls of universities. His official calling had been proconsular and
administrative, his heart's calling was the pursuit of interests
developed in the islands, and Davidson had given him the opportunity of furthering his research. It was Davidson's gift that
although he was himself a scholar of traditional mould with
developed interests in colonial history and contemporary politics,
he had the sensitivity and perception to see that there was a whole
unexplored world of culture-contact and pre-European history in
the Pacific with its own methodology and rationale.

That Harry Maude responded to the opportunity provided
him is evident from the new emphasis which developed in the
Department. Whereas Davidson believed Pacific historians should
be concerned with the problems of islanders rather than the
problems of colonial powers his own advances in that direction
did not go beyond participant history. With Maude it was different. While Harry also wrote participant history he came to be
primarily interested in the cross-cultural dimension of Pacific
history. He early claimed the American movement into 'ethnohistory' as the parallel of his own interests and borrowed the term.
His influence on and encouragement of scholars such as the
Crocombes, Dening and others was apparent. It is no doubt significant that through his contributions, and also the editorship of
Murray Groves, the *Journal of the Polynesian Society* became an
acceptable medium of publication for the Pacific historian. Hither-

to Pacific history had largely been confined to the exclusively historical journals.

Harry's hope that the history of the Pacific Islands would one day be written by Pacific Islanders themselves as well as by expatriates is one with which we can sympathize, and it reflects his emphasis on the importance of indigenous source material, both written vernacular and oral. His essay into Rarotongan history with Marjorie Tuainekore Crocombe was a significant pilot study in showing the importance of drawing on the skills of historically-minded islanders, and Marjorie Crocombe's own practice as a historian owes much to that experience. It is perhaps fitting that this book closes with a chapter in which island-born scholars have combined with an expatriate scholar in elucidating the story of their past.

When Harry Maude retired from the Department of Pacific History and from his position as co-editor of *The Journal of Pacific History,* his colleagues and friends planned to present him with a *Festschrift* to be edited by the late Professor Davidson. Following Jim Davidson's untimely death I agreed to carry on this project. For various reasons it was decided to limit invitations to those scholars here represented, mostly senior colleagues working in the kindred fields of Pacific history, anthropology and prehistory with a vital concern with the kind of changes in the Pacific which have interested Harry.

With Harry's own classic study of the Gilbertese *boti* in mind contributors were asked to select an institution or distinctive social feature, preferably a central one, in a Pacific culture and trace its evolution in the culture-contact situation. Those not at home in this field were able to select other topics in Harry's field of interest which would contribute to a view of changing society in the Pacific Islands. The response was excellent. A number of distinguished scholars, Professor R. G. Crocombe, Mrs Marjorie Crocombe, Professor William Davenport, Dr Ernest S. Dodge, Professor Sir Raymond Firth, Professor Murray Groves, Dr Gerd Koch, Father Patrick O'Reilly and Professor Saul Riesenberg, all would have liked to contribute but their already heavy commitments did not allow this in 1975-76. They were unanimous in recording their friendship with Harry and their respect for his work. Professor Jack Golson actually prepared a paper on the history of the sweet potato in the New Guinea Highlands, but regretfully felt that it should not be published until further experiments could be carried out.

A number of other friends and colleagues, on hearing of the *Festschrift,* wrote expressing their willingness to assist. It is hoped that those not invited to contribute will realize that it was not possible to plan a book which would cater for the interests of all

of Harry's wide circle. Harry's former Ph.D. students in particular
join with me and the present members of the Department of
Pacific and Southeast Asian History in offering this garland of
scholarly papers to Harry on his seventieth birthday. In another
sense their own work is a continuing *Festschrift,* reflecting as it
does Harry's interests and his influence on their approach to
scholarly problems in the Pacific.

In editing this volume my main concern has been to standardize
the text in the interests of internal consistency and balance of
contributions. Words from islands languages have been italicized
except when used as titles (frequently hybridized forms such as
luluai) or borrowed in the English language (e.g. mana). Capitaliza-
tion has been avoided as much as possible and glottal stops and
other linguistic points have been confined to those languages where
their usage has become official. Proper names of islands generally
follow the spelling of the editors of the *Geographical Handbook
Series* published by the Naval Intelligence Division of the British
Admiralty in 1945 except where the island governments concerned
have given official rulings since that date.

I must here thank the contributors for their assistance in completing their papers expeditiously and sometimes under unfavour-
able conditions. More than one paper was partly written in the
field. Even at this time, as the copy goes to the publishers, two of
the contributors are involved in the historic trip of Hawaii's
voyaging canoe *Hokule'a* on its way to Tahiti and another has
gone ahead to prepare for the canoe's arrival.

Besides those whose names appear, a number of others have
given of their time and expertise to produce this volume. Winifred
Mumford, of the Department of Prehistory (Pacific Studies,
A.N.U.), assisted with the Figures and drew those of canoe sails.
Lio Pancino of the Department of Human Geography assisted with
the maps and drew the endpapers; Keith Mitchell of the same
Department arranged the Gilbertese genealogical tables. Many
present and former members of the Department of Pacific and
Southeast Asian History wished to participate in some way or other
to honour Harry. I am particularly grateful for the support of Dr
Caroline Ralston of Macquarie University, Sydney, as a representative of Harry's former students in the Department, for assisting
me with the editorship of this volume. Mrs Jennifer Terrell, for
long associated with Harry on *The Journal of Pacific History,* has
read the manuscript and given me the benefit of her professional
advice. Mrs Norah Forster, besides her own contribution, has compiled and checked the general bibliography and ensured the
accuracy of reference citations. Mrs Robyn Walker made her
special contribution the typing of the entire manuscript.

Canberra   *Niel Gunson*
April 1976

Harry Maude: shy proconsul dedicated Pacific historian

ROBERT LANGDON

In the early hours (G.M.T.) of 27 October 1937, while King George VI and most of his loyal subjects in Great Britain were sleeping off the excitement of the previous day's official opening of Parliament, an enthusiastic young officer of the British Colonial Service was making history on his sovereign's behalf on the opposite side of the world. The scene was McKean Island, a small, circular, coral pancake of a place, 350 km south of the equator and about 480 km east of the international dateline—a place so far removed from Buckingham Palace and the meridian of Greenwich that there it was not yet three o'clock on the previous afternoon. The young officer was Henry Evans Maude, Native Lands Commissioner for the Gilbert Islands, hereafter referred to as Harry. His historic feat consisted of taking physical possession of McKean Island—a somewhat Gilbertian performance in truth, but as things turned out, the last expansionist thrust of His Britannic Majesty's Empire. With the help of his Gilbertese companions, Harry built a cairn with coral stones, erected a flagstaff and hoisted the Union Jack. He also had a notice board nailed to the staff to inform anyone who might care to dispute the point that McKean Island was British territory. Then he sailed away in H.M.C.S. *Nimanoa,* leaving the island in the care of the numerous brown rats and frigate birds that had long been its only inhabitants.

McKean was the eighth island that Harry had added to the British Empire in the space of ten days. Its annexation came at the end of a tour of the uninhabited, little-known Phoenix group eastward of the Gilberts, which he had suggested could be used to resettle several hundred land-hungry Gilbertese. The object of the tour was to ascertain which of the islands would be best suited for resettlement and to leave physical evidence on each of their incorporation within the boundaries of the Gilbert and Ellice Islands Colony.

In due course, Harry's voyage of reconnaissance and his eight acts of territorial aggrandizement were followed by the migration to three of the Phoenix Islands of more than 700 Gilbertese. Later again, Harry was rewarded for his enterprise by a grateful monarch, or at least in his name by his chief Pacific representative. This was Sir Harry Luke, the irrespressible and foot-loose Governor of Fiji

1

and High Commissioner for the Western Pacific, whose second title gave him an excellent excuse for visiting remote corners of the South Seas. In his book, *From a South Seas Diary, 1938-42,* Sir Harry recorded the British Crown's recognition of his namesake's services. Under date of 11 July 1939 he wrote:

> We arrived at Beru [southern Gilbert Islands] in the morning and landed in uniform for a big meeting in the government *maneaba,* at which I presented the M.B.E. to Maude, the Native Lands Commissioner for the Gilberts and Officer in Charge of the Phoenix Islands Settlements Scheme, of which he is the originator. But first, with the proper ritual, I was installed on the sacred Stone of Chiefs, Ati-n-toka, on which only the head of the senior clan, the Karongoa-n-Uea, or the direct representative of the King of England as Overlord is allowed to sit . . . Lunched with the Maudes in their nice native house; Mrs Maude is doing valuable work in developing Gilbertese arts and crafts and in marketing the excellent local hats, fans and baskets.

Sir Harry Luke's reference to Harry (and also to his wife Honor) is the first to appear in Pacific literature. It is also one of the last, for although Harry spent nearly twenty years in the Pacific as an administrator, he was either too shy and self-effacing (as he still is) to be noticed by itinerant authors, or he was visiting some far-flung corner of the island world to which itinerant authors did not penetrate.

It is evident from listening to him reminisce or from reading his many published reports and papers that remote isolated islands always had a fascination for him, and that, no matter how many new ones he visited, he approached them all with the same excitement. For him, each new island seems to have touched 'a virginity of sense'—as Robert Louis Stevenson said could only happen with one's first Pacific landfall. This delight in islands—this feeling of affinity with them—undoubtedly stems from a lonely childhood, which was spent in India during the still-splendid days of the British raj. It was at Bankipore, a suburb of Patna, that Harry was born on 1 October 1906 into an ancient English family, whose various branches can be traced back many centuries in the peerage and in *Burke's Landed Gentry.* The family has an ancestral tree beginning with one Eustacius de Monte Alto, said to have come from northern Italy to join William the Conqueror's invasion of England and to have been rewarded by being made Baron de Montalt of Hawarden Castle. His name was later corrupted to Maude. The youngest son of the fourth baron, Andomar Maude, is celebrated in the family annals for capturing King William the Lion of Scotland (1143-1214) in a border affray. This is the traditional explanation for the signet ring that Harry wears depicting a Scottish lion behind bars. His only noteworthy relative connected with the Pacific was Thomas Hallett, the midshipman of the *Bounty* who was asleep on an arms chest while the plot for mutiny was being hatched.

Most of Harry's immediate ancestors and relatives occupied prominent positions in India, either in the East India Company or in the Indian Civil Service. Harry's father, Sir Walter Maude, K.C.I.E., C.S.I., retired to England when Harry was only four years old. But he returned to India soon afterwards to become President of the Legislative Council of Bihar and Orissa. Harry recalls that his family lived in an enormous house with seventy or so servants. He was the youngest of seven children, of whom the five preceding him were sisters. As his father was generally pre-occupied with affairs of state and his mother with social and war work, for which she was made an O.B.E., and as his youngest sister was about six years his senior, it is scarcely surprising that Harry grew up a shy, timid, lonely boy. At the age of eleven, Harry went to St Pauls School, Darjeeling. About eighteen months later, with the First World War over, he was sent 'home' to attend preparatory school, and then, at fourteen, to be enrolled at his father's old school, Highgate. Meanwhile Harry had become an omnivorous reader—*The Swiss Family Robinson,* Ballantyne's *The Coral Island* and Stevenson being among his early favourites. His reading also included solid Everyman's Library classics such as Bede's *Ecclesiastical History* and Thucydides' *History of the Peloponnesian War,* which his mother bought and pressed upon him.

At Highgate Harry allegedly broke a contemporary record by being caned three times in one day, with six strokes each time. Such punishment must have toughened him up a bit and made him more of a mixer, for he became captain of the school's shooting VIII and head of his house. But despite his delight in reading, he was otherwise a 'scholarly dunce', as he puts it, and he left Highgate in July 1925 without having passed the London matriculation examination. The headmaster wrote somewhat despairingly to his father, then living in retirement in Jersey. Harry was 'a nice boy', he said, but one who was 'unfortunately behind the door when the good Lord was doling out the brains'.

In consternation about his future, Harry mulled over various schemes for earning a living without academic attainments. A job in the Indian Railways and a farming venture in Cochabamba, Bolivia, were among those considered. Finally, he resolved to sail to the Argentine in a cattle boat in the hope of becoming a *vaquero.* His father, however, got wind of this, and set him to work with a tutor in a last effort to get him into university. After six months Harry succeeded in passing the College Previous Examination—or what he himself calls the 'gentleman's entrance'—into Jesus College, Cambridge.

In his first year Harry gained his Blue for shooting and second class honours in economics. Then an event occurred which gave his life a new dimension. While on holiday in Jersey, he became engaged to Honor Courtney King, who had lived there since the age of eight. He had first met her several years earlier. Under the influence of Stevenson, Melville, Stoddard and other such authors whose books he had been reading, Harry persuaded Honor that they should make their future home in the South Seas. Their engagement formalities were not completed without difficulty, however, for Harry recalls that on being locked in a room with Honor's mother to seek her blessing on his betrothal, he was too shy to ask her anything.

Back at Cambridge, Harry switched to anthropology, in which a course on the Pacific was being given for the first time. The romance of the Islands had now gripped him and, with Honor already sharing his interest in the same books, the study of what was generally looked on as a stodgy subject became a joy. He romped through the works of Radcliffe-Brown, Malinowski, Haddon, Codrington and Pitt-Rivers, besides those of many of the authors listed in the back of *Stewart's Handbook of the Pacific Islands,* then the only Pacific bibliography. The anthropology lecturer was a certain Tommy Hodson, formerly of the Indian Civil Service, who gave tutorials in his house once a week and regaled his twelve students with an endless flow of Rabelaisian stories.

In his final examinations, as part of his oral, Harry had to give a half-hour lecture. Malinowski and Sir Hubert Murray, the Lieutenant-Governor of Papua, were in the front row. Despite these formidable auditors Harry's lecture was apparently a success for he emerged from Cambridge with a good honours degree. A history of Highgate, his old alma mater, records the details in these terms: 'Cl.2, Div.II, Pt I, Econ. Trip.; Cl.2, Div.I, Arch. and Anthrop, Trip., M.A.'.

With Cambridge behind him, Harry applied forthwith for admission to the Colonial Service and, with Stevenson guiding him, specified the Gilbert Islands as his field of preference. Since only one person had previously asked to serve in these remote, almost-unheard-of islands, his wish was readily accommodated, and he was appointed a cadet within a month or two of coming down from Cambridge. He and Honor were married soon afterwards, and they set sail for the antipodes on 20 September 1929. In Melbourne they joined the phosphate ship *Nauru Chief* and continued on to Ocean Island, then the headquarters of the Gilbert and Ellice Islands Colony. En route the only islands to appear on the horizon to touch Harry's 'virginity of sense' were the Chesterfields, to the north-west of New Caledonia, and Santa Ana, off the eastern end of San Cristobal. Ocean Island was reached in mid-

November. From afar, it looked like an upturned canoe, but once ashore, much of it proved to be a moonlike expanse of exhausted phosphate diggings, the result of twenty-eight years of extraction work by the British Phosphate Commissioners and two predecessor companies.

The Resident Commissioner, Arthur Grimble, who had interviewed and approved both Harry and Honor in London, was still on leave when they arrived. His deputy was a model of bureaucratic procrastination. By the time Grimble returned, about 150 files of internal correspondence had to be hidden under his bed where they remained until the need to act on them had passed. Harry thus learnt his first important lesson in the mystique of administration: if you let sleeping dogs lie, they eventually die. Meanwhile, he was initiated into the mysteries of sub-accountancy and postal work, and sent as the government representative on a voyage to the southern Gilberts to recruit labourers for the phosphate deposits. The voyage, the first of several 'recruits', gave him a taste of Islands life as he had imagined it. The secret of being a good recruiting officer, he soon learned, was to get the islanders in a good humour. One old hand did this with conjuring tricks; another had a repertoire of much-appreciated 'blue' stories. But things could get 'sticky'. After a week or two of moving from island to island, the labourers were apt to get mixed up with each others' wives. Then fists might fly, or knives. Harry recalls one man with a slit neck and a jugular vein spouting like a fountain. Another had a knife buried to the handle between his eyes. The knife somehow missed the brain, and the victim achieved the distinction of being written up in the *British Medical Journal* with a photograph of the knife still in position.

In May 1930 Harry was sent to Beru as Acting District Officer, Southern Gilbert Islands. As such, at the age of twenty-three years and eight months, he was addressed respectfully as the 'Old Man' while his young bride had to accustom herself to being called 'The Old Woman'. His district consisted of six atolls—Beru, Tabiteuea, Nikunau, Onotoa, Tamana and Arorae—with a total population of about 10,000. Harry had been at his new post only three months when word arrived of some strange troubles on Onotoa. A native magistrate on that island reported that the people had 'suppressed' the law, and that he himself was afraid to punish anyone for fear of starting disorder. 'I beg you, my chief, to help me', he said, and he went on to complain about a Gilbertese pastor who had predicted the end of the world. The pastor had said, among other things, that the 'King' would descend, that the wind would blow furiously, and that a thunderbolt would fall. Not only that, the government station and the Roman Catholic settlements would be destroyed, the Protestants with their church would ascend to heaven, and a certain Catholic saint would be seen 'scuttling round' the Catholic church. Somewhat mystified, Harry set out for Onotoa in the mission ship *John Williams,* accompanied by Honor and the Reverend G. H. Eastman, the head missionary of the London Missionary Society. The story of the strange and turbulent religious movement that was subsequently unfolded to them and of how Harry reorganized the island government, how Honor protected a dozen or so terrified Catholics, how Eastman advised the island's traditional leaders to seek the government's forgiveness for their excesses, and how Harry, on a raised dais and in a loud voice, ordered some recalcitrant wrongdoers to appear before him in the name of His Majesty King George V and such of his titles as he could remember—all this is told in Harry's paper 'The Swords of Gabriel', first published in 1967. There was no opportunity to write it up in detail at the time. At Nikunau, the next island, a brutal murder had been committed, and the 'Old Man' had to hasten on to investigate the crime and apprehend its perpetrator.

But life was not all high drama. There was also time for Harry to pursue his anthropological interests. Honor was a great help to him in this. Being an outgoing person, her ability to speak Gilbertese—whether grammatically correct or not—improved apace, and she could thus make many inquiries where Harry's shyness still left him tongue-tied. Two papers in the *Journal of the Polynesian Society* in 1931 and 1932 put the name Maude into print (jointly) for the first time. The first was on adoption in the Gilbert Islands; the second, a much more substantial piece, was entitled 'The Social Organization of Banaba or Ocean Island, Central Pacific'. The latter has preserved for the Banabans much knowledge about their own former customs that would otherwise have long been forgotten. But it was the last paper of its kind that Harry was to write. After several years in the Gilberts he had begun to move away from an anthropological outlook to one with a historical base. Having come to know many of the villagers of the outer islands, he began to realize that they were as diverse in their character, motivations and conduct as a corresponding group of Europeans. To search, therefore, for universally valid laws for human conduct, as many anthropologists seemed to do, was to keep going down a pathway that led nowhere. On the other hand, Harry did feel that everything he saw around him was firmly rooted in history, and he reasoned that if he had a firm grasp of what had happened in the Gilberts in the past he could gain a fair understanding of the Gilbertese character.

As the opportunities for historical research in the Gilberts were minimal, it is not surprising that no further papers emanated from Harry's pen for several years. In any case, as his experience in-

creased, he had more and more important tasks to keep him occupied. His *curriculum vitae* for the period gives some idea of his
activities. Between March 1931 and March 1935 he was a Census
Officer taking the first Colony census; Acting Administrative
Officer, Southern Gilberts; Acting Native Lands Commissioner;
acting and then substantive Administrative Officer, Ocean Island;
Acting Secretary to Government; Administrative Officer, Central
and Northern Gilberts; and finally Native Lands Commissioner,
Gilbert Islands. During the same period, he passed the law examination prescribed for cadets as well as one in the Gilbertese
language (higher standard). The latter had its moment of drama.
Faced with the prospect of appearing before Resident Commissioner Grimble, as chairman of examiners, and a dozen or so
elderly Gilbertese, Harry worked himself into such a state of panic
that a police officer, to calm him, mixed him a stiff drink. It was
a gin and tonic, half-and-half, which imbued Harry with the
necessary courage, but caused him to fall asleep halfway through
his examination. Grimble, however, proved tolerant about this
and Harry was duly awarded his linguistic spurs—which meant
more pay—after proving his ability to write a letter in Gilbertese.

Grimble by this time had been in the Colony for eighteen
years. He had contracted amoebic dysentery and had become convinced that his superiors had left him to rot in a colonial back-
water. In his last year or so, in an effort to introduce a uniform
code of laws for the Colony, he promulgated what were called
'Regulations for the Good Order and Cleanliness of the Gilbert
and Ellice Islands'. The Regulations were generally of mission
origin, and were drawn together from all islands of the Colony.
The Chief Judicial Commissioner in Fiji later described them as
'spartan in character and draconian in their severity'. Dancing, for
example, was prohibited on all days except Wednesdays, Saturdays
and non-religious public holidays, and even then it could only be
held in the *maneaba* between the hours of 6 p.m. and 9 p.m. At
9 p.m. on such days the village policeman was required to sound
his conch beside the *maneaba* as a signal for the dancing to cease,
and fifteen minutes later he was to sound a second signal. Any
person then found absent from his house was liable to punishment.
Card games were prohibited without the knowledge and consent
of the *kaubure* (village councillor); women could not play any
games with men unless accompanied by a proper guardian; dogs
had to be tied up at sunset; husbands and wives could not live
apart without consulting the *kaubure;* and so on.

Harry was strongly opposed to many of the Regulations, which
filled the Colony's gaols and kept the islanders poor through paying
fines. After Grimble's departure in 1933 he strenuously urged
their repeal. He got nowhere until May 1935, when he left the

Colony on his first leave to England. At Nauru his ship was joined by the anthropologist, Camilla Wedgwood, to whom Harry gave a copy of the Regulations. She passed them on to an uncle, Colonel Wedgwood, a member of the British Parliament, who took them to the Colonial Secretary. As a result, orders went out that something must be done about them. A couple of years later, after Harry had returned to the Colony, he was instructed to amend and redraft the entire code. He set about this task by personally visiting each of the sixteen islands and ascertaining, at a series of public meetings, what the islanders themselves considered reasonable and necessary. The upshot was that more than one hundred of the old Regulations were rescinded and most of the remainder substantially modified. 'The day the people were freed', as Harry describes it, is one that he now looks back on with happiness and pride.

Harry's absence from the Colony after departing on his first leave lasted about two years—twice as long as he expected. The first twelve months, comprising accumulated leave and travelling time, were largely spent in searching libraries and archives for historical material on the Gilberts. He then left London to return to the Pacific, but was asked to go to Honolulu to represent the Gilbert and Ellice Islands at a conference on education in the Pacific—the first such meeting ever held of representatives from the Pacific Islands. The *Pacific Islands Monthly* reported that Harry gave 'an illuminating and exhaustive paper on native life, administration and the education situation in his territory' and that everyone who heard it was convinced that the G.E.I.C. Administration, although 'far removed from the crossroads of the Western world', had much to teach other Western territories. *P.I.M.* added that Harry had found 'masses of material' in the Hawaiian archives that threw light on the history of the Gilberts in the nineteenth century, and that he was 'working assiduously with his typewriter on it'.

Harry was still in Honolulu when he received word that the G.E.I.C. Administration had recommended a proposal that he had long campaigned for. This was that the Phoenix Islands should be officially investigated as a possible home for land-starved Gilbertese. Harry naturally expected that he would soon become involved in this investigation. But on reaching Suva en route to the Gilberts, he was dismayed to learn that he had been transferred, on health grounds, to the post of District Officer in Zanzibar, East Africa. *P.I.M.* reported, with an air of finality, that his transfer would be greatly regretted in the Gilberts by Europeans and natives alike, and that he had presented his 'extensive and unique collection' of Gilbertese and Ellice Islands artefacts and curios to the Auckland War Memorial Museum. The move proved to be only temporary, however, for less than a year later *P.I.M.* announced that he would soon return to the Gilberts and that this would give satisfaction 'to all concerned'.

Resuming duty in his old post of Native Lands Commissioner in July 1937, Harry was immediately assigned to elaborate on his Phoenix Islands proposal. On the one hand, he was asked to report on the causes and extent of over-population and land hunger in the Colony. On the other, he was charged with visiting the Phoenix Islands—which had recently been incorporated within the Colony's boundaries by an Order in Council—to ascertain their potential for settlement. This assignment, besides leading to his eight flag-planting exploits, resulted in a comprehensive report which enabled him to use some of his historical gleanings to good advantage. The report, which was written on Ocean Island, included a detailed plan of how a settlement scheme could be carried out. It was exacting but exciting work, for the Phoenix Islands had stirred Harry's imagination. 'The romance of these little lone islands . . . ' he later wrote, 'had quite taken possession of me and I felt that I could not rest till I had seen them the home of a contented and prosperous community . . . I could still hear the crash of the waves on Sydney's reefs and the cries of the white terns circling over the lagoon at Gardner.'

Shortly after completing his report Harry said farewell to Honor for several months. While she went down to Auckland he himself departed for Tamana, one of the southernmost of the Gilberts, where various land matters required attention. Harry was the first European to live on Tamana for many decades, and he greatly enjoyed the experience. Besides participating in the islanders' games, contests and community singing, he taught them deck tennis, which they took to with wild enthusiasm. After three months a warship appeared off the island and fired three guns. The islanders to a man took to the bush, thinking the Japanese had come. But as Harry could see a White Ensign flying, he stiffened his upper lip, so to speak, and went out to see what the ship was making a fuss about. It proved to be a New Zealand warship, whose amicable captain greeted him. 'Congratulations, Maude', he said, 'your wife bore you a son in Auckland two and a half months ago.'

A week later a schooner carried Harry back to Ocean Island where he was reunited with Honor and met his small son, Alaric. He also learned that the Phoenix Islands Settlement Scheme had been approved, and that he had been appointed officer in charge to carry it out. The story of how the scheme was carried out—interrupted by an 'exploratory expedition' on Harry's part to Fanning, Washington and Christmas Islands—is told in Harry's book *Of Islands and Men*. But the book does not tell how, in the course of his duties, he slipped a disc, became bed-ridden, and was finally ordered to Suva and then to Auckland for treatment. He reached Auckland in October 1939, about a month after the Second World War was declared, and was not well enough to resume duty until the following February. When he did, it was not in the Gilberts, but in Suva, as an assistant to Harry Vaskess, the long-reigning Secretary to the Western Pacific High Commission. Harry's chief task at this time called for much delving in the Commission's archives and was his first real effort as a research historian. It resulted in the compilation of a report on the Phoenix and Line Islands 'with special reference to the question of British sovereignty'. This issue had suddenly become important because the Americans had asserted claims to some of the islands, and the Foreign Office was anxious to know exactly where Britain stood.

After six months Harry was given another, completely different, task. This was to go to Pitcairn, the *Bounty* island, to frame a constitution and a code of laws, and to open a post office. The idea of the post office was to provide Pitcairn with a means of raising revenue. Honor and Alaric were included in this expedition and the three travelled to Pitcairn via Wellington in the ship *Akaroa*. As things turned out, Harry had plenty of time for his work. With the war in Europe becoming more intense and the torpedoing of ships more commonplace, Naval headquarters in Wellington refused to allow ships to call at Pitcairn for fear that an enemy vessel might be lurking in the vicinity. Eight months passed before the Maudes could get off the island again. Harry employed some of his enforced leisure in collecting more than a thousand stone adzes that had been left on the island by the *Bounty* mutineers' Polynesian predecessors. He also persuaded the Pitcairners to allow the *Bounty*'s rudder, which had been found on the sea bed several years earlier, to be crated up for dispatch to the High Commission, which deposited it in the Fiji Museum, Suva. Meanwhile Honor, an inveterate gardener, chanced to dig up the *Bounty* wedding ring which had been lost more than a century before. Not surprisingly, Pitcairn left its mark on the Maudes. Years later it inspired Harry, as a historian, to write two of his best-known papers, 'In Search of a Home' and 'Tahitian Interlude', as well as a meticulous fifty-six page history of Pitcairn. Pitcairn, for its part, has greatly profited from the sale of postage stamps. On the Maudes' arrival there the local treasury contained only £70— derived from the sale of gun licences over the previous fifteen years. Three years later, the island had a bank balance of more than £50,000. As for the Constitution and Code of Laws of Pitcairn Island, this document, as finally published, was not one drawn up by a European 'expert' and thrust on the islanders. It represented the unanimous decision of the islanders themselves, having been framed by an elected committee, discussed at meetings of the people, and ultimately signed by every man and woman over eighteen as 'what we want'. Harry saw his role as merely that of adviser and draughtsman for, as in the Gilbert Islands, it was his conviction that the procedures and laws by which the people were governed should be decided by themselves.

The Maudes finally left Pitcairn in an American ship which took them to Panama. From there they travelled to Suva via Mexico City, Guatemala (where a shipload of Gilbertese 'black-birds' had once worked as labourers), Brownsville, Texas (where Honor was much photographed by the Press after being mistaken for Madame Lupescu, the mistress of Rumania's king), Dallas, Los Angeles and Honolulu. Back in Suva, Harry and his family were installed in Government House, affectionately known as the 'Western Pacific Boarding House'. But before long Sir Harry Luke announced that he wanted Harry to go to Tonga for a few months to act as British Agent and Consul. Harry protested that he did not possess tails, but his superior was equal to this. 'When you get to Tonga', Sir Harry said, 'inform Her Majesty [Queen Sālote] that owing to wartime austerity in England, the use of formal attire at the Court of St James has been abolished by royal edict, and you, as representative of the British Crown in Tonga, will be precluded from the use of tails in Nuku'alofa.' Harry recalls that he passed on this message with 'fear and trembling', not to the Queen but to her consort Tungī, who was also Premier. 'Thank God for that, I always hated them', Tungī, said, and within an hour a similar royal edict on the wearing of formal dress in Tonga was issued from the Tongan court.

In Queen Sālote Harry found a person of similar temperament to himself—shy, nervous and, initially, reserved. His first audience with her would have been a speechless fiasco on both sides had not the down-to-earth Tungī intervened. Thereafter, the Queen and the Maudes became close friends, and Alaric, then three, was a frequent visitor to the palace. When Harry's term as Agent and Consul expired, the Queen made a special request that he should remain in Tonga an extra month, and she provided a furnished house for the purpose. He was then seconded to the Tongan Civil Service, as the Queen wanted his advice on how the service could be reorganized. Harry produced a typically thorough report. One of his recommendations—a fairly radical one for the time—was that Tongans should be trained to take over all key posts from Euro-peans. The recommendation was in line with the tenor of several talks that Harry had had with Tungī in which he remembers dis-cussing the notion of an Oceania freed from European political domination. Harry firmly believed that all islanders had the right to govern themselves in their own way, and it was undoubtedly because of his conviction on this that he was chosen for his Tongan mission. He recalls that at that time Britain still had extra-territorial jurisdiction over European residents in Tonga—a relic of tutelage, he thought, that should be abolished.

On leaving Tonga the Maudes sailed to New Zealand en route for Suva. They arrived in Auckland just in time to hear of the Japanese attack on Pearl Harbor. Alarm over this persuaded Harry to leave Honor and Alaric in Auckland and to return to Suva alone. By then the Japanese had occupied Tarawa, the future capital of the Gilbert and Ellice Islands, and one of Harry's first tasks was to do what he could to help evacuate the Europeans still in the Colony but not in Japanese hands. He was also sent to Levuka to set up headquarters to administer the Colony's affairs, as far as this could still be done. Another task was to attend to a request from the Banabans—the people of Ocean Island—to buy an island for them with their accumulated phosphate royalties against the day when their own island would be nothing but an empty shell. This was how Rabi Island, the Banabans' present home, was acquired. Harry negotiated its purchase for $25,000, after Lever Bros, in the panic of the time, had agreed to sell. At about the same time, Rabi's neighbour, Kioa, was bought at auction for the people of Vaitupu, in the Ellice group; and Harry also had a hand in buying Niulakita, the southernmost of the Ellice group, from Burns Philp. Another of his tasks was to draw up a list of provisions required in case 'Government House' had to be transferred to one of the huge caverns then being built at Tamavua, a Suva suburb, in the event of a Japanese invasion.

In September 1942 Harry was sent to Fanning Island to deal with a strike by Gilbertese labourers on the Burns Philp plantations there. A year later he flew to Honolulu where he was attached to the intelligence section of the U.S. Fifth Amphibious Force, under Rear Admiral Turner at Pearl Harbor, engaged in preparing plans for the recapture of the Gilbert Islands. One of his tasks was to write a booklet for issue to the American forces composing GALVANIC, the code name for this operation. The booklet included hints on food, drink, fishing, fish poisoning, sunburn, and par-ticularly 'contacts with natives'.

Harry's next assignment was to have preceded the occupation of the Gilberts by landing at Abemama from a submarine. But before this could take place he was redirected by Pacific Fleet headquarters at Noumea to Pitcairn to explain to the islanders the necessity for building a radio transmitter on their island to assist the Allied cause. Harry reached the island by U.S. transport from New Zealand. It took two attempts. The first was frustrated because the ship's propeller fell off. The ship was then towed by a passing vessel into the tail of a hurricane near the Cook Islands until the towing cable broke. After that she was rescued by a tug from Wellington, which took three weeks to tow her to dry dock for repairs. By the time Harry finally reached Pitcairn, carried out his mission there, and returned to Pearl Harbor via San Francisco, the Gilberts had been recaptured and the Americans no longer required his services. He therefore returned to work with the Western Pacific High Commission.

His first mission was to investigate further possibilities for Gilbertese resettlement after the war. This involved yet another tour to little-known islands in the Central Pacific. From Honolulu Harry went on what the U.S. Air Force called the 'milk run', first to Christmas Island, then to the American base on Borabora, and from there, via Tongareva, to the American base on Aitutaki. A couple of sea voyages followed. The first, in a schooner skippered by the renowned 'Andy' Thompson, of Rarotonga, took him to Mauke, Atiu, and Rarotonga. On the second he went to Pitcairn once more, through the Austral group, and thence past Mangareva and Hereheretue to Tahiti. In Tahiti the crew disappeared for a week, each with a Tahitian girl friend. After the gendarmerie had rounded them up, the voyage continued—to Caroline, Vostok and Flint Islands, Tongareva, Manihiki, Rakahanga, Pukapuka, Nassau and Suwarrow. The first three and last two of these islands were examined for their colonization possibilities. Then it was back to Aitutaki, where a Catalina flying-boat arrived from Fiji to return Harry to Suva and his long-separated family.

For the next fifteen or sixteen months there were no more excursions to out-of-the-way places—just work of one kind or another at the Western Pacific High Commission. In December 1944 Harry became Acting Secretary to the Commission for a couple of months. His principal task during the whole period was to draw up a blueprint for the postwar reorganization of the Gilbert and Ellice Islands. This was completed on 27 June 1945 and later published. Soon after its completion Harry was asked to go to the Gilberts as Acting Resident Commissioner.

With Honor and Alaric he returned to the Gilberts in November 1945 for the first time in six years. Although his report on postwar reorganization had recommended Abemama as the colony's future capital, Tarawa, scene of a horrific battle against the Japanese, was then being used as such, and was eventually preferred, because of a better passage into its lagoon. The Maudes arrived there in time to greet 1,000 or so Banabans and Gilbertese who had just been rescued from Kusaie in the Caroline Islands, where the Japanese had deported them at the beginning of the war. As there was neither food nor housing on Ocean Island, the Banabans were taken soon afterwards to Rabi, with the option of returning to Ocean after two years.

Harry's next important task was to go to London to advise both the Colonial and the Foreign Offices on the question of sovereignty over the Phoenix and Line Islands. This issue had again arisen because the Americans, having become apprehensive over the lack of protection for their west coast, were laying claim to twenty-two of them. From London Harry went on to Washington as a member of a British delegation to discuss the sovereignty issue.

Back in the Pacific Harry resumed duty at the Western Pacific High Commission in Suva. A month or two later word arrived from Rabi of alleged serious differences of opinion between the Banabans and the British officer-in-charge, who requested a detachment of police to maintain order. With Fiji's Assistant Colonial Secretary, P. D. (Paddy) Macdonald, a former colleague in the Gilberts, Harry was asked to go to Rabi forthwith to investigate. This assignment resulted in the publication of yet another comprehensive Maude report in which nine major reasons were listed as the cause of the Banabans' discontent. None of these blamed the Banabans for what had happened. The growth of the phosphate industry, Harry said, had dislocated their traditional economy and had turned them into dole-fed hangers-on of the British Phosphate Commissioners. There had been a marked decline in their physical and moral condition in the seventeen years he had known them. Urgent measures were therefore needed to save the Banabans from sinking into a state of indolence and apathy, and Harry recommended that everything should be done to persuade them to build up a new life on Rabi.

After Harry had delivered his views on the Banaban question the Western Pacific High Commissioner, Sir Alexander Grantham, offered him the choice of two important posts. He could either become Secretary to the Western Pacific High Commission or go to the Gilbert and Ellice Islands Colony as Resident Commissioner. Because of his affection for the atolls and their people, Harry chose the latter and returned to Tarawa in October 1946. He had been back only seven or eight months, however, when it became opportune for him to take six months accumulated leave—his first long leave since before the war. He and his family made their way to Suva. But before their furlough could properly begin, there were still two important jobs to be done. One was to go to Rabi again with Paddy Macdonald to fulfil the government's promise to the Banabans on where they were to live. After three days of discussions a secret ballot was held in which eighty-seven per cent of the islanders voted to remain on Rabi, and the rest opted to move to Ocean Island. After two more days, however, all of the minority group also decided to stay where they were.

The other job that Harry still had to attend to concerned the perennial problem of providing living room for the increasing Gilbertese population. The High Commission in Suva was already negotiating the purchase of Christmas Island from a French company with the idea of making it available to land-hungry Gilbertese; and Harry was now asked to go to Sydney to try to negotiate the purchase of Fanning and Washington Islands for the same purpose. As the two islands were owned by Burns Philp, he had to confront one of the toughest businessmen in the Pacific, 'Holy Joe' Mitchell, the company's indestructible general manager. Mitchell proved to be 'a bit miffed' by the fact that co-operatives were being established in the Gilberts, which made it unattractive for his company to resume its prewar trade in those islands. But he eventually agreed to sell Fanning and Washington for £100,000. With this promise the Maudes went on to London where Harry hoped to obtain the necessary money from the British Government's Colonial Development Committee. These hopes, however, were soon dashed by the arrival of a letter from a newly-appointed officer in the Gilberts who claimed that the Gilbertese had plenty of land. It was just being inadequately used, he said. Harry was distressed at being thus foiled by an inexperienced officer in his attempt to buy what he felt were two badly needed islands for the Gilbertese. Indeed, his strong feelings over this matter were among the factors that prompted him to launch into a new career.

While Harry was on leave a conference was held in Canberra which led, a year or so later, to the establishment of the South Pacific Commission. The Commission was envisaged as an international body supported by the six metropolitan powers with colonial interests in the Pacific. Its purpose would be to advise the member governments on matters affecting the economic and social development of their territories, to organize and carry out research on their behalf, and to provide technical assistance. In the war-weary but optimistic atmosphere of the time, the concept of the Commission appealed to Harry. Colonialism, he had come to think, would soon be as outmoded as slavery, and he felt it was time to hasten the emancipation of the dependent island territories while providing them with technical and other assistance through an international organization. He therefore let it be known that he would be interested in one of the three top posts in the Commission—that of Deputy Secretary-General. Five months after returning to Tarawa he learned that he had been accepted for the post, and after only two more months he left the Gilberts to take it up. This was in November 1948. Harry's term of office as Resident Commissioner thus lasted just over two years, but his actual period in residence was only about half that time. Colleagues

who were then in the Gilberts recall that he was still as shy as
ever, and that he never seemed comfortable in the top post.
Harry's own reminiscences bear out this assessment, for he speaks
of being 'segregated in the febrile atmosphere of an expatriate
headquarters station from the ordinary Gilbertese villagers' and
of being obliged by the etiquette of his office to entertain his
fellow Europeans. Clearly his own preference would have been to
spend his leisure with the islanders, discussing their customs,
traditions and such like.

Harry's great interest in Gilbertese custom and tradition was a
point on which he dwelt when writing a farewell message to the
islanders in the vernacular news-magazine, *Tero,* another of his
innovations. The message summarized what he and Honor had
done and had tried to do during their stay in the Colony. Looking
back now over the things he enumerated, Harry sees the foundation
of the Colony's co-operative movement as his proudest achievement. He recalls that when he first went to the Colony all commercial activity was in the hands of Australian and Japanese
wholesale trading firms selling through European or Chinese retail
traders. When he left seventeen years later all commerce was in
the hands of native-run co-operative societies, operating on every
island and jointly owning the Colony Co-operative Wholesale
Society. The Society (which has since greatly expanded) had
grown out of a single retail co-operative that Harry had founded
on Beru in 1931, and of which there were thirty-four similar
co-operatives throughout the Colony within three years.

Economic progress for the islanders was an essential part of
Harry's philosophy. He made this clear in a last admonition to
the Gilbertese leaders then in training just before his departure
from Tarawa. 'Political advancement towards self-government is
not enough', he said, 'in fact it may prove to be a handicap,
unless it is balanced by a corresponding advance in the economic
and cultural spheres.' And it was in this belief that he joined the
South Pacific Commission.

The small band of men who made up the foundation secretariat
and Research Council of the Commission assembled in Noumea,
which had been chosen as the Commission's headquarters. In
February 1949 Harry and three of his new associates attended the
Ninth Pacific Science Congress in Auckland where Harry pre-
sented papers on the co-operative movement in the Gilbert and
Ellice Islands and on the Phoenix Islands Settlement Scheme.
Immediately afterwards there was a fact-finding and familiarization
tour of the Pacific. This took Harry to a number of places that
he had not previously seen—Tulagi, Honiara, Lae, Port Moresby,
Aitape, Goroka, and the capital of what was then Dutch New
Guinea, Hollandia. Back in Noumea Harry attended a session of

the S.P.C. and the first meeting of its Research Council. By this time he had discovered that the post of Deputy Secretary-General did not offer him the scope that he had expected. It was little more than a senior clerical job—one that was painlessly abolished a few years later. In the circumstances Harry was fortunate in being asked to take over the post of Executive Officer for Social Development, which had not then been filled. He agreed, and thus became one of three officers responsible for the execution of the Commission's programme—the others being in charge of economic development and health.

In his new post Harry could visualize a vast range of projects that could be undertaken for the benefit of the Pacific Islanders. One of the first that he helped to organize was a community development project on Moturiki Island, Fiji. This was an experimental attempt to raise the living standard of a selected community by their own efforts, without compulsion or legislative enactments. Other projects which were soon approved included a plan to extend the use of visual aids in teaching in the Pacific Islands; a study to ensure more efficient teaching methods in the Islands vernaculars; a survey of Islands languages; and an investigation of the most suitable buildings for the tropics, especially for schools. A little later surveys were also commissioned on co-operatives, on facilities for professional and technical training in the Islands, and on the research in social anthropology that was still needed in Polynesia, Micronesia and Melanesia. These and similar projects brought Harry into increasing contact with the scholarly world. Two noted anthropologists, Felix Keesing and A. P. Elkin, were asked to undertake the survey on anthropology; the linguist A. D. Capell was commissioned to report on Islands languages; and the Fiji historian R. A. Derrick was assigned to do the survey on professional and technical training. Harry himself made a survey of co-operatives in the Cook Islands in July and August 1951 at the invitation of the New Zealand Administration; and later he did a similar study in the New Hebrides in association with the French anthropologist Jean Guiart.

In the midst of all these activities Harry's headquarters remained in Sydney. This was because Sydney was more convenient than Noumea for the research contacts essential for his work and for travel throughout the islands. As time went on, it was also found to be especially suitable for the production of visual aids and elementary literature which became an important function of the Social Development Section. To help in the literary work, Harry recruited Bruce Roberts, a specialist from Southern Rhodesia, who took charge of what became known as the South Pacific Literature Bureau. Harry's other colleagues included two able women, Helen Sheils and Nancy Phelan. The latter, now a well-known author, wrote her first book, *Atoll Holiday*, following a prolonged visit to the Gilbert Islands with Helen Sheils. Harry wrote a nostalgic foreword to it.

With many talented and well-informed people to deal with, Harry felt that he 'really blossomed out' in Sydney after the restricted intellectual life of the Islands. His work kept him busy. Conferences were held every six months; there was a concomitant number of reports to write; and a lot of literature had to be seen through the press. One of Harry's reports to the Research Council, with its recommendations on projects and activities, was sent to the Caribbean Commission as a model. But despite all the hard work some people began to wonder whether it was all worth while —whether the Commission was really achieving what its planners had envisaged. The *Pacific Islands Monthly* complained on one occasion that the Commission was 'not near enough to the cold earth', and that it took too little account of the vagaries of politics and of human nature. *P.I.M.* did not deny that the Research Council was doing an excellent job and that its Literature Bureau was producing an 'increasing stream of books, pamphlets and reports'. 'But', it said, 'what actually is being accomplished in the realm of practical administration in the South Pacific's 14 or more territories as a result of this costly set up . . .? Is the South Pacific Commission really changing and improving the texture of Islands life?'

There were undoubtedly times when Harry also felt that the Commission was not doing enough to change and improve things. Yet there were considerable difficulties to contend with. The Commission, as he now puts it, was 'not a super-government with overriding powers of its own', but only an advisory body to the territorial governments. The European administrators, moreover, were apt to accord a low priority to recommendations in his own 'Cinderella sphere' of social development. And there were the attitudes of some of the member-government's commissioners to live with, also. Harry recalls, for example, that he failed 'spectacularly' when he suggested a conference to try to give the Islanders a sense of pride in their own history. The idea was emphatically squashed by a commissioner who said: 'Pamper and cosset dependent subjects if you will, but don't assist them to recapture a pride in their ancestral heritage'. Despite this rebuff, Harry did succeed in launching a couple of projects aimed at rescuing some of the Islanders' historical heritage from extinction. One was a project to locate and ensure the preservation of valuable manuscripts on the Islands by having photocopies made of them. The material sought for included grammars, dictionaries, vernacular texts, collections of folklore, family records, and such like. When such items were located, they were borrowed for microfilming and then returned to their owners. The other project aimed to build up a central library of recorded music, chants, ceremonies, speeches on historical occasions, etc. The manuscripts project was particularly successful and resulted in the filming of seventy separate items, which were listed from time to time in the Commission's quarterly, the *South Pacific Bulletin*. The *Bulletin* also became the vehicle for the publication of another Maude-inspired idea—a regular bibliography of scholarly books, articles and papers on the Islands. At first, the bibliography could easily be made to fit into one or two columns. But as time went on it grew longer and longer. Finally, in 1954, there came the publication of the *Bibliography of Bibliographies of the South Pacific*, in which Ida Leeson, a former Mitchell Librarian, listed Islands bibliographies by area and subject.

The principal reason for the increasing activity in the field of Pacific bibliography was that as the fifties advanced, several universities took a greater interest in South Seas affairs. Pre-eminent among these was the newly-established Australian National University in Canberra, with its unique Research School of Pacific Studies. Harry had frequent occasion to visit Canberra to consult scholars in the Research School. Among these was Jim Davidson, the Foundation Professor of Pacific History, whom Harry had first met in Wellington in 1941. Another was Oskar Spate, the holder of the Chair of Geography and a specialist on India, who was consulted on the status of the Indian universities on behalf of the Fiji Government. Professor W. D. Borrie and Dr Norma McArthur, of the Department of Demography, were sought for their help in carrying out censuses in the Islands. Thus it was that Harry had some interesting and influential A.N.U. friends when, in April 1955, the South Pacific Commission acquired its third Secretary-General, an American, who moved the Social Development Section to Noumea. This development marked another turning-point in Harry's career. Having exhausted his 'six original thoughts', as he puts it, he decided to take up a senior position that Professor Davidson had offered him a couple of years earlier in the Department of Pacific History.

Harry's resignation from the S.P.C. took effect from 31 December 1955. But he continued with the Commission in an acting capacity for the first few months of 1956, pending the appointment of a successor. Then, being almost fifty years of age, he was eligible to take pre-retirement leave from the British Colonial Service, from which he had been on secondment throughout his S.P.C. career. Harry spent most of his pre-retirement leave reading up Pacific history in the Mitchell Library, Sydney. With typical modesty, he felt that he knew virtually nothing about the subject. Also, after having written little but officialese for more than a

c

quarter of a century, he tried his hand at a more literary form of composition—something more appropriate to a future Pacific historian. Two efforts in this new vein, based on gleanings from the Mitchell Library, were published in the *Pacific Islands Monthly* for October and November 1956. Their subjects indicate that Harry was still as young at heart as when he first went to the Pacific. One article was on Louis Becke—'the writer who lived his own Pacific romances'. The other was entitled 'Stevenson in the South Seas: even the cabin boy wrote a book'.

Harry joined the A.N.U. on 1 January 1957. For a while he was at a loss to know where to begin. Having been given a room, he recalls that he was left to his own devices for six weeks, and being as shy as ever, he was unable to discover where the library was or how one went about posting a letter. Moreover, as a former civil servant, he expected instructions from his head of department as to what he should do. Word of this eccentricity eventually reached Jim Davidson, who is reputed to have said: 'I suppose he'll do whatever he wants to do.' This 'directive' was duly relayed to Harry, who thereupon got to work on the first of the long stream of punctiliously researched papers that have since made his name renowned wherever Pacific history is read and practised. Honor, too, settled down happily to work on her own speciality, the esoteric art of Oceanic string figures. She has since prepared five monographs and several articles, some based on her own field work and others in collaboration with Sir Raymond Firth, Kenneth Emory, Camilla Wedgwood and Christa de Coppet.

The principal details of the remainder of Harry's career to date are fairly simply told. In June 1959 he was promoted to the permanency of a Senior Fellowship at the A.N.U. and in 1963 he became a Professorial Fellow. Meanwhile, besides writing his numerous papers, he supervised Ph.D. students, carried on a helpful correspondence with an ever-widening circle of Pacific scholars, and suggested and encouraged a variety of projects for the benefit of Pacific scholarship. His enthusiasm for Pacific history and his persuasiveness in attracting other people to study it eventually created a number of rods for his own back. First, having realized with other Pacific historians that there were not enough outlets for the publication of their articles, Harry got to work and did most of the preliminary drafting for *The Journal of Pacific History*, which he edited with Jim Davidson. The first issue of the *Journal* appeared in 1966. Harry then felt that if the study of Pacific history was to prosper, some kind of centre was needed to ensure that unique manuscripts on the islands were not destroyed or lost. He also envisaged that the centre should be able to make such documents readily available to scholars. Having interested the Mitchell Library and the library of the University of Hawaii in this idea, Harry expanded his thoughts in another characteristic report, 'The Documentary Basis for Pacific Studies: a report on progress and desiderata'. The upshot was the establishment of the Pacific Manuscripts Bureau within the Research School of Pacific Studies with the support, initially, of four libraries, and later five. But this was by no means all. Harry felt that much valuable research time was being wasted by Pacific scholars because of the lack of bibliographies, serials indexes, manuscript catalogues, and similar research tools. The result was his paper 'Searching for Sources' for *The Journal of Pacific History*. It was also the genesis of the Pacific Monograph Series, published by the Australian National University Press. The first volume of this series was a catalogue of published and unpublished theses on the Pacific Islands.

The *Pacific History Series* (published by the A.N.U. Press), of which Harry has been general editor since 1968, was also his idea. Its purpose is to provide scholars with easy access to important, previously unpublished manuscripts and long-out-of-print books, expertly annotated. Nine volumes have so far been published.

Harry retired from the University in 1970, but his enthusiasm for Pacific studies has continued unabated. He played an important part in a U.N.E.S.C.O. conference on Oceanic cultures in Canberra in January 1971, and some time later he went to Suva for a specialist meeting on the same subject. In 1973 he had a big hand in organizing another U.N.E.S.C.O. conference on 'Source Materials Related to Research in the Pacific Area', at which he delivered papers on Pacific documentation and Pacific bibliography. Another important contribution to the future of Pacific studies that year was the sale of his unique library of more than 10,000 Pacific books, pamphlets and periodicals to the University of Adelaide. The collection had been gathered together over about thirty-five years, and was especially strong on the Central Pacific. The university recognized Harry's work with an Honorary Professorship.

In the last year or two, Harry has frequently threatened to curtail his activities in the Pacific field when he reaches his seventieth birthday on 1 October 1976. But with the publication in his honour of this large volume of essays by a wide range of admiring scholars, it is hard to imagine that these threats will have to be taken seriously.

Bibliography of the writings of H. E. Maude, 1931-76

Entries for each year are in alphabetical order according to title.

1931

(With H. C. Maude), 'Adoption in the Gilbert Islands'. *J.P.S.*, vol. 40, no. 4, pp. 225-35.

1932

(With H. C. Maude), 'The Social Organization of Banaba or Ocean Island, Central Pacific'. *J.P.S.*, vol. 41, no. 4, pp. 262-301.

Report on the Census of the Gilbert Islands, 1931. Ocean Island, Gilbert and Ellice Islands Colony.

1936

Culture Change and Education in the Gilbert and Ellice Islands. (Paper delivered to the Seminar-Conference on Education in Pacific Countries, Honolulu, sponsored by the University of Hawaii and Yale University.) 10 pp.

(With H. C. Maude), 'String Figures from the Gilbert Islands'. *J.P.S.*, vol. 45, nos 178-80, Memoir Supplements, pp. 1-40.

1937

Report on the Colonization of the Phoenix Islands by the Surplus Population of the Gilbert and Ellice Islands. [Confidential]. Suva, Fiji, Government Press. 31 pp.

(With H. C. Maude), 'String Figures from the Gilbert Islands'. *J.P.S.*, vol. 46, nos 181-2, Memoir Supplements, pp. 41-56.

1938

(With H. C. Maude), 'String Figures from the Gilbert Islands'. *J.P.S.*, vol. 47, nos 186-8, Memoir Supplements, pp. 57-72.

1940

Report on the Phoenix and Line Islands with Special Reference to the Question of British Sovereignty. [Secret]. Suva, Fiji, Government Printer. 54 pp.

1941

'The Gilbert and Ellice Islands Colony'. *Pan-Pacific*, vol. 5, no. 2, pp. 6-7, 21.

'Instructions for the Guidance of the Local Government of Pitcairn Island'. *Western Pacific High Commission Gazette,* no. 54, pp. 359-85.

1942

Instructions for the Guidance of the Local Government of Pitcairn Island. Suva, Fiji, Government Printer. 28 pp.

Report on the Public Service of the Kingdom of Tonga, with Recommendations for Reorganization. Suva, Fiji, Government Printer. 31 pp.

1943

Notes on the Gilbert Islands for the Use of U.S. Forces. [Restricted]. [Honolulu], Intelligence Section, Fifth Amphibious Force. 13 pp.

1945

Gilbert and Ellice Islands Colony. Memorandum on Post-War Reorganization and Administrative Policy. Auckland. 39 pp.

1946

Gilbert and Ellice Islands Colony. Memorandum on the Future of the Banaban Population of Ocean Island: With Special Relation to Their Lands and Funds. Auckland. 30 pp.

1949

The Co-operative Movement in the Gilbert and Ellice Islands. (Paper first delivered to the Seventh Pacific Science Congress, Auckland, Feb. 1949.) South Pacific Commission Technical Paper No. 1. Sydney, South Pacific Commission. 14 pp.

1950

'The Co-operative Movement in the Gilbert and Ellice Islands'. Supplement to *South Pacific,* vol. 4, no. 6. 10 pp. (Reprinted from South Pacific Commission Technical Paper No. 1, 1949.)

'Mass Education through Co-operation—the Development of the Co-operative Movement in the Gilbert and Ellice Islands'. *Mass Education Bulletin,* vol. 2, no. 1, pp. 10-14.

'Social Development in the South Pacific'. *South Pacific,* vol. 4, no. 5, pp. 73-84.

1951

'Co-operatives in the Gilbert and Ellice Islands'. *Venture,* vol. 3, no. 9, pp. 4-5. (Based on *The Co-operative Movement in the Gilbert and Ellice Islands,* 1949.)

'Those Henderson Island Mysteries'. *P.I.M.,* vol. 21, no. 10, pp. 62-3.

1952

'The Colonization of the Phoenix Islands'. *J.P.S.,* vol. 61, nos 1 & 2, pp. 62-89.

'The Co-operative Movement in the Pacific Islands'. *Papers and a Brief Summary of Proceedings: 1952 Congress of Queensland Co-*

operatives Held in Brisbane on March 25th and 26th. Brisbane, [Co-operative Union of Queensland]. 9 pp.

'The Work of the Social Development Section of the South Pacific Commission'. Royal Society of New Zealand, *Report of the Seventh Science Congress, Christchurch, May 15-21 (inclusive), 1951.* [Christchurch], pp. 182-5.

1953
'The British Central Pacific Islands: A Report on Land Classification and Utilization'. *Proceedings of the Seventh Pacific Science Congress of the Pacific Science Association* (Auckland and Christchurch, 1947), vol. 6, pp. 89-97. [Auckland], Whitcombe & Tombs.

'Colonization Experiments in the Central Pacific'. *Proceedings of the Seventh Pacific Science Congress . . . ,* vol. 7, pp. 627-8. Christchurch, Pegasus Press.

'The Co-operative Movement in the Gilbert and Ellice Islands'. *Proceedings of the Seventh Pacific Science Congress . . . ,* vol. 7, pp. 63-76. (First appeared as South Pacific Commission Technical Paper No. 1, 1949.)

The Role of the Social Sciences in the Welfare of the Peoples of the South Pacific Commission Area. (Paper delivered to the Eighth Pacific Science Congress of the Pacific Science Association, Quezon City, Philippines.) Unpaged.

Rural Community Projects in the South Pacific. (Paper delivered to the Eighth Pacific Science Congress . . .) Unpaged.

1954
Preface to Ida Leeson, *A Bibliography of Bibliographies of the South Pacific,* published under the auspices of the South Pacific Commission. Melbourne, Oxford University Press, pp. vii-viii.

1955
'Co-operative Movements in the Territories within the Area of the South Pacific Commission'. Horace Plunkett Foundation, *Year Book of Agricultural Co-operation.* Oxford, Basil Blackwell, pp. 10-18.

1956
'Louis Becke, 1855-1913. The Writer who Lived His Own Pacific Romances'. *P.I.M.,* vol. 27, no. 3, pp. 87, 111, 113.

'Stevenson in the South Seas. Even the Cabin-Boy Wrote a Book'. *P.I.M.,* vol. 27, no. 4, p. 83.

1957
'Sovereignty over Christmas Island'. *The Australian Outlook,* vol. 11, no. 3, pp. 31-7.

1958

Foreword to Nancy Phelan, *Atoll Holiday*. Sydney, Angus and Robertson, pp. vii-xiii.

'In Search of a Home: From the Mutiny to Pitcairn Island (1789-1790)'. *J.P.S.*, vol. 67, no. 2, pp. 104-31.

'Islands of the South Seas'. *The Times* (London), 5 August, p. 7.

(With H. C. Maude), *String Figures from the Gilbert Islands*. Memoirs of the Polynesian Society, no. 13. Wellington, The Polynesian Society. VIII, 161 pp. (Pages 1-72 of the Memoir appeared in *J.P.S.*, vols 45-7, 1936-38.)

1959

'Spanish Discoveries in the Central Pacific: A Study in Identification'. *J.P.S.*, vol. 68, no. 4, pp. 115-40.

'Tahitian Interlude. The Migration of the Pitcairn Islanders to the Motherland in 1831'. *J.P.S.*, vol. 68, no. 2, pp. 284-326.

'The Tahitian Pork Trade: 1800-1830'. *Journal de la Société des Océanistes*, vol. 15, no. 15, pp. 55-95.

1960

Review of *Adams of the Bounty* by Erle Wilson. *J.P.S.*, vol. 69, no. 2, pp. 177-8.

'In Search of a Home: From the Mutiny to Pitcairn Island (1789-1790)'. [Revised edition]. Smithsonian Institution, Washington, *Annual Report for the Year Ended June 30, 1959*, pp. 533-62. (Reprinted as Publication 4411 of the Smithsonian Institution.)

1961

'The Pitcairn Commemorative Stamp Issue, 1961'. *Crown Agents Stamp Bulletin*, no. 346, pp. 20-4.

'Post-Spanish Discoveries in the Central Pacific'. *J.P.S.*, vol. 70, no. 1, pp. 67-111.

1962

(With Marjorie Tuainekore Crocombe), 'Rarotongan Sandalwood. The Visit of Goodenough to Rarotonga in 1814'. *J.P.S.*, vol. 71, no. 1, pp. 32-56. (Originally prepared as a paper for the Symposium on Ethnohistory in the Pacific at the Tenth Pacific Science Congress, Honolulu, 1961, with the title: 'Rarotongan Sandalwood: An Ethnohistorical Reconstruction'.)

1963

Discussion on Roy A. Rappaport, 'Aspects of Man's Influence upon Island Ecosystems: Alteration and Control', *in* F. R. Fosberg (ed.), *Man's Place in the Island Ecosystem. A Symposium* (held at the Tenth Pacific Science Congress of the Pacific Science Association, Honolulu, 1961). Honolulu, Bishop Museum Press, pp. 171-4.

The Evolution of the Gilbertese Boti: *An Ethnohistorical Inter-pretation.* Memoirs of the Polynesian Society, no. 35. Wellington, The Polynesian Society. 68 pp. (Reprinted from *J.P.S.*, vol. 72, no. 1 (1963), Supplement; originally prepared as a paper for the Symposium on Ethnohistory in the Pacific at the Tenth Pacific Science Congress, Honolulu, 1961.)

'The South Pacific Commission'. *Australia's Neighbours*, 4th series, no. 5, pp. 1-4.

1964

'Beachcombers and Castaways'. *J.P.S.*, vol. 73, no. 3, pp. 254-93.

'The History of Pitcairn Island', *in* A. S. C. Ross, A. W. Moverley *et al., The Pitcairnese Language.* London, Andre Deutsch, pp. 45-101.

Review of *Pandora's Last Voyage* by Geoffrey Rawson. *J.P.S.*, vol. 73, no. 2, pp. 240-1.

'Some Quotations about the Pitcairnese Language', *in* Ross, Moverley *et. al., op. cit.*, pp. 118-20.

'The Voyage of the *Pandora*'s Tender'. *The Mariner's Mirror,* vol. 50, no. 3, pp. 217-35.

1965

(With Ida Leeson), 'The Coconut Oil Trade of the Gilbert Islands'. *J.P.S.*, vol. 74, no. 4, pp. 396-437.

1966

'Bibliography of Current Publications, Part 1—Books'. *J.P.H.*, vol. 1, pp. 212-17.

Review of *A Complete History of Guam* by Paul Carano and Pedro C. Sanchez. *J.P.H.*, vol. 1, pp. 243-5.

'The Cruise of the Whaler "Gypsy" '. *J.P.H.*, vol. 1, pp. 193-4.

'The Edwards Papers'. *J.P.H.*, vol. 1, pp. 184-5.

'Maconochie, Hawaii and the East India Company'. *J.P.H.*, vol. 1, pp. 194-9.

(With Edward Doran, Jr), 'The Precedence of Tarawa Atoll'. *Annals of the Association of American Geographers*, vol. 56, no. 2, pp. 269-89.

Review of *Who Caused the Mutiny on the 'Bounty'?* by Madge Darby and *The Causes of the Bounty Mutiny: Some Comments on a Book by Madge Darby* by Rolf du Rietz. *J.P.H.*, vol. 1, pp. 246-7.

'William Douglas Campbell (1770-1827)' *in Australian Dictionary of Biography*, vol. I, pp. 208-9. [Carlton, Vic.], Melbourne University Press.

1967
'Bibliography of Current Publications, Part 1—Books'. *J.P.H.*, vol. 2, pp. 198-205.

The Documentary Basis for Pacific Studies: A Report on Progress and Desiderata. Canberra, Research School of Pacific Studies, Australian National University. 48 pp.

'George Hunn Nobbs (1799-1884)' and 'Thomas Raine (1745-1860)', in *Australian Dictionary of Biography*, vol. 2, pp. 288-9, 359-60. [Carlton, Vic.], Melbourne University Press.

'Louis Becke: The Traders' Historian' (review article of *Louis Becke* by A. Grove Day). *J.P.H.*, vol. 2, pp. 225-7.

Review of *New England and the South Seas* by Ernest S. Dodge and *The Voice of the Whaleman. With an Account of the Nicholson Whaling Collection* by Stuart C. Sherman. *J.P.H.*, vol. 2, pp. 238-9.

'Pitcairn Island' and 'Tonga Islands' in *Encyclopaedia Britannica* (new ed.), vol. 17, p. 1116; vol. 22, pp. 72-3. Chicago, Encyclopaedia Britannica, Inc.

(With R. J. Lampert), 'The Stalactite Fish Hooks of Ocean Island'. *J.P.S.*, vol. 76, no. 4, pp. 415-26.

'The Swords of Gabriel: A Study in Participant History'. *J.P.H.*, vol. 2, pp. 113-36.

'Two Letters of Robert Louis Stevenson'. *J.P.H.*, vol. 2, pp. 183-8.

1968
'Bibliography of Current Publications, Part 1—Books'. *J.P.H.*, vol. 3, pp. 193-201.

Foreword to W. E. Giles (Deryck Scarr, ed.), *A Cruize in a Queensland Labour Vessel to the South Seas,* Pacific History Series, no. 1. Canberra, Australian National University Press, pp. vii-ix.

Of Islands and Men: Studies in Pacific History. Melbourne, Oxford University Press. xxii, 397 pp.

'The Pacific Manuscripts Bureau'. *J.P.H.*, vol. 3, pp. 191-2.

'Searching for Sources'. *J.P.H.*, vol. 3, pp. 210-23.

Review of *The Story of the Solomons* by Charles Fox. *J.P.H.*, vol. 3, pp. 226-7.

Foreword to R. G. and Marjorie Crocombe, *The Works of Ta'unga: Records of a Polynesian Traveller in the South Seas, 1833-1896,* Pacific History Series, no. 2. Canberra, Australian National University Press, pp. ix-xiii.

1969
'Bibliography of Current Publications, Part 1—Books'. *J.P.H.* vol. 4, pp. 178-87.

Foreword to Philip A. Snow, *A Bibliography of Fiji, Tonga and Rotuma.* Canberra, Australian National University Press, pp. vii-x.

'East Indiamen in the Pacific, 1788-1825'. *J.P.H.*, vol. 4, pp. 158-9.

Review of *Missionary Adventures in the South Pacific* by David and Leona Crawford, *The Native Polity of Ponape* by Saul H. Riesenberg and *Porakiet: A Kapingamarangi Colony on Ponape* by Michael D. Lieber. *J.P.H.*, vol. 4, pp. 230-1.

1970

'Baiteke and Binoke of Abemama: Arbiters of Change in the Gilbert Islands', *in* J. W. Davidson and Deryck Scarr (eds), *Pacific Islands Portraits.* Canberra, Australian National University Press, pp. 201-24.

Foreword to Nancy Viviani, *Nauru: Phosphate and Political Progress.* Canberra, Australian National University Press, pp. vii-x.

Preface to Diane Dickson and Carol Dossor (comps), *World Catalogue of Theses on the Pacific Islands.* Canberra, Australian National University Press, pp. v-vii.

1971

'The Cultural Setting', *in* Honor (H. C.) Maude, *The String Figures of Nauru Island.* (See H. C. Maude 1971.) pp. ix-xix.

'The Documentary Basis for Pacific Studies', *in* Library Association of Australia, *Proceedings 15th Biennial Conference, Adelaide, 25th-29th August, 1969.* Sydney, pp. 274-85.

'Documentary Resources for the Study of Pacific Islands Cultures', *in* Australian National Advisory Committee for UNESCO, *Meeting on Studies of Oceanic Cultures: Australian National University—January 1971.* Canberra, Australian National Advisory Committee for UNESCO, pp. 199-209.

Review of *Norfolk Island: An Outline of Its History* by Merval Hoare. *J.P.H.*, vol. 6, pp. 238-9.

'Pacific History—Past, Present and Future'. *J.P.H.*, vol. 6, pp. 3-24.

'South Pacific. Independence and Regionalism in the South Sea Islands'. *The Round Table,* no. 243, pp. 369-81.

Foreword to Andrew Cheyne (Dorothy Shineberg, ed.), *The Trading Voyages of Andrew Cheyne, 1841-1844,* Pacific History Series, no. 3. Canberra, Australian National University Press, pp. vii-ix.

(With H. C. Maude), 'Traditional Social Organisation', *in* Martin G. Silverman, *Disconcerting Issue. Meaning and Struggle in a Resettled Pacific Community.* Chicago, University of Chicago

Press, pp. 23-47. (Reprint, with slight modifications, of 'The Social Organization of Banaba or Ocean Island, Central Pacific', 1932.)

1972

Foreword to James F. O'Connell (Saul H. Riesenberg, ed.), *A Residence of Eleven Years in New Holland and the Caroline Islands*, Pacific History Series, no. 4. Canberra, Australian National University Press, pp. vii-x.

(With H. C. Maude), 'String Figures', *in Encyclopaedia of Papua and New Guinea*, vol. 2, pp. 1102-4. [Carlton, Vic.], Melbourne University Press in association with the University of Papua and New Guinea.

1973

'Baiteke and Binoka of Abemama . . .', *in* Davidson and Scarr (eds), *Pacific Islands Portraits* (corrected paperback ed.). Canberra, Australian National University Press, pp. 201-24 (*q.v.* 1970).

'Bibliographic Control of Pacific Manuscripts', *in* Australian National Commission for UNESCO, *Australian UNESCO Seminar: Source Materials Related to Research in the Pacific Area: National Library of Australia, September 1971.* Canberra, Australian Government Publishing Service, pp. 70-83.

'James Wightman Davidson'. *J.P.H.*, vol. 8, pp. 5-9.

'Pacific Documentation: An Introductory Survey', *in* Australian National Commission for UNESCO, *op. cit.*, pp. 9-22.

'The Raiatean Chief Auna and the Conversion of Hawaii'. *J.P.H.*, vol. 8, pp. 188-91.

Foreword to William T. Wawn (Peter Corris, ed.), *The South Sea Islanders and the Queensland Labour Trade,* Pacific History Series, no. 5. Canberra, Australian National University Press, pp. ix-xi.

Foreword to Willowdean Chatterson Handy, *Thunder from the Sea.* Canberra, Australian National University Press, pp. v-vii.

1974

Foreword to Edward Robarts (Greg Dening, ed.), *The Marquesan Journal of Edward Robarts 1797-1824,* Pacific History Series, no. 6. Canberra, Australian National University Press, pp. vii-x.

Foreword to Jean Baptiste Octave Mouton (Peter Biskup, ed.), *The New Guinea Memoirs of Jean Baptiste Octave Mouton,* Pacific History Series, no. 7. Canberra, Australian National University Press, pp. ix-xi.

1975

'Nouvelles d'Australie et de Nouvelle Zélande'. *Cahiers d'Histoire du Pacifique,* no. 2, pp. 54-6.

1976

'Charles Smith (1816-1897)', *in Australian Dictionary of Biography*, vol. 6, pp. 141-2. [Carlton, Vic.], Melbourne University Press.

Foreword, Endnotes and Bibliography to *Sous l'Equateur du Pacifique,* by Ernest Sabatier, translated by Ursula Nixon *(Astride the Equator).* Melbourne, Oxford University Press, pp. v-viii, 353-86.

1977

Foreword to Luelen Bernart (John L. Fischer, Saul H. Riesenberg and Marjorie G. Whiting, eds), *The Book of Luelen,* Pacific History Series, no. 8. Canberra, Australian National University Press, pp. vii-xii.

Foreword to David Cargill (Albert J. Schütz, ed.), *The Diaries and Correspondence of David Cargill, 1832-1843,* Pacific History Series, no. 10. Canberra, Australian National University Press, pp. vii-x.

The Evolution of the Gilbertese Boti: *An Ethnohistorical Interpretation,* reprinted from the Memoirs of the Polynesian Society, no. 35, with permission. Suva, Institute of Pacific Studies and Gilbert Islands Extension Centre, University of the South Pacific 68 [2] pp.

Forthcoming

Books

The Grimble Book. Canberra, Australian National University Press.

The Island World of Yesterday (essays and articles). Melbourne, Oxford University Press.

The Peruvian Slave Trade in Polynesia, 1862-1863.

Articles

'The Construction of the Gilbertese *Maneaba'.*

'The Evolution of Island Government in the Gilberts'.

H. C. Maude

As Harry and Honor Maude have worked together so closely during their years in the Pacific, it was considered appropriate to include here the following bibliography of Honor Maude's separately-published work.

1967

(With Camilla H. Wedgwood), 'String Figures from Northern New Guinea'. *Oceania,* vol. 37, no. 3, pp. 202-29.

1968
(With G. Koch), *Mikronesier (Gilbert-Inseln, Tabiteuea) Faden-spiele*. Begleitveröffentlichung zu Film E883 der Encyclopaedia Cinematographica. Göttingen, Institut für den Wissenschaftlichen Film. 29 pp.

————— *Mikronesier (Gilbert-Inseln, Onotoa) Fadenspiele*. Begleitveröffentlichung zu Film E884 der Encyclopaedia Cinematographica. Göttingen, Institut für den Wissenschaftlichen Film. 25 pp.

1969
(With G. Koch), *Polynesier (Ellice-Inseln, Niutao) Fadenspiele*. Begleitveröffentlichung zu Film E885 der Encyclopaedia Cinematographica. Göttingen, Institut für den Wissenschaftlichen Film. 22 pp.

1970
(With Raymond Firth), *Tikopia String Figures*, Royal Anthropological Institute Occasional Papers, no. 29. London, Royal Anthropological Institute of Great Britain and Ireland. 64 pp.

1971
The String Figures of Nauru Island, South Australian Libraries Board, Occasional Papers in Asian and Pacific Studies, no. 2. Adelaide, Libraries Board of South Australia. xxxii, 155 pp.

Forthcoming

(With Kenneth P. Emory), *The String Figures of the Tuamotu Islands*. Paris, O.R.S.T.O.M. Monograph Series.

(With Raymond Firth and Christa de Coppet), *String Figures from the Solomon Islands*. Sydney, *Oceania* Monograph Series.

The Pacific as an artefact

O. H. K. SPATE

'The Pacific' is a European artefact; not so the peoples who inhabit its shores and islands—rather, they are themselves artificers. Right at the start of any discussion of Pacific historiography we must try to make sure—and not just as a matter of areal definition —which 'Pacific' and which history we are treating. In the last resort I believe all history is one, all its topical or thematic species, all the regional, national, local, family, personal histories going to build up the history of the Family of Man. So vast a synthesis is obviously unattainable, except at the risk of gross superficiality; yet, if we are to be more than chroniclers of small and smaller beer, we must at least try to retain this feeling of 'the altogetherness of all things'. In practice of course we have to use manageable isolates, filing-boxes for data and questions and ideas; and one of these, a very large one, is labelled 'the Pacific'.[1]

Here we have, to begin with, two distinct histories, or genera, each of them sub-divisible into species. There is 'The History of the Pacific', of the Ocean as an Ocean; and there is 'The History of Pacific Peoples', which in practice (we shall try to see why) usually comes down to 'of Pacific Islanders'. I shall often refer to these as the Oceanic and the Insular histories. They differ to some extent, often quite considerably, in materials and method; and— importantly—in scale, which itself may involve differences in treatment and structure: small animals, perfect in their kind, may not need the stout endoskeleton necessary to the larger vertebrates. Distinct as they are, the two of course interpenetrate: they have not that specific distinction—that crossing produces infertility. Phosphate is a factor in Oceanic, even world, history as well as in the history of Nauru. It would be distastrous if their interplay, potentially so fertile, were to be inhibited by academic exclusiveness or by ethnocentricity, of whatever coloration.

Much has been written on the History of the Pacific, but so far it has been mainly in terms of its exploration or of colonial policies and geopolitics, or merely anecdotal; very little in the broad economic and social terms so magnificently exemplified in Pierre and Huguette Chaunu's *Séville et l'Atlantique* and set out in Lucien Febvre's introduction to that book:

> these studies of maritime relations, these reconstructions of the histories of oceans considered as real entities, historic personalities,

primary factors in the collective effort of mankind; these novel studies that generations of historians, lacking neither industry nor intelligence, have not dreamt of giving us . . .[2]

So far this has been a dominantly European history in the writing, and largely in the making; and this is natural enough when one considers how vast are those northern and eastern sectors of the Ocean which are utterly void of land and people, how discrete are the flecks of lava and coral and population in the rest, which nevertheless Europeans and Americans—and Japanese—have crossed by webs of communications, transforming them into a field of economic and military power. This History of the Ocean, moreover, must take into account the adjacent land masses, though here the question of spatial and societal limits is indeed a tricky one.

The History of Pacific Peoples has not been quite so exclusively Euro-dominated, either in the events or the historiography. It is also perhaps not quite so recent as we tend to think; there were heroes before Agamemnon. But as a coherent discipline, fully adopting modern canons of scholarship and yet marked by a strong empathy, it is still young. It will assuredly become more and more important: only by a loving study of the individual lives will we reach an intimate understanding of the family. As for the limits of this Insular history, of course the Japanese or, say, the Aleuts are 'Pacific peoples', but in practice this field of Pacific history has come to mean that of the Islanders of Oceania. The other peoples are marginal to the Ocean, not embraced in it; their activities, until very modern times even those of the Japanese, have been thalassic, in the bordering seas, not truly oceanic; they have strong continental links. The Islanders, until the coming of the Europeans, had their whole history (as distinct from their remoter origins) in the Pacific; their contacts with any other world had so long been lost, their adaptation to and of their watery environment was so complete, that they had developed self-contained and self-sustaining cultures: their groups had internal contacts, but collectively were not only a distinct but also an isolated segment of mankind.

Operationally separated as they may be, the two histories have more in common than a local habitation and a name. The Oceanic history is vast in scale, the Insular may sometimes be a microhistory, in which for instance significant economic change can be measured in tens or even units of people or acres; but in time of record they share a recency, a lack of depth on the time-scale. In fact, so far as precise dating goes, one could say that for any particular island the two were born on the same day—the day the first canoes came off, the first ship's boat scraped the sand. But of course both had long pre- or proto-histories. The Oceanic has an intellectual prehistory going back to Greek concepts of the figure and size of the earth, and a more immediate gestation in the political, economic, and technological configuration of Iberia, the Mediterranean and the Levant in the fifteenth century. The Insular Pacific has a material prehistory, the exciting new frontier of archaeology, and a rich spiritual and aesthetic proto-history, that of myth, legend, and saga.

And both have their besetting dangers. That of the Oceanic, whether in its older geopolitical or in its new socio-economic trend, may reduce the human story to the unrolling or the interactions of grey impersonal forces: see, for example, the Spanish adventure in the Philippines as no more than the interface between silver-gorged New Spain and silver-famished China, or the Galleon as merely a technical device for transferring values between the two. As for the Insular, its practitioners may on occasion not see the Ocean for the Islands, may be content to be marooned in the tight but so safe confines of their little atoll of knowledge, regardless of the sweep of the currents which bring life to the isles.

So much as proem. In the rest of this paper I propose to say something of the setting, temporal and spatial, appropriate to a History of the Pacific, a first sketch of a frame of reference; then, no longer as practitioner but as observer, to reflect on some problems which seem to me to face the writers of History of the Pacific Peoples. This volume on the whole reflects the Island more than the Ocean theme; most fittingly, for indubitably the Founding Fathers of the former's tradition, in its modern shape, were Jim Davidson and Harry Maude, and its spirit is beautifully encapsulated in the very title of Harry's book, *Of Islands and Men*. The present writer is, by ambition if not by achievement, an Oceanic rather than an Insular historian, and it is also fitting that there should be some representation of this older approach; for more than one essay in *Of Islands and Men* shows that their author is also entirely at home in the Oceanic mode: *docte sermones utriusque linguae*.

Strictly speaking, there was no such thing as 'the Pacific' until in 1520-21 Fernão de Magalhãis, better known as Magellan, traversed the huge expanse of waters, which then received its name. Eight years earlier, at a moment which in the saga of the New World ranks only second to the landfall of Columbus, Balboa had gazed not on the Pacific but on the Mar del Sur, the South Sea; and so the Ocean was usually styled in common speech, and very often on maps and in academic discourse, for nearly three centuries. Charles de Brosses, for example, in his influential *Histoire des Navigations aux Terres Australes* (1756), uses 'Mar du Sud' exactly twice as often as 'Pacifique', and in his supporting documents the proportion is not two but seven to one. A hundred years later, however, while 'South Sea(s)' was (and indeed still is) common enough, its geographical significance has been restricted,[3] and its connotation has taken on a literary, often a romantic tinge; already by the mid-nineteenth century the standard term in the world of commerce and affairs is 'Pacific', more especially for the Ocean itself rather than its islands. 'South Sea' held its own for the whole Ocean until the fur-traders following Cook, and after them the whalers, brought European ships in numbers into the seas far north of the Equator, till then scarcely traversed except by the annual Galleons from Manila to Acapulco.

What sea lay before him Balboa did not really know, though presumably beyond it lay the true Indies and Cathay; just to be sure he claimed, with vast panache and formality,

> real and corporeal and actual possession of these seas and lands and coasts and ports and islands of the south, and all their annexures and kingdoms and provinces to them pertaining . . . in the name of the Kings of Castile present or to come, whose is that empire and lordship over these Indies, islands and Tierra Firme northern and austral . . . whether within or without the tropics of Cancer and Capricorn . . . until the final day of judgement of mortal man.[4]

A comprehensive assertion, leaving no gaps; but still the Mar del Sur, the claims of His Catholic Majesty notwithstanding, was the greatest blank on the European map of the world, which already by 1513 was more comprehensive than the previously superior Sinic world-map.[5] This far side of the globe was only a vast void— although, significantly, it *could* be thought of as merely a narrow gap—across which Magellan had carried a thin line marked with only three island-dots: a track almost lost in a waste of mystery and darkness.

And yet, and of course, Europeans were not in truth the first discoverers: since few even of the remoter islands of the Pacific were uninhabited when Europeans came upon them (a marked contrast to the Atlantic), there were discoveries of which we know nothing, except that they had happened. The drama of exploration and exploitation was played out upon an already peopled stage; the priorities of our conventional exploration histories are intra-European priorities, only in rare cases absolutes.

To Europeans in the brief interval between Columbus and Magellan, then, where is now the Pacific was only a nameless naked space between the known to the east and the known to the west; simply the convexity of the sphere, of greater or lesser extent according as one followed the Ptolemaic or the more modern (really more ancient!) estimates of the figure of the Earth. But for those who lived on its continental shores there was an objective phenomenon: here a mysterious and limitless expanse of strangely salt water, a barrier; there an avenue for active trade, but a trade littoral or at best thalassic, not oceanic. And for those who lived on the islands 'lost over its blue expanse like handfuls of confetti floating on a lake',[6] the Ocean was, if not a highway, then at least a net of local ways with a few widely-known nodes, within an extensive but closed system of navigation. Clearly, it cannot always have been closed on all sides, at least not to one-way and perhaps one-time passage: in default of spontaneous generation, the Islanders must have come from somewhere, though the whence and the how are still matters of sometimes acrimonious debate.

But this was not yet 'the Pacific': neither the littoral dwellers, seamen though they might be, nor those whom we must anachronistically style 'Pacific Islanders', had any recognition of anything remotely approaching such an entity: they could not do so, since they were not aware of its bounds, and to be comprehended a thing must be bounded. The seventy or so islands which Tupaia named to Cook range from Rotuma to Hiva Oa and Pitcairn; this covers a respectable section of the Central Pacific, but still only a very small fraction indeed of the whole. Of these islands Tupaia had visited only twelve, and the most distant seems to have been Mangaia, say 1,000 km from Tahiti.[7] The Ocean proper, exclusive of its bordering seas, covers some 166,000,000 km²—nine per cent more than the total land surface of the earth; and it was this expanse that Europeans and Americans traversed, charted, named and recorded: in this primary sense, as well as a geopolitical one, the Pacific is a European artefact.

European excursion into the Pacific proper did not begin until the eighteenth century; before that there had been mere forays which passed through and stayed not, leaving no doubt on something over a score of islands memories of a potent and mysterious apparition, a few tools and trinkets, perhaps a few babies. The Manila Galleon routes were desert tracks, with the one oasis of Guam. Although by and large the buccaneers followed the Galleon course and so found nothing new, Dutch voyages—Schouten's and Tasman's—did indicate the existence of other oases. The three serious attempts at incursion, by Mendaña and Quiros, were abortive, and while their reports were not forgotten, they were so imprecise as regards location as to obscure rather than to enhance knowledge. These three apart, the voyages were simply traverses, made as speedily as might be.

Things were much the same with Roggeveen, Byron, Wallis, and Carteret; but then, in the mid-century, began the era of incursions, formal and well-publicized expeditions, carefully prepared, and taking their time about it; prestigious in the strictest sense. So far as Britain and France were concerned, the rivalry was ostensibly, and in large part really, for the advancement of knowledge; yet always with a keen eye to the main chance in commercial and geopolitical advantage. Cook and Bougainville usher in this phase; in three or four decades, by 1800-10, the main lineaments of the Island groups had been established, although there was much detail work left for the very notable expeditions mounted in the next five decades, mainly by the French and Russians, but with the United States taking a hand with Wilkes. But these are carry-overs: from around the turn of the century incursion is succeeded by the invasion of whalers, missionaries, traders, who set up fixed bases, sketchy and squalid as they might be, and who, however transient as individuals, nonetheless formed an economic and social force that had come to stay.

In 1700, then, European knowledge of the Pacific was practically confined to its margins, and even then with great gaps: all the eastern coasts of New Holland were *terrae incognitae,* and all the north from southern Japan to southern California. Available Russian maps were extremely primitive, and the entirely mythical Gamaland (south of Alaska) survived until 1750 on a map produced by Delisle and Buache, names of great repute in the geographical world.[8] Exploitation of the known margins was well advanced, either by Spanish colonization in the Americas and the Philippines, or by the great Dutch and English Companies trading to the East; but real knowledge was very unequal, or unequally accessible. Already by the early seventeenth century the merchants, missionaries, and scholars of Europe had at command a great volume of information on 'Asia East by South';[9] but a hundred years later the Spanish American empire, at least on its Pacific side, was to all intents no more accessible to the outside inquirer than were those of China and Japan; the monopoly of Seville kept out legal trade. On the purely academic side there was of course the great succession of Spanish histories of the Indies, but very little indeed was available on current conditions away from the Caribbean. Apart from one or two sports such as the scoundrelly but vivid English priest-errant Thomas Gage,[10] the reporters were buccaneers who had sacked a few petty ports in Peru or New Spain, or had traversed the Isthmus, either on raids such as Henry Morgan's on Panama City in 1671, or on the run from Spanish forces; and few of these men had anything like Dampier's objective and inquiring spirit. For the Pacific coast, it is probably no exaggeration to say that it was not until French shipping came to Chile and Peru as an emergency measure during the War of the Spanish Succession that reports became available from intelligent and informed observers who were neither Spanish nor hostile; and the best known of these, Frézier, visited only the coasts south of Callao.[11]

Still, however inadequate or distorted the information on the content of the Pacific littorals, their outlines (with the gaps men-

tioned) were known: the maps were there. It was otherwise with
the truly Oceanic Pacific. Although in the two and a half centuries between Magellan and Cook probably as many as 450 European ships crossed the Pacific,[12] perhaps 350 or more of these were
the regular Manila Galleons, which even on their southern (west-
bound) leg passed north of the island groups, except Hawaii. In
the west, indeed, Iberian mariners and missionaries had established the geography of the Marianas before 1700, and either by
visit or report the Spaniards knew of the western Carolines; but
much of this was the work of only the previous two decades.
Further east, several of the Marshalls and Gilberts had been
sighted by the Spaniards, and occasional contact made with their
people; but knowledge was so vague and restricted that some had
to be 'discovered' more than once.[13]

One little group of high islands, Saipan, Tinian, Rota, Guam,
at the southern end of the Marianas, was indeed well known, and
exercised an almost magnetic attraction for the scurvy-ridden
crews, buccaneers or privateers, following in the westwards track
of the Galleon. Pigafetta says that Magellan wished to get supplies
at Guam, but the Ladrones robbed so much that this was impossible; but since he recovered a stolen skiff, burning forty or fifty
houses, it is not likely that he came away empty-handed.[14] Despite
Legazpi's formal annexation of Guam in 1565, and its continued
use as a supply-point for the Galleons from Acapulco, actual
colonization did not begin until the landing of Father Sanvitores,
S.J., in 1668; by 1695 conquest and conversion were complete;
those of the Chamorros who were left—perhaps a tenth—were safely
Christian. But in the century between Legazpi and Sanvitores,
English or Dutch interlopers on the Galleon track were keenly
aware of the value of the group: Guam or its neighbours were visited
by Drake, Cavendish, van Noort, Spilbergen, and the Nassau Fleet;
after 1668 by the buccaneers Eaton and Cowley (1685), Swan and
Dampier (1686), not to mention Anson's stay at Tinian.[15] In effect,
these were the only Oceanic islands generally and really known,
and in an odd way Guam, so distant from every continent, seems
to have been almost extra-territorial both for Europe and the
Pacific: the colony 'welcomes any ships that come, friend or foe,
in times of war or peace . . . [and] takes no part in the quarrels
of European peoples . . . '[16] Reading between the lines of Carano
and Sanchez, one suspects that this cordiality was enforced, the
Governor having little strength and hence no option.

For the rest, knowledge was scrappy indeed. The northern
coasts of New Guinea had been traced by de Retes as early as
1545, and in 1606 Torres had sailed through the strait which
Dalrymple named after him over 150 years later; but the in-
sularity of New Guinea, though sometimes suspected and even

shown on maps, was not fully a part of the common stock of European knowledge in 1700.[17] The matter, if not the strait, had been left open by the Dutch, who by this time were the experts on this part of the world; Tasman, sent in 1644 to see if a passage between New Guinea and New Holland existed, had turned back just too soon. Two years earlier, however, he had gone along the northern shores of New Ireland and New Britain and thus set a limit to any hypothetical projection of New Holland northwards into the Pacific.

Since Magellan's day, Europeans had seen a total of some three score islands east and north of New Guinea—fewer than those named by Tupaia, though spread over a much wider area. Landings had been made on about two dozen. The remote and tiny Henderson and Ducie, east from Pitcairn, had astonishingly enough been seen by Quiros; but considering the vast number of islands, the full list of sightings is short. Three of the largest and most important groups—the Society, Samoan, and Hawaiian Islands—as well as the largest single island, New Caledonia, had not been seen by Europeans, as of record, by 1700. What, apart from vague and shifting outlines, scattered dots on maps, was actually known? The answer must be, not a great deal; in Humboldt's words,

> The Pacific no longer appeared as it had done to Magellan, a desert waste, it was now animated by islands, which, however, for want of exact astronomical observations, appeared to have no fixed position, but floated from place to place over the charts.[18]

Tasman named his major discovery 'Staten Landt' because it might be connected with Le Maire's Staten Land off Tierra del Fuego (Nieuw Zeeland was a later geographers' name); he had been in hostile contact with Maoris in canoes, but made no landings; on a couple of Tongan islands he did land briefly, but had scarcely more than glimpsed Fiji. The longest stays had been those of Mendaña and his lieutenants in the Solomons in 1568—six or seven months; Mendaña again, with Quiros, at Ndeni in 1595—six or seven weeks; and Quiros at Espíritu Santo (Tierra Austrialia) in 1606—six weeks. Theirs were the only reports based on more than a few hours stay; Lope Martín and his fellow mutineers were marooned on Ujelang in 1566, and the crew of Mendaña's missing *Santa Ysabel* must indeed have lived on San Cristobal for some weeks, but none survived to tell the tale.[19] For the next century and a half, nobody attempted a sojourn. Mendaña and Quiros gave a great deal of detail, much of it ecstatic, about the lands and peoples they had found; but their Christian Utopias had failed wretchedly, and for practical men and practical purposes, their lyrical estimates of Pacific potentialities must have been discounted by the extraordinary vagueness of their longitudes:

wherever they were, they were wonderful, but wherever were they?

Still, these were the most serious and extended reports available; the rest had to be picked out from the journals of less dedicated voyagers. One can get something of their flavour from the marginal notes in de Brosses:

> I. Salomon fertile en or . . . Nations de trois couleurs . . . Perfidie des insulaires . . . Accouplement des tortues . . . il n'y a point de peuple qui se nourisse habituellement de chair humaine . . . Histoire d'une prétendue colonie européenne établie dans l'intérieur de la Magellanique . . . Histoire du solitaire de l'isle Jean Fernand, qui a donné lieu au roman de Robinson Crusoë ["qu'on lit encore volontiers"!] . . . Idoles des insulaires . . . Docilité des habitans . . . Leurs femmes se fardent . . . Haute taille des habitans. Leur méchante physionomie . . . Trahison des femmes . . . Description de l'oiseau de Paradis . . . Mauvaise nation des mille Isles . . . Entrepôt à former à Jean Fernand . . .

There is of course much more in his text; some travellers, from Pigafetta to Dampier, were good and alert observers; but it does not really amount to much. Perhaps the thing that most struck the seamen was the excellence of the neat and handy canoes; for the rest, Islanders were by and large judged by their readiness to exchange fresh provisions for trade trinkets. Yet we have already, long before Bougainville, and Diderot's Nouvelle Cythère, a faint hint of the Noble Savage, drawn from Le Maire: Man lives 'as in that first age the poets speak so much of . . . simple, as Nature made him'—along with savages, in Magellanica and New Holland, who are less noble by far, but whom we should yet 'not consider as pure animals', even if so far they are just about that. After all, 'every animal, man as well as brute, is born equally savage' and will remain so if left to himself; but even among brute beasts, how many are capable of domestication . . . '[20] The Enlightenment has still some way to go.

There was also a known and dominant route: around Magellanica, and then with the Trades across the Ocean, perhaps after some plundering up the American coast, and striking either into the southern limb of the Galleon track to Guam, or holding farther south for Batavia. Beyond this, only the outlines of the Pacific shores, disappearing into vagueness in the north, and mere spots of land, disjointed strips of coast. But in the commercial rivalries of the later seventeenth century, in the turmoil of the War of the Spanish Succession, pressures were building up which would bring about the second and greatest European opening of the Pacific, first by the great systematic voyages after mid-century, then by wider and freer economic enterprise than that of Crown or Company monopolies. In the process the artefact, rough-hewn in 1700, took on an ever more coherent outline, until by 1800 its shape was clear, and needed only a little polishing, a little shading in of the fine detail.

This opening was to bring Europeans, for the first time but for the unhappy experiences of Mendaña and Quiros, into intimate contact with those whose ancestors had carried out an earlier expansion: a diaspora more limited than the European one in actual area covered, but relative to the technical resources available for its achievement, an even greater one. This was the Oceanian expansion into the uttermost isles, the last major migration of mankind into a previously unpeopled realm. The prologues have been spoken, the actors have been brought on to the stage; and we may now turn to consider some of the problems involved in producing the drama called History of the Pacific Peoples.

A basic factor is scale: excluding New Guinea and New Zealand, all the islands of the Pacific have a total land area of about 127,000 km² (49,000 square miles) and under 2,500,000 people;[21] even adding those greater islands, this amounts to a mere sliver of the dry land of the earth. Moreover, these trifling totals are fragmented, sub-fragmented, sub-sub-fragmented, and strewn over something like one-fifth of the earth's surface. The time-scale of human history also is shorter than that for any other major division of the world: for the Islands, even going back to the earliest pre-historic radio-carbon date yet known, it begins only between 3,000 and 4,000 years ago for Watom (New Britain), but in islands east of Tonga is not much over half that.[22] Much shorter is the recorded involvement with the world at large: it dates from A.D. 1520, and until after 1770 was slight indeed. And the internal power of the Pacific Island world, in any material sense, is obviously minimal.

These are clearly limiting factors, in the sense that if we take a major objective of historiography to be the building of a picture or mosaic of the world-past (and this is something like a greatest common measure of many definitions of history-writing), then no matter how well the Pacific historian does his job, it will look like a very small contribution. It is true that other than purely quantitative values count: Ratu Sir Lala Sukuna seems to me to have had political skills fully equal to those of a Salisbury or a Parnell (to go no higher), and vastly greater than those of a Randolph Churchill, who yet made some figure in the world; and a great actor is great whether playing to fifty or five thousand people. But in the nature of the case, there will not be anything like the quanta of generalizable data that are found in vastly more populous, longer-recorded, and more complexly institutionalized societies.[23] What can be done, even within these limitations, is shown by what is perhaps the finest creative historical writing yet stemming from the Pacific, albeit in fictional form: W. C. Handy's *Thunder from the Sea*.[24] Here the particular and general do meet and marry; Pakoko's character and fate are held in perfect balance, both as Marquesan and as man. Such work has more than a local reference.

Moreover, for making the tiles of the mosaic, the small scale and the fragmentation have, at least seemingly, their advantages: units manageable in size, like the geologist's hand-specimens but yet *in situ;* the neat ready-made boundaries of islands; spans of written record so short that one can cover a large sector of their total time, perhaps all of it. And there's the rub: the insular Pacific is so splendidly splittable into Ph.D. topics that it is a very fine training ground in the mechanics; but where do we go from here?

The question has a peculiar poignancy in the Pacific because of the language problem. Certainly there are still useful topics which could be dealt with through two or three European languages; but increasingly the style and conduct, whether reactive or autonomous, of the Islanders themselves is seen as an essential factor in the understanding of the Pacific past; not least by the rising generations of students attracted to the Island-orientation pioneered by Maude and Davidson. And, obviously, to write with real authority in such a context, one should be at home in the speech of the people concerned. Unfortunately, in the Islands the local language is a very unversatile tool of trade. Owing to the small number of their speakers and the recency of their enscripting, the Islands languages are not of much use anywhere else, apart from transferability within Polynesia itself; so the specialist becomes a fine needle trapped in the groove of the monographophone. Yet, without the language, it will be difficult indeed to capture the whole spirit of the people. It may of course be objected: can an outsider ever catch 'the whole spirit of the people'? In an absolute sense, of course not; but then in an absolute sense we have to admit defeat in almost any department of human endeavour. We can make approximations, and (given of course technical competence) these will be valid and valuable to the degree in which empathy has been attained. Language is a very potent, often an indispensable, aid to the attainment of empathy.

Some might put the objection more brutally: why should Europeans write Islands history, or indeed should they do so at all? Such questions carry extreme implications, but one does find them hinted at: 'One cannot understand the feeling of Ruritanity unless one is a Ruritanian oneself', and it is implied that one cannot even comment usefully. The answer to the second is 'No' only if one wishes to bring back the Tower of Babel; the end would be a tribal solipsism. As to why Europeans should write Islands or any other non-European history, the simple answer, and a sufficient one (though far from the only one), is that of Herodotus and Terence: intellectual curiosity, or if you like just curiosity, and a common human feeling.

More seriously, there is an inner and an outer view of everything, and in so far as reality can be more than superficially apprehended, it can only be by the marriage of the two. Islanders of course should be best at the inner view—though they must grasp the outer too, to find their just place in the world; but since at this stage, unfortunately, only a very few Islanders have a thorough training in historical method, Europeans cannot help but make the running; otherwise the history goes by default, and its very raw material may be lost. But the outsider looking in must be aware of limitations, and beware of possibly distorting presuppositions: for instance, some folk have a propensity to throw the word 'feudal' around regardless. And one thrust of the outsider's activities should be to train Islanders to take over—what?

Certainly not the exclusive rights to the writing of Islands history, but just as certainly a role which is more than simply explaining their own view of themselves and their story, and what it was like to be on the receiving end of colonialism; providing raw material, in fact. (After all, even the Victorians did as a rule make the gesture of beginning with a rehash of the traditional history, or what they took to be such; after that the intellectual work could begin.) But so far, we would only be using Islanders to straighten out our own external view, and they have the right to much more than this—the right to have their own view of their history built in as a functional, indeed a foundational, part of the structure.

At this point, the problems are concerned not so much with building the 'mosaic of the world-past' as with the fashioning of individual pieces—though of course they must eventually match up. To the people concerned, this is likely to mean the use of history for identity-finding or nation-building. This is an ancient role for history; often an honourable one; sometimes, when the canons of honesty are not observed, the reverse. Initially the results are likely to be rough, not always properly critical of doubtful elements in the national story, and more or less nationalistically biased. Yet we want to be sure that the materials are sound and will match, and this not just in the interests of the world-mosaic but in the interests of the nation itself: for there is no point in producing a brightly-coloured tile which will be rejected by the pattern, and it is very much in a nation's interest to have a just pride, but not at all in that interest for it to have a legendary inflation of its weight in the scheme of things.

Here the outsider can only assist, and if the approach is too didactic it will either be rejected or will go too far in shaping the product to conform with the nice norms of Academe. His own work (if he has empathy) will probably be far more effective than exhortations to a supra-national view: that is a luxury for the arrived and assured, and when the chips are down not likely to last long even with them. There may be confrontations and rejections; biases there are bound to be. There will be a lot of trial and error, which is a homely term for dialectic interplay; and it is not so much a matter of cancelling out biases, to form a colourless consensus, as of seeing where this interplay will take us.

I do not want to be thought of as suggesting that there should be a dichotomous share-out, the Islander taking the 'inner' or local function, the European relating it to outside world forces and trends: this is simply mining for raw material again. Far from this, I think that in the long run Pacific historiography will not have done its job until Island-born and trained historians take on European themes in their own right—these last four words applying to both the Islanders and the themes. This means that historians from Fiji or Tonga should for example tackle John Wesley as well as the *Lotu Weseli na Viti;* be able and willing to consider Sir Basil Thomson as a political figure in England, not only as the supplanter of Shirley Baker. This is probably a long way ahead, and of course is always likely to be limited by paucity of numbers; but it should be our ideal, a community of scholars drawn from both cultures, each of whom can move in either with a reasonable, even if not quite equal, assurance. I think that in the long term this would be attainable, and I know that it would be most fruitful.

The small numerical scale of Pacific societies, even if they are all added together, does impose limitations. Because of the field's small bulk in world affairs, historians of the Insular Pacific may not have a great impact on the world's view of itself and its past; but they have unusual opportunities for fascinating interdisciplinary work with prehistorians and anthropologists, sociologists and economists, geographers and political scientists. Until recently, indeed, the smallness of scale and the thinness of the governmental structures with which the Islands endeavoured to come to terms, but not capitulatory terms, with 'the modern world' offered another compensation, and one of much attraction for lively minds. To an altogether unusual degree, the Pacific historian had the possibility not only of writing but also of helping to make the history of the Islands, and this in almost startlingly direct fashion: and once more we must place jointly in the forefront the names of Jim Davidson and Harry Maude. That with Independence such opportunities fall into the discard is itself a tribute to their success. A new artefact is in the shaping, one more native to the limited soil and all but limitless waters of the Pacific.

I am conscious that my own substantive contribution, so far as it goes, will be very much in the History of the Pacific, an Oceanic history, and not in the History of the Pacific Peoples; and that these few precepts are very much those of the outsider looking in. I can only plead that the looker-on does sometimes see more of the game; and that the preceptual function has been the prerogative, or arrogative, of age in many societies—and in none more markedly than in those of the South Seas. Happy they who, like Harry Maude, have sufficient generosity and breadth of vision, remain sufficiently young in heart and mind, to balance deftly on the seesaw, to be at home on the Ocean, in the Islands.

NOTES AND REFERENCES

1 A few paragraphs of this essay are from a symposium on the historiography of the Pacific, held at the Australian National University, and also appear in a forthcoming work, *The Historical Discipline and Culture in Australasia*, edited for the University of Queensland Press by Dr John Moses.
2 Chaunu 1955-59:I, xv.
3 See the quotation of 1840 in *The Oxford English Dictionary*, X, 485, *s.v.* South Sea. The Pacific south of 30°S. is still 'Mar del Sur' in the map of Oceania in the *Enciclopedia Universal Ilustrada*, Espasa-Calpe, Madrid 1964, T. 39.
4 Hernández de Oviedo in Medina 1914:I, 92-3. Technically, at this time Ferdinand of Aragon was Administrator of Castile for his insane daughter, Juana la Loca.
5 See the Korean world-map of 1402 in Needham 1959:554-5 and pl.CDXII.
6 Cumberland 1954:5.
7 Cook 1968:I, 291-4; cf. Lewthwaite 1967:81-4, and Lewis 1972:293-8.
8 Lebedev and Grekov 1967:171-5; Dahlgren 1916: figs 17, 20, 21, 23.
9 Lach 1965:I, Book Two, and Epilogue.
10 Gage 1648.
11 Frézier 1716/1717.
12 Langdon 1969.
13 Sharp 1960:13-42 *passim;* Maude 1968:50-63.
14 Pigafetta, in Nowell 1962:129, 132.
15 Carano and Sanchez 1964:Chs 2-3 *passim.*
16 de Brosses 1756:II, 198-9. In keeping, the Spanish Governor in 1898 was unaware of the war with the United States until the arrival of an American warship. Carano and Sanchez 1964:170-5.
17 See *inter alia* (and there are many *alia!*) Jack-Hinton 1969:175-83, 222, 239, and maps XXIV-XXVIII, XXXI, XXXIII; Cortesão and Teixeira da Mota 1960:IV, 414 A & B, 419 C & E.
18 von Humboldt 1864:II, 649.
19 Green 1973:14-31.
20 de Brosses 1756:II, 347, 374-5.
21 Figures compiled from *Webster's New Geographical Dictionary*, Springfield (Mass.) [Bell, London], 1972. They include the Bonins, the Eastern Pacific Islands from Guadelupe and Clipperton to Juan Fernandez, and Bougainville, but exclude New Guinea and attached islands (Manus, Admiralties), Norfolk and Lord Howe, and the Chathams.
22 Ambrose and Green 1972:31; Shutler 1971:13-27.
23 cf. Toynbee 1934:I, 445-6, and comment in Spate 1965:214-15.
24 Canberra 1973. *Moby Dick* might be cited, but has hardly so specific a historical referend.

The Pacific navigators' debt to the ancient seafarers of Asia

Polynesian and Micronesian maritime technology are here re-considered in the context of voyaging in the Asian seas. Evidence about early voyaging is scanty to say the least and, for the remote times with which we are concerned, largely circumstantial, so that any propositions advanced will necessarily be tentative. Accumulating data, however, would seem to confirm that from Mesolithic times seagoing, including deep-sea fishing, has been far more extensive than was once believed.[1]

The earliest evidence of sail so far extant is a clay model from Eridu dated about 3500 B.C., and resembling in form the later Assyrian hide-covered *quffa*. The sail itself is unfortunately not shown.[2]

The next is a high ended cat-rigged ship (i.e. mast stepped in the bow) depicted on a pre-dynastic Egyptian vase of around 3000 B.C., which possibly represents a foreign Semitic type from across the Red Sea.[3] A huge third millennium B.C. baked brick dockyard, possibly with sluice gates, with terracotta models of sailing ships and advanced stone anchors, has been excavated at Lothal on the Indian Ocean—dramatic evidence of the Indus civilization's high development of maritime commerce on the Arabian Sea.[4]

Dunn, referring to the isolation of insular Southeast Asia by rising sea levels at the close of the Pleistocene, postulates the effective bridging of the gap so formed by advances in the maritime arts between 3000 and 1000 B.C., citing the appearance in the archipelagos of innovative ceramic and other traditions.[5] Golson proposes the South China Sea as the ultimate origin of such oversea expansion and Ling, who quotes a literary reference to Chinese seagoing rafts of the third millennium B.C., concurs.[6] It is noteworthy that this expansion falls entirely within the era of sail.[7]

Giant leaps forward were made into Micronesia (the colonization of the Marianas by 1500 B.C.) and into western Polynesia (Fiji and Tonga prior to 1000 B.C.) which are not unreasonably instanced by Golson as pointing to 'a high order of maritime technology'.[8] Indeed the Marianas lie 1,000 miles to windward of the Philippines and more than 400 from the nearest 'stepping stone' atoll. The 400-mile-wide trench between eastern Melanesia and Fiji is (as shown by computer simulation experiments) most unlikely to have yielded to accidental drifts.[9]

The people responsible for this explosive maritime expansion which in the Indian Ocean reached as far as Madagascar seem to have been speakers of Austronesian languages; West Austronesian in Indonesia, Malaysia, Madagascar, the Philippines and western Micronesia; East Austronesian or Oceanic in parts of coastal New Guinea, most of Melanesia, the whole of eastern Micronesia and all Polynesia.[10]

Between 1400 and 1200 B.C., we find a 'mobile group of Austronesian seafarers and traders'[11] associated with the Lapita style of pottery, rapidly establishing coastal settlements along the Melanesian chain and, shortly thereafter, in Tonga and Samoa.[12] It seems to have been in Tonga and Samoa that they developed, in relative isolation, the culture we now know as 'Polynesian'.[13]

Less clear at present is the Micronesian picture. The western islands (the Marianas, Yap, Palau) have cultural and linguistic affinities with Indonesia and the Philippines.[14] The rest of Micronesia (central and eastern Carolines, the Marshalls and Gilberts) has as yet been little investigated archaeologically, but the languages appear to share with Polynesian a common origin in eastern Melanesia, more specifically, in the New Hebrides.[15]

A second explosive maritime expansion on an even vaster scale was the settlement of all eastern Polynesia, including its most distant outposts, beginning from the Samoan region early in the Christian era and completed well before the end of the first millennium A.D.[16]

The computer simulation experiments referred to above[17] demonstrated the inadequacy of a drift hypothesis to explain either the initial colonization of eastern Polynesia from western Polynesia or the subsequent occupation of Hawaii and New Zealand. Intentionally navigated, though perhaps one-way, voyages would have been necessary. But simulated navigated experiments (exploratory probes or their sequelae) did satisfactorily account for all these long sea crossings where drifts could, for practical purposes, be ruled out. In the other direction drifts down-wind from Samoa, but not Tonga, reached the Polynesian outliers—in line with linguistic evidence linking the outliers with Samoa rather than Tonga.[18]

Strong presumptive evidence for the Lapita people's possession of seaworthy vessels and reliable methods of navigation has been provided by Ambrose and Green, who found that obsidian used in the manufacture of flake artefacts in a 1000 B.C. Santa Cruz Reef Island Lapita site had been transported 2,400 miles from

New Britain, a journey that included a least distance across open ocean of 200 miles.[19]

When we turn to deductions about the character of the Lapita ships, linguistic and distributive evidence points to vessels stabilized by outriggers[20] and double-hulled craft[21] as having been the main vehicles. This seems a reasonable enough deduction since the distribution of outrigger canoes of all types, double canoes (and the majority of advanced sailing rafts), is coincident with that of the Austronesian speaking peoples and their areas of contact.[22] Early as it began, the main Austronesian expansion belongs to the era of sail, since man's use of wind power extends back at least to the mid-fourth millennium B.C.[23]

It is impossible to discuss the various types of sea craft met with in Oceania without reference to those of Indonesia, India, Madagascar and East Africa[24] and, we might add, South China.[25] Regrettably there is no direct evidence to date as to the method of construction of the ancient craft of eastern Asia, since no old shipwrecks have yet been located and excavated anywhere in the area,[26] and only remains of vessels themselves can unequivocally reveal constructional features.

We do have relatively early evidence for the persistence of a remarkably uniform tradition in the Middle Eastern-Mediterranean area from at least 1800 B.C. to A.D. 500. This was the laying of planks edge to edge and joining them to each other with mortice and tenon joints and wooden dowels, to form a carvel shell generally without caulking, into which frames and ribs were subsequently inserted. The earliest examples so far known, two Nile boats buried in the sand near the pyramid of Sesostris III (1878 B.C.-1842 B.C.), had no keels. Later examples, such as a Canaanite ship of 1200 B.C., and a merchantman that sank off Kyrenia in the fourth century B.C., had keels, stem and stern posts, but were otherwise constructed exactly like the Egyptian boats.[27] This shell-first tradition of carvel shipbuilding was replaced in the Mediterranean by the frame-first method after about A.D. 500.[28]

The innovation of setting up frames before constructing the shell was never adopted in the eastern seas or the Pacific, where the shell-first post-inserted frame style did not even begin to be replaced until modern times and still persists in Indonesia.[29]

But while the early Middle East-Mediterranean and eastern Asiatic-Pacific areas had shell-first construction in common, they were poles apart in one highly significant feature. The Indian, Persian and Arab shipwrights and the craftsmen who built the Polynesian voyaging canoes did not construct their shells by mortice, tenon and pegging, but sewed their hull planks edge to edge together.[30]

The sewing together of planking has important implications regarding antiquity. While the innumerable, necessarily perfectly circular holes that were needed to receive the Mediterranean-type dowels could conceivably be drilled with stone-tipped tools, the universal provenance of the technique strongly suggests the general use of metal drills.

The eastern sewn-plank construction also required that holes be bored or burnt through the planking for threading sinew, leather or cord. But these apertures need not have been particularly regular in shape. Stone, bone or shell-tipped drills would have been quite adequate to make them as, indeed, they were found to be by the Neolithic Polynesians and Gilbertese. We have even a direct statement on the matter. The para-Micronesian Ninigo Islanders informed me that in former times they had lashed or sewed together the strakes of their canoes but, since acquiring metal drills, they had abandoned the method in favour of boring holes and hammering in wooden dowels.[31]

Whatever may have been the ancestry of the Mediterranean mortice-and-tenon boat (possibly from building up the sides of dugouts), the eastern sewn-plank method represents a separate tradition,[32] and it is difficult to avoid the conclusion that this originated in the substitution of wood (once planks could be split off and adzed into shape) for the sewn-hide or bark that had preceded it as boats' 'skin' during the millennia of the Mesolithic.[33] Asia is believed by Hornell to have been the home of the skin boat, and the origin of its circum-Arctic distribution, which includes, as well as the Eskimo and north Siberian craft, the ancient craft of Norway and the British Isles.[34] Suggestive of transition from sewn hide to sewn plank has been the excavation in Yorkshire of fragments of three Bronze Age boats, dated around 1500 B.C., that were built of broad planks sewed together edgewise. It is, however, certainly on Asia's southern and south-eastern littoral and in Oceania that we find the sewn-plank tradition to be most widespread, persistent and advanced.

The sequence, sewn bark, sewn hide, sewn planks can also be observed in the Americas, though here the planked boat reached only a primitive stage. We may instance the Eskimo *umiak* and the Plains Indians' bull boat; the bark canoes of both continents; the sewn-plank *dalca* of the waters between Chiloé and the Taitao Peninsula.[35]

All Micronesian and Polynesian craft were fitted with outriggers or else were double canoes. In the former case, they were always single outriggers, that is, fitted on one side only.[36] Indonesian outriggers are more often double, that is, fitted on both sides, but there are many exceptions.[37]

Summing up their monumental *Canoes of Oceania,* Haddon
and Hornell conclude on watercraft construction that:

> Certain curious features suggest that the vehicles used by the proto-
> Polynesians had frames and were plank-built, rather than ordinary
> dugout hulls with strakes. For example: the U-shaped inserted frames
> or spreaders of Hawaiian canoes tied to cleats on the inner side of
> the dugout hull: the V-shaped spreaders of Niue, which may or not
> be sewn to the hull without cleats: the inserted frames of large
> Fijian craft tied to cleats . . . the true V-shaped frames of the canoes
> of the Tuamotus and Gilberts, sewn directly to the hull planking.
> Some of the more important of these examples are truly marginal, as
> in Hawaii and the Tuamotus, and are thus presumably ancient,
> whereas others are sporadic.[38]

This list could be extended to include the 'riblike projections'
left to strengthen double canoes in the southern Cooks, while other
sewn-plank vessels with inserted frames were the larger Samoan
and Ellice Island outriggers, the Tahitian double voyaging canoes
(*pahi*) and an outrigger *pahi,* possibly from Tubuai.[39]

The major portion of the maritime technology of Oceania,
whether Lapita-Polynesian or Micronesian, would appear to have
originated in, or been modified and mediated via, the archipelagos
of Indonesia, the Philippines and the South China Sea. Lack of
data is generally a deterrent to dogmatic assertions as to origin
versus transmission. Apart from sewn-plank and sewn-strake construction, there are several features characteristic of the area: advanced dugouts; outriggers, double and single; double-hulled
canoes; the technique of 'shunting';[40] dagger board steering of
sailing rafts; certain sails; perhaps some navigational methods.

Authorities differ mainly in the emphasis they place on one
or other part of Southeast Asia, Haddon and Hornell, for instance, stressing Indonesia's role and Ling that of the South China
Sea littoral and islands.[41]

The primacy of the dugout or the bark/skin-covered boat remains an open question; though absolute primacy, which might
well vary geographically, would seem of less importance in the
development of water craft than the adaptations and elaborations
necessary for serious seagoing. Hornell instances the vestigial
frames of some Malabar Coast dugouts and some British lacustrine
finds as suggestive of dugouts being a later development from
skin/bark-covered boats.[42] Brøgger and Shetelig strongly support
this sequence for Scandinavia.[43] The evidence from Australia is
perhaps significant, in view of the continent's relative isolation.
Bark canoes of all stages of complexity, from frameless to elaborately framed, were built, but there were no locally developed
dugouts;[44] yet ground stone axes suitable for dugout construction
had been available for at least 20,000 years.[45] Leaving aside ques-

tions of origin, Hornell, referring to India and the 'Malay Archipelago', points out that 'dugouts here attained their highest and most elaborate development and greatest multiplicity of form'.[46]

The stabilizing devices, the outrigger and the double canoe, are virtually confined to the provenance of the Austronesian speaking peoples. The unresolved question of the relative ages of double and single outriggers does not concern us here;[47] it is the origin and *raison d'être* of outrigger and double canoes that bear more closely on Indo-Pacific seagoing.

If it be conceded, as Hornell asserts, that the highest, most elaborate and varied forms of dugouts evolved in the heart of the Austronesian region,[48] then we might logically expect some connection between the slenderness of dugout hulls enforced by the proportions of tree trunks, and the development of stabilizing devices in precisely the same area. The obvious origin of double outriggers, single outriggers and double-hulled canoes alike would then be the need to supply stability when dugout craft ventured out to sea under sail.[49]

Hornell, rather surprisingly, sees outriggers quite otherwise, as extensions of the poling platforms of Southeast Asian river craft,[50] an hypothesis that would not explain the occurrence of the double canoe throughout exactly the same area.[51] It would seem more likely that once the tradition of stabilizing narrow hulls with outriggers or by juxtaposition had become established, certain advantages of what today are called multihulls would have become apparent—namely, speed, lightness, flexibility and ease of driving.

This is exactly what appears to have happened. If we are correct in supposing stabilizing devices to have originated with the putting to sea of sailing dugouts, they were, not unnaturally, applied to the sewn-plank vessels of the same vast culture area. In fact, our earliest pictorial record of craft with outriggers is the majority of the substantial sewn-plank merchantmen depicted in the eighth century A.D. Borobudur carvings in Java.[52] Among other Pacific double canoes, the enormous Fijian *drua,* with complements of 200 warriors and sailors, were of essentially similar sewn-strake construction.[53]

Apart from Fiji and Indonesia, sewn-plank outriggers or double canoes are found throughout the whole Austronesian area, as in Polynesia and the Micronesian Gilberts and Marshalls, Ceylon and Madagascar.[54] As early as A.D. 23, Strabo mentions a double outrigger ship which is regarded by Needham as of Indonesian origin.[55]

The alternative stabilizing mechanism (unavailable for dugouts but easy for planked boats), increasing beam to support sail, was, in fact, adopted in Indonesia literally side by side with the outrigger. Thus, of the Borobudur ships, four had outriggers to

E

port, one to starboard and two had no outriggers at all.[56] The *knabat bogolu* of the Mentawei Islands were sometimes fitted with outriggers, sometimes not.[57]

Doran has coined the useful term 'shunting' for vessels that work to windward by reversing ends instead of tacking through the eye of the wind.[58] The bows and sterns of shunting craft must be identical and interchangeable and the steering device transferable from the former stern to the new one. The vessel's sides, on the contrary, need not be symmetrical. Where the shunter is an outrigger canoe or a double canoe with hulls of unequal size (as in Fiji) the outrigger or its equivalent is always kept to windward.

Tacking boats, unlike 'shunters', have permanent bows and sterns that are usually morphologically distinct. Their steering devices are generally permanently attached to the stern.

Shunting is yet another Austronesian contribution to seagoing, being distributed symmetrically about Indonesia—west to Ceylon and Madagascar and east throughout Micronesia, Melanesia and parts of Polynesia.[59] Our first literary record of a shunting vessel is from the ex-naval officer Pliny in A.D. 75. Needham considers that it was probably from Sumatra.[60]

Despite its presumed (on distributional grounds) Indonesian origin, shunting is not used on double outriggers which, we have seen, are the most usual outrigger types in Indonesia and the Philippines today. This tends to favour Doran's hypothesis of relatively recent change from single outriggers to double, the site of the innovation being Indonesia.[61]

In the Pacific all Chinese vessels, the older Polynesian double canoes of Tonga and Samoa, all those of Hawaii and Tahiti, the outrigger canoes of Samoa and Tahiti were tacked.[62] Shunting double canoes, Fijian adaptations from Micronesian outriggers, replaced the equal-hulled Polynesian tacking double canoes in Tonga, Samoa and probably the New Hebrides in the late eighteenth century.[63]

This change, which was accompanied by innovations in rig, would appear to represent an Indonesian-Micronesian intrusion into western Polynesia that, in general, did not proceed farther east. An intriguing enigma is how it came about that the equal-hulled double canoes of the Tuamotus, in the heart of eastern Polynesia, were shunted rather than tacked![64]

Boats are generally steered by side-to-side movements of rudders or steering oars. But there is an alternative method which involves altering the relationship between the hull's centre of lateral resistance and the sail's centre of effort. If a dagger board or large paddle be lowered down into the water towards the stern, it increases the effective draft and the craft will turn downwind; towards the bow, upwind.

The application of this principle to steering appears to be another product of the Austronesian speaking zone, with the possibility open of its independent development in South America. It is used most often in sailing rafts (insertion of dagger boards between the logs) but is also applied in certain Pacific canoes.

Sailing rafts steered by inserted dagger boards seem to have originated in South China in remote times and are recorded in Taiwan from the twelfth century A.D.[65] There is an illustration of a sophisticated early nineteenth-century craft of the same type from Vietnam.[66] The flying fish sailing catamaran (log raft) of the Coromandel coast of India was steered in the same manner.[67] The only other place where sailing rafts steered by dagger boards have been reported was on the coasts of Ecuador/Peru at first contact.[68] Since the Chinese-Taiwanese-Vietnamese dagger board sailing rafts certainly antedate European contact with the Americas, the likelihood of trans-Pacific contact has been raised. While the question remains unsettled, it must be pointed out that dagger board steering was not used on any of the sailing rafts of the insular Pacific.[69]

In at least two Pacific archipelagos, however, the principle of altering course by raising and lowering the steering paddle was applied. One was Fiji, on the great *drua* double canoes;[70] the other was, and is, in para-Micronesian Ninigo, where two-masted mat-sailed outriggers up to fifty-two feet in length are so steered.[71]

In regard to sails and rig, there seems no reason to question the generally accepted temporal primacy of the square sail (the term refers to any rectangular sail set symmetrically on its mast), like that depicted on the Egyptian vase of 3000 B.C.[72] One may doubt that the transition to fore-and-aft rig necessarily increased windward efficiency, but it undoubtedly reduced the risk of capsize in small and medium sized craft. A number of modifications in the fore-and-aft direction took place.[73] At the risk of over-simplification we will confine ourselves to considering the one that seems most relevant to the Indo-Pacific area, the canted square sail. This is the rig portrayed on the Borobudur Javan ships of the eighth century A.D. It is still in use in, for example, the Philippine Moro *vinta*, some Bugis and Madurese prahus and on Ninigo.[74]

But outside the Austronesian world altogether we find exactly the same canted square sail on two types of middle Nile craft, the *naggar* and the *dongola markab*.[75] In which area, then, did the rig originate? Needham, judging canted square sails to have been in use in the Indian Ocean in the third century B.C., inclines towards the view that they were a product of the Indian-Indonesian and Sino-Thai culture area.[76] But this is by no means beyond dispute.

Egyptian ships carried laterally elongated square sails with top and bottom yards from the second millennium B.C. onwards, in place of their earlier tall rectangular sails.[77] To tilt this classical Egyptian square sail, and so produce the canted square sail still extant in the middle Nile, would have required but minor modifications in hoisting tackle and none at all in the sails or yards themselves.

A suggestive pointer is the distribution of the bipod mast, which is virtually limited to ancient Egypt and Southeast Asia. Such masts would be most advantageous on papyrus reed-bundle boats, the predominant river craft of ancient Egypt,[78] in order to straddle the weak centre of the hull and distribute sailing stresses between the lateral reed bundles.[79] The bipod mast was retained on many if not most of the wooden seagoing ships of Egypt.[80] It is a characteristic feature of many of the craft of insular Southeast Asia, in which its presumed *raison d'être*, the necessities imposed in masting a reed-bundle boat, is lacking.[81] Only in these two regions (except for Lake Titicaca and the Tuamotus) is the bipod mast recorded.[82]

It would appear most probable, then, that somewhere in the Egyptian/Red Sea culture area, the classical Egyptian square sail was rehoisted asymmetrically to produce a canted square sail, and that this revolutionary step towards fore-and-aft rig spread across the Indian Ocean into Indonesia.

The Indonesian boomed lateen sail would appear to be a natural development from the canted square sail, and one whose undisputed Indonesian origin rests on its present and past recorded distribution: Indonesia, and its 'offshoot' the Coromandel Coast in the west; Micronesia and western Polynesia in the east.[83]

Three main types of lateen sail are known. Mediterranean and Indian Ocean lateens are both loose-footed (boomless), the difference being that the latter has a short luff, while the former (and the Peruvian variety) are triangular. Indonesian/Micronesian lateens (and the rather primitive western Polynesian ones) are triangular and have booms as well as yards.

Like the canted square sail, the Indonesian boomed lateen has in many areas been ousted by rigs of European origin. The fishing prahus of Raas, however, that appear regularly off the Kimberley coast of Australia, are still so rigged.[84] Boomed lateens are the universal rig of Micronesia—the Carolines, Marshalls and Gilberts —today,[85] and in the vanished 'flying proas' of the Marianas, first described by Magellan in 1521.[86] In Micronesia they are used in conjunction with the technique of shunting. Boomed lateens, together with shunting, were introduced into Fiji in pre-European contact times, presumably from Micronesia (because of the as-

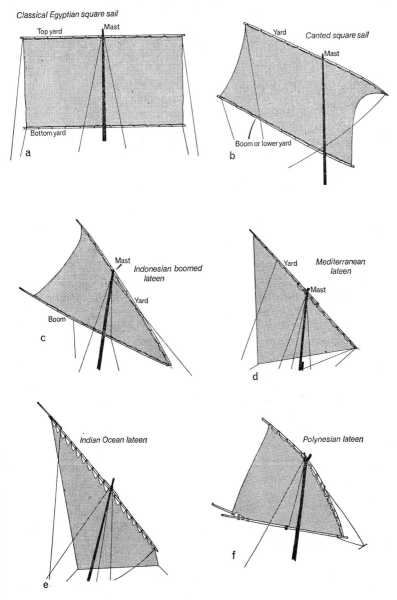

Fig. 1   Ancient sail types

sociation with shunting) and thence during the late eighteenth century into Tonga and Samoa.[87] In Tonga and Samoa they replaced a more primitive form of boomed lateen where the yard was supported in a crutch in the mast.[88]

In Polynesia, where remoteness might lead us to anticipate uniformity, the very reverse is true; complexity seems the rule and anomalies abound. However, the two millennia between the Lapita incursions and the completion of eastern Polynesian settlement allowed ample time for development and degeneration of rigs and for as yet unguessable complexities of contact to have occurred.

It has been customary to classify the rigs of Oceania into 'oceanic lateens' and 'oceanic spritsails'.[89] The first is a not unreasonable division though it blurs the distinction between simple Polynesian boomed lateens and the more sophisticated Indonesian-Micronesian boomed lateens. But the application of the term 'sprit', generally regarded as a spar crossing a sail diagonally to a spar which supports a sail's margin is misleading; it invites comparison with unrelated types of European sail and tends to obscure possible relationships between indigenous rigs. Thus the inverted triangular sail, so common in Polynesia, fits into neither category of lateen or sprit.

Undue emphasis seems to have been placed on the presence or absence of masts separate from sail-supporting spars, when this seems to have been largely a matter of convenience and the size and function of the vessel. For instance, in Samoa and in Tahiti both masted and unmasted rigs were simultaneously in use on double and outrigger canoes respectively.[90]

A provisional reclassification based on sail shape might prove more rewarding. Three types of sail, of uncertain relationship, appear to have been widespread in Polynesia; they may be tentatively classified into simple Polynesian lateens, triangular apex-down sails spread by spars at the margins, and claw sails.

The simple Polynesian lateens were boomed lateens, frequently supported by a forked mast-head crutch, thus being difficult to lower. Examples include the pre-eighteenth century Tongan double canoe (*tongiaki*), first recorded by Schouten in 1619; its almost identical Samoan counterpart, the *va'a tele* and the double canoes of the Tokelaus and the Ellice Islands.[91] The Goodenough Island *waga* similarly sported a simple lateen with the yard held in a mast crutch.[92]

The eighteenth-century intrusion of the true Indonesian-Micronesian boomed lateen hoisted by a halyard, together with shunting and unequal-hulled double canoes, into Tonga and Samoa from Fiji, where the cluster of traits seems to have owed its inspiration to Micronesia, has already been noted.

In triangular apex-down sails spread by spars at the margins, one of the marginal spars may double as a mast. Typical of this category is the mastless sail (*la*) of the Samoan *soatu* outrigger, the mastless New Zealand sail, *ra kautu*, the masted sails of Manihiki

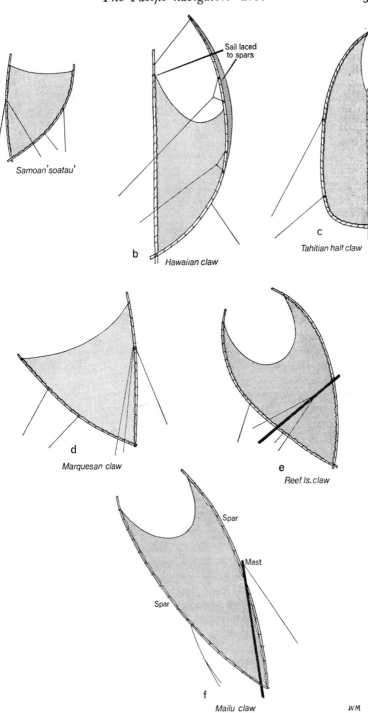

Fig. 2 Pacific sail types

and the mastless lake sails of the Polynesian outlier, Rennell.[93] None of these inverted triangular sails bears the slightest resemblance to any kind of lateen, or spritsail for that matter. The possibility cannot be discounted that some may be simple developments from plaited palm fronds. However, in view of the antiquity of sails in Oceania and the fact that some (e.g. the *soatau*) occur along with Polynesian lateens and others (e.g. in New Zealand) in places where the use of sail was declining, the inverted triangle seems more likely to be, at least sometimes, a simplified or degenerate form of the third type—the claw sail.

The claw sail is an original and sophisticated sail design and one whose geographical distribution is marginal in Polynesia (including outlier Polynesia). It was probably used on Pentecost in the New Hebrides and it survives today among certain south-east Papuan speakers of East Austronesian languages. In eastern Polynesia it has always been recorded as mastless; in the west, on the Polynesian outlier Taumako and among the Motu and Mailu of Papua, it is set on a mast. The claw sail of Hawaii may be used to illustrate the shape. What may at first sight appear to be a fanciful shape reveals itself on analysis to be highly functional. The tapering off of the sail towards the claw tips ensures that the area the luff and leach spars have to support should decrease in exact proportion to the distance from the point of attachment of the spars.

This allows efficient operation with far lighter spars and masting, less elaborate bracing and, in general, much less weight and stress aloft than any other shape would impose. These are no small considerations when one considers the weight of a wet mat sail in a light outrigger or double canoe.[94]

It is the unique 'engineering' of the claw sail which suggests that it should provisionally be classified as a distinct type—despite the discontinuity in its distribution from Tahiti to Tuamako. However, the claw sail's claim to possible antiquity as a Polynesian, and very probably an East Austronesian artefact, rests on this same marginal distribution.

The claw sails of eastern Polynesia include the Hawaiian *la,* described above, where the fore boom *(kia* or *pou)* doubles as a mast. The Tahitian 'half claw' sail was, according to Hornell, 'in its essentials . . . strictly comparable with the old Hawaiian sail'.[95] Like the Hawaiian it was usually set without a separate mast; not invariably, however, for Webber on Cook's third voyage illustrated a *tipairua* with a standing mast.[96] A Marquesan sail was sketched by Hodges in 1774. Hornell describes it as 'almost identical with that of Hawaii'.[97]

The Tuamotuan double canoes which, unlike nearly all the rest in eastern Polynesia, were shunted, possessed a somewhat aberrant rig which defies neat classification. The sail is an inverted triangle and not a claw, but Tahitian affinities are suggested by the curve of the boom and the masting, which is reminiscent of Webber's *tipairua*.[98]

The middle-eastern and western Polynesian archipelagos are dominated by vertical triangular sails, some of which, we have suggested, might be simplified derivatives of true claw sails, together with Polynesian or later Micronesian type lateens. The claw sail reappears in the Polynesian outliers Taumako and the neighbouring Santa Cruz Reef Islands, but this time it is masted.[99]

The pandanus *gabani* sail formerly used on Pentecost Island in the New Hebrides also appears to have been a claw sail, being described by Haddon as 'triangular in outline with a concave upper margin'.[100]

Even farther west, the masted claw sail is still used by the East Austronesian-speaking Mailu and Motu people of south-east Papua, whose settlements are believed to have been established about the time of Christ.[101] It is perhaps significant that this same region is one of the last strongholds of that other characteristically East Austronesian artefact, the double canoe.[102]

In contrast to the plethora of information we have about Southeast Asian boats and rigs, almost nothing is known about navigation. Even though non-instrumental navigation is widely practised to this day on the sizeable seas of the Indonesian archipelago, its methodology has never been systematically studied. We have to look to the Indian Ocean and beyond for data.

It is impossible to guess at present at what times and places watercraft became seaworthy enough to leave off hugging dangerous coasts and be able to seek security offshore. Probably this stage was attained in some areas with skin boats and rafts in the Mesolithic age.[103] Once man had ventured over the empty sea horizon, however, the arts of navigating by patient observation of every available natural sign would have been learned apace.

Once the multifarious techniques of navigating by the unaided senses had been evolved and perfected, no matter how long ago, they would change but little over subsequent ages, except to be amplified by prolonged observation of the heavens or modified in response to local conditions. Finally, of course, they were outmoded by the advent of mathematical and instrumental technology, typified by the introduction of the magnetic compass on Chinese and probably Indian ships, sometime between 850 and 1000 A.D.[104] From then on the ancient navigating techniques fell into decline, but are still not all forgotten in the few places where they continue to be practised, notably in parts of the Pacific and Indonesia.[105] Explanations for their sporadic survival despite European contact, because of the systems' incompatibility, are advanced else-where.[106]

The early date, 1500 B.C., of Marianas settlement over least distances of 400 miles between islands brings home to us how very remote are the times when navigational techniques must already have been well tested and precise.[107] Since our earliest data on navigation are much later than this and are but scanty records, the conservatism and stability, postulated above, of ancient navigation and the widespread diffusion of its practices[108] are about the only factors in our favour when we seek to draw conclusions from con-temporary survivals.

The Buddhist pilgrimages of A.D. 380 from China to India involved voyages that were dependent on fully oceanic naviga-tion,[109] but we know nothing of the nature or antiquity of the methods used. Some clue to their nature may perhaps be deduced from fragments garnered elsewhere. Thus Herodotus around 500 B.C. makes casual mention of the use of the sounding lead armed with tallow to bring up specimens of the bottom—a technique only outdated by the echo-sounder.[110] A Roman poem of the first century A.D. refers to seamen judging latitude by the height of the circumpolar stars.[111] Another pointer towards the relative uni-formity of non-instrumental navigation is a passage in the fourth century A.D. *Gatakamala,* which says of the famous Indian pilot Suparaga:

> He knew the courses of the stars and could always readily orient himself; he also had a deep knowledge of the value of signs . . . of good and bad weather. He distinguished the regions of the ocean by the fish, by the colour of the water, by the nature of the bottom, by the birds, the mountains (landmarks) and other indications.[112]

Although soundings have little place in abyssal Pacific waters, apart from the useful 'screens' of deep reefs,[113] all the rest of these accounts have a familiar ring to students of Polynesian and Micro-nesian navigation.[114]

Less seems to have been recorded of today's technology than even these ancient fragments. The Raas and Madurese fishermen, who make landfall on eight-foot-high Ashmore Reef 100 miles out in the Arafura Sea before proceeding to trochus grounds off Wes-tern Australia, navigate in part by taking careful back bearings on departure and by noting sea colour and wave form.[115] The prahu captains of Ujung Pandang (Makassar) make use of winds in their orientation.[116]

In view of this paucity of information, the only one of the source areas of Pacific navigation for which data is available is the Indian Ocean, upon which, perforce, we must concentrate.

Apart from Babylonian and other Middle-Eastern deluge myths, a fifth-century B.C. Indian account quotes the Buddha as saying 'Long ago ocean-going merchants were wont to plunge forth upon the sea, on board a ship, taking with them a shore-sighting bird'. The same custom is mentioned by Pliny in the first century A.D. as being practised by the seamen of Ceylon, who were said to lack skill at star steering.[117]

The carrying of messages between islands by tame frigate birds is well documented for the Pacific.[118] Tongan traditions of tame tropic birds finding new land have been recorded and Hornell cites a Samoan creation myth to the same effect.[119] However, apart from the possible and legendary discoveries made by following the flight paths of migrating birds, the main value of birds to contemporary Pacific navigators is in 'expanding' the target range of islands.[120] The carrying of shore-sighting birds aboard ship might have been more appropriate to the early periods of exploratory probes.

Though it is impossible to separate wind directions from their ultimate stellar and solar determinants, the system of dividing the horizon by named winds was so universal as to deserve special mention. The Greeks had an eight-fold wind rose, probably inherited from the Phoenicians, oriented by the due south sun at noon, and displayed on the Tower of Winds in Athens. From 400 B.C. or earlier the sun's positions at equinoxes and solstices, supplemented by 'companion' points, gave rise to a twelve-fold directional system, which continued to co-exist with the eight-fold one.[121]

The famous *Muhīt* (The Ocean), compiled in 1553 by the Turkish admiral Sīdī 'Alī ibn Husain from a compendium of earlier Arab sources going back, according to Needham, to the ninth century A.D., says about winds: 'The principal winds are four, according to the Arabs, the Northern, Southern, Eastern and Western; those between them are called sidewinds (*Nokeba*); but the pilots call them by names taken from the rising and setting of certain stars'.[122]

In Oceania wind 'compasses' are documented from, among other places, the Carolines, the Cooks, Pukapuka, Tahiti, Fiji and the Santa Cruz Reef Islands.[123]

By Sīdī 'Alī's day the magnetic compass had long been in general use, but certain passages in the *Muhīt* clearly demonstrate that it was antedated in the Indian Ocean by a star compass.[124] The horizon is divided into thirty-two divisions, every one of which is named after a particular constellation.[125] Such a compass card from an Arab work on navigation, the *Majid Kitāb*, is described and illustrated by Prinsep. 'The card may be divided into two great parts, the eastern and western, in which the same names of stars occur in direct and inverse order—on the east with the prefix *mutalá,* or "rising place of", on the west with that of *magīb* or "setting place of" '.[126]

The resemblance to the Carolinian star compass of Micronesia is uncanny. Here again thirty-two horizon star points are the norm on most islands, and prefixes signifying rising or setting precede the star name.[127] On Puluwat, for instance, *daane* is rising (east) and *doloni* is setting (west).[128]

A significant correspondence between the two star compasses is that both make exactly the same error (in strict astronomical terms) in the star regarded as indicating the east-west line. The *Muhīt* states that the rising and setting points of the Eagle (Aquila) are due east and west;[129] the Carolinians also take Altair (in Aquila) as a true east-west star. Both are wrong because Altair rises and sets $8\frac{1}{2}°$ north of the true east-west line.[130]

A difference between the Carolinian star compass and the *Muhīt* star points is that the azimuths of the latter are correct for the mid-thirteenth century, when the Pole Star was far from its present position;[131] the Carolinian system is in use today and includes the Pole Star among its points.

The Arabs found true north by measuring in finger-breadths, *isbah,* approximately $1\frac{1}{2}°$, the half way point between the rising and setting positions of the Little Bear. The Chinese navigators of the same period had an analagous method of measurement in finger-breadths, *chih,* equalling $2°$, but used a different reference constellation.[132]

The Arab star compass was also of more northerly derivation than the Carolinian. The southern pole took its name from Canopus (*Soheil*),[133] but many of the *Muhīt* stars in the southern quadrant cannot be identified with any certainty, and the name of at least one (*tir*) is not Arabic at all. In the Carolines five star points are indicated by different positions of the Southern Cross; none of these, with the possible exception of *Hamárein,* seem to have been included in the Arab star compass.[134] Nevertheless, no fewer than eighteen out of the thirty-two star points appear identical in the two systems.

The height of the Pole Star or its substitutes, that corresponds with the mariner's latitude, was estimated in finger-breadths, *isbah,* by the Arabs, and $\frac{1}{2}°$ larger finger-breadths, *chih,* by the Chinese.[135]

On Satawal in the Carolines the height of the Pole Star, as judged by eye and expressed in conceptualized breadfruit-picking poles (*ey-ass*), was said, by the senior navigators Namonour and Epimai, to be half an *ey-ass* at Satawal and one *ey-ass* at Saipan. These proportions are correct, since the latitude and hence the height of the Pole Star at Saipan is exactly double that at Satawal —15° as against 7½°. One *ey-ass* then, clearly equals 15°.[136]

It is clear from any number of references that the Arabs were wont to make their long east-west voyages by reference to the rising and falling of the substitute Pole Stars.[137] Such long distance latitude sailing is not documented, as far as I know, for the Pacific, but knowledge of latitude would be equally useful to the navigator of Oceania.

The longer Asian sea routes were confined largely to the Northern Hemisphere. The Carolines also being north of the equator, it is natural that estimates of the Pole Star's height at different islands should be retained in the navigators' repertoire. But south of the equator Polaris is no longer visible and, with its companions, unavailable for latitude determination.

Latitude estimating in the South Pacific was by reference to stars that culminated in the zenith of particular islands, that is, that passed directly overhead in their latitude: 'the *fanakenga* star that points down to an island, its overhead star'.[138] It may reasonably be assumed that we owe the navigational application of this concept to the Polynesians of the South Pacific, though the Carolinians used it also.[139]

The *Muhīt* mentions a 'circle of height', which Prinsep in a footnote presumed was 'any circle passing through the *Zenith* of a place, on which altitudes above the horizon are measured'.[140] There is no evidence of which I am aware, however, of the Arabs or their Indian and Persian predecessors having used the zenith star to determine latitude.

Other navigational techniques will only be revealed by the collection of field data in Indonesia and contiguous archipelagos, which possess the world's richest residue of varied and ancient traditions in maritime technology; above all, non-instrumental methods of navigation are there still extant. When compared and contrasted with those surviving in Oceania, they may be expected to throw light upon otherwise irrecoverable aspects of the seagoing heritage of mankind. But this must be done quickly because, once modernization has fully taken hold, this irreplaceable store of knowledge will be lost forever.

NOTES AND REFERENCES

1 Dart 1957 and 1960; Brøgger and Shetelig 1951; Bass 1972:12.
2 Needham 1971:607 fn. 6; Barnett 1958:221; Bass 1972:12.
3 Hornell 1946b:225; Bass 1972:13.
4 Bass 1972:15; Shaw 1972:89.
5 Dunn 1970:1048-50.
6 Golson 1972a:20; Ling 1956:51.
7 Needham, Barnett, Bass, *op. cit.*
8 Golson 1972a:20.

64   *The Changing Pacific*

9 Levison, Ward and Webb 1973:44-5, 52.
10 Bellwood 1975:10, 11.
11 *ibid.*:13.
12 R. C. Green in Bellwood 1975:20.
13 Groube 1971:278-316; R. C. Green in Bellwood 1975:21. The related groups in the New Hebrides, Fiji, etc., were in varying degrees submerged by later movements from the New Guinea region (Golson 1972a:20). A puzzle yet unresolved is that, though Lapita pottery seems related to certain ceramic traditions in insular Southeast Asia and the Marianas, Polynesian languages are derived from Eastern Melanesian, and not in any direct way from the Southeast Asian region (Bellwood 1975:13, 15).
14 Bellwood 1975:16.
15 *ibid.*:17; Golson 1972b:15.
16 Sinoto 1970; Bellwood 1975:15.
17 Levison *et al.* 1973:59-61.
18 Pawley 1967.
19 Ambrose and Green 1972:32.
20 Pawley and Green 1971:8-9; Bellwood 1975:11.
21 Ling 1969:263; Haddon 1920:77; R. C. Green, pers. comm. 1975.
22 Hornell 1946a:253; Haddon and Hornell 1938:15-16; Doran 1974:134-5; Ling 1969:269-72; Doran 1971, fig. 7.19.
23 See the Eridu boat, above.
24 Haddon and Hornell 1938:13.
25 Needham 1971:353, 393; Ling 1956, 1968, 1969.
26 Bass 1972:10.
27 Bass 1972:33; DeVries and Katzev 1972:50-3.
28 Throckmorton 1972:70. At least two distinct traditions separate from the Mediterranean seem to have developed in Western Europe: the Celtic pre-framed carvel, which probably included the Atlantic ships of the Veneti, so admired by Caesar (Marsden 1972:120-2) and the Iron Age Baltic clinker (lapstrake) shell-first type, which reached such perfection in the Viking ships (Hornell 1946b:195-7).
29 Hornell 1946b:194; A. Horridge, pers. comm. and photograph 1975.
30 Hornell 1946b:231, 192, 256-9.
31 Haidak, Itilon and others in Lewis, field notes 1969.
32 Hornell 1946b:231.
33 Dart 1957:4; Brøgger and Shetelig 1951:24; Marstrander 1963.
34 Hornell 1946b:166-7, 178; Brøgger and Shetelig, and Marstrander *op. cit.*; Case 1969.
35 Hornell 1946b:112-80; Edwards 1965:21.
36 Haddon and Hornell 1938:15, 41.
37 Single outriggers occur in Kai Basar (Nooteboom 1932:211), South Sulawesi, some Java villages, at Bantam (Palm 1962:217-70), on some Sumatran *jellore*, a 19th-century warship from Mentawei Island, and in model form (Haddon 1920:78-9).
38 Haddon and Hornell 1938:40.
39 Hornell 1936:171, 232-46, 137-9, 122-4. We are here concerned with deep sea vessels proper, and hence are concentrating on the plank-frame level of technology. The very widespread distribution of dugouts, as well as rafts and some reed bundle boats, through the Pacific, suggests that Polynesian seafarer-craftsmen would be acquainted with many kinds of these smaller craft, which would be far better suited to exploiting lagoon and inshore marine resources than the somewhat cumbersome 50-100 foot voyaging canoes (Haddon and Hornell 1938:43; Banks 1962:364). Haddon and Hornell warn against uncritical application of concepts of marginal diffusion, based on residual or purely local canoe types, to the specialized ocean-going craft themselves, since the later and more sophisticated types might well diffuse farthest over the empty ocean (1938:12, 13).
40 Doran 1974:130.
41 Haddon and Hornell 1938:13; Hornell 1946b:253; Haddon 1920; Ling 1956, 1968, 1969.
42 Hornell 1946b:187.
43 Brøgger and Shetelig 1951:33.

44 Hornell 1946b:181-6; Mathews 1908:1-16.
45 White 1967:152.
46 Hornell 1946b:187.
47 See Hornell 1946b:269, and Doran 1974:130-40, for opposing views.
48 Hornell 1946b:187.
49 Outriggerless dugouts do in some places carry sail, but rarely more than as a down-wind alternative to paddling as in the catboats of Cayman Brac and the Jamaican fishing canoes, that sail out on the land breeze and back on the afternoon trades (pers. observation, 1949). The outriggerless dugouts with auxiliary sail that replaced the *te puke* of the Santa Cruz Outer Reef Islands was a post-Second World War introduction from the northern Solomons (Silas Sitai, pers. comm. 1968).
50 Hornell 1946b:265-7.
51 Doran 1974:134-5.
52 Haddon 1920:100.
53 Hornell 1936:325-6.
54 Doran 1974:134-5; Hornell 1936; Hornell 1946b:257.
55 Needham 1971:612.
56 Haddon 1920:100.
57 *ibid.*:74, 78-9.
58 See n. 40 above.
59 Hornell 1943:42; Doran 1974:134-5; Haddon and Hornell 1936-8.
60 Needham 1971:612.
61 Doran 1974:130-40.
62 Tacking outriggers have permanent distinct bows and sterns and long buoyant outriggers that do not 'bury' when they are to leeward.
63 Hornell 1936:241, 265-73.
64 *ibid.*:92.
65 Needham 1971:393, 551; Ling 1956:47, 35.
66 Ling 1956:pl.2.
67 Hornell 1946b:66-82.
68 Edwards 1972:885.
69 Hornell 1936:appropriate sections; Edwards 1972:884.
70 Nyret, pers. comm. 1972.
71 Lewis, field notes 1969.
72 Hornell, and Bass, *op. cit.*
73 See Needham 1971, diag. p. 606.
74 Haddon 1920:100; Doran 1972:144-59; A. Horridge, pers. comm. 1975; Lewis 1972:267.
75 Needham 1971:608-9; Hornell 1946b:214.
76 Needham 1971:617.
77 Bass 1972:18, 19.
78 Hornell 1946b:46-7, 225, 227.
79 cf. contemporary practice on Lake Titicaca (Bass 1972:15, 16).
80 Hornell 1946b:225; Bass 1972:16.
81 Hornell 1946b:226, 228.
82 *ibid.*:228.
83 *ibid.*:66-80; Hornell 1936.
84 N. Graham, pers. comm. and photographs 1971.
85 Hornell 1936. The Indonesian quarter rudder is used on central Carolinian *wa* (Lewis, field notes 1973).
86 Needham 1971:611.
87 Hornell 1936:241, 265-73.
88 Melanesian rigs, many of which are of great interest, have been omitted from the argument for lack of space.
89 Needham 1971:606.
90 Hornell 1936:230, 241, 118, 131.
91 *ibid.*:266, 338-9.
92 Haddon 1937:273-4.
93 Hornell 1936:230 *et seq.*; 208-10, 184; Haddon 1937:63 fig. 44.
94 Hipour, pers. comm. 1973; Iotiebata, pers. comm. 1969. A modern Hawaiian attempted reconstruction of an ancient Polynesian double voyaging canoe has paid a heavy price in broken spars and impaired weatherliness for

failing to make her sails claw-shaped. She is now being re-rigged correctly (B. Finney, pers. comm. 1975).

95 Hornell 1936:122.
96 *ibid.*:119, fig. 81, 131, fig. 87.
97 *ibid.*:40.
98 *ibid.*:131, 86.
99 Haddon 1937:49.
100 *ibid.*:34.
101 Bellwood 1975:13; Golson 1972a:19.
102 Haddon 1937:227, 231-40.
103 Dart 1957:1-6; Ling 1956:45-52; Brøgger and Shetelig 1951:14.
104 Needham 1971:576.
105 Lewis 1972; Dick 1975; N. Graham, J. Fox, pers. comm. 1975.
106 Lewis 1972:69-70, 142-4.
107 Golson 1972a. The limitations of the accidental drift hypothesis in explaining long windward crossings in the Pacific, has already been noted (see Levison *et al.* 1973).
108 Lewis 1972:11.
109 Needham 1971:555.
110 Taylor 1971:35.
111 *ibid.*: 46-7.
112 Needham 1971:555.
113 Gladwin 1970:162.
114 See Lewis 1972.
115 N. Graham and J. Fox, pers. comm. 1975.
116 H. Dick, pers. comm. 1975.
117 Hornell 1946a:143.
118 Lewis 1972:165-6.
119 *ibid.*:169; Hornell 1946a:143.
120 Lewis 1972:173, 162-72, 217-22.
121 Taylor 1971:6-7, 14-15.
122 von Hammer 1834:548; Needham 1971:571 fn. *Muhīt* references are to years and page numbers of von Hammer's trans. in *Journal of the Asiatic Society of Bengal*, which published extracts between 1834-38.
123 Lewis 1972:73-7; Koch 1971:153.
124 Prinsep 1836:788.
125 *ibid.*:768. In the related (to navigation) realm of cosmology, the *Muhīt's* nine convex skies comprehended one within the other, whose centre is the earth (von Hammer 1838:767), is a concept apparently identical with the nine-domed Tuamotuan heaven illustrated by Henry (Lewis 1974:135).
126 Prinsep 1836.
127 Lewis 1972:63.
128 Goodenough 1953:19.
129 von Hammer 1838:768-9.
130 Lewis 1972:65.
131 Prinsep 1838:775.
132 Needham 1971:571-3.
133 Canopus is a particularly important southern steering star in the Polynesian Santa Cruz Reef Islands (Lewis 1972:49).
134 Prinsep 1838:775, 777; 1836:790, 791.
135 Needham 1971:571.
136 Lewis, field notes collected 1973.
137 Needham 1971:572.
138 Ve'ehala of Tonga, cited by Lewis 1972:236.
139 Lewis 1972:233-42.
140 von Hammer 1838:768. Prinsep's italics.

Post-contact changes in Gilbertese *maneaba* organization

On 8 April 1841 Captain W. L. Hudson of the U.S.S. *Peacock* dispatched a party of eighty officers and men to Utiroa village on Tabiteuea Island. His purpose was to punish the natives, who were believed to have killed seaman John Anderson the previous day, and to ensure against the recurrence of similar hostile incidents between the Gilbert Islanders and future foreign visitors. Some twelve Tabitueans were killed, three hundred village houses destroyed, and the community meeting house, or *maneaba*, was left 'entirely in ashes'. There is not the slightest hint from the historical record whether this 'salutary lesson', as Commander Wilkes later described it, resulted in any significant changes in Gilbertese attitudes towards outsiders. Later, however, both attitudinal and ultimately cultural changes—which were deliberately promoted by a handful of traders, missionaries, and government officials—led to major transformations of traditional Gilbertese social institutions. Powerful ideological and political weapons, fuelled by a mutual desire on the part of Gilbertese and expatriate Europeans for economic growth, consequently succeeded in bringing about changes where gunpowder and the torch appear to have failed.[1]

The Gilbertese *maneaba*, appropriately characterized by Sabatier as 'le chef-d'oeuvre du génie gilbertin' and by the first elected chief minister the Honourable Naboua T. Ratieta from Marakei Island as 'the heart of our culture and traditions',[2] symbolizes the intellectual kernel of Gilbertese culture. The *maneaba*, and its system of *boti* or formal seating divisions, also provides an excellent focus for the study and analysis of cultural dynamics.

Sufficient ethnohistorical evidence is available to indicate that the Gilbertese *boti* first appeared as an important feature of *maneaba* organization as a direct result of the coming of Samoans to Beru Island about A.D. 1400. Maude's careful reconstruction of the oral history relating to the formation, diffusion, and eventual decline of the *boti,* as part of the larger *maneaba* complex, provides the most complete picture of *maneaba* organization up until the turn of the twentieth century.[3] It must be emphasized, however, that large community meeting houses existed in the Gilbert Islands before the Samoans introduced and institutionalized the *boti* customs and, most importantly, that the *maneaba* still serves

F

as a focal point of Gilbertese social organization following the 'decay' of the *boti* and the many social adaptations required to accommodate foreign religious and political influences.

I shall stretch the organic analogy a bit further and argue, on the basis of the available ethnographic and ethnohistorical evidence, that the *boti* represented a compatible social transplantation that brought the pre-contact culture to a state of florescence. The inevitable disappearance of the *boti* as a focal principle of *maneaba* organization, and the subsequent incorporation of foreign religious and political functions into the *maneaba* governmental structure, attest to the symbolic significance of the *maneaba* as the heart and genius of Gilbertese culture.

Since only men, who are seated along a rectangular line which demarcates the seating area inside the building, speak before important assemblies of the people, it would be tempting to classify the Gilbertese *maneaba* as a variety of so-called men's houses found elsewhere in Micronesia and Melanesia. The late Father Sabatier translated the word *maneaba* as that 'which holds, surrounds the people', and he also offers examples of how it may be used as a prefix to denote either a cobweb or an enclosure.[4] The American philologist Hale reported in an inconspicuous but important footnote that 'this word [Maneapa] was so written at the time; we have since thought that it should perhaps be Uma-ni-apa, literally, house of the town, or town house'.[5] If Hale could have read Stevenson, who visited Abemama Island some forty years later, he might indeed have adopted this translation. Stevenson was awed when he saw King Binoka's workers construct Stevenson's 'city' consisting of no less than two 'Maniaps'.[6] Stevenson, in other words, used the term 'Maniap' to describe a Gilbertese house. He was, of course, only correct in so far as the roof of the typical Gilbertese house (*te uma* or nowadays *te auti*) resembles a miniaturized version of a *maneaba* roof structure.

It is not very difficult to understand why an observer in the Gilberts might possibly conclude that the *maneaba* represents a larger version of the family dwelling. At any given time one can observe people camping in the *maneaba*. A casual visitor from parts of Borneo or Southeast Asia might even conclude that he is looking at a slightly different version of a land Dayak long house. Families may be seen to occupy different sections of the *maneaba;* they have their mosquito nets tied into place along the outer roof line, their private pandanus mats may cover sections of the floor, and women may be seen to prepare food in a small hearth dug in the vicinity immediately outside the *maneaba* building itself. It would take either extended observation of the behaviour of such *maneaba* dwellers or minimum interview facility in the Gilbertese language to discover that, in fact, these families use the *maneaba* only as a temporary shelter while away from their own village. That is to say, any person or family who uses the *maneaba* as a household or dwelling will do so only on a temporary basis and while away from home. The methodological point to be made here is a simple one. Only a combination of linguistic analysis, information carefully gathered through participant observation, and the sifting of oral and written historical sources enables us to explain the meaning and significance of the *maneaba*.

Whether a Gilbertese village district is large or small, it has at least one *maneaba*. Large village districts, and there are some one hundred and thirty seven such districts in the entire sixteen-island archipelago, may in addition to the village district *maneaba* include sub-village or hamlet meeting houses. It is also common for villages and hamlets to have *maneaba* buildings that principally serve as gathering places for different religious congregations, governmental agencies, or any other special interest groups. It is a conservative estimate that, at the time of writing, there are at least three hundred *maneaba* buildings in the Gilbert Islands. The physical size of these buildings varies considerably, but they all share, with a few notable exceptions, a common design.[7] The largest *maneaba* in the entire archipelago is found on North Tabiteuea Island. It was, paradoxically, designed in accordance with traditional principles by a German priest of the Sacred Heart Mission.

In 1965 I witnessed the rethatching of a village *maneaba* on South Tabiteuea Island. This permitted me to both measure some of the critical dimensions of an average sized *maneaba* and learn more about ceremonials during the celebration held at the completion of the village effort at rethatching the *maneaba*. The celebration held when rethatching has been completed parallels that held at the erection of a new *maneaba*. The celebration is referred to as *te koro maneaba* and literally means 'the cutting of the *maneaba*'. It is a celebration which is held at every erection of a meeting house on a new site. Celebrations are regularly held thereafter every five or seven years, or as the roof structure requires repair and rethatching.

The Buariki village *maneaba* on South Tabiteuea, called Tabontebike after its namesake on Beru Island, is a medium-sized building. According to the 1964 census, there were seventy-seven households and a total village district populace of 386 persons who belonged to the Buariki village district. The village *maneaba*, however, usually is built to house four or five times the number of persons who actually reside in, and most frequently use, the building.

To begin with, one must realize that the building itself basically consists of a large roof held one metre above the ground by

massive coral support pillars. Consequently, the *maneaba* is completely open at the base since there are no walls, windows, or
doors. A person walking alongside a *maneaba* cannot see more
than the first two rows of people seated on the very outside under
the roofline. All speakers before the assembly must stand, and it
is quite impossible to be a spectator or participant while outside
the building itself. The *maneaba*, through its genius of construction, privately encircles participants and excludes, both from view
and from hearing, persons who are not seated under the giant
roof. Although the massive support pillars measure about one and
a half metres in height, the eaves of the gigantic roof extend down
about half a metre so as to require every person, except children,
to crouch down when entering or leaving the *maneaba* structure.

The roof of the Tabontebike *maneaba* at Buariki measures as
follows: width sixteen metres; length thirty-three metres; vertical
height nine metres; and a roof slope of approximately forty-five
degrees. These measurements yield a total roof area of 936 m², and
covering a floor area of 528 m². The roof itself requires 4,812
pieces of hand-manufactured pandanus thatch, hundreds of metres
of hand-made coconut sennit coir, and a variety of roughly shaped
pandanus and coconut tree logs. It takes from five to six months
to procure and prepare the thatch required for a roof, and the
entire building or repair process demands countless hours of
physical labour by all able-bodied men, women, and children.

The *maneaba* floor is covered with small crushed coral rocks.
These, in turn, are overlaid with hand-woven coconut leaf mats,
which are soaked for weeks in salt water to make them both
pliable and more durable, and finely woven pandanus mats which
are carried to and from the *maneaba* by individual participants.
The large hand-carved coral rock pillars, formerly cut from exposed reef areas with tridacna-shell adzes, that are used to support
the roof structure represent hundreds of hours of hard labour. It
is not altogether surprising, therefore, that many villages wish-
fully dream of the day when their village *maneaba*, like many of
those found on Tarawa Island and on Butaritari Island, may be
covered with a 'tin roof' supported by cement pillars, and have
more 'permanent' cement floors.

The completion of a new *maneaba*, or the rethatching of an
old one, is followed by yet another collective expenditure of labour.
Large quantities of food are prepared and served to guests from
other villages who are invited to share in the commemoration of
the collective labour and accomplishment. Since a social gathering
may last from three days to an entire month, and all invited
guests and their families must be cared for as long as they choose
to remain, the seemingly simple act of constructing a community
meeting house immediately takes on additional social significance.

While the enormous expenditure of labour itself serves to symbolize the prosperity and vigour of the people in a particular village, the 'opening ceremony' has much broader social significance: it brings people from different village districts together to celebrate and to reconfirm many kinship and social relationships. It is also a time for competitive dancing, singing, and, more seriously, the reaffirmation of a multitude of social traditions. One of these traditions, which was publicly upheld and sanctioned as a cardinal principle of *maneaba* organization during my most recent visit to Tabiteuea Island in 1975, concerns the rules of seating arrangements. One of the first and foremost of these principles is that nobody, except by invitation or while performing a public dance or singing, seats himself at the centre portion of the *maneaba;* people are always seated in such a fashion that a large rectangular space remains unoccupied during social gatherings and formal meetings. This rectangular space, referred to as *nuka n te maneaba* (literally, 'the middle or centre portion') is conceptualized as a kind of neutral social space. *Maneaba* functionaries, usually those who display prestations of food or tobacco, may place these in the centre for public viewing. Different dance groups may also occupy the centre during a performance and a speaker may venture into the space to emphasize a point. But the space is not to be used for any other purpose. Logic would dictate, as seemed warranted during the celebrations of the Queen's birthday at Buariki in 1975, that the pressure to accommodate people in overcrowded sections along the edges of the *maneaba* would result in an expansion inward of *boti* divisions and thereby permit persons to sit closer to the centre of the building. But no one trespassed the centre rectangle. The principle and custom of *boti* sitting locations overrides logic but reaffirms an organizational principle introduced into the Southern Gilberts by Samoans some six centuries ago.

According to Maude, 'the literal meaning of *boti* is "a place in the *maneaba* reserved for the members of the clan" but by extension it used to designate the clan itself, quite apart from its maneaba sitting place'.[8] In the past, persons were required to demonstrate publicly, through proofs of descent and kinship affiliation, their precise genealogical relationships to the original *boti* founder. Whether a new *boti* was founded peacefully, as when the first *maneaba* was erected by the Samoan settlers in Beru Island, or by an act of military conquest, fissioning, partitioning, or any other means as described by Maude, were previously matters of critical importance. Accurate knowledge of clan genealogies was, in other words, prerequisite to obtaining seating rights in any *maneaba*.[9]

Maude's discussion of the *boti* treats the problem of seating privileges with exceptional clarity. According to Maude, the very first *boti* divisions were established in the Tabontebike *maneaba* on Beru Island. These divisions were enlarged and contracted with the growth and decline in *boti* membership. As the *boti* system became firmly institutionalized among the other island societies in the archipelago, and especially among the gerontocratic societies in the Southern Gilberts, the patterns first established on Beru Island were adapted by the other island societies. New *boti*, created to accommodate a multitude of persons who were not directly related to the original *boti* founders on Beru Island, were established when needed. All oral traditions confirm that this indeed is what occurred. Careful comparison of the names used to designate *boti* divisions among individual *maneaba* lend additional support to this interpretation.

The great emphasis formerly placed on patrilineal descent, as the sole criterion of *boti* membership, may have led Maude to speak of the *boti* in the post-contact culture as in a state of 'decay'. This is so because only a few genealogical 'experts' in the preliterate society would be able to decide whether to include or exclude individual claimants from any particular *boti* on grounds of their consanguineal relationships to a founder.[10] Such a principle has historically only been workable in royal lineages, and even here with considerable difficulty, and the principle of allocating seating rights by demonstrating descent from a *boti* founder was doomed to extinction in a rapidly growing and politically changing culture.

The final incorporation of the sixteen autonomous island societies into one colony required the Gilbertese—at the hamlet, village, and island levels of organization—to accommodate themselves to new and foreign notions about the allocation of authority and the conduct of government. At the turn of the twentieth century, it is evident that the Gilbertese people, who had already abandoned much of their ceremonial life at the sometimes forceful requests of missionaries, quickly adapted to the foreign imposition of island councils, island and lands courts, and a judicial structure whose authority derived from a central yet still a foreign government.[11] But although many pre-contact governmental functions of the *boti* were partially removed from the *maneaba* complex itself, the traditional system of gerontocratic government in the Southern Gilberts continued, if in altered form. *Boti* membership no longer had to be diligently contested by complicated genealogical proofs of descent ties to quasimythological founders. It became sufficient to show kinship relationships to an existing *boti* member. A person seats himself in *boti* locations defined in accordance with

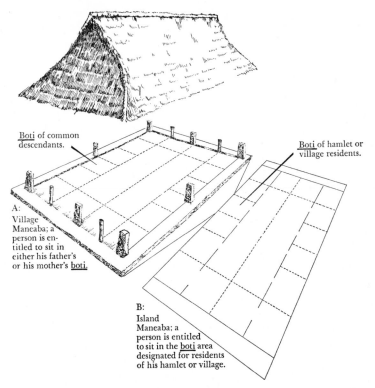

Boti of common descendants.

Boti of hamlet or village residents.

A:
Village Maneaba; a person is entitled to sit in either his father's or his mother's boti.

B:
Island Maneaba; a person is entitled to sit in the boti area designated for residents of his hamlet or village.

Fig. 3 Principal types of *maneaba* organization on Tabiteuea Island

ancient principles no longer remembered beyond the common-place assertion that 'this is our custom'.

The general rule, which affiliates every individual with a particular *boti* division in his village *maneaba* and extends to seating privileges in the island *maneaba*, is based on membership affiliation. At the hamlet or village level, a person seats himself in the *boti* division of either his father, his mother, or his spouse. In the island *maneaba*, he sits in the *boti* allocated to his village (Figure 3). In the first instance, the principle of affiliation is based on the recognition of 'shallow' consanguineal or direct affinal ties. At the island level, a person sits together with those who, like himself, own land in a particular locality and who claim common membership in a village *maneaba*. Neither of these seating arrangements requires feats of genealogical memory nor a detailed knowledge of how these customs were derived in the first place.

In 1965 I met the old men of Buatoa village on South Tabiteuea Island to discuss the *boti* divisions within Baribo *maneaba*. There were several good reasons to suspect that their *maneaba* would be suitable for these more detailed inquiries. I had previously visited all the *maneaba* buildings on South Tabiteuea Island before selecting this particular village for further inquiries. On my first visit, the people of Buatoa, unlike the Gilbertese people on both Nonouti and Tamana, where I had spent almost a year prior to this visit, cherished their local reputation among fellow islanders for being very traditional. If there were any continuities with pre-contact *maneaba* customs, it was felt that this village would be a good place to focus a study. At first glance, the residents most certainly knew more traditional dances, lived more isolated from acculturative influences, and evidently enjoyed a kind of social cohesiveness unaffected by religious factions or any of the other signs of Western influence often seen elsewhere in Gilbertese villages.

On the first day I met the representative elders from each of the *boti*. As soon as we began to work on the naming of individual *boti* divisions, however, the assembly broke into heated argument. The debate, which focused on the proper designation of boundaries for particular *boti* divisions, became very emotional and, in fact, I finally suggested—on the grounds that the inquiry was not intended to cause bad feelings among the people—that we perhaps should forgo any further discussion of *boti* customs. The assembly broke up, but not before an invitation had been issued for another meeting on the following morning. We met thereafter for three full days and the people now assumed a less combative and more serious interest in relating information about the *boti*. A representative speaker systematically pointed out the names of each *boti* division, together with the names of ancestors and the names of mythological deities associated with each division. The entire procedure did not seem to depart radically from what one might have witnessed some hundred years earlier. The first and second speakers were assigned as expected (that is, they were assigned in complete accordance with the principles described by Maude) and very little was really missing except perhaps for the refinements associated with the elaborate ceremonials described for the pre-contact period.

On the second visit to Buatoa in 1975, no ceremonies took place and I did not meet with the elders in the *maneaba*. Persons who had stood out as knowledgeable only ten years earlier now appeared unable to discuss intelligently various cardinal principles of *maneaba* organization. But neither the *boti* divisions, nor the general principles of *maneaba* cermonial organization, had in fact disappeared. Something else was happening, or had already happened, which could explain the apparent lack of adherence to previously observed *maneaba* customs. Could it be that the flourishing ceremonials observed just ten years ago had fallen into decay, or disuse? I thought not. However, an explanation for the lack of *maneaba* ceremony, and especially for the inability or unwillingness of elders to display publicly knowledge that they previously possessed, had to be sought in a rather unexpected place. As it turned out, comparison of the census figures available for 1964 and 1973 showed a noticeable decline in the number of village residents of *unimane* status, those persons or 'old men' who by custom represent and speak for a particular *boti*. The village had, within a short ten-year period, become a village essentially governed by *rorobuaka* or 'men of the warrior generation', who were heads of households but who would not as yet be recognized as influential enough to represent their kinsmen before an assembly of *unimane* or high status male elders. In addition to age and sex composition in the population structure, other important forces of change had contributed to the temporary lack of emphasis and interest in ceremonials.[12] First, a large majority of villages had changed their affiliation from Roman Catholicism and Protestantism to the Bahá'i faith. The Bahá'i congregation, which only enjoyed a small following in the 1960s, had established a mission station on the main atoll across from Buatoa village. Several householders had already established permanent residence on the main island and others were 'commuting' regularly to the Bahá'i settlement to visit relatives and to participate in religious assembly meetings. These particular villagers were adapting to circumstances analogous to those facing Gilbertese in less isolated villages nearly one hundred years ago. As for the reasons in the major shift in religious affiliations among the Buatoa villagers, I was consistently told that the converts preferred the Bahá'i faith for two reasons: first, because Bahá'i missionaries did not require monetary contributions from the villages but, in fact, generously contributed both food and medicine to the people; and second, the Bahá'i faith did not require people to observe the Sabbath. On the basis of these rather fundamental religious changes it would be reasonable to suggest that the *maneaba* organization at Buatoa is headed for extinction. Subsequent interviews with government officials who have always attempted to ameliorate relations between disputing religious factions led me to suspect that the picture was, however, far more complicated than this.[13] According to the representatives of the government, the people in this particular village were placing excessive demands upon the government for a new school, for economic assistance to pay for a new 'tin roof' on the *maneaba,* and for outright economic handouts which would permit them to construct a water supply system from a distant well to the village in addition to government maintenance of the recently constructed causeways.

This long series of separate but interrelated economic demands for government support of village activities were not made at government headquarters. They were formally presented and insisted upon during each and every visit of government officials to the village. These officials, as it turned out, were entertained and dealt with in accordance with traditional *maneaba* etiquette. One such custom treats the visitors to 'entertainment' by the choir, dancing exhibitions, and a lavish meal. It is expected that the persons so entertained will reciprocate with generous gifts of tobacco, cloth, tea, or even a cash contribution. The people of Buatoa knew exactly when and where to present a united front and they ingeniously placed government officials in the secondary role of outsider and stranger during all deliberations concerning village matters.

Maude modestly concluded his detailed ethnohistorical study of the Gilbertese *boti* by stating 'that a process of ethnohistorical reconstruction may help us to gain a truer picture of a culture, or some part of it, than we can expect to obtain by direct field observation and interrogation alone'.[14] This conclusion, which addresses itself to a methodological point, is strengthened by the assumption that 'the translation and interpretation (of oral traditions) usually necessitates a knowledge both of the local language and the local culture'.[15] Although Maude himself knew both the Gilbertese language and Gilbertese culture intimately he de-emphasized the role of that valuable knowledge in the formulation of the hypothesis and hinted in no uncertain terms that 'progress in this field will be slow until adequately trained Pacific Islanders themselves take over the work'.[16]

In this brief essay I have suggested that any explanation of culture, or any institution such as the Gilbertese *maneaba,* necessarily must weigh every single fact from both diachronic and synchronic perspectives. Any methodological debate as to the relative merit of ethnohistorical versus observational analysis is unproductive. One example must suffice to further illustrate and summarize the point. In 1975 I showed a copy of Maude's monograph, together with my notes previously collected in Buatoa village in 1965, to my hosts. Their response to the reproduction in Maude's monograph of the ink drawing of the Utiroa *maneaba* on North Tabiteuea by a member of the Wilkes expedition was unexpected. The picture, which shows a group of people assembled in the *maneaba,* uniformly met with negative expressions of 'It is a lie, it is a lie'. The Buatoa villagers viewed with disbelief the depiction of men attired only above the waist and the appearance of a naked girl in the lower right hand side of the drawing. Whether the Gilbertese in the past century went about naked is, of course, a proposition that can only be properly tested by

searching historical sources for mention of nakedness or the published accounts of Europeans about the appearance of natives.
Since European romanticists, and especially consumers of literature
written about South Sea Islanders, expected to read accounts of
erotic and carefree Islanders, one might at first suspect that published accounts dealing with nakedness and social behaviour would
be unreliable. Nevertheless, the accounts by visiting whalers, missionaries, scientists, and writers all permit the conclusion that
nakedness was tolerated, if not uniformly resorted to in everyday
appearance. The Gilbertese word *bekan,* derived from the English
'pagan', is today used as a synonym for both heathenness and
nakedness. The fact of previous nakedness can be established by
ethnohistorical reconstruction but could never be noticed by direct
field observation. The two approaches are complementary.

The Buatoa villagers approached the presentation of diagrams
of *boti* divisions quite differently. At first they were awed by the
fact that this information was available to outsiders and not part
of the literature in their own language, that somebody knew
something about them that they themselves did not have direct
access to. When I juxtaposed my own diagrams, collected from the
same village in 1965, with Maude's diagrams of the early *boti*
divisions, the people were extremely interested in studying the
differences and similarities between the *boti* divisions of Beru
Island *maneaba* and the divisions observed of their own *maneaba*
ten years ago and today. It was talking about Maude's earlier work
on Beru Island and comparing previous field notes with what
people knew and practised today that brought the point home: a
cultural account is by definition a statement about process. This,
by definition, implies consideration of both the past and the present. If a study focuses exclusively upon the past, it will necessarily
invite speculation about extinction and decay of cultural institutions and social customs. Any account based exclusively upon
field observation will inevitably rely excessively upon functional
explanations.[17]

NOTES AND REFERENCES

I would like to thank Bernd Lambert (Anthropology Department, Cornell
University) and Anne and Keith Chambers (Anthropology Department,
University of California at Berkeley) for their cogent criticisms and sug-
gestions during the preparation of this essay.
1 See, e.g., Brady 1975; Maude and Leeson 1965; Lundsgaarde 1968.
2 Sabatier 1939:88; Gilbert and Ellice Islands House of Assembly: Official
Report, 3rd Session, 26 Nov.-12 Dec., 1974:346.
3 Maude 1963.
4 Sabatier 1954.
5 Hale 1846:26.
6 See Stevenson 1900; Mrs Stevenson 1914.
7 The definitive descriptive study of Gilbertese material culture, which in-

cludes excellent descriptions of house building and *maneaba* construction techniques, is that of Koch 1965. Earlier and quite good descriptions of *maneaba* buildings are found in Wilkes 1845, and Krämer 1906. It remains for future researchers to investigate the similarities and differences between the Gilbertese *maneaba*, the Samoan *fono*, and other analogous forms of meeting house organization in other Pacific Island societies.

8 Maude 1963:11.

9 The following excerpt from the deliberations of G.E.I.C. House of Assembly, published as *Atoll Pioneer Supplement 14*, 29 May 1975:15, illustrates some current Gilbertese views on the subjects of their own culture history and, in particular, how easy it may be to confuse mythological and historical events. Allowance must be made for the fact that the published excerpt represents a truncated and translated version of what must have been a lively and extensive debate.

'Mr. Tetoa Ubaitoi (Nikunau) moved the next motion that Government is requested to invite all storytellers of the Gilbertese genealogy from the outer islands to come to Tarawa to compile the true Gilbertese genealogy that can be used in schools. He said that it is important for young people these days to know about their past, myths and tradition. People from outside have come to this country to learn and write about our stories, social pattern of living and visits had been made to Makin, Maiana, Abemama, Nikunau and Tamana. He said he was ashamed that people from Asian countries know our traditional stories better than we do.

'Mr. Ingitae Tobeba (Tamana) said he opposed the motion because *Gilbertese stories have no truth in them and no version agrees with the other*. It would appear that if we undertake this exercise, *we will be teaching our youth nothing but a pack of lies* . . .

'Mr. Tom Sione (Niutao) also opposed the motion because it only asks for the compilation of Gilbertese stories but not Ellice. Mrs Tekarei Russel said she would support it on one condition only—that no argument occur over the question whose land was first created by God, Nareau. She like to see our students at the USP to return at the end of their course and do research work before producing a publication on the subject which can be accepted in school.

'Mr. Sione Tui Kleis (Niu) said *the situation is like the time when children of Israel declared themselves as the only true people of God*. He objected because it was better to have a written record of each island than one common version which is likely to work towards the advantage of one or two islands.

'The Minister of Education, Training and Culture, The Hon Roniti Teiwaki, said Government had to oppose it because there are problems some of which have already been expressed by previous speakers. There is the question of the story to be accepted and others. He assured Members that Government would try and record stories from each island so that work could be continued by USP students who may wish to take up the task.

'The Speaker put the question on it and it was lost . . . ' (emphases added).

10 For a more detailed discussion of Gilbertese kinship principles, see Lundsgaarde and Silverman 1972. Silverman 1971 treats changes in Banaban-Gilbertese social organization.

11 See, e.g., Lundsgaarde 1970.

12 The unpublished Provisional Report of the 1973 G.E.I.C. Census, examined on Tabiteuea Island, revealed that only 12 males of *unimane* status in the age category of 50 years and above resided in the Tewei census district. The census district includes the Buatoa village population together with those Gilbertese who have settled on the main part of the atoll generally spoken of as Tewai. Only 13 men in 1973 would qualify for *rorobuaka* status or fit the age category between 40 and 49 years. Buatoa village, like other villages on South Tabiteua, has not only been depopulated but the general age profile represents a skewed unimodal frequency curve that is dominated by the relatively large number of young people in the popula-

tion. 'Young persons'—including, by Gilbertese standards, persons well into their 40s—assume the secondary role of spectators rather than as principals in *maneaba* affairs. It remains for future studies to show how demographic variables correlate with changes (which may be entirely cyclical) in various aspects of social organization.

13 See, e.g., Maude's very delightful account of how he personally helped to defuse a potentially dangerous religious conflict on Onotoa Island in 1930 (Maude 1967).

14 Maude 1963:54.

15 *ibid.*:6.

16 *idem.* It seems premature to conclude categorically that scientific and scholarly insight will be improved once people begin to study their own culture. It is one thing to guard against the dangers of ethnocentricity and quite another matter to assume that membership in a particular culture *a priori* confers analytical insights that cannot be acquired by outsiders. The many problems, some of which are fundamental epistemological issues facing all scholarly and scientific inquiries, have been elegantly exposed, if not entirely resolved, by Pike 1971.

17 See, e.g., Leach 1954 for a critique of functional explanation and an innovative theoretical approach to the analysis of social organization as a process.

Uean abara: the high chiefs of Butaritari and Makin as kinsmen and office-holders

The anthropologists Max Gluckman and Aidan W. Southall have noted that many monarchies in southern and eastern Africa, and in medieval Europe, were subject to periodic rebellions and accession wars in which a disaffected party aimed at replacing the king or his heir with another member of the royal family, while leaving the kingship unaltered as an institution.[1] A revolt might be precipitated by the ambition of a prince, by the desire of his followers and near kinsmen to advance their own fortunes, by the cruel behaviour of the reigning monarch, or even by natural disasters, which were blamed on his ritual unworthiness. 'Complicated, variable, and flexible rules of succession' often allowed several pretenders to make legitimate claims to the throne.[2] Among the Bemba and certain other Central African peoples, for example, there was potentially a contradiction between the norm of matrilineal primogeniture, which required succession by the sons of certain titled princesses, and another norm holding that a king should be succeeded by a near kinsman. A kingship rotating among two or three dynasties was apparently introduced as a compromise solution in the Fulani emirates of northern Nigeria and in early medieval Scotland, although the succession was often contested here as well.[3] Regardless of how the throne had been acquired, however, the new ruler consolidated his position by appointing close relatives and loyal henchmen to many important posts.[4]

Recurrent accession wars have been interpreted mainly in the light of functionalist theory. Gluckman regarded them as a means of reintegrating a fundamentally unchanging social order because they emphasized the prestige of the kingship even when they removed an unworthy incumbent. The hope that a local chief might seize supreme power may have deterred outlying provinces from seceding and kept them oriented to events in the capital. The entire country was unified as a single social system under the aegis of the victorious claimant and his followers.[5] Werbner has partially refuted this explanation by pointing to structural changes occurring in the nineteenth century Bemba kingdom under the cover of political oscillations.[6] The Bemba, according to this point of view, engaged in civil wars, not in order to maintain their society in a state of equilibrium, but because they found it necessary to devise a new administrative system to handle trade with the Arabs, raiding by South African Ngoni and other wandering tribes, and their own territorial expansion.

Even if the functional explanation for recurrent conflicts is rejected, however, such conflicts can provide insight into the social structure and into native theories of government. For, as Gluckman puts it, 'conflicts of organizing principles, expressed in disputes and quarrels, are not merely disruptive breakdowns in social organization but are attributes of society itself'.[7] Because any particular society is likely to have characteristic ways of dispersing rights among territorial sections or the branches of a ruling descent group, the alignment of rival forces in an accession war may be fairly predictable. Once membership in a royal lineage has increased beyond a certain point, the criteria for selecting an ideal legitimate heir are also likely to be distributed among several pretenders. Each of them lays stress on the criteria that apply to him and gathers what adherents he can to make good his claim. After the accession war, the state will probably be centralized again along traditional lines, perhaps with some adjustment to changing conditions and some surviving peripheral power centres. Centralization may mean that some segments of the ruling descent group are no longer considered as belonging to the aristocracy. In a society like that of the northern Gilbert Islands, where affiliation with descent groups, land rights, and social status were normally transmitted through both males and females, the exclusion of some of the chief's collaterals from the upper social stratum is necessary if the aristocracy is not to proliferate endlessly.[8]

Legalistic arguments over the rules of succession may mask a fundamental contradiction between the norms of kinship, which apply to members of the dynasty as they do to commoners, and the conception of the kingship as a unique office serving the entire society. Lloyd Fallers proposed the hypothesis that the simultaneous structuring of authority within a society in terms of both corporate lineages and the state is productive of strain and instability.[9] Members of a descent group are often obligated to assist one another on roughly equal terms, so the ruler's brothers and cousins may well expect to share fully in the prerequisites of authority. From the ruler's point of view, however, his kinsmen are indispensable allies but also potentially dangerous rivals unless subordinated.[10] On the other hand, precedence within the royal descent group may be fixed in theory on genealogical grounds, yet be difficult to establish in practice amid shifting political, military, and economic circumstances. In Polynesia, despite the importance of primogeniture as the basis for authority, a variety of legitimate claims could be advanced by pretenders fighting over the succession.[11] Recognition as chief depended on the maintenance of quasi-kinship relationships to many people outside the circle of the ruler's immediate kindred. The willingness to override the claims of strict primogeniture may have been reflected in beliefs that not all charismatic power (mana) over human beings and natural forces was inherited directly from chiefly ancestors; some chiefs possessed more than others and hence were more effective.[12] On Butaritari and Makin the questions of whether the chief ought to share power with his kinsmen or pass it intact to his eldest son, and whether the chieftainship belonged to a particular descent group or to society as a whole, were argued in meeting houses and on battlefields from the legendary beginnings of the high chieftainship until after its abolition.[13]

The atoll of Butaritari and the reef island of Makin, the northernmost of the Gilbert Islands, were never conquered by the warriors from Beru who spread a particular meeting-house (*maneaba*) organization throughout the rest of the Gilberts around 1650.[14] The two northern islands instead developed, or retained, a stratified society on the Micronesian pattern culminating in a high chief who reigned over both islands. The high chief's powers were sharply restricted by the small size of the society—Butaritari and Makin had a combined population of about 2,000 in the middle of the nineteenth century[15]—and by the authority of ten autonomous councils of village elders. Nevertheless, his privileges and responsibilities, and the taboos that separated him from ordinary folk, all recall practices associated with chieftainship on a grander scale elsewhere in Polynesia and Micronesia.

The high chief's office provided the society with a degree of centralization, particularly in economic affairs. The system of land tenure depended ultimately on the high chief, since he or his collateral kinsmen had superior rights to most of the estates on the two islands.[16] The chief's role as redistributor of atoll taro (*Cyrtosperma chamissonis*) corms and other foodstuffs, and of imported goods and money after 1850, has been discussed elsewhere.[17] There is some evidence that the houses of the high chief and his brothers were centres for the cultivation and preservation of traditional knowledge of all kinds, which Gilbertese regard almost as a form of material property. The high chief was also the representative and symbol of his society in its dealings with the outside world. He always had the duty of caring for strangers, whether they were refugees who would settle permanently in one of the villages and ultimately acquire land rights there, perhaps with the chief's assistance, or temporary visitors who needed lodging and passage on the next ship home. Richard Randell, the first resident trader in the Gilberts, established his headquarters on Butaritari in 1846 partly because he was assured of the high chief's protection.[18]

The authority of the high chief to settle conflicts within the society and to regulate social relations generally were based mainly on the fear of the supernatural force inherent in him and were exercised irregularly. Disrespect or criticism of the chief—even in his absence—and certain kinds of intimate contact with his person made the offender *maraia,* that is, subject to a variety of misfortunes, of which falling out of a coconut tree and the illness or death of one's children were considered typical. The awe in which he was held—and his position outside the network of kinship—made it possible for the high chief to reconcile a quarrel between two brothers without cost to the honour of either, to force parents to forgive a daughter who had eloped, and to lead a runaway wife back to her husband's house. Even the mention of the chief's name could be a deterrent to aggression. The high chief seldom punished offences committed by his subjects against one another, or mixed in their disputes except as mediator. Before the establishment of the British Protectorate, however, he was much readier than other people to avenge by force (or occasionally by the confiscation of land) real or imagined injuries he or his kinsmen had suffered. The chief usually sought vengeance for crimes generally recognized—the murder of relatives, adultery, and theft—but, since his kinsmen and dependent commoners were normally stronger than any other descent groups, he could inflict greater damage than anyone else. He could also extend the definition of these offences, especially adultery, to comprehend merely symbolic acts. Stevenson relates the story, which is still remembered, of a man who was executed or assassinated by a brother and two henchmen of Chief Kaiea I (reigned 1852-79) for insulting the high chief, who in this case did not wait for supernatural forces to inflict punishment.[19]

The etiquette that surrounded the high chief symbolized the social distance between him and other people. There was a taboo against anyone's using a kinship term to refer to him, for example. (Gilbertese kinship terms are never used in address.) Although his name could be used in ordinary conversation, he was often called *uean abara,* 'the chief of our land'. Nor was it safe for a man to finish the food the chief left on his plate, or for an individual of either sex to touch the ruler's head. People left the road when they encountered the high chief and, in this century, got off their bicycles when they passed his house. Several people told me that the magic with which Na Kaiea II (who died in 1954) had been treated in his youth made them acutely anxious when they had occasion to visit him. Furthermore, Na Kaiea did not approve commoners visiting him without bringing a gift of food, or unaccompanied by an aristocrat.

G

The status of the high chief's nearest kinsmen resembled his in many respects, however. Indeed, the term *uea*, translated as 'high chief', actually means just 'member of the chiefly status level', and is also applied to the high chief's children, his siblings, and often his siblings' children. Kinsmen of lower rank were supposed to refer to them as 'chief of our land', too, rather than by kin terms. They too could serve as mediators; when I inquired after the origin of land titles I was told of an occasion when an unnamed *uea* (but not the high chief himself) had persuaded the members of a descent group to accept a plot of land as compensation instead of taking vengeance for the murder of a stranger living with them. One of the marks of the high chief's status was his unique right of receiving prestations (*uaroko*) of *Cyrtosperma* from almost all the estates on the two islands. At least in the nineteenth and twentieth centuries, however, the full siblings of the high chief were invested with domains (the Gilbertese word is *te mwii*, which literally means 'inheritance') consisting of scattered estates in several villages. The aristocrats and commoners holding land rights in each domain were supposed to attend their petty chief's life-crisis feasts and to follow him into the high chief's presence with their gifts of *Cyrtosperma*.[20] The petty chiefs were often tempted to redistribute the prestations themselves, instead of forwarding them to the high chief, and to recruit followers for a try at seizing the chieftainship. The temptation to rebel must have been acute in the second generation, when the old chief's brothers' sons were scheduled to lose their domains to the new chiefs' brothers. A high chief could generally rely on his full brothers, whose fortunes rose or fell with his own. His sisters also seem to have been on his side, even in opposition to their husbands' kinsmen. Half-brothers or father's brothers' sons were potential rivals, however. High chiefs sometimes tried to neutralize their father's brothers' sons by turning them into brothers-in-law but they often had to fight them anyway.

A good deal is known about the accession wars, rebellions, and other disputes over the high chieftainship that occurred in the past two centuries or so. Kaiea II had the history, genealogy, and traditional mnemonic songs of Butaritari-Makin written down around 1952. The high chief and his genealogical experts were obviously concerned that this knowledge might be forgotten, although they also wanted to arm themselves with unchallengeable data to present to a lands commission. The manuscript history was made available to me through the kindness of Mr Richard Turpin, who has held several posts of responsibility in the Colony government.[21] The history, which would fill about seventy printed pages, begins with the creation of the world and includes a number of myths, but ends with realistic accounts of the accession wars of about six generations ago. Although there is no reason to doubt that many of the incidents in the latter part of the history actually occurred, they are even more significant as reflections of the native experts' thinking about their own social structure. They represent the North Gilbertese equivalent of the Beru traditions that H. E. Maude used to such advantage in *The Evolution of the Gilbertese Boti* (1963).

The story of the high chiefs begins with Rairaueana—the name means 'the overturning of his chieftainship' (see Figure 4)— the son of Teimauri and Nei Rakentai, who conquered Butaritari and Makin at the head of a band of warriors from Tarawa, Abaiang, and Marakei, the islands immediately to the south. The tradition of this conquest may not be good history—the heroes kill incredible numbers of their opponents—but it does reflect recurrent themes in the struggle over the chieftainship. The 'normal' order of succession was violated at the outset, for example: Rairaueana, although an eldest son and a conqueror, did not actually become high chief. He had been initiated by the method called Ukeukenei or Baremau, which creates an extremely 'violent and quarrelsome spirit' in a young man, as Grimble was later to hear from Butaritari informants.[22] Warriors like Rairaueana were almost beyond rational social control. Rairaueana's mother had induced him to invade the north by convincing him that he would find opponents worth fighting there. When, after the conquest, he tried to kill his own brothers, she persuaded him to make war on the land of Bukiroro, nowadays identified with the Marshalls,[23]

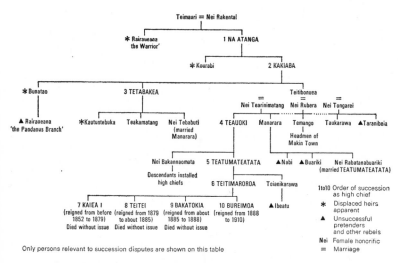

Fig. 4   The high-chiefly line of Butaritari and Makin before the establishment of the British Protectorate

and turned the high chieftainship over to his younger brother Na Atanga. Later violence in the high chiefly dynasty was also confined to the generation of potential successors. Real or classificatory parents were never attacked, even when they took sides in the dispute.

The high chieftainship and the position of headman of Makin Town, the main village on Makin Island, were apparently the only statuses in the society that were supposed to be inherited by patrilineal primogeniture. Wilkes's statement that the high chief was normally succeeded by the eldest son of his highest-ranking wife is confirmed by native traditions.[24] In default of sons, the high chief's eldest full brother succeeded him. The respect for seniority was so great that in two instances when the chief's eldest child was a daughter she had formally to renounce her rights in favour of her brother. The elder sister of the high chief Teatumateatata (Figure 4) is supposed to have said that her brother could have the chieftainship but that she would keep the aristocracy; her descendants, as the leading aristocrats, made the decisive speech at the installation of the high chiefs, warning the new ruler not to oppress his subjects. An eldest son was likely to react violently when he did not receive the food presentations to which he was entitled as his father's heir. And some people, at least, were prepared to support him just because he was the legitimate successor. At one point in the history, the legitimists are called 'those whose minds were straight'.

Succession to the high chieftainship was anything but automatic before the advent of British rule, however. Almost every legitimate heir was challenged either by a younger brother or by a son of one of his father's full brothers. Like an ordinary father, an old chief sometimes tried to disinherit an elder son who lived at a distance in favour of a younger one who showed greater filial devotion by remaining near by. In one of the best-remembered cases of disinheritance, which will be described below, the beneficiary was the chief's brother's son—but this act of generosity was considered unnatural by the native historian. Since in the general kinship system genealogical seniority seems not to have counted for much after a generation, the sons of a chief's father's younger brothers may have been quite unwilling to subordinate themselves to him. An elder brother who wanted to reassert his rights, or a father's brother's son who undertook to depose a reigning chief, needed to secure the support of the people of the district in which he resided. He recruited followers for the accession war through conspicuous generosity and friendliness. One dispossessed heir attacked Butaritari with a troop from the island of Marakei, but, perhaps out of shame for employing these 'mercenaries', disguised himself by blackening his face and cutting off his hair.

Two cases of attempted usurpation—one successful, the other not—should clarify the process of rebellion. Teauoki, whom the natives of Butaritari later considered the most illustrious man their island had ever produced,[25] gained the chieftainship through the favour of his father's eldest brother, the high chief Tetabakea, and through his own victory over Tetabakea's sons. Teauoki was advised by his own father to insinuate himself into Tetabakea's good graces when the old chief lay ill. Teauoki took his wives to spend nights with Tetabakea, although it was believed that even thinking about sex would slow the chief's recovery. Afterwards the chief allowed himself to be taken to Teauoki's land to convalesce. Now, a man who has had sexual access to a classificatory son's wife is expected to make the husband a gift called *te bora*. Tetabakea's *bora* was neither a plot of land nor a *Cyrtosperma* garden, but the high chieftainship and the lives of his sons.

Teauoki began to murder Tetabakea's sons one by one with their father's connivance. At each new moon another man would die, and Tetabakea would remove another pebble marker from his coconut shell. The victim's brothers and the people all thought that the killings had grown out of personal quarrels between kinsmen and were thus of no concern to anyone else. Once the survivors suspected Teauoki of aiming at the high chieftainship, they banded together under the leadership of the eldest brother to wage war against the pretender. Most men fought on the side of the heirs, who, as the historian puts it, 'had power to hold the office (*nakoa*) of chief because it surely belonged to them'. The word *maka*, which I have translated as 'power', has the same supernatural connotations as mana, its possible cognate in other Oceanic languages. Teauoki was, in fact, forced to flee Butaritari temporarily with his allies after being severely wounded. On his return, he was permitted to settle on an isolated islet, where he spent his time in fishing and in training his younger brothers. He made a habit of giving the choicest part of his catch to the large Butaritari descent groups, in order to put them under obligation to himself. When his brothers had grown into warriors, he assembled his allies and resumed the battle. After many days of fighting, Tetabakea's eldest son was killed and his forces scattered. Teauoki was now assured of the high chieftainship.

Before his death Teauoki asked his only surviving full brother, Manarara, to act as regent for Teauoki's eldest son and heir, Teatumateatata, who was still too young to rule. Manarara eventually tried to transfer the high chieftainship to two of his own sons. Most of the people showed their willingness to accept the substitution by making the customary gifts of food to the two usurpers. Manarara's sons, however, thought that they had to put the true chief out of the way in order to attain the full renown of the office. They planned to wait until everyone had assembled at Butaritari Town for dances and games, and then assassinate Teatumateatata in the meeting house. Teatumateatata, who was living on Makin at the time, was warned of the plot by his father's half-brother, Temango. The young high chief crossed over to Butaritari, supposedly to attend the festival, and, assisted by three of his brothers, a sister's husband, and two followers, killed Manarara's sons the day before he himself was scheduled to die. Once his rivals were dead Teatumateatata helped to bury them, for they had been, after all, his classificatory brothers and the full brothers of his principal wife. The wife, whose first loyalty clearly lay with her brothers, then threw her own infant son by Teatumateatata into the grave 'to fill it'. This insult made Teatumateatata so angry that he threw dirt on the baby, which fortunately was rescued by a bystander.

The victorious high chief, whether he was the legitimate heir or a usurper, reserved the attributes of chieftainship for himself, his siblings, and his children. The chief's brothers and sisters, and all of his children except the eldest son, became the founders of aristocratic descent groups holding residual title to estates cultivated by native or immigrant commoners.[26] The ruler also tried to assume control over the outlying villages, which were semi-autonomous. In every village but one the wealthiest and most powerful descent group, that of the village headman, is descended from one of Teatumateatata's children or sibling's children. (The exception is Makin Town, whose two headmen are descended from Teatumateatata's ally, Temango.) The defeated claimants, their allies, and most of the other collateral descendants of former chiefs were reduced to the rank of commoners. The last two realignments of status levels are associated with Teauoki and his son Teatumateatata. They not only correspond to events in the traditional history, but are attested by genealogies and land records, and may be referred to in an early description of Butaritari and Makin. Hale, the ethnographer of the United States Exploring Expedition of 1841, learned from a beachcomber that:

> Teauoki, the grandfather of the reigning king, and a mighty warrior, succeeded in concentrating in his own hands the sovereign power, which was before lodged with the whole body of the gentry or petty chiefs . . . His descendants constitute the *ioomata* [*inaomata*, literally 'free people'—one of the terms used for aristocrats], and share among them the supremacy, though there is one that retains especially the title of head chief (*ueea*).[27]

Tradition calls Teatumateatata's battle against Manarara's sons 'the war which overturned the aristocracy'. The composition of the aristocracy remained fairly stable in the nineteenth century, partly

because widespread sterility reduced the number of potential contenders for the high chieftainship and thus made accession wars
unnecessary.

The high chiefs retained much of their authority until long
after the establishment of the British Protectorate in 1892, even
though the government tended to regard the chieftainship as an
anachronism. C. R. Swayne, the first Resident Commissioner of
the Gilbert and Ellice Islands, made the high chief and one of
the co-headmen of Makin Town responsible for maintaining order
on Butaritari and Makin respectively.[28] However, his successor,
W. Telfer Campbell, who strove (in Macdonald's words) 'to
achieve efficient control over the islanders' lives', withdrew recognition from the chiefs in the Northern Gilberts and administered
all the islands through appointed village wardens (*kaubure*).[29]
The Revised Native Laws of 1917 formally abolished the position
of high chief.[30] Nevertheless the high chief Na Kaiea II (reigned
1912-54) remained easily the most influential man on his two
islands. He not only performed his traditional duties of protecting
persons threatened with violence, settling family quarrels, and
providing food for strangers, but also made arbitrary decisions on
such matters as the location of the co-operative store. The Native
Magistrates found it quite difficult to carry out measures to which
he was opposed.[31] As a matter of fact, members of the high-chiefly
family or their affines occupied the post of Magistrate for much of
the time between the 1920s and the 1950s. Some people felt that
permitting Na Koriri (reigned 1954-59) to serve as Magistrate
while actually holding the high chieftainship gave him too much
power: his immunity from criticism as high chief inhibited complaints against his actions as Magistrate. The Native Government
Ordinance of 1941 recognized the high chieftainship as a ceremonial position, and required the Resident Commissioner's consent for the installation of a successor—a provision that was to have
serious consequences for Butaritari-Makin society.[32]

The traditional land tenure system, which entitled the high
chief occasionally to harvest the coconuts from almost every estate
on the two islands, and the aristocrats' authority to organize presentations of food to him, remained intact until Arthur Grimble's
visit as Lands Commissioner in 1922. Grimble sought to end the
payment of what he considered tribute, and to pave the way toward
individual ownership of land, by assigning the high chief Na
Kaiea II a quarter of every plot from which he had had the right
to collect coconuts and dividing the other three-quarters between
the aristocratic and commoner co-owners.[33] Na Kaiea allotted all
the Quarters to his own domain and to those of his full brother
and full sister at first, but was later persuaded to reassign a relatively small number to his paternal half-brother and half-sister.[34]

The creation of the Quarters put a stop to the general collection of coconuts on the high chief's behalf. The presentations of food by descent groups continued, but gradually became restricted to those groups whose estates lay in the high chief's personal domain.

The high chieftainship was eventually doomed by the ambiguities surrounding the succession. Before the coming of the British flag, those ambiguities would have been resolved by violence, by a movement among the people at large to present *Cyrtosperma* to one of the contenders, or by a formal decision on the part of the aristocratic descent groups founded by Teauoki's children. In the twentieth century the authority to make major decisions concerning the chieftainship was thought to be vested in the traditional councils of the two principal villages, Makin Town and Butaritari Town, augmented for the occasion by elders from the other villages on each island. The men and women of the chiefly dynasty descended from Na Bureimoa (reigned 1888-1910) and his only child and successor Nan Tabu (reigned 1910-12) also had a voice in choosing the high chief, who would become head of their descent group and manager of their collective property. The last word, of course, belonged to the Resident Commissioner.

Nan Tabu's eldest child was a daughter, Nei Tabanou, but she renounced the high chieftainship in favour of her full brother, Na Kaiea II (see Figure 5). When Na Kaiea died childless in 1954, his logical successor was his half-brother Na Koriri (the son of Nan Tabu by his second wife), who was a respected man of mature years. At the death of Na Koriri himself in 1959, there was talk on Makin of making either Nei Tabanou's granddaughter Nei Neri or Na Koriri's sister's son Na Binauea high chief. The Butaritari council, however, pre-empted the choice by electing Na Koriri's eldest son Na Uraura.

Real trouble occurred in 1963 when Na Uraura died unexpectedly leaving only young children. The Butaritari and Makin councils, meeting separately, agreed to offer the chieftainship to Nei Neri, and immediately sent a delegation to Tarawa, where she was living, to escort her to Butaritari. The Resident Commissioner, V. J. Andersen, arrived later at Butaritari to confirm her succession. The descendants of Nan Tabu's second wife, however, who had objections to Nei Neri, persuaded Anderson not to recognize her until further discussions could be held. Some of them later told me that they had proposed alternative candidates, including Nei Neri's sister, but that the elders had unreasonably insisted on Nei Neri herself. The elders say that everyone, except for the 'chiefs' themselves and some people related to them by marriage or fosterage, agreed that Nei Neri, as the eldest representative of the senior line descended from Nei Tabanou, had

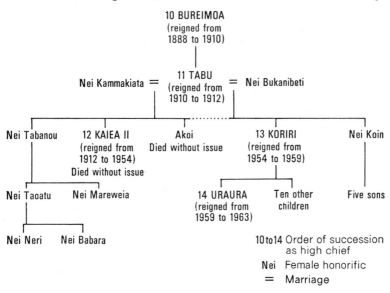

Fig. 5   Recent high chiefs of Butaritari and Makin

the strongest claim to succeed. Finally Andersen gave the 'chiefs' and the elders just one more day to agree on a successor. When they proved unable to do so, he declared the high chieftainship abolished. (He may also have felt that constitutional changes would be easier to introduce if no traditional chiefs remained.)

The disappearance of the high chieftainship not only left the problem of the Quarters unsettled, but in fact aggravated it. In 1968 a Gilbertese Lands Commissioner almost caused a riot on Makin when he tried to turn over to Nan Tabu's descendants the Quarters of the *Cyrtosperma* gardens which they had been awarded on paper long before. The Quarters of the coconut lands, however, remained in the hands of the 'chiefs' and of those persons who had either bought them from the 'chiefs' or received them in return for fostering the 'chiefs'' children or for other reasons. Almost everyone else believed that the Quarters had actually been assigned to the title (*te ara*, literally 'the name') of high chief and should not now be considered a family estate. In the absence of a high chief, they thought that the Quarters, which I heard referred to as 'the very flesh of our lands', should be returned to the estates from which they had been taken. In November 1970, just after my own arrival on Makin, about a dozen elders came over from Butaritari to discuss petitioning the government for the return of the Quarters. The speeches that some of the Butaritari and Makin elders delivered in the meeting house the next day contained most of the arguments for considering the high chieftainship as an office separate from the kinship status of its occupant, and incidentally showed that legend and history had not lost their relevance for the islanders. One of the old men from Butaritari opened the discussion by dwelling on the benefits that the old people had derived from the high chieftainship. As long as there was a high chief, he said, Makin and Butaritari had been joined together as a single society and no descent group or faction could prevent the emergence of a consensus. Another stressed that since all the natives of the two islands shared the same genealogies, all were kinsmen of the high chief and entitled to a share of his property. 'We are all Nei Rakentai', he said, referring to Rairaueana's mother, 'and we are all Teauoki and Teatumateatata'. After the meeting, a local man put another argument into the mouth of Grimble, the Lands Commissioner who had secured the Quarters for the high chief in the first place. Legend now has it that Na Kaiea boasted to Grimble that he, the chief, owned both the land and the people. Grimble is supposed to have replied with the rhetorical question, 'Did you fight by yourself then?'—a comment about the old-time wars that would occur more readily to a Gilbertese than to an Englishman. The high chief's kinsmen make the cogent point that to surrender the Quarters would leave them with no patrimony from their chiefly ancestors. They contend that Teauoki would never have left the chieftainship to just one of his children and allowed the rest to starve. In short, the dispute between 'chiefs' and people rests squarely on a contradiction in the social structure itself.

The existence of a unique office in a society where almost all roles were based on consanguinity, affinity, or various types of adoption and fosterage was bound to create difficulties. For the people at large the high chief was an office-holder—*uean abara*—who could unify them because in one sense he stood outside the kinship system and in another was related to all of his subjects. The high chief could not be referred to by a kinship term and did not belong to any descent group, but everyone was obligated to attend his children's rites of passage. On the other hand, his real and classificatory siblings partially shared his status and could make claims on him as a kinsman. In the absence of an administrative system, he could not assure himself of the chieftainship or rule without them, but there seems to have been a belief that a real chief would find ways of distinguishing himself from his brothers. This may be the reason why the traditional history puts such stress on the personal duels that chiefs fought with their rivals, and on a chief's determination to proceed directly to his objective, like the chiefly canoe which could not return to shore once its sail had been hoisted. The historian also appears to be saying that a person not bound by the obligations of kinship is likely to kill his young brothers or be willing to bury his son alive. It is clear from Stevenson's account of Na Kaiea I[35] and some more recent incidents that aggressive behaviour was expected from the high chiefs and their near kinsmen and kinswomen. The violence and the accession wars might have been suppressed if the society could have devised a concept of authority not resting on kinship or the negation of kinship. There was no place for such concepts in the traditional culture, however.

NOTES AND REFERENCES

1 Gluckman 1963, 1965; Southall 1956.
2 Gluckman 1965:138-9, 163-6.
3 Gluckman 1965:161-2; Mackie 1964:42-3.
4 Gluckman 1965:105-6.
5 *ibid.*:140-1.
6 Werbner 1967.
7 Gluckman 1965:142.
8 Goody 1966:30.
9 Fallers 1965:227-8; Goody 1966:39.
10 Fallers 1965:228-31.
11 Goldman 1970:24.
12 Firth 1940.
13 My first period of research on Makin, from June 1959 to October 1961, was sponsored by the Tri-Institutional Pacific Program (Yale University, the University of Hawaii, and the Bernice P. Bishop Museum), under a grant from the Carnegie Foundation. I returned to the Gilbert Islands from October 1970 to August 1971, and again from June to August 1972, with the support of the National Science Foundation (Grant GS-27381). Except for two months spent on Maiana in 1971, and some weeks spent waiting for ships and planes on Tarawa, the second and third field trips were again devoted to research on Makin. An earlier version of this chapter was presented under the title 'A Cycle of Rebellion in Micronesia' as part of a Symposium on the Structure of Cognatic Societies (George N. Appell, chairman) at the 1967 meeting of the American Anthropological Association, Washington.
14 Maude 1963:14.
15 Lambert 1975.
16 Lambert 1971.
17 Lambert 1966.
18 Maude and Leeson 1965:415.
19 Stevenson 1900:217-18.
20 Lambert 1966:164-5.
21 Kaiea II, Ana Boki-ni-Karaki Na Kaiea [Na Kaiea's book of stories], n.d. MS. in possession of author.
22 Arthur Grimble, Education, Butaritari, boys, n.d. MS. in possession of H. E. Maude, Canberra.
23 Grimble 1921:54.
24 Wilkes 1845:V, 85.
25 *ibid.*:100.
26 Lambert 1971.
27 Hale 1846:101.
28 Macdonald 1971:30.
29 *ibid.*:41.
30 *ibid.*:81.
31 *ibid.*:86.
32 *ibid.*:174-5.
33 B. C. Cartland, Butaritari/Makin land tenure, 1953. MS. in District Office, Tarawa.
34 *idem.*
35 Stevenson 1900:211-12.

Some problems in the understanding of oceanic kinship

MARTIN G. SILVERMAN*

At the moment of writing the Banaban people are engaged in legal action against the British Phosphate Commission and the British Government, over the way the Ocean Island phosphate was appropriated and the Banaban people have been administered. I do not think that it is stretching the point to say that there is at least an intellectual connection between the theoretical issues discussed in this paper, and the terms of what is now an action at law.[1]

In the social sciences we make much of 'social relations'. What are social relations? Good reasons abound for worrying about the problem of definition. At the same time, there are good reasons to be cautious about defining such subject matter prematurely. One of the reasons enjoining caution is that the construction of universally applicable definitions may lead attention away from the real internal unities in what we are trying to understand. The drawing of lines—what is separate from what, what is not separate from what, and how—is a very tricky business.

Let us assume that in capitalist ideology, an elemental separation is made between 'persons' (or 'individuals') and 'things'. This separation also entails the separation of individuals from one another, and of things from one another. Where 'something' appears to be neither a person nor a thing, or is on the borderline between them, there is a problem.

---

* This essay is very speculative in nature. It may thus appear to be foreign to Harry Maude's work, to his careful attention to detail and to the criticism of sources. Yet the speculation is directed toward an end we share: the understanding of a people's historical action in terms of the assumptions they bring to and take from that action. It was Maude who taught me that the objectives of anthropological and historical scholarship can meet at this point. Perhaps he will forgive the more ambitious statements, especially as they are part of an attempt to understand the people of Ocean Island, now resident on Rabi Island in Fiji, whom he knew so well, and to whom he so kindly introduced me.

I have no 'data' to add to earlier things I have written about the Banabans (e.g. Silverman 1970, 1971, 1976). I would rather like to take up a few threads from earlier work—including a 'revisit' to the paper by Honor and Harry Maude (1932)—and place those threads in a rather different analytic context, which might, among other things, facilitate comparison with related societies.

Social relations fill the spaces between individuals. One can imagine a chart with individuals as dots, and different lines running between them. The lines indicate social relations of the same or of different kinds, of greater or lesser intensity, frequency, or whatever. Social relations as relations may be characterized in respect of things ('property rights', for example), but as social relations they are pre-eminently relations between persons. The persons they are between appear as more real than, and prior to, that which fills the space between them.

'Social relations' is a derived category, and an uncomfortable one. If a social relation appears to be like a person (*l'état c'est moi*), it is open to the criticism of personification. If a social relation appears like a thing (the market), it is open to a number of criticisms: objectification, hypostasization, reification. I think that I can essentially change my relations to other individuals without either essentially changing myself, or essentially changing those other individuals. If people can essentially change themselves, does it follow that their relationships with one another will change also? Perhaps yes, perhaps no.

The separation of individuals from social relations underlies such notions as equal rights before the law. It also underlies the notion that there is an individual who remains the same individual, in an essential sense, as he or she engages in different social relations. It is much easier to imagine an individual without social relations than it is to imagine social relations without individuals. In the latter case, 'social relations' would appear only as abstractions—which, analytically, they are anyway. In the former case, the individual would not appear as an abstraction in the same sense. Robinson Crusoe was not an abstraction (conceding him an aesthetic reality); he was alone. The reality of the individual is not the same as the reality of the social relation. The individual is a concrete reality, and is at the same time the knowing and responsible subject.

Given the elemental nature of the separation of persons and things, and the very problematic nature of social relations, it should come as no surprise to find schools of social science which take up the terms: that the correct orientation of the study of human behaviour is the study of individuals; that the correct orientation of the study of human behaviour is the study of things, such as technology in the narrow sense. The two approaches seem antithetical to one another, and are antithetical to one another, but as opposite sides of the same coin. It is surely difficult to challenge the point that one should explain what is less real (relations) in terms of what is more real (individuals). It is difficult to challenge such an assumption without challenging the ideology which frames the options themselves.

At one important level, individuals, social relations and things appear separable from one another. The critical exception seems to lie in consanguineal kinship (and in relations similar in form to it). In consanguineal kinship, an internal substance—blood—is the foundation of the relation. Blood is a thing-like yet living reality in the real individual.[2] At this level kinship relations contrast with market or contractual 'relations', in which individuals (ideologically) voluntarily exchange things which are separable from them, without exchanging their selves. I may indeed regard my employer as 'owning me', but that is a very counter-ideological notion.

Looked at from its own perspective, the consanguineal relation is more real than, say, a relation of buyer and seller. My consanguine and I are 'of the same blood'. But at the same time, we each individually have (or, more tellingly, 'possess') that blood. And here we come to that unresolved paradox: the most unbreakable relations are the most real, and the most real are grounded in a substance internal to the individual. But consanguinity and relations similar in form to it are 'accidents of birth'. Indeed, economically, they function as obstacles to a 'perfect labour market', since decisions concerning where to take a job and what job to take, are complicated by such 'irrational' considerations as extra-nuclear family kinship ties. Once we get beyond the simple world of individuals and things, reality is an accident.

Kinship relations are more real than market relations in so far as they are 'internalized to' the individual. Market or contractual relations, it seems to me, appear more real when they appear most like kinship: the 'university tradition', 'the corporate family'. Action, in the world of contract, has the appearance of an exchange of things between individuals. Action, in the world of kinship, has the appearance of the enactment of a relationship—but, once more, quite possibly between individuals. We might turn the phraseology around: action which has the appearance of the enactment of a 'real' relationship indicates to us the existence of something like kinship. Action which has the appearance of the exchange of things separable from individuals, between individuals, indicates to us the existence of something like contract or the market.

The relations between persons and things are not the same in the two options considered at this level. The birthday present between kin is not equivalent to the delivery of a typewriter from a typewriter manufacturer. When they do appear as equivalent, then either the kin relation becomes suspect as such, or one is really accepting the proposition that IBM is your friend. The fact of this relationship between persons and things in the kinship context is probably one reason why we can make intellectual contact with relations in other societies, but it also contains a limitation, as we will see.

The internalization to the individual of the kin relation (blood) sets up the possibility of the mutual substitutability of kin and contractual relations, once the individual is taken as the privileged point of reference. On the one hand, kin relations and contractual relations are radically different from one another. The relations between individuals, social relations and things are not the same for both. But, on the other hand, given the separation of individuals, social relations and things, kin relations and contractual relations are not radically different from one another. Both can be constructed in terms of individuals, engaged in 'relations' (as patterns of behaviour) which occur between them, exchanging things separable from them. It becomes possible to construct 'the good parent' or 'the good spouse' along the same lines as 'the good employer', 'the good employee', or 'the good mechanic'. And, indeed, certain people have the option of substituting one for the other—for example, hiring a housekeeper and a sexual partner versus marriage; buying washing machines and vacuum cleaners versus hiring a housekeeper . . .

The real separation of persons, social relations and things means the absence of any inherent connection between them. Socially, relations between them must be established, relations between what is already separated. Analytically, having made the separation, we re-generate for ourselves the problem of their interrelations in another way. We ask which is more determinate, or speak somewhat mysteriously of 'feedback' or 'dialectic'. It is very easy to sidestep the larger question: under what conditions do those separations occur?

My simple concept of pre-colonial Banaban society is this: the 'elemental separation' of the same order as the separation of persons and things in capitalist ideology was the separation between relationships of different kinds. These relationships, as relationships, included aspects of persons, things, and behaviours. Within a relationship, the clearest separation of aspects such as persons, things and behaviours occurred in the context of conflict. Furthermore, relationships were real. In this essay I will not discuss the differences between relationships of different kinds, but rather these shared features. The essay is very much of the 'what if' genre.

In a society that does not produce commodities, one would not expect all 'things' to be considered of the same order. In *The Social Organization of Banaba or Ocean Island, Central Pacific,* H. C. Maude and H. E. Maude discuss access to and inheritance patterns regarding a number of things, including lands (considered parts of hamlets, but usually passing from parent to child); water-caves (within hamlets); the meeting houses, spirit houses and terraces of village districts (and we may add, fishing rights on their foreshores, where applicable), and things and activities tied up with the 'ritual system' which linked units at various levels.

In retrospect, one sort of discussion is striking by its absence in this context: a discussion of access to a variety of other things. With such careful ethnographers on matters such as this as the Maudes, one can justifiably assume a good reason for the absence of such a discussion. The 'things' they do talk about form part of a single but differentiated system of 'things' which are *sine qua non* conditions of production and reproduction, 'reproduction' being considered here in the enlarged Marxist sense of 'reproduction of the conditions of production'.

How can we speak of people's 'relations to' these conditions?

Gilbertese, which is spoken by the Banabans, features a contrast which seems to be generally the same as that described by Oliver for Tahitian:

> It would not be practicable to draw up an exhaustive list of the innumerable types of goods that circulated among the Maohis. Even formulating a list of the principal categories of such goods raises methodological problems that I am unable to solve . . . The language does, however, contain the widespread Polynesian *o-a* contrast, the so-called markers of alienability which occur as parts of most possessives.[3] Briefly stated, *o* is used for possession which is intimate, innate or permanent, while *a* is used for possession which is incidental or transient.[4]

In his work, *The Structure of Gilbertese*, published in 1951, Cowell observes: 'There are two classes of nouns distinguished by their ability to take a suffixed or a prefixed possessive pronoun'.[5] He lists the nouns which take the suffixed possessive pronouns as: (a) parts of the body and of things (e.g., my arm; his, her, its side); (b) physical and mental attributes (e.g., your sickness, their opinion); (c) gerunds (e.g., our coming); (d) terms of relationship except two referring to relatives in general, one for ancestors, and one for parents; (e) 'personal possessions, the derivation of which is purely vernacular of which the most common are . . . ' words meaning canoe, house, skirt, hat, cane, mat, land, food, drink, garland and residence; and (f) quantitative nouns (e.g., many, total) when followed by an animal noun.[6] Cowell goes on to observe:

> The use of the possessive with the gerund gives rise to difficulty. A quotation from a popular song will clarify—
> *Ai   nano   ra   tangiram   irou!*
> How   deep (is) the loving-of-you   by-me!
> Idiomatic English would read—
> How deep is my love for you!

If it is remembered that the *possessive* nounal suffix denotes possession by the person to whom the noun refers there should be no difficulty.[7]

The linguistic interpretation of 'possession' in Gilbertese awaits the publication of work on the language as a whole, particularly given Cowell's last observation and related usages. I should note that there are some 'nouns' which differ in meaning according to whether the suffixed or prefixed form is used, the differences seeming to follow the same general logic. Apparently new usages indicate that the contrast is a live one: for example, *wina*, 'his her, its teeth'; *ana wi*, 'his, her keys';[8] *tamami*, 'your (pl.) father'; *ami tama*, 'your (pl.) Catholic priest'.

One can think of the relation indicated by the suffix much as Oliver does: inalienable, intimate, innate, permanent. The examples given by Cowell in (e) include things closely associated with the body, house and residence, canoes—and land. And 'kinship terms', with a few exceptions. Thus 'my land' is constructed according to the same form as 'my mother', 'my arm', 'my garland', etc.

The clue provided here, although there are still uninterpreted loose ends, is that there are two kinds of relationship 'between' a person or persons and the 'it' to which a person relates: one which suggests inalienability, innateness, permanence, attachedness; one which suggests alienability, separation.[9] Your land and your kin (at least your more particular sorts of kin, e.g., 'father' and 'mother', yes; 'parents', no) among other things, fall into the 'inalienable' pattern.

The situation with regard to water-caves and the terraces and foreshores of village districts is unclear to me, and is complex when it comes to ritual rights. As far as the latter are concerned, however, there is a term used in the sense of 'rights' of this sort which is also used for 'behaviour, way, custom, manner', and which takes the possessive suffix. Interestingly enough, the term used with the prefixed form these days means 'sect'. A text recorded on Ocean Island by Sir Arthur Grimble uses the suffix to refer to some particular ritual rights *vis-à-vis* their holder.[10]

Now for the problem of interpretation. If we say something like: 'Generally speaking, people had access to things which are *sine qua non* conditions of production and reproduction through their father and their mother', or some similar phraseology, this might suggest a number of options: for example, a mother-child relation, which involves rights to land, and to certain ritual prerogatives. Or let us say that we are on the ground and we start our analysis with two real people, Temanna and Uoman. We define a relation between them as being a mother-child relation, and we could describe it as being a relation of 'mutual affection',

H

or 'hate', or whatever. And we perhaps note that the relation 'functions' in regard to land, or involves rights in respect to land.

Here the ambiguity in the history of Western law is itself instructive. Does 'property' refer to 'the thing itself', or to a bundle of rights between persons in respect of a thing? In the Introduction to *Cheshire's Modern Law of Real Property,* we read of:

> the invention and development by the common law of the doctrine of an estate in the land as something distinct from the land itself, a distinction which has enabled proprietary rights to be moulded with a flexibility wholly unknown to the legal systems that derive from Rome.[11]

In this respect at least, the Banaban view may have been closer to that derived from Rome than from the conditions of English feudalism. For what if the land, or rather the specific lands, constitute part of the 'relationship' itself? That is to say, the notion of social relation we would have to use would have to include in its very essence something which may appear to us as a separable thing. Lands under this interpretation do not only symbolize a relationship. Nor are they 'only' things to which access is gained through a relationship. Nor do they only underlie (as it were) a relationship. Lands are constitutive of relationships, but of relationships which are not contractual in our sense. Thus as we look at a relationship (or at least some kinds of relationships), one of the things we literally have to look at is the lands. It can even be misleading to say that people have a relation to land, thus positing people, land, and a relation between them.

From the perspective of a 'social relation' of this sort, the separation of persons and land is not something which occurs simply because persons and lands are 'not the same'. The separation of persons and land is made when someone or some group makes it: most conspicuously, in situations of conflict.

The 'stable' state of affairs to the Banaban people is an internal relation between them, within a social relation. When a specific internal relation becomes sundered (for example, land passing outside parent-child inheritance channels), that calls for special explanation. And when 'things' appear outside social relations, those things have to be placed within them. On the latter point I have in mind the rights which I have grouped together as 'ritual incorporation': rights to initiate dealings with strangers to the island; porpoise, turtle or *urua* fish stranded on the foreshores; some flotsam and jetsam. Their transmission and division (in the case of objects) between groups brought them into a relationship, as the action of dealing with them gave life to some of the relations. Operating on the assumption that all things on Ocean Island were produced or appropriated within social relations, these would have been things which initially were not.

In the Maudes' description of the kinds of land conveyances customary on Ocean Island in times of peace (information is too incomplete to say much about warfare), there are some conveyances which we may well interpret as involving a separation of people from their lands: land passing from a murderer to the family of the murdered man; land passing from adulterer to cuckold. And:

> On a famine occurring, those who were destitute would go and live with those who had food or were skilled fishermen. These people would look after them throughout the famine and when it was over were entitled to take all their lands under the title of *te aba ni kamaiu* (the land of life-giving). The destitute might continue to use the products of their old land sufficient to maintain them, but in any case the land passed irrevocably on their death.
>
> Should a betrothed boy break off his engagement to a girl after having commenced sexual relations with her, four or five lands would normally pass from his family to hers under the title of *te aba n iein* (the land of marriage). One or two lands would often pass on a boy terminating his engagement even if no sexual intercourse had taken place. Should the girl break off her engagement no land would pass. On Banaba it was customary for betrothals to take place at a very early age, often as soon as the child was born.
>
> Should it be generally considered that certain lands had got into the wrong hands resort could be had to a custom known as *te aba ni butirake* (land of the asking). A girl would bind wreaths on the old man or woman who had obtained the land in question and he (or she) was then compelled by this custom to give the girl a piece or pieces of land. Should there be no good reason for the binding of the wreaths the old man might satisfy the island by presenting a minute plot of land, but should it be general opinion that the girl or her family were the rightful owners of certain lands in his possession he would be expected to give them up with a good grace.
>
> Should an individual kill any tame frigate or other bird belonging to another, one piece of land would be conveyed by the killer to the owner of the bird under the title of *nenebo-n te man* (the blood payment for animals) . . . Should an individual offend against any social convention for which a transfer of land was considered a fitting penalty, a meeting of his hamlet would be held and the offender ordered to forfeit certain of his lands to the person injured. If the affair was serious and beyond the control of the hamlet a meeting of the village district, or even of the whole island, would be held at which the trouble could be ventilated and appropriate measures for restoring the status quo discussed.[12]

I would like to take seriously the notion of 'restoring the status quo'. The transfers of land here can be interpreted as compensations for a loss in a relationship, a loss of persons and things closely tied to production and reproduction, although the role of frigate birds is unclear.

The destitute, in times of famine, were in effect forfeiting the possibility of their own reproduction in exchange for food, since their children (if any) would have no land to inherit from them. I did not find it appropriate to inquire deeply into this situation, hence I can only speculate on its interpretation. Given the Banaban stress on sharing food among kin, this condition was perhaps most likely to arise if in a famine people could not get food in the 'usual' way from their relatives who had it. Alternatively, some people may have taken advantage of their own relative prosperity to acquire land from others. In either case, a full kin relation may have been being denied (or was absent) and the famine would have been more comparable with warfare.

It is not inconceivable that 'the land of asking' might have been a way of restoring some of these lands to their original owners at a later time. One Banaban friend astute in traditional matters told me rather mysteriously that people who had lost land rights in an area might even now turn up at celebrations involving people who still had land rights in that area. This is itself part of a pattern: the most spectacular instance of people allegedly losing their ritual rights is in fact fraught with ambiguities. People are not surprised if a child adopted from his or her original parents without receiving land from them (and thus their 'child' 'only' in the sense of sharing blood) wants to relate to them positively. The general point may be this: once a productive or reproductive 'inalienable' or 'part' is taken out of the relationship within which it occurred, traces of that inalienability remain.

In a previous work I referred to the *ceteris paribus* ('other things being equal') indigenous model of traditional Banaban social structure. In this model the bilateral descendants of X live on territory Y and conduct a set of ritual activities, Z. The distribution or circulation of descent, people on a territory, and rights in ritual activities, coincides. In actuality these 'three' distributions rarely coincide. As was pointed out, different pictures of the social structure can be constructed by the people if they start from different points: from descent, from land and territory, from ritual activities.[13] I think the logic behind this is the same as that behind the construction of relationships in general. For various purposes people can emphasize different aspects of relationships—blood, land, particular kinds of behaviour, rights and obligations—as being the most crucial or determinate. They may even take a much stronger interest in one aspect rather than in another. But these are emphases, or interests, within a pre-given configuration of inalienabilities or inherencies. The different emphases become most relevant to action when particular inalienabilities are denied by some people to others.

How systematic such denials were awaits more historical research. Given some materials from the early colonial period, I have tended toward the interpretation that some of the disputes over traditional rights among Banabans on Rabi were not radically different in form from what occurred pre-colonially.

The Maudes observed:

> The mwenga [sleeping house] in its typical form was known as a *bata* and consisted of a rectangular roof of pandanus thatch supported well above the ground on four posts and containing a loft entered by a trapdoor. In this loft the family kept their valuables, more or less secure from the attacks of their enemies. Besides the bata, a family would also possess a small open-sided, thatched shed forming a roof over the *umum* or cooking oven and a store-room for miscellaneous objects which were not likely to be stolen.[14]

While we know little of the incidence of theft, or the kinds of goods involved, this at least says something about people's expectations, and allows us to re-pose the issue of inherence and inalienability.

The 'pre-given configuration of inalienabilities or inherencies', in a concrete relationship, had to be protected against threat. This is no more—or less—of a paradox than the notion of 'denial of natural rights'.

Consider a related matter. When I asked Banabans about their traditional custom in general, or about descent and kinship, they often directed my attention to certain family gatherings which had to do with life-transitions, particularly marriage. I have interpreted the activities (including exchanges) at these gatherings in simple 'functionalist' fashion as symbolizing the solidarity of groups, as publicly reaffirming relationships, and so forth. These interpretations are, I think, correct as far as they go. But if we think of those activities as symbolizing or demonstrating something, that asserts a passive role for them. It may be better to think of those activities as 'energizing' those relations, as 'keeping them up' (or keeping them from becoming disassociated) in a more literal sense. That is to say: these relationships are real, but are of a kind of reality which requires concrete activity in order for that reality to continue. In this light, when Banabans talk of 'making a [kin relation] disappear', we may have to interpret them literally.

Given the theory that relationships are real, ignoring the fact of relationship is something like ignoring the fact that the sun rises in the morning. One can possibly do both, but doing both is very different from, in an encounter in a shop, the shop-assistant and myself ignoring the fact that I am an Associate Professor. But ignoring them is less different from both of us ignoring the fact that I am married. Relationships which are real are more obstinate. They are more difficult to 'contextualize', and if they are, everybody knows it.

In this light I should criticize some aspects of my earlier ethnography. My account could be read to indicate that, in a situation of change, the Banabans were characterized by 'imperfect differentiation'. Religious and village groups on Rabi, for example, were partially recruited along kinship lines; kinship allegiances had the potentiality to threaten, and often did threaten, the solidarity of the newer forms of groups. The reference model is that of an older social science, in which persons could with fair ease 'change hats' in different situations (I am son to my parents, seller to a buyer . . .). This 'ideal type' situation rests on the kind of separation of persons, things, and social relations discussed earlier. I am son to my parents and seller to a buyer, yet I have an anchor in reality in that there is my separated self, independent of activities in which I engage, which is the same as I act in both kinds of relation, a separated and autonomous self which is the paramount reality. As a seller to a buyer I do not have a 'real relationship' with a buyer, unless that relationship becomes 'more than merely' a relation between buyer and seller. As son to my parents I have a real relationship, yet one which is, really, an 'accident of birth'.

We may see what the Banabans were doing as a positive rather than, if implicitly, a negative thing. At least many of them, much of the time, were resisting a construction of reality and society which presupposed a split of the same sort between the person (or self) and social relations, and a fictionalizing of those relations: they were trying to act in an unalienated way, in an alienated and alienating 'environment'.

Thus when Banabans listened to outsiders in 'official positions' who were dealing with the Banabans' grievances against the colonial government and the phosphate company, and asked those officials what they really thought themselves about those grievances, the Banabans were not playing a trick, as at least one official suggested. Officialdom 'differentiates' between personal views and the requirements of official behaviour, between 'the office' and 'the man'. Officials themselves sometimes indicated that the official position was one thing, and that their personal opinions were something else. Such a 'differentiation' can also be described as separation and alienation: when there is this sort of difference, what does that mean for the official? A separation, an alienation, of a public part of the self from a private part of the self, of work from thought, and so forth. To describe the Banabans' refusal to embrace such a world as a 'difficulty' misidentifies where the difficulty truly lies.

If social relations in the enlarged sense constitute the basis of social reality—if a basis with fragilities of its own—then both individuality and collectivity are defined in reference to them.[15] Real Banaban groups do not simply just exist or form. Their forming or functioning cannot be presupposed even in the same way that the relation between blood and land can be presupposed. Groupness implies a very active ordering of the system of relationships within groups, which always must go beyond the groups. Given this construction of reality, to have stable, multifunctional groups may indeed require a very active re-ordering of systems of relationships, which means a re-ordering of reality itself. This may partially explain why recent Banaban attempts to build such groups have been so closely identified with Christian sects.

If relationships are both real and are constituted as internal relations of persons, things and behaviours, a few other observations may be brought into a single pattern. Some people say that in the old days, and perhaps even now, certain infractions of custom in the meeting houses would be followed by something terrible happening to the miscreant. People who said this did not seem to have a particular theory, for example, that ancestors or. their ghosts punished those who broke their laws. The lack of explanation might lead one to assert a sort of 'mysterious punishment'. But the level of mystery may be no greater than the general recognition that if one's arm moves two miles, so will one's legs. If there is a unity between the meeting house, its past and present incumbents, what they do and have done, not identifying the precise 'mechanism of cause and effect', or a precise 'agent', is not really a problem. One could also think of things which happen at a distance between kin, when what one does affects the other. How is this possible? If the relationship is itself a continuous reality, such things might become more explicable.

If social relations are real and persons and 'material things' are part of that reality, then what appears to us as a concern with not only holding on to, but perhaps also increasing, one's 'social network' and one's 'landholdings', might have something to do with holding on to and increasing the piece of reality (as it were) in which one is directly implicated, and implicated as an active, re-creating agent.

Here a 'political' and a 'theoretical' point come together. The separation which capitalist ideology makes between persons, things and social relations has a very powerful consequence, and that consequence is one of the rationales of the separation. I can construct my 'relationship' to a 'thing' without even drawing a line between myself and the direct producers, or original owners, of that thing. If I use Banaban phosphate which comes from Banaban lands, that does not really place me in any 'relationship' with the Banabans. If it does place me in a relationship with them, it is not a real relationship—at least not as real a relationship as I have with my kin; even less real than the relationship that I have with the company which sold me the phosphate. Thus the Banabans' situation is not my own: they live in a different world.

At least for a long time the Banabans have taken the charitable point of view that when enough people learned about the facts of their case, wrongs would be righted, obligations would be met. The people who appropriated their phosphate were much more than only 'buyers' or even 'lessees'.

With many peoples such as the traditional Banabans, one of the reasons why the 'economy' appears 'embedded in social relations' is that material things are, literally, part of social relations. The 'economy' appears more distinct where—tautologically—material things appear more separable from social relations and from persons. Different constructions of social relations appear as people's relations to their means of production are different.[16]

The next question is clear: do some of us as social scientists operate with a concept of social relations which is itself part of that system of relations which is oppressing the Banabans? I criticize myself first for failing to see the implications of this question earlier.

The relations between persons, things and social relations were an issue for both Marx and Mauss. It was indeed Mauss who wrote:

> We live in a society where there is a marked distinction (although nowadays the distinction is criticized by lawyers themselves) between real and personal law, between things and persons. This distinction is fundamental; it is the very condition of part of our system of property, alienation and exchange. Yet it is foreign to the customs we have been studying.[17]

Sahlins, in an essay which I have found so useful for the formulation of the above, remarks:

> Since Mauss, and in part by way of rapprochement with modern economics, anthropology has become more consistently rational in its treatment of exchange. Reciprocity is contract pure and mainly secular, sanctioned perhaps by a mixture of considerations of which a carefully calculated self-interest is not the least . . . Mauss seems in this regard much more like Marx in the first chapter of *Capital*: if it can be said without disrespect, more animistic. One quarter of corn is exchangeable for X hundredweight iron. What is it in these things, so obviously different, that is equal? Precisely, the question was, for Marx, what *in these things* brings them into agreement?— and not what is it about these parties to the exchange? Similarly, for Mauss; 'What force is there in the thing given that makes the beneficiary reciprocate?' And the same kind of answer, from 'intrinsic' properties: here the *hau,* if there the socially necessary labor

time. Yet 'animistic' is manifestly an improper characterization of the thought involved. If Mauss, like Marx, concentrated singularly on the anthropomorphic qualities of the things exchanged, rather than the (thinglike?) qualities of the people, it was because each saw in the transactions respectively at issue a determinate form and epoch of alienation: mystic alienation of the donor in primitive reciprocity, alienation of human social labor in commodity production . . . They thus share the supreme merit, unknown to most 'Economic Anthropology', of taking exchange as it is historically presented, not as a natural category explicable by a certain eternal disposition of humanity.[18]

Consider one of Ollman's points:

> In *Capital,* Marx tries to measure value, to chart out where it goes, and to detail the forms it takes, but he devotes little time to uncovering its basic character. His chief concern is with a question other political economists have never asked: 'Why is labor represented by the value of its product and labor time by the magnitude of that value'.[19] Rather than presenting the case that value is labor, he is attempting to explain why in our era labor is expressed as value.[20]

Marx's explanation, of course, identifies precisely the necessity of the relationships between 'the parties to the exchange', that is, the relations of production.

It may get us closer to at least one side of Mauss' 'totalizing' intentions to tilt the general idea toward production, and to argue for the virtue of taking production and reproduction as 'historically presented, not as a natural category explicable by a certain eternal disposition of humanity'. In this regard, I think Sahlins presents a better clue in his paper 'The Spirit of the Gift' than in his papers on the 'Domestic Mode of Production': ' "Everything happens as if" the Maori people knew a broad concept, a general principle of productiveness, *hau*'.[21]

Might we contemplate embedding Mauss' notion of 'total prestation'[22] in a notion of 'total reproduction' for some Oceanic societies? Such a move might solve one of the problems which Sahlins gets into in the first Domestic Mode of Production paper, when he observes:

> the convenient identification of 'domestic group' with 'family' that I allow myself is too loose and imprecise. The domestic group in these primitive societies is usually a family system, but this is not always so, and where it is, the term 'family' must cover a variety of specific forms.[23]

If social relations are relations within which persons, material things and behaviours are internally (and not necessarily 'mystically') related, then we can entertain the possibility that a certain position in production-reproduction defines certain relations as 'kinship relations'. The appearance of 'kinship relations' as, quintessentially, 'genealogical relations', may thus structurally coincide with the appearance of 'labour' as, quintessentially, labour-power which is sold as a commodity to capital.

One may recognize that 'kinship functions in primitive societies both as production-relations and as relations for the propagation of the species'.[24] But to speak of kinship as having 'a much larger number of functions' in one range of societies as opposed to 'our own societies'[25] would thus have to be seen at best as a form of shorthand. Otherwise it may well represent a failure to make 'kinship' itself problematic enough.

NOTES AND REFERENCES

1 For ease of presentation, I do not further cite the theoretical sources on which I am drawing. The first part draws on Steve Barnett and Martin G. Silverman, 'The person in capitalist ideology' in a forthcoming work, *The Cultural Basis of Social Relations,* edited by Lee Guemple, in which the relevant citations are made to works by Karl Marx, Sir Henry Sumner Maine, C. B. Macpherson, Louis Dumont, David Schneider, and others. A provocative discussion of 'social relations' occurs in Balibar 1970, a work important in the development of this essay; cf. also Godelier 1972. The question of the reality of kinship relationships is raised in Schneider 1968, on which I draw heavily in the first part. The problem of the relation between concepts of person and social relations for Oceania was broached in Read 1955, on which I draw heavily in the second part. It has recently been posed in another analytic framework by Vern Carroll and Michael Lieber, with whom I have had numerous discussions. Much of what I am doing theoretically in this paper constitutes a sort of 're-contextualization' of points raised by them; see, e.g., their papers in Lieber 1977, as well as that by Eric Schwimmer. Marshall Sahlins' 'reading' of Mauss and the Maori certainly informs the second part (Sahlins 1972). The notion of 'internal relations' is borrowed from Ollman 1971.

2 See Schneider 1968.

3 Oliver's footnote 5 refers to Ralph G. White and Ariihau a Terupe, *Linguistic Check-Sketch for Tahitian* (Tahiti 1958): 57. Oliver notes: 'I have not examined the older textual material with enough attention to this aspect to be able to list which items were "alienable" (incidental or transient) and which items "inalienable" (intimate, innate or permanent) . . .'

4 Oliver 1975:II, 587, 1133.

5 Cowell 1951:16.

6 *ibid.*:33.

7 *ibid.*:35.

8 This example is cited in *A Gilbertese Grammar and Vocabulary* (Sacred-Heart Mission, Gilbert Islands, n.d.):18.

9 It might also be possible to regard the prefixed form as indicating 'unmarked possession', while the suffixed form marks inalienability. Some of the complexities in the issue derive from the possibility of using both forms, for terms relevant to this discussion. For example, *kai* in the sense of 'tree' or 'stick' takes the prefixed form when it belongs to a person, and this might suggest alienability. But with the suffix it means 'punishment'. At the same time, -*kai* as a numeral classifier is used for trees, shrubs, land-sections and fish hooks (cf. Cowell 1951:24), which is at least one indication that the issue of production is not being arbitrarily imposed.

10 cf. Maude 1971[1932]:337-8. The interpretation here is complex since, where the suffix is used, it is used in phrases to describe the rights, with key words which can take the suffix anyway, e.g. 'canoe', 'food (to be eaten by the person referred to)', 'material for anointing', 'garland'. (A term for a dance form, *ruoiam,* is suffixed, but I am not sure of how possession is

otherwise expressed with regard to it.) Of course, the fact that many of these rights do involve 'things' which are otherwise suffixed is itself significant.

11 Cheshire 1972:97.

12 Maude 1971[1932]:44-6.

13 Silverman 1971:55ff.

14 Maude 1971[1932]:28.

15 This is a better account than that in Silverman 1971, which refers to 'individual' and 'group' frames of reference on Rabi. Those frames of reference are themselves marked vis-à-vis a taken-for-granted relational frame of reference, which is one reason why they present problems. The point should have been apparent given the contemporary difference between the 'attitude toward authority' in 'kinship' versus newer kinds of relations. Authority is less problematic in 'kinship relations' since they are, according to this interpretation, more real than the others.

16 Given what is presented here, this should be taken as an assertion. The reconstruction of the organization of production on Ocean Island remains to be formulated, although I will be presenting some partial analysis anon. As a technical note: some of the issues focus on the relations between different relationships (different 'kinship' relationships vis-à-vis one another, and 'kinship' and 'descent' relationships vis-à-vis one another). These relationships appear as different yet linked, and the reproduction of all kinds of real relationships is normally necessary for the reproduction of any one kind of relationship. The concept of 'reproduction' allows us to integrate 'human' and 'material' reproduction, and to move from an emphasis on the 'sociology of exchange' to an emphasis on the political economy of production.

17 Mauss 1970[1925]:46.

18 Sahlins 1972:180-1, references omitted.

19 Footnote omitted; Marx 1967[1867]:80.

20 Ollman 1971:176.

21 Sahlins 1972:168.

22 Mauss 1970[1925].

23 Sahlins 1974:77; cf. also Godelier 1972.

24 Godelier 1972:94, fn. 189.

25 ibid.:95.

Norms of Tahitian land tenure: ancient and modern

DOUGLAS OLIVER*

The subject of land tenure in ancient Tahiti[3] is obscure, to say the least. As a system of overlapping rights it was probably no more complex than the European systems prevailing at that time, but the European observers who reported anything about it—and not many did—either misunderstood or oversimplified its actual workings. In addition, most subsequent attempts to delineate it—the system having undergone far-reaching changes under early European influence and later under European political control—have been obfuscated by application of terms like 'feudal', and rendered suspect by their authors' tendency to fill in the gaps in the Tahitian data with data from other Polynesian societies (an expedient that might be warranted in some instances, but could be partly or wholly fallacious).

The two kinds of social units in ancient Tahiti with which territory was most universally and exclusively associated were *kin-congregations* and *tribes*. I apply the former label to residential, co-worshipping groups of people that consisted of a core of consanguines, along with a fringe of other individuals who had become attached to them as spouses, refugees, or bond-friends. The focus of such a group was a *marae*, or temple, at which the members

* The pleasure I feel in dedicating this paper to the pre-eminent historian of the Pacific Islands is tinged somewhat with the regret that it is not history in the sense he might wish it to be. In fact, it is not even comparison, which anthropologists sometimes purvey under the (mistaken) impression that they are writing history. What follows is nothing more than juxtaposition: a reconstruction from archaic written sources of some indigenous land-related customs of the people who inhabited the Society Islands during the second half of the eighteenth century,[1] followed by a summary of some equivalent customs I observed during my field studies of two rural Society Islands communities in 1954-55 and 1959-60.[2] As for what transpired during the century and a half in between—how the ancient customs were transformed into the ones I observed—I have scarcely touched on that. Such a history would require not only a well-nigh endless sifting of myriad archives, but also reports about numerous local events that probably have never been recorded. This paper will form part of a monograph, now being written, which will bear a title something like, 'Two Tahitian Villages: an exercise in comparison'. As its title indicates, this paper includes no generalizations about the economics or sociology of modern land tenure in the communities, nor any indication of the amount of parcel fragmentation, etc. that has occurred since colonial title registration began.

(usually only the adult males or their priestly representatives) communicated—including presentation of offerings—with their tutelar spirits, who included, typically, one or more ancestral ghosts. Kin-congregation temples varied widely in size, in architecture, and in accessories, but they all included these features: a stone rest for the spirit(s) during the religious service, a fixed place for the principal officiant(s), an altar for offerings, and a space for the worshippers. (The spirits' place ranged in size and form from a single slab to huge platforms or multi-stepped pyramids; the officiants' place consisted usually of one or more basalt uprights.) In addition, each temple had associated with it, more or less exclusively, one or more tracts of clearly demarcated land (and in some cases, adjacent portions of lagoon or sea). And as I see it, anyone who was acknowledged by the congregation's leaders to be a fellow member, either by birth from a prior member or by 'adoption',[4] was entitled to use-rights in its temple-associated territory. Also, any non-member married to a kin-congregation's member enjoyed use-rights in such territory—rights that continued after the member-spouse's decease provided he or she did not marry and live with a non-member elsewhere. However, in keeping with the pervasively hierarchic ordering of ancient Tahitian society, the territorial use-rights of a kin-congregation's members were markedly differentiated—for example, those of an eldest sibling (especially if male) enjoyed precedence over those of younger ones, and those of a head member of a senior line over those of the head of a cadet line.[5]

When in the course of time a kin-congregation proliferated, the additional residences built to accommodate the increase were usually located quite widely apart and at some considerable distance from the 'parental' ones—in other words, the most typical settlement pattern of that era was of the type now called 'dispersed'. This residential movement was usually accompanied (or preceded?) by dispersion of the emigrés' gardens and groves, to which they thus came to acquire distinctive use-rights. Indeed it seems likely that continual and uncontested use by a sub-unit of any portion of a kin-congregation's territory served to enhance its rights over it, with or without a shift of residence.

After a few generations of this kind of differentiation the territory of a kin-congregation, like the group itself, would have become segmented into numerous subdivisions, each with its own temple and fairly exclusive land boundaries. In the ordinary course of events, however, the kin-congregation as a whole, represented by the head of its senior sub-group—in effect, the kin-congregation's 'chief'—continued to have residual rights in all the kin-congregation's territory—rights that were periodically acknowledged by the sub-units in the form of first-fruits presented to that chief at the 'ancestral' temple, partly for token redistribution and partly for offerings to the group's tutelar spirits (who were concerned with the productivity of the kin-congregation territory as a whole). In addition, the chief of a kin-congregation was entitled to impose a *rahui* over resources of its territory from time to time—that is, a prohibition against, say, the eating of its coconuts or the catching of its fish. It seems likely that the senior member of each sub-unit of a kin-congregation possessed similar rights over his unit's territorial subdivision, but about that the sources are silent.

In addition to the process of internal differentiation just described, some kin-congregations underwent dispersion and differentiation through 'colonial' expansion. That is to say, it sometimes happened that one or more members of a kin-congregation left the home territory altogther and established a new settlement elsewhere, perhaps by migration into an uninhabited and unclaimed area or by successful conquest. Where that occurred, and if communication with the homeland could be maintained, the 'colonials' usually continued to acknowledge their ties with the homeland by rendering first-fruits to the kin-congregation chief at the ancestral temple. Moreover, their derivation from and allegiance to the larger unit were concretely symbolized in their own temple, into which was built a 'corner' stone taken from the ancestral temple.

It goes without saying that among the many kin-congregations into which ancient Tahitian society was divided the potency of the residual territorial entitlements just mentioned must have varied quite widely—for example, according to the size and scatter of each one's sub-units, the degree of amity or enmity among its sub-unit heads, the personality of its current senior chief. Nevertheless, the ideological model just summarized remained available, to be followed or ignored as circumstances or ambitions decreed.

In listing the criteria for membership in a kin-congregation I mentioned the rights accruing to a member's spouse, the reference having been to a spouse from elsewhere. It should be noted that in many if not most marriages, and particularly between persons of the lower social classes,[6] both spouses were likely to have belonged to the same kin-congregation—although, except for upper-class persons, some of whom married 'close in' in order to preserve 'purity' of line, most persons were at pains to avoid reproductive mating with consanguines. In other words, kin-congregations were not exogamous *per se,* and most of them were probably wide enough in span, and localized enough in distribution, to permit and encourage matings between fellow members. When, however, a husband and wife did belong to distinct kin-congregations their progeny acquired entitlements in the kin-congregations of both. Thus individuals could, and evidently did, inherit entitlements in the territories of numerous kin-congregations—but the potency of such rights would of course have depended upon the claimants' ability to validate them genealogically and the uses actually made of them. In most cases, probably, an individual of middle- or lower-class status maintained effective inherited use-rights only in the territory of his or her residence, or if married elsewhere only in that of his birth. Some high-ranking *arii* made a practice of revisiting the various kin-congregation territories in which they possessed entitlements in order to maintain them there, but there seems not to have been any formal procedure whereby lowlier persons could keep their claims 'warm'.

The second kind of ancient Tahitian social unit possessing important territorial domains was, for want of a distinctive native label, what I shall call a *tribe*—a unit all of whose members resided contiguously[7] and under the leadership of someone—a chief—who himself was not under the leadership of any other chief. Leadership of the kind I refer to embraced acknowledged and effective command over the goods and services of people, including war-making and periodic levies of objects and labour. The comprehensiveness and absoluteness of that command varied not only with the character of the tribal chiefs but also with the strength of sub-tribal units—and even, it appears, with regional differences in opinion about chiefs' rights. That is to say, some tribes were ruled totally and despotically, and others only partially and with laxity.

This may have been the position during the era of Tahiti's initial settlement when each kin-congregation was an autonomous tribe, but by the time Europeans arrived on the scene none of the tribes then extant comprised less than three or four distinct kin-congregations, with the result that each of them contained two or more levels of administrative leadership, to which corresponded a like number of levels of territorial rights. A tribal chief's authority over the territories of other kin-congregations within his domain may not have been as direct or as priestly or as supernaturally sanctioned as over his own, but at the very least he received tribute, through their own chiefs, in the form of food and other objects produced in those territories, and, through their own chiefs, was able to impose *rahui* over them. Moreover, each tribe also had its temple, which on occasion served as a religious centre for the tribe as a whole. In some cases the kin-congregation temple of the tribal chief doubled as tribal temple as well; in others a separate and distinct tribal temple was constructed for this purpose.

All the territorial entitlements so far mentioned pertained to social groups or to individuals as heads of such groups. It should also be added that some ancient Tahitians, notably some tribal chiefs and members of their immediate families, individually possessed full, undivided, rights over certain tracts of land, from which each obtained some or most of his daily food. Most of these chiefly lands constituted those parts of a chief's kin-congregation land that had become identified with his lineal ascendants by use over time, but some of them had been acquired by extra-tribal conquest, or by dispossession of former intra-tribal members as punishment for some misdeed (most typically, for *lèse-majesté*).

The above reconstruction of ancient Tahitian land tenure is not in accord with one put forward by some ethnologists, who viewed that society as having been stratified more discontinuously and along more ethnic lines. Those writers, having accepted certain liturgical myths more historically and literally than I am inclined to do, perceived the three major social classes into which the society was stratified as having been different and distinctive with respect to land ownership as well, namely: the aristocratic *hui arii*, a race of immigrant conquerors, who owned the most favoured coastal lands and lagoons; the yeomen *pue raatira*, who owned the less favoured but still productive lands bordering those of the *hui arii;* and the commoner *manahune,* survivors of the Islands' original, conquered inhabitants, who lived inland and who 'owned no land'.

Ancient Tahitian society was indeed stratified (cf. above, p. 111), but not—I believe—on this basis, and not with the kind of land tenure attributions just reported. In my view, most of the larger, widely ramified kin-congregations would have included *arii, raatira,* and *manahune* members. And although the *hui arii* of a kin-congregation might, had they wished, have enjoyed more pre-emptive rights than lower-class members over their jointly-owned territory, the difference in entitlements was a matter of degree and not of kind. Moreover, although it occasionally happened that an individual was banished from his tribal territory for some offence or other, and was hence 'landless'—at least temporarily—in that particular area, an ancient Tahitian's kin ties (and hence land-use rights) were so widely ramified, it would in my opinion have been quite exceptional for any exile to have had no rights to any land anywhere.

Needless to say, the land tenure régime I have just summarized has undergone some major transformations since Europeans appeared on the scene—first, as a result of unification of the Islands' twenty or more eighteenth-century tribes into four European-style 'kingdoms' (Tahiti - Moorea - Tetiaroa - Mehetia, Huahine - Maiao, Raiatea - Tahaa, and Borabora - Maupiti); later as an aspect of French colonial control. A full historical account of the land tenure changes accompanying these developments would require a whole volume (and one well worth compiling) but I shall sketch only enough of it to provide a background for the situation that prevailed in 1954-55, when I carried out field studies in two communities there, one on Huahine (one of the archipelago's Leeward Islands), and one on Moorea (one of the archipelago's Windward Islands).

The Windward Islands (Tahiti, Moorea, Mehetia, and Tetiaroa) became a French Protectorate in 1842. By then some of their lands had already been acquired by Europeans, and those remaining in Tahitians' hands had become, *de facto,* identified fairly exclusively with co-residential kin groups that were much narrower in span than the earlier pagan kin-congregations had been. Meanwhile, the kind of 'citizenship' estate earlier associated with tribal membership had become attenuated nearly to the point of nonexistence through the coalescence of the former tribes into the larger and less functional political units represented by the new kingdoms. In connection with the latter change, the 'chiefly lands' referred to above had become apanages (*farii hau*) of the offices of the district chiefs (*tavana,* from English 'governor'), who by 1842 had come to be representatives and subordinates of the monarch. Also, by this time the land rights of the monarch (Aimata, Queen Pomare IV) had become reduced to those pertaining to a few explicitly royal apanages and to a small number of her kin units.

French officials exerted first their influence and then their authority in an effort to Westernize land tenure in the Windward Islands. The process began in 1852 with a law of the Tahitian Kingdom that ordered the registration, by district,[8] of every distinct land parcel (French *terre;* Tahitian *fenua*) according to its native name, its geographic boundaries, its approximate area, and the name(s) of its principal owner(s). Separate registers were to be kept for privately owned and official apanage lands. With respect to the former, an owner was evidently identified with the head, usually male, of the household having most active, locally acknowledged usehold rights in the parcel in question. (No provision was made at that time for the rights, if any, of absent, co-owning collaterals, nor for minors for whom the parcel might have been held in trust.) With respect to the apanages—the parcels known as *farii hau*—these were intended to provide for the subsistence of the district chiefs and their families—in amounts 'in keeping with their superior social status', and were declared to be subject to alienation only after approval by the Protectorate's legislative assembly.[9]

Once recorded (presumably by each district's local officials) the lists were required to be checked for accuracy and authenticity by a commission consisting of the Protectorate's official interpreter, a member of the Protectorate High Court, the district's chief local judge and its oldest Tahitian citizen. After approval by this commission one copy of each list (in Tahitian) was deposited with the Tahitian High Court (*Toohitu*) and another (in French) with the Protectorate Lands Office (*Service des Domaines*). Thereafter, all

J

changes in a parcel's boundaries and ownership were required to
be recorded in a separate register lodged with the High Court.

All very sensible and orderly, from the colonizers' point of
view. Notwithstanding, many of the Tahitians of that time failed
to register their land holdings, either from negligence or ignorance
of the law. In fact, many had still not done so by 1880, when the
Windward Islands were formally annexed, so that the French
authorities issued another decree (24 August 1887), which revised
the registration procedure somewhat and contained sanctions
against non-registration. By this decree, all lands in the colony
were initially viewed as if belonging to the Lands Office. Thereupon, a title deed was handed over to each officially acknowledged
owner, and all parcels not so allocated were classified temporarily
as 'district lands'.

The decree allowed the claimants to the latter a year in which
to lodge their claims, failing which these lands were to become
domaines. To lodge a claim, the claimant was required to state
his officially registered name, the name and area of the parcel,
and the names of all parcels bordering it. This information had
to be presented at a meeting of the district's council and inscribed
on a public notice. If after three months no opposition to the
claim had been lodged with the Lands Office, it was declared to be
authentic, the claimant was given a title deed, and the parcel was
registered in the Lands Office. On the other hand, if an opposing
claim were lodged within the specified period the district council
in question was empowered to decide between the rival claimants
—which it did, it would appear, mainly on the basis of genealogical
evidence.

Titles to the traditional *farii hau* parcels were handled in the
same manner. In addition, all those areas on which had been built
public structures, such as churches, schools and Administration
offices, were declared to belong to the colonial administration or
to the district in question.

And finally, all parcels unclaimed or otherwise unattributed
were declared to be Territory *domaine*. The decree of 1887 also
established the principle that, after a specified lapse of time, all
future claims and counter-claims would have to be considered
according to standard civil-law procedures.

In the Leeward Islands the history of land registration followed
a different course, inasmuch as these islands did not come under
direct French rule until 1888. During the preceding eight decades
each of the petty kingdoms comprising these islands had its own
law codes (inspired mainly by missionaries of the London Missionary Society) and these served to formalize land tenure régimes
that incorporated elements of ancient Tahitian ideas about kin-
communality and social hierarchy, along with European ones

about individual private ownership, land buying and selling, and church property.[10]

One of France's first official acts in the Leeward Islands was to issue a decree (22 December 1898) establishing a procedure for attributing and registering land ownership. By it the authorities appointed a commission in each of the Leewards' major sub-divisions (*arrondissements*) to receive and review land claims.[11] As a first step each claimant declared his claim before the commission, which caused it to be published in the *Journal Officiel*. After that a period of six months was allowed to permit other parties to submit counter-claims. If none was submitted the commission nevertheless inquired closely into the bases of the claim and approved it only if they considered it to be justified (presumably, on the basis of genealogy or clear proof of purchase or gift). If a counter-claim was submitted the commission scrutinized that in the same manner, and either decided in favour of one of the claimants or, if neither claim was considered strong enough, declared the parcel to be Administration *domaine*. As a further safeguard the commission's decisions were permitted to be appealed against before a special court, consisting of judges and chiefs, before final approval and registration.

Eventually, both Windward and Leeward Islands were mapped to show the boundaries, place-names, area (in hectares), and current owner(s) of each tract of land[12] recognized as being a separately owned parcel (French, *terre;* Tahitian, *fenua*); and new boundary markers were set up when necessary.[13]

According to the principles that seem to have governed these initial attributions, the listed owner (*propriétaire*) of a parcel—or fraction thereof—was the head, usually the eldest male, of the household currently exercising uncontested use-rights over it—or the 'heirs' of that head if he were but recently deceased. Obviously this definition of land ownership constituted some narrowing of the usages that prevailed in pre-European times. It did not, for example, take into account any residual rights of more-senior-line collaterals, nor any joint-use rights of absent siblings. As such, however, it reflected realistically the changes in land use practice that had come about during the previous decades of depopulation and European influence.

Also, in identifying parcels with specific households the commissioners and judges seem to have given much weight to the presence of the burial sites of the claimants' ancestors. In instances of disagreement and challenge, where all the parties were able to provide equally persuasive 'proofs' of ownership, the issues seem to have been settled by adopting one of three solutions: by dividing the parcel among the claimants (in some cases into minute fractions of the original tracts); by awarding ownership to the oldest surviving 'heir' of an agreed 'original' owner, in the terms governing inheritance set forth in the *Code Civil*;[14] or by attributing equal-part ownership to two or more claimants or sets of claimants (Tahitian, *tomite,* from English committee). Regarding these latter, many parcels were also attributed to two or more *tomite,* not as a result of contesting claims but by mutual agreement of the parties themselves—in cases, for example, where two or more households had been peacefully sharing the use of a parcel and did not wish to divide it.

From this distance in time it is impossible to reconstruct all the specific changes the initial land registrations served to introduce or perpetuate, but two general ones can be listed.

First, by defining 'ownership' more narrowly and more exclusively than the traditional principles had done, the registration focused people's land use rights upon smaller geographic areas, and reduced or extinguished their rights elsewhere. In doing so, the registrations served to decrease the size and sharpen the boundaries of their kin corporations.

Second, by attributing ownership principally to specific individuals or heirs of individuals, the registration could have disenfranchised altogether some other persons who possessed rights according to older usages.[15] It may in fact have done so in some instances; however, in view of the principle traditionally practised and now officially recognized whereby children inherited from both parents, this disability would not have led to the foundation of perpetually landless family lines.

One ancient feature of Tahitian land tenure, which neither time nor European influence and legislation has altered, is the Tahitians' respect for the boundary stones *(ofai otia)* that anciently served to mark land-parcel boundaries not otherwise delimited for example, by streams or cliffs or conspicuous trees. Low stone posts were also set up to mark the new boundaries delimited during the initial colonial land registrations, and these, like the ancient ones, were sacrosanct to all of the Tahitians I queried on the subject. Many of these informants knew some of the stones to be venerable (those from heathen times, *tau etene*) and others more recent, but all of them considered both kinds of boundary stones to possess (or be?) mana (power)—whether derived from the ancient gods (now collectively identified as Satan, *Tatani*) or from more recent but deceased (and potentially vengeful) chiefs and judges. I discovered no Tahitian who would have had the audacity to move a boundary stone. And I was cited examples, even by the best educated of my informants (including those who disavowed Satan's role in the matter), of individuals who had become ill or crippled through having accidentally moved or damaged one of them.

Meanwhile, the French *Code Civil* was applied to govern the ways in which full ownership of a parcel could be transferred, namely, by inheritance (*succession*), testament, gift, purchase or barter, 'prescription acquisitive', and uncontested occupation of thirty or more years.

French laws governing inheritance were (and are) precise, detailed, and—for metropolitan French society, at least—exhaustive. Among other things, they defined *filiation* more narrowly than the traditional Tahitian usages (for example, by reducing the inheritance rights of illegitimate and 'unrecognized' offspring), and in the absence of offspring they specified with mathematical precision the fractional residual rights of ascendants, of collaterals, of spouses, etc. Fortunately (for the ethnographer!) the nearly endless possibilities envisaged by the *Code* had very little relevance for the communities I studied, where virtually every landowner since the initial registration has had either offspring or siblings to whom his or her land titles did or could devolve. And in the few instances I knew about where that was not the case, the owner in question usually (purposely) avoided wider distribution by making a will.[16]

With respect to land transaction by 'gift', the *Code* served to substantiate and formalize some previous ceremonial transactions to a degree beyond the intent of the original donors (and at the same time it perpetuated an aspect of class stratification in a society that had otherwise become more egalitarian in its official ideals). I refer here to a situation that prevailed—and still does—in some districts, namely, the ownership of large parcels of prime land by absentee descendants of former *arii*. As the Tahitian colonial society became more egalitarian the traditional *arii* lost even their symbolic, residual proprietorship over their former subjects' lands, and would have retained rights only over their own family lands but for the rhetoric of some of their former subjects or others of like class. That is to say, even well into the colonial era, it often happened that when a member of the disappearing but still respected *arii* class went visiting, his local host, if of inferior social status, conventionally greeted him (or her) with traditional, hyperbolic phrases of hospitality, including the invitation to 'consider all my lands to be your own'—and some of the visitors did just that when colonial land registration took place. (Something similar occurred with respect to some early European visitors, but fewer of these ceremonial transfers seem to have been perpetuated.)

The purchasing (and bartering) of land that was sanctioned by the *Code* was probably unknown in pre-European Tahiti, but had become a common transaction by the time the *Code* began to be applied. It is highly likely that many of the instances of 'purchase' (by Europeans and Chinese especially) that the initial registrations recorded—and hence officially sanctioned—were never intended by their Tahitian 'sellers' to be such; or were 'sold' under duress of one kind or another (while drunk, or under threat of arrest for non-payment of debt).[17]

In any case, the purchase of land had become commonplace in the communities I studied but the sellers were no longer gullible, open-handed marks.

The French Administration also set up procedures for dividing a parcel into two or more separate ones. 'To divide or not to divide' is an issue that probably all adult Tahitians are conscious of, and most of those with whom I discussed it held strong views favouring one solution or the other. Some more general reasons given for these views are 'moral'—'it is better, more Tahitian, for kinfolk to keep together and share their land' versus 'every [nuclear] family ought to have separate land, in order to avoid conflict and quarrels'. Other general reasons for taking either stand are economic—'people produce more by co-operating', versus 'a man is more certain of his earnings if he does not have to depend upon others'. Informants also volunteered more specific, situational reasons for wanting to divide or not divide—for example, a desire to cease trying to work with an uncongenial brother or sister's husband; a wish to continue working with a congenial and industrious cousin.

In addition, there were certain technological factors that influenced people's decisions to divide or not to divide. One such was vanilla-growing; in the communities I knew it was rare for two or more adults from different households to co-operate in growing vanilla beans in the same garden. And, since a vanilla production cycle lasted six or more years from planting to depletion a person wishing to grow the crop could expect to be met with reluctance or outright refusal from his co-proprietors when proposing such a long-term tie-up of what in most such instances was the most fertile part of their jointly-owned land. Hence, the impulse in this kind of situation was to divide.

With copra production it was usually the reverse, especially with respect to already-producing groves (which, at the time of my visits, was the state of most of them). With such groves the original investment of labour, in ground-clearing and planting, had long since been made, and current production consisted only of keeping the ground vegetation reasonably low and harvesting the nuts as they ripened. (In other words, no current producer was impelled to control a specific piece of land continuously for a long period of time in order to obtain returns for his own original investment of labour, etc.) Thus, the co-proprietors of such a parcel found it feasible and reasonable to divide harvest rights on a time basis (*opu i te faufaa*) rather than divide the land (*vavahi i te fenua*); and in the absence of other, non-economic, reasons for dividing they found it less of a bother, and hence highly preferable, to leave things as they were.

Dividing land not only involved negotiation and initiative—bargaining sessions with co-proprietors and trips to Administration centres—but was expensive as well. The services of a surveyor were required to lay out and map the new boundaries, and those of a notary—and sometimes a lawyer—to formalize the deal.

The *Code* also sanctioned various kinds of arrangements for the temporary transfer of use-rights in land and in objects associated with land—houses, trees, etc. Many of these arrangements were not practised and had no relevance in the communities I studied, and some of the local transactions of this nature were without exact parallels in the *Code*. There follows a brief description of the more tangible kinds of arrangements I found in operation there.

Fixed-rate lease was a transaction which, when applied to land (territory), involved different types of rights—some explicit, some implicit—according to context. For example, when land was leased for vanilla-growing, the lease-time was usually for an explicitly-stated period of nine years; and although the contract, usually written, did not specify such, the lessee was understood to have the right of sub-leasing and of using the fruit of trees already growing there. On the other hand, it is questionable that he had the right to cut down, say, a breadfruit tree or coconut palm without explicit permission of the lessor. As for growing other cash crops, I know of only one instance of land having been leased for such purposes—in this case, pineapples—and the period was also nine years. To the best of my knowledge no one in those communities had ever leased land for growing coconuts, the growing and producing cycle having been considered too long (up to fifty years). Nor did I hear of any instance of leasing land for money, for growing food crops—a scandalous suggestion to my informants.

One of the communities studied contained two parcels of Administration *domaines*. One was leased by the current chief (*Tavana*), the other by his predecessor (in both cases at low rents—transparently, a perquisite of office). Rents were paid yearly and the agreements were evidently for unspecified and indefinite donations, and entailed no restrictions on use, either of soil or of trees already growing there. In the other community studied a parcel of *domaine* (and its Administration-owned house) was inhabited by a Public Works official; I was unable to discover whether he paid rent.

In one of my communities most houses were built on lots comprising a parcel owned by a Chinese living on Raiatea, who charged a token rental of ten francs per annum. The houses themselves were owned either by the residents themselves or by absentee kinsmen (who usually charged no money rent).

Share-crop lease was a type of transaction which took place mainly in connection with coconut- and vanilla-growing. For coconuts the conventional arrangement was for the lessee to acquire the right to harvest the nuts (for a specified or indefinite period of time), process them into copra, sell the copra, and pay the lessor one half of his net profits (after deducting out-of-pocket costs of drying, bagging and transporting—but not of the labour expended by himself or his unpaid, usually household, helpers).[18] For vanilla share-cropping two kinds of arrangement obtained. By one of them the lessee took over uncleared land—usually by written contract and for a period of nine years; cleared, planted, and harvested it, and paid the lessor a specified percentage (typically, twenty per cent) of the price received for the ripe beans. The other arrangement was for the lessee to lease an already-planted garden, and thereafter keep it weeded, pollinate the plants, and harvest the beans—again, for a specified or indefinite period of time. The rent paid for this kind of leasing was a fraction of the price received for the beans (fifty per cent in one community, thirty per cent in the other) with no deductions allowed, or in fact claimed, for labour or other production 'costs'.

Crop purchase, a somewhat anomalous type of transaction, involved outright sale, at a price fixed in advance, of harvesting rights of a crop for a specified time period. It was applied mainly to coconuts—only rarely to vanilla—and the price was usually based on that received for the previous harvest.

Food-growing 'lease', as implied above, was a conventional practice in the communities I studied by which landowners permitted others to grow food crops on their land, in return for the planting, by the users, of a few coconut palms (which was viewed as a 'permanent' improvement to the land). The assumption behind this practice was that the taro and other food crops produced would be eaten by the growers themselves. I heard of no instance where any part of such harvests was sold by the grower, but failed to inquire whether that would have altered the arrangement, had it occurred.

In addition to these more or less explicit and formalized lease transactions the Tahitians I studied practised and concurred in various informal and more or less implicit arrangements respecting use of land and its resources by persons other than the owners themselves.

First, there was the right of transit, which owners usually permitted neighbours to exercise. The only situations I heard of in which this right was limited were during vanilla harvest seasons, when some growers tried to discourage passage through their gardens, on the assumption that the passer-by might steal some beans. Some of the more anxious vanilla-growers went so far as to put up 'keep-out' marks at the entrance to trails leading through their gardens, but this action was popularly considered to be either unnecessarily hard and selfish, or ridiculous.

Second was the right whereby most owners permitted their fellow villagers to take a few coconuts, breadfruit, or mangoes (but not bananas or coffee beans) from their land for home use (but, emphatically, not for sale); and the same degree of permissiveness extended to firewood and palm fronds (used for thatch). If an owner wished to restrict such rights he put up keep-out marks (a strip of frond tied around the trunk of the tree in question); but as in the case of transit-blocking such measures were unpopular—and in fact not often required or resorted to.

Large trees to be used for house construction or for canoe hulls were a different matter. Before obtaining such as these it was necessary for the taker to obtain consent of the land owner, and sometimes to pay a price, which—again—was usually higher if the end-product was intended for sale.

Most owners were anything but permissive about allowing neighbours' pigs or cattle access to their lands. Cattle were in fact no great problem; their owners usually kept them tied up or fenced in. But some residents allowed their pigs free range, or found it difficult to confine them, and these animals often played havoc with garden crops. When that occurred the garden owners either killed them or brought suit against their owners, or both— usually to the accompaniment of mutual ill-feeling.

Next, there was the kind of land use-rights practised in connection with the hunting of wild pigs. It was customary, I was told, for the successful hunter to give some of the animal's flesh to the owner of the land on which it was killed. (And just as customary, it was added, for the hunter to forgo doing so unless the land owner could prove that the killing had taken place on his land!)

Finally, there remains the question of use-rights in waterways. In the communities studied, when a stream flowed through a land parcel it was generally considered to be part of the parcel, and its resources, if any—mainly crayfish and shrimps—were held to belong to the parcel's owner, and to require his permission before fishing there. (Also, it was considered necessary to share the catch with the owner if it were 'large' enough—how large I could not discover.) With streams forming boundaries between parcels, the matter of ownership was open to question—and to some argument, I was informed, when large catches of crayfish were made. However, this latter situation occurred too infrequently, it would appear, for any consensus to have developed concerning its rights and wrongs.[19]

The types of rights and transactions exercised by the villagers I studied with respect to private lands and their appurtenances are here summarized.[20]

First, there were *proprietary rights*. Parcels of land were officially owned either by a sole proprietor or the heirs of a sole proprietor, or by two or more name-specified joint proprietors and their respective heirs. A sole proprietor was empowered to lease all or part of his parcel or to dispose of it by sale or (within limits) by gift. A joint proprietor possessed similar rights of lease and disposal over his fraction of a parcel—usually, but not always in practice, after agreement with the other joint owner(s). With respect to the heirs of a deceased sole or joint proprietor, their respective proprietary rights in the parcel, or fraction of the parcel, were proportional to their number—for example, each of three heirs held a one-third proprietary interest in the parcel, or fraction of the parcel—and each had rights of lease or disposal over his portion. In the case of parcels held by two or more proprietors, they could make use of its soil and other resources either by serial allotment of time (as with coconut harvesting) or by informal territorial subdivision.

By following official procedures, a parcel could be territorially divided into two or more separate parcels, either by its sole proprietor, or by agreement among all its co-proprietors, or by judicial order.

Inheritance rights refer to the rights to a whole parcel, or fraction thereof, held by all the heirs of a living proprietor as identified and defined by French laws of succession. They entail rights of use and lease but not of disposal, and even their use- and lease-rights are subject to consent of the parcel's proprietor. The French *Code* extends inheritance rights to spouses, to ascendants, and to collaterals of various degrees of kinship, but since land registration was first instituted in the communities I studied inheritance rights have in practice been exercised or claimed only by the offspring (legitimate, or illegitimate and 'recognized') and siblings of a proprietor; and it is in this limited, but ethnographically relevant, sense that I use the term. Some Tahitians I knew were aware of some of the ramifications of inheritance contained in the *Code* but considered them irrelevant, or even inapplicable to themselves. Indeed, many of them were so uninformed about the inclusion of spouses among an individual's potential heirs that they complained about their supposed exclusion.

In this connection the word *tomite*, as used by Tahitians, was the social unit comprising all persons holding proprietary or inheritance rights to that fraction of a parcel that had been apportioned, either officially or by unofficial agreement among a parcel's co-proprietors.

Familial rights is a label I have invented to apply to a category of land-use rights that are not explicitly defined in the *Code* but that were distinctly conceptualized and practised in the communities I studied. I refer to the special and more or less exclusive uses made of a proprietor's land by all members of his or her household—including spouse, offspring (legitimate, illegitimate and foster), ascendants, and any other persons—kin or not—residing more or less permanently in the household. Familial rights did not include rights of lease or disposal, but they served to empower the holder to freer use of the land and its resources than was permitted, say, to the proprietor's siblings residing elsewhere. (In other words, familial rights superseded inheritance rights under some circumstances.) Moreover, even for those few of my informants who knew about a spouse's legal rights as a potential heir, it was her (or his) identity as a familial-rights holder that defined her (or his) use of the proprietor's land.

There was of course some differentiation of land-use rights among familial rights-holders—for example, a spouse's having usually been 'stronger' than, say, an unmarried offspring—although instances of disagreement did occasionally occur; but the kinds of common use-rights possessed by all its resident members set each household off from all others in this respect.

Lease rights refer to the types of rights that a proprietor transferred to someone for temporary periods and limited kinds of use in return for some material kind of consideration ('rent').[21] The period could be for a few months, a whole year, several years (nine being the usual term), the time it took to plant and harvest a food garden or specific cash crop, or indefinitely. The kinds of use included planting and harvesting gardens or cash crops, harvesting already growing coconuts, pollinating and harvesting already planted vanilla, and residing—either in houses already built or in those built by the lessee. The rents paid for lease rights were in the form of money (either a fixed amount, or a specified sharing of profits), or of food-bearing trees planted on the leasehold by the lessee.

Finally, *neighbour rights*—I found it to be the practice in both of the communities studied for proprietors and tenants to extend certain land-use rights to their community mates with a degree of permissiveness beyond that offered to outsiders (except of course to outsiders who were kinsmen or friends). These included rights of transit; of occasional collection of coconuts, breadfruit, mangoes, firewood and some building material; of hunting; and of fishing. The successful hunter or fisherman was expected to pay some 'rent' in the form of part of the catch, but the only 'rent' charged for use of the other rights was the implicit expectation of reciprocity should the need arise—all of which may sound very nebulous but which was shown to be solidly tangible by the angry reactions I witnessed to some instances when outsiders were known or suspected of making use of such rights.

Except for the brief references to the Administration *domaines* that were leased by some residents, all the above description applies to privately owned land. In the communities I studied there were also to be found parcels owned by other social units: by the Administration (for example, the lots on which the schools were built), by the Protestant mission, and by the local Protestant parish. During my visits questions arose among the local residents concerning the appropriate allocation of use-rights to all of these, but space will not permit further discussion.

NOTES AND REFERENCES

1 Abstracted from Oliver 1975.
2 Note well the limited applicability of that summary. That is, had I included, say, urban centres like Papeete or more remote rural communities like Maupiti and Maiao (cf. Hooper 1966 and Finney 1964) my summary of 'modern' land tenure would have had to include several other norms and practices. For more extensive coverage, including economic aspects of Tahitian land tenure, see Panoff 1964 and 1970.
3 By 'ancient' Tahiti I mean the era from about 1750 to about 1800—i.e., that immediately preceding and during the period of the first European visits and before those visits had, directly or indirectly, brought about radical changes in the indigenous society. And by 'Tahiti' I include all of the islands that have come to be known as the Society Islands. The customs I attribute to that era may have been, and indeed probably were, prevalent before then—but about that there is no reliable evidence.
4 There appears to have existed a nuptial-like rite that was performed for validating an outsider's 'adoption' to congregation membership.
5 There is some evidence to suggest that a male's use-rights outweighed those of his sisters and that this inequality extended to the latters' progeny, but this is not altogether firm.
6 Ancient Tahitian society was stratified into three social classes: an upper caste, the *hui arii*, members of the senior segments of venerable kin-congregations; the *pue raatira*, the senior members of less distinguished kin-congregations and of less-than-senior segments of the more venerable ones; and the *manahune*, 'commoners', who comprised the remaining and largest proportion of the population. As in all other societies structured according to aristocratic principles, class membership entailed both privileges and responsibilities, ceremonial and practical, with forceful emphasis, in this society, against a person's reproductive mating with members of a lower class. This proscription was enforced mainly among the *hui arii*, but seems to have curtailed to some extent marriages between *pue raatira* and *manahune* as well.
7 That is, except for two parts of a sub-tribal division in Tahiti's southern peninsula, which were separated by a separate sub-tribe.
8 The colonial administration districts (Tahitian *mataeinaa*) into which the Islands were and are subdivided (at that time Tahiti had seventeen, Moorea four) were in most cases perpetuations of ancient tribal or sub-tribal divisions.
9 The clause in quotes is taken (in translation) from Pambrun 1958, upon which much of the historical summary of this and following paragraphs is

based. The other secondary source I have used extensively in this historical précis is Newbury 1956, an excellent Ph.D. dissertation which—most unfortunately—has not been published in full.

10 During much of this period the Leeward Islands constituted a British Protectorate—without, however, much more British involvement than was required to discourage other nations from seizing them.

11 Each commission was composed of five or more Tahitian residents of the subdivision, including one or two judges and district chiefs.

12 By French law, lagoon and sea areas were no longer subject to private ownership (but see n. 19 below).

13 The type of real property system thus applied goes under the label of Régime Hypothécaire du Code Civil, to distinguish it from the Régime de l'Immatriculation ou du Livre Foncier. In 1955 the former operated in Metropolitan France, Martinique, Guadeloupe, Réunion, New Caledonia, in parts of Sénégal, and in French Polynesia. The latter was in force in French dependencies elsewhere. The principal difference between the two régimes lies in the form in which lands are identified and registered in the official records—the former being done so by name(s) of the owner(s), the second by the name of each land parcel (Pambrun 1958).

14 *Code civil annoté d'après la doctrine et la jurisprudence*, 61st ed., Petits codes Dalloz, Paris 1962.

15 During the drafting of the 1887 Decree, referred to earlier, a suggestion was made in Privy Council that attributions be recorded in the names of whole land-using groups, but this was turned down on the grounds that it would perpetuate land indivisibility (Newbury 1956).

16 There were some parcels of land in the communities I studied whose post-registration ownership histories I was unable to trace, because of their owners—or joint owners—having left the community and lost contact with their former lands and neighbours. In some of these cases, in which actual transfer of ownership had not been recorded in the Lands Office, it could be that ownership rights had devolved along more unusual lines—e.g., from owner to distant collaterals—but the heritances I knew about followed the paths just noted.

17 In fact, when I was inquiring into the histories of specific land parcels and came to those owned by Europeans or by descendants of Europeans, the standard explanation given me by my Tahitian informants (including, in one case, a mix-blood descendant of one of them!) was that the land in question had been acquired for a pittance and usually by guile, lubricated with alcohol. Such may in fact have been the case—although I cannot document it one way or another.

18 I failed to inquire whether the lessee deducted any if he dried the crop in his own dryer.

19 As noted earlier, with the application of French law, private ownership of lagoon and ocean water areas was abolished. And although the Tahitians I knew respected this ruling with regard to fishing rights—indeed, they were no longer aware that the land tenure practices of their pre-European ancestors included lagoon fishing rights as well—they were uninformed or unpersuaded about some other aspects of this law.

20 In what follows I employ some familiar labels in ways that may be unfamiliar to many readers. I regret having to resort to this inconvenient practice, but have had to do so in order to clarify my own ideas about this complex subject. Hopefully it will add clarity to my written description of it as well.

21 Lessees were often empowered by local convention to sub-let their leaseholds, and in the communities I studied they occasionally did so.

Division of food and labour at the far ends of Polynesia

KENNETH P. EMORY

During a stay on the island of Napuka in the Tuamotuan Archipelago of French Polynesia I witnessed and recorded the equal division and distribution of food among the total of one hundred and ninety-two inhabitants of more than a year old.

The writer, Clifford Gessler, as my companion, and I were set ashore from the sampan *Islander* in the course of the Bernice P. Bishop Museum Mangarevan Expedition to continue my earlier researches on the island.[1] Gessler in his book *Road My Body Goes*[2] gives a graphic and detailed account of our days there, 16 May to 29 July 1934, including the activities pursuant to the division of food I am describing. These observations, being outside the scope of my *Material Culture of the Tuamotu Archipelago*,[3] have remained unpublished.

On 31 May 1934 the trading schooner *Ruahatu* appeared to take copra aboard. As compensation for the villagers who helped weigh and load the copra the crew gave several sacks of flour. A week later this flour was mixed with water and kneaded into dough, without any leavening (yeast), shaped into rolls six inches long and an inch in diameter, then wrapped in coconut-leaflet packages, and baked in ground ovens. Flour cooked in this way was called *fara rotika*. The entire batch made at this time was then immediately eaten and was in such quantity that many of the people soon suffered from extreme constipation. They came to us requesting medicine to relieve their headaches. It was then that I suggested eating papayas (*Carica papaya*) to counteract the over-consumption of the *fara rotika*.

The recommendation was carried out on 12 June when canoes were dispatched to bring back papayas from a forest on the islet of Tematahoa where they grew. They returned with a quantity of green and ripe papayas, which were dumped on the beach for distribution. These papayas were distributed in two rows, one of green papayas and the other of ripe papayas set at right angles to the other. In each row were eight piles, called a *pou* (heap). The distribution into these piles was carried out by men and women, boys and girls. Each person had to complete his chosen row setting down the papayas one at a time in succession on the eight piles.

When the distribution was nearly complete, the man in charge kept a careful watch and was the one person who laid the last of the papayas on the *pou*. Several green and ripe papayas left over, because there were fewer than eight, were reserved for the chief.

Now followed the division of each *pou* into six portions, *tuhanga*, each of which would constitute a share for four people. These *tuhanga* were laid out at right angles to the *pou* and their redistribution was carried out in the same manner as the first distribution. If a family numbered eight persons, they would remove two *tuhanga* for transporting to their house. If the share falling to one, two, or three persons was to be taken directly from the *tuhanga* distribution pile, the pile was then divided into four equal piles called *pu-rare* (single shares) in the same manner as the larger piles.

In the particular distribution of 12 June, I recorded, each person received four ripe papayas and three green papayas. There were sixteen papayas in each *tuhanga* of ripe papayas and twelve in each *tuhanga* of green papayas. So that, in all, 1,344 papayas were divided into one hundred and ninety-two equal shares. We were told that sometimes each *pou* was divided into three *tuhanga* and each *tuhanga* into eight *pu-rare*. This combination, too, would result in one hundred and ninety-two equal shares.

Gessler in his chapter 'The Harvest' in *Road My Body Goes* describes the first time we saw papayas collected and divided on 23 and 24 May, when each person received four ripe and four green papayas; and then the later flour episode.[4]

This division of food must have been arrived at empirically, since the Napukans had not been schooled in multiplication or division. It seems obviously based on thinking in terms of fours and may go back to the custom of tying coconuts in bunches of four (called an *amui* in Tahiti) for easy handling, or in pairs, one for each hand.

One morning I observed all the middle-aged men gathered to begin work on erecting a house. The head man held in his hand a number of pebbles equal to the number of men needed. Calling out a name, he set down a pebble when he was answered. At the end of the roll call any men whose names had not been called spoke up and an additional stone for each was placed on the heap. The stones left in the hands of the head man then represented the number of men needed still lacking. I suppose that the work which had been set aside for these was then apportioned among those available.

While at the Polynesian inhabited atoll of Kapingamarangi in the Caroline Islands in 1947 and in 1950, our field party witnessed and recorded the division of fish resulting from community fishing drives with community nets. While I have described this activity at some length in *Kapingamarangi: Social and Religious Life on a Polynesian Atoll*,[5] I did not include our records of specific fish drives and divisions of their hauls into equal shares for the participants. I believe a presentation of these records will give a better grasp of this aspect of their food economy.

In 1947 small fishing groups went out with nets and traps as Dr Buck has described on an expedition he accompanied in which fish were driven into a net trap.[6] Twenty-eight participants from both Touhou and Werua joined in the drive. The fish, which were of all kinds, were equally distributed on the gravel beach of Motukerekere islet into twenty-eight heaps for equal shares.

Dr Buck and I both joined the small group of twelve men which went out with a trap on Saturday morning 30 August 1947. Buck has recorded this expedition and the division of just over five hundred fish into twelve equal piles, one for each of the participants.[7] The main group left before daylight. We followed an hour later, arriving at Pumatehati as they were finishing a breakfast of some small fish they had already caught and roasted on hot pebbles of a freshly made ground oven. The party was composed of King David, aged 61; Taikuru, aged 61; Rimari, aged 65; Tiroina, aged 51; Topiki, aged 45; Hakatekoi, aged 48; Tawhera, aged 52; and three others. None of these were brothers, or fathers and sons, but all lived at Touhou.

During the afternoon of Wednesday 1 October 1947 a flock of sea birds over the lagoon signalled a school of fish. The Werua people launched three large canoes, loaded in fish nets and fishermen, to go in pursuit. They drove the fish into shallow water against a beach, then placed a net across a gap made in their ranks towards the deeper waters of the lagoon. The fish rushed into the net. The canoes returned at sunset. When within 200 yards of Werua, they broke into a race for shore, chanting the while an ancient chant. The lagoon shore of both Touhou and Werua were lined as usual with spectators, waiting to learn the outcome of the fishing and also to witness the race which they know would take place when such a large party returned.

In 1950 we witnessed a remarkable method of driving schools of fish into a net. This was done not by a sweep of leaves but merely by the shadow of a rope half an inch thick, manned at rather wide intervals by the men handling it. The first drive was carried out when the net used in conjunction with it was completed in July 1950. This net was made in two weeks at the men's house at Touhou and required 600 fathoms of coconut-fibre twine, *tirahira*. A Christian prayer was said before the commencement of the work and at the end. It was estimated that this net would last for two years if much used, three years if used lightly.

On Monday 17 July 1950 at 5 o'clock in the morning, as it was just light enough to see, I heard movements at the men's house. Investigating, I learned that the village canoe was being launched to initiate the net. I woke Hetata, King David's son, to prepare his canoe so that Dr Miller, he, and I could go along. Forty-five men went out, altogether, in thirteen canoes. The three of us returned at 11 a.m. because Dr Miller had a patient waiting for him. During the day the new net was set about ten times and eight hundred and one fish were taken. The fish were divided into eighty-two shares (*tuhongo*) of nine fish each (one large fish, one medium fish, seven small fish). The balance of sixty-three fish was donated to a feast for those who made the net. The women brought *sakaroi* pudding for this feast. I did not learn exactly why the division was into eighty-two shares; I believe now it was on the basis of the number of house groups; that is, one share to those living in one house. But it may have been on the basis of one share for each participant in making the net and one share for each member of the fishing expedition. Upon the completion of the distribution, two young girls from the family of each recipient came with freshly plaited coconut-leaf baskets into which the fish were placed to be carried to their houses.

On another fishing expedition, on 29 July 1950, forty-seven men in fourteen canoes went out with rope and the net called *kupega manu* (bird net). Those in the canoe carrying the net, *ti kau ti waka kupenga* (the people of the net canoe) were in charge of the expedition and the division of the haul. Tirongorongo, the leader, was in this canoe. We joined them at noon. During the day they set the net on the reef north of the pass, four times for *paua* (rabbit fish) and other small fish, and one time for *kina,* a kind of mackerel.

The men then proceeded to Pumatehati islet to make the division on a sandy spit. The fish were distributed evenly, two by two, over four parallel rows of piles, thirteen piles in three rows and eight piles in the last row. The piles were set so that about two feet separated them. The *paua* and like fish were distributed evenly over forty-seven piles, then the *kina*. It was found then that each pile had sixteen *paua* or the like, and four *kina*. Seventeen *kina* were left over and four *paua*. Twelve of these *kina* were divided evenly between the owners of the three ropes. Roheti was the owner of one, Alfred of another. The remaining five *kina* and the four *paua* were given to Dr Miller and me. The men said that in the old days, the remaining piles would have been reserved for their gods. Thus we have the division of six hundred and sixty-

K

three *paua* and two hundred and five *kina,* a total of eight hundred and sixty-eight fish.[8]

On 31 July 1950 fifty-seven people went out setting the net five times for *kina,* and bringing in a total of two hundred and eighty-five, or five *kina* apiece. They returned just after sunset, the long canoe of each village racing.[9]

On 2 August 1950 a larger number of men than usual went out with the net. The haul resulted in one *kina* and four other fish apiece.

On 5 August 1950 thirty-three men went out net fishing, setting the net about seven times. They caught six hundred and thirty-four fish of all kinds, but all rather small. The distribution gave nineteen fish to each participant.

The largest expedition which we saw go out took place on 10 August 1950. Werua village sent forty-seven men in five canoes, and Touhou, fifty-seven men (counting Dr Miller and me) in nine canoes; fourteen in the large village canoe, eight in one canoe, seven in each of two canoes, six in one canoe, five in each of two canoes, three in one canoe, and two in one canoe. The Touhou group caught about 300 *kina*. The net was put down five times. The first time, all the fish escaped owing to a blunder on the part of one of the young men, who was sharply reprimanded by Tirongorongo; the second time a good haul was made; the third time the fish all escaped; the fourth time part of the school escaped; the fifth time a good haul was made. These fish were for the feast dedicating the completion of the pier. It was found that each inhabitant had two *paua* and one *kina* fish.

These are subsequent expeditions which I noted. On Saturday 26 August 1950 sixteen hundred fish were caught with the net, the largest number taken in one day during our stay. These were for a community feast, welcoming the Spanish priest, and presumably, bidding Dr Miller and myself goodbye. It so happened that the boat that was to pick us up was delayed for three months! On 2 September they made a small haul with the net. On 16 September the haul with the net was about five hundred fish. They went out again on 30 September. On 21 October four canoes went out with the net, and caught only eleven fish. The men explained that this was too small a number to divide, so they gave the entire haul to Miller and me, to our embarrassment. This ended the season of driving fish with a rope.

The division of food witnessed at Napuka, although made with new and introduced foods, and the division of fish at Kapinga-marangi, were surely in accord with the islanders' ancient methods of apportioning food, as well as of organizing labour to obtain it. Whether these methods are still practised I cannot say, but it would not be surprising if they are.

NOTES AND REFERENCES

1 Gregory 1930-31, 1935.
2 Gessler 1937.
3 Emory 1975.
4 Gessler 1937:91-100, 107-9. A photo facing p. 77 was taken of the distribution of 12 June 1934.
5 Emory 1965.
6 Buck 1950:226-8.
7 *ibid.*:228-30.
8 I was able to record on 16 mm colour film the rounding up of the *kina*, the landing at Pumatehati islet, and the sailing of the fleet homeward.
9 Also recorded in moving pictures.

Institutions of violence in the Marquesas

GREG DENING

E ika ta was a Marquesan phrase meaning 'to go fishing'. Marquesans fished for more than shark and bonito. They 'fished' for *heana*, the victims that were sacrificed and sometimes eaten. At times of major social crisis, such as the death of a *haka'iki* (chief) or *tau'a* (priest) or at the failure of a breadfruit crop, or at a celebratory and *tapu* moment in the life of the *haka'iki's* first-born, raiding parties would go out to snatch enemies from their fishing canoes, or capture them as they wandered alone along the shore or deep in the valleys. If the raiding parties went by canoe, as they mostly did, they followed all the ritual preparations and sang all the chants that belonged to fishing for the most *tapu* of catches, the turtle. *Heana,* when caught, were brought back, a large hook in their mouth, baskets of bait tied to their limbs, their bodies painted red in token of the *tapu* fish of which they were part. They were carried to the *me'ae* with fishing chants and either hung as sacrifices from the trees or ceremonially eaten by *tau'a* and *haka'iki* and *toa* (warrior).[1]

One can only guess at the number of *heana* that were caught each year. In the periods in which there is documentation by witnesses to *ta ika,* 1798-1805, 1832-1837, probably eighty to one hundred men, women and children were taken and eaten or sacrificed each year among the six principal islands of the Marquesas. For example, William Pascoe Crook recorded the exploits of Teinae, *haka'iki* of Vaitahu on Tahuata, in the period August 1798 to May 1799. On 6 September Teinae went fishing for *heana* at the death of the *tau'a* of Vaitahu. His canoes flew the white *tapa* streamers of a turtle hunt. On their prows were the skulls of *heana* already caught. In the morning they were back from Hiva Oa with four *heana.* They had caught three men and a woman of the Pikina on the south-east coast of Hiva Oa. The bodies were flung on the beach, tied hand and foot to long poles. When the men and boys had mocked the corpses and played with them, two bodies were taken to be hung on the *me'ae* and two were taken to be eaten. In November Teinae and his brothers went fishing again, this time among the Tepue people of Hiva Oa. Fourteen men and women were caught and brought back alive to Vaitahu. At Vaitahu their captors either killed them and ate them or bartered them with others to do the same.

In March 1799 Teinae made two more raids on Hiva Oa. This time they were not so much stealthy fishing trips for *heana* as large-scale expeditions with hundreds of warriors in dozens of canoes. In the first they returned with only one victim. In the second the Pikina of Hiva Oa, who had killed four of Teinae's allies, were surprised at night and slaughtered wholesale. A large number of corpses was brought back to Vaitahu. At Vaitahu itself four Pikina begging for ornaments of war to go to battle were killed and eaten by Teinae's youngest brother.[2]

There were other periods, almost as frenzied in their killings, while Keattonnue and Temoana were *haka'iki* of Taiohae at Nukuhiva 1813-42, and Iotete and Maheono were *haka'iki* at Vaitahu 1830-45.[3] The function of such systems of violence is more comfortably understood in the library than perhaps its purposes could be understood by its victims. There was no pool of *heana* living side by side with the rest of the community, as seems to have been the case in Tahiti. Occasionally victims would be taken from within some wider tribal grouping because they had broken some *tapu* or were suspect of being the cause of some social disorder. The greater number were taken from among traditional enemies. Since the poorer people, the *kikino,* the dark skinned, were more likely to be collecting food along the shore or to be in their canoes fishing at night, they were more likely to become *heana* than the *tapu* group. The *tapu* class also had networks of relations by blood and by marriage through most of the valleys of the islands on whom to call for protection if they were taken. The men among the *tapu* class were more likely to be taken or killed in formal battle than to be caught by one of the fishing parties.

William Pascoe Crook, who lived alone at Tahuata and Nukuhiva for eighteen months in 1798-99, was the first to report this violent side of Marquesan society. Josiah Roberts and his mate Magee had reported the violent clashes between themselves and the inhabitants of Vaitahu, and that most disorganized ship of the British navy, H.M.S. *Daedalus,* had two unhappy visits to the Marquesas during which they feared attack. But the violence between the *Jefferson* and the *Daedalus* and the Marquesans sprang from the disorder and distrust of contact, not the aggression of the Marquesans.[4] The shooting of an islander by one of Cook's guards on the *Resolution* and the death of a woman by a careless shot from the *London* were of the same cause. There was hardly a visiting ship in the first forty years after Cook's arrival that did not report some incident between crew and Marquesan. But only Marquesans were killed and only in the case of Josiah Roberts were they killed because they tried to attack a vessel.

Before David Porter's arrival at Nukuhiva in 1813 in the U.S.S. *Essex* the violent side of Marquesan society was known through W. P. Crook's private reports, from the talk of beachcombers such as Edward Robarts with ships' captains, and from the publications of the Russian expedition under Johann von Krusenstern. With their tattoos and bizarre headdresses, the Marquesans looked as wild and as savage as they were reputed to be, but before 1813 reserved their savagery for themselves. Porter's own savage occupation of Nukuhiva was a turning point. Not only did the Happa and the Taipi react effectively to his sorties against them, in the end they had the satisfaction of knowing they had driven off the remnants of his men. The *Greenwich,* one of Porter's captive whalers, was burnt and four of Lieutenant Gamble's men were killed. For the first time their numbers and their skills in ambuscade were effective.

Porter's visit coincided with the development of the sandalwood trade in the Marquesas. Captain William Rogers in the *Hunter* had first exploited the wood and alerted sandalwooders in Canton to his discovery in 1812. In those months just before the British blockaded Canton the *Lydia,* the *America* and the *Pennsylvania Packet* all took loads from Nukuhiva, Hiva Oa and Tahuata.[5] Porter discovered Lieutenant John Maury at Nukuhiva. He had been left to collect wood for the *Pennsylvania Packet's* return. Tradition in the Maury family had it that John Maury had been left with five others, four of whom had been killed by the Marquesans. John Maury and a companion were believed to have escaped by building themselves a platform in the trees where they were fed by friendly islanders. Whatever the fantasy in that tradition, at least one of the men left by the American sandalwooders was killed. The reason is not known. The escape of the captive whaler *Seringapatam* alerted Sydney traders and the end of the blockade at Canton allowed the news of sandalwood in the Marquesas to get to Boston and Salem. From 1813 to 1826 the number of sandalwooders increased greatly. The arithmetic of violence also took an upward turn. Attempts were made to cut off the ships *Lydia, Queen Charlotte, Endeavour* and *Bordelais.* The Marquesans succeeded in wrecking the *Matilda* at Ua Huka, killing the boat crews of the *Flying Fish, Mary, Coquette,* of another American vessel and of a French whaler.

There is no knowing what was in the Marquesans' minds when they attacked these boats, other than that they wanted the whalers' or the sailors' muskets. Those Marquesans who lived in more isolated valleys were rarely visited by ships except the sandalwooders, and probably felt they had no other means of acquiring these treasures than by violence. That they ate those they killed was a common sailor's assumption, despite the comforting lower deck myth that the Marquesans found Europeans too salty for their taste. That they killed in order to eat is more doubtful. There is never a suggestion in the description of these attacks that the Marquesans saw their victims as *heana* or their attacks as *ta ika*. Of the thirty or forty beachcombers who were killed in the Marquesas 1798-1880 almost all died because they had flaunted some *tapu*, stolen some Marquesan property or quarrelled in their drunkenness. Only in one instance, the murder of a Spanish beachcomber after the Peruvian slave traders had stolen Marquesans from Ua Pou, is there evidence that the Marquesans shared the logic of those who bombarded their valleys or took hostages and made one white man responsible for the actions of others. Some of the beachcombers were eaten. None, so far as is known, were sacrificed. The French killed by Iotete's men at Tahuata in 1842 and by Pakoko's men at Nukuhiva in 1845 were seen as trespassing enemies, and such of their bodies as were taken were mocked and treated as trophies of hate. Lieutenant Halley and his men at Tahuata were killed in ambush on one of Halley's forays. The five soldiers at Nukuhiva were killed as they washed their linen in a place forbidden to them. Pakoko's men carried some of the latter off to their *me'ae,* but there is no evidence that they had gone fishing for them.[6]

The violence Marquesans showed to outsiders (*te aoe*) was different from the violence they showed to themselves (*te enata*). *Te aoe* were fair game. They stood outside both the systems of obligation and of right, and in so far as they controlled their relations with *te enata* violently with their guns were subject to the same violence. Being a *heana* belonged to *te enata,* the Men. If it seemed a doubtful privilege, it was nonetheless invested with prestige. *Heana* were equated with *haka'iki* in the level of Havaiki to which they were destined to go after their death. Their numbers proclaimed and established the power of the *haka'iki* and *tau'a* who sought them.

Whatever the function of *ta ika,* the search for *heana* was an integral part of Marquesan society. The role of *haka'iki* was inconceivable without the legitimation which the sacrifices made of his office. The *haka'iki* was at the centre of Marquesan society in time and space. In time, because to him belonged the *atua,* the deified ancestors going back in a line to the Men's beginnings, because the rhythm of his social life established the cycles of feasts and exchanges that drew the Men together, and because in his first-born was the pledge of continuity. In space, because the *tapu* system was a social map in which the elements of the physical and social environment were related in their sacredness and separateness to the *haka'iki.* The capture of *heana* and their sacrifice at the *me'ae* that belonged to the *haka'iki* and his line were pledges of solidarity and continuity.

In the Marquesas there was no overthrow of the *tapu* system in one dramatic gesture as in Hawaii, and the tribal groupings were too divided in their mutual hostility to follow the example of only one *haka'iki* if he were converted to Christianity. Both the London Missionary Society and the American Hawaiian Mission failed to win converts. In 1845 at Tahuata, after the social trauma that followed the deposition of Iotete as *haka'iki* by the French, and when depopulation had stripped many valleys of their people, there was a sort of religious convulsion as the people accepted the catechetical book printed by the Sacred Hearts missionary, Mgr Baudichon, and with Maheono, the French replacement for Iotete, ritually broke their *tapu* by having the women mount the *paepae* in the *tapu* enclosures, or eat with men, or hang their *pareu* (waist clothes) over the door of the chapels and have the men walk under them. These ceremonies were conducted with a frenzy of excitement. None could read the books. None could be said to have really accepted the Christian teaching. The new fervour collapsed quickly.[7] The *tapu* system now broken, a social and religious vacuum was left. Tahuata entered on a period of listless hopelessness. Maheono tried to re-establish his lost power as *haka'iki* by savagely looking for *heana*, but he had long traded his traditional symbols for European and lost his central position in time and space by looking for the ways in which he could accumulate wealth in muskets and clothing rather than distribute it in exchange and feast. His *heana* were savage murders and his fishing without social meaning.

This convulsive religious movement was repeated in Nukuhiva after the conversion of Temoana in 1853. Although Temoana subsided into drunken lethargy rather than relapsed into active heathenism, in nearly all the valleys of the island a frenzy of killings and an orgy of eating flesh followed the high excitement of the overthrow of the *tapu* and the rejection of the old ways. Again, the violence was socially meaningless. It was internecine and orgiastic. There was no fishing. Those killed were as likely to be neighbours as enemies. The murders were not softened with ceremony or their purpose played out in ritual. The *tau'a* were gone and the *tapu* were kept for inner fears.

Death was always present in vivid ways among the Marquesans and perhaps it displays an ethnocentrism to feel dismayed by the killings. The dead rested among the living, in their houses or by their houses in their hangers of display. They were memorialized in *koina*, feasts, with great frequency. The feasts were a social register in their size and frequency. Aggression was also a prominent feature of their life. There was the overt aggression in their endemic ways and their raiding of enemy for *heana*. Formal display of aggression by men in their preparations for battle was highly valued. In a sense, more significant were the aggressions played out in sorcery, not so much against tribal enemies but with enemies within the same communal group. Disposal of human waste and of objects that had touched or come from the head and genitals had a complex social etiquette for the Marquesans. They feared that those things might get into the hands of sorcerers who might use them to kill or make them sick. The Marquesan penchant for creating *tuhuna* or specialists extended to very numerous and precise categories of sorcerers.[8]

Heana who were sacrificed or eaten probably had no opportunity nor felt the need to observe the nice distinction of being killed because they supported the status of the *haka'iki* and the structures of Marquesan society, and being killed because these same structures had broken down and they were exposed to the latent aggression in Marquesan society. Yet there are extraordinary events in the 1860s and 1870s on Hiva Oa and Fatuhiva that need explanation. The records of the Hawaiian Mission and of the Sacred Hearts fathers provide the story, too detailed to reproduce here. Both the Hawaiians and the priests traced its beginning to the making of coconut toddy by beachcombers and the subsequent debauches by the Marquesans that ended in more and more violence and killings. Zachariah Hapuku made a station report for Atuona 1865-67 in which he recorded the following events: 15 June 1861 Tiviuta of Atuona slain and eaten; 12 August 1862 Titiwehi of the Etuoho cooked by people of Atuona and eaten, ten saved; 30 August 1862 Tutepuu of Atuona cooked by Hanamenu; 19 December 1864 Titihai cooked by Atuona people; 26 October 1865 Teitipatai of Atuona cooked by Etuoho; 18 December 1865 Ohaihai of Hanatetuua cooked by Atuona; 4 January 1866 Houpo of Haamau cooked by Atuona; 25 May 1866 Pehitumoe of Haamau eaten by Atuona. He also mentions Peni of Tahiti shot to death 22 December 1864; Waitei slain by his son 9 October 1866; Tupipi slain by a chief 20 December 1866; and two others who were killed in 1866. For 1868-69 Kekela reported from Puamau that in six months seven had been killed, among them a father by his first-born son, a son by his mother. In the next valley five had been killed in the same time.[9] The population of Puamau at the time was about five hundred men, women and children. Between 1861 and 1880 when the French made a show of strength and dispossessed the Hiva Oans of their arms, and forbade them to leave their valleys or to make liquor and put them to building roads, the missionary records some two hundred and eighty violent killings. Often the killings are in the context of wars that flared up between traditional enemies. More often as the population in each separate valley dwindled to two hundred and less, the killings were within families. After years in the Marquesan field, the Hawaiian missionaries seemed free of the need to embellish the killings with horror, but in their simple descriptions one senses there is an extravagance of violence and aggressive cruelty that they did not need to exaggerate. Where in fishing for *heana* there was mocking of the dead, but no torture of the living, now captives, even the very young, were torn apart while they lived. Where before the eating of flesh was selective in the parts eaten and in the individuals eating, now there were extraordinary scenes of debauch around the bodies. Where before the chants and rituals dominated *ta ika,* now they were gone altogether and the killings followed on rage liberated by drink or careless hate.

The quiet that followed these upheavals was matched by the silence of the valleys. Fifteen populated valleys of Tahuata were reduced to three or four, and everywhere the ruined *paepae* and *me'ae* marked a growing desolation. Visitors, including Robert Louis Stevenson, spoke of the sounds heightened by the quiet, the thump of a falling coconut, the clatter of pebbles in the surf. They felt vaguely threatened by lonely figures that moved silently through the thickets with faces and bodies still marked by their tattooed signs of savagery. The Men's independent and democratic spirit which had so often been described by outsiders and had so often been the despair of administrators and missionaries was now seen to be masked by a sullen, distant look. After the traumas of the 1840s and 1850s, the Men had made no revival of their old ways. They made no attempt to give new life to their old roles of priest and chief, or to their old systems of stability in their feasts, or to their old systems of control in their *tapu.* The violence that once sustained them now destroyed them.

NOTES AND REFERENCES

1 Gerard Chaulet, Notices Géographiques, Ethnographiques et religieuses, MS. 1873, Archives of the Congregation of the Sacred Hearts of Jesus and Mary, Rome. Charles Noury, Notes pour servir à l'ethnologie, MS. 1849, Société des Etudes Océaniennes, Papeete.
2 William Pascoe Crook, Account of the Marquesas Islands, M.L., MS. 1799.
3 Robert Thomson, Letter to Secretary of L.M.S., 16 April 1840, L.M.S. South Seas, Incoming Letters; Richard Armstrong, Letters and Journals 1832-33, Benjamin Parker, Letters and Journals 1832-33, William P. Alexander, Letters and Journals 1832-33, Hawaiian Children's Mission Library, Honolulu; Gerard Chaulet, Notice Historique Religieuse sur les Iles Marquises, MS. 1873, Archives CSSJ, Rome.
4 Bernard Magee, Journal of a Voyage of the Ship Jefferson 1791-1794, MS. 1791, Massachusetts Historical Society, Boston.
5 John Child, Journal of a Voyage from Boston to the South Seas and Canton, MS. 1810, Massachusetts Historical Society, Boston.
6 Saturnin Fournier, Journal en Ephémérides 1838-42, MS. 1838, Archives CSSJ Rome; Almaric, Etablissement de Noukouhiva October 26, 1844-

January 28, 1844, Oceanie A20, Carton 4, Archives de France d'Outre-Mer, Paris.

[7] Paul Baudichon, Journal, MS. 1844, Archives CSSJ, Rome.

[8] Thomas C. Lawson, Manuscript letters and notes pertaining to . . . the Marquesas, sent . . . to Mr Damon, Seamen's Chaplain, Oahu, Sandwich Islands, between 1861-1867, Bernice P. Bishop Museum, Honolulu.

[9] Zachariah Hapuku, Station Reports, Atuona 1865-67, MS. 1865; Abraham Kekela, Letters 1857-80, MS. 1857, Hawaiian Mission Society Library, Honolulu.

Symbolic slaying in Niue: post-European changes in a dramatic ritual complex

KATHARINE LUOMALA

The study of Polynesian use of puppets, marionettes and other moving and movable figures led me to investigate the farewell ceremony held for Edwin M. Loeb on his departure in 1924 from Niue Island, Polynesia, during which he was required to spear an effigy in human form suspended between trees.[1] The anthropologist, it seems to me, only partially recognized the significance of the ceremony held for him and twice in earlier decades for Niueans.

This article assembles data on Niue ethnohistorical traditions and concepts of aboriginal and Christian origin expressed in myths, chants, customs and ritual in order to demonstrate that the 1924 ceremony had elements of both primitive drama and a farewell rite of passage with multiple, intertwined strands of symbolism. First of all, the effigy represented the mutual friendship and loyalty that had bound spear-thrower and village. The spear-thrower's act severed that bond, destroyed mutual obligations between him and village, and rendered him an outcast, free to go elsewhere. The effigy also symbolized not only a warrior who, tradition claims, had died because of a companion's betrayal, but the traitor himself whom villagers had then killed and eaten. Further, the effigy being named Limaua, Two Hands, stood for a fearful sea god who when slain always reappeared. Additionally the effigy may represent an ineffectual king to be killed because his mana had failed to protect his people from drought and famine. Not surprisingly, reference to the former Niuean custom of slaying a weak ruler-magician occurs in Frazer's *The Golden Bough* in connection with his interpretation of the scene in Diana's sacred grove at Nemi, Italy.[2] Christianity in Niue inevitably added new strands, such as those perhaps linking the effigy with Jesus or Judas. The intermingled strands, some now too tangled or frayed to separate and identify, have a martial colouring because feuding formerly was almost incessant between island moieties, villages, and even members of the same village.

Evident in this ceremonial complex is the structure distinguished by van Gennep for rites of passage, whatever their immediate, overt purpose.[3] Initial rites separate the individual (and others like

142

him) from the society in which he has a certain status. His old mode
of life is dead or dying. Liminal, or threshold, rites mark a transition, full of magical danger, between his old life and his preparation for rebirth in the new. Finally, rites incorporate him into
his new status; and society, the crisis over, resumes a normal
routine. In the Niuean farewell rite of passage the central figure
from one point of view was not the departing individual honoured
by the ceremony but the effigy, or, rather, who or what it symbolized. Only with this in mind is the design clear.

The leave-taking ceremony with the ritual of hurling a spear
through the suspended effigy of Limaua has been held at least
three times in the modern era but dates and circumstances are
reported for only two.[4] In 1891 when Nemaia, a native mission
teacher, was leaving Tuapa village for Mutalau village, Tuapa
invited the Mutalau villagers to his farewell party. In 1924 Loeb
was leaving Anakule which he had rented in a *kaina,* the home
place or hamlet of an extended family, to return to the United
States. People of his adopted *kaina,* deciding to hold 'an old
fashioned "killing the god" ceremony', invited as guests their
relatives from near-by Aliutu (now Alofi), and white residents on
Niue. For the occasion Aliutu men made the effigy: Tuapa men
had made their own.[5]

On the festive day in 1924, after a dance and feast, four men
appeared with the effigy, heavily cloth-wrapped, on their shoulders.
Behind them, Aliutu men chanted, danced, and brandished real
spears or substitutes. Limaua was then suspended in mid-air on a
rope between two coconut trees. As his final wrappings fell away
and he was exposed to full view, the crowd hushed.

The anthropologist, about a hundred yards from the image,
was told to throw a heavy branch given him through its chest. But,
as he prepared to cast his spear, warriors, performing the war
dance and waving weapons, rushed at him from behind the effigy.
He missed the throw, to the crowd's disappointment. On the second
throw, conditions having been arranged to ensure success, he
struck his spear 'full force onto the face of the *tupua* [god]. A cry
of joy arose, and the god who a moment before had been moving
violently up and down on his line, was now left inanimate.'[6]

The spear-thrower's landlord 'then took the part of the dead
god, and calmly stretched himself full length on the ground. Here
he was mourned over as a fallen *toa* [warrior], to the sound of the
customary *tagi* [lament], *"Ko e mate toa he ha."* [Why did the
warrior die?]. A song evidently composed for quite a different
occasion, the meaning or significance of which is no longer remembered.'[7]

In 1891 Tuapa hosts asked their Mutalau guests, not Nemaia
himself, to slay the god. Followed by people dancing (presumably

a war dance), the hosts carried a large effigy of Limaua, tapa-covered and made of *puka* wood (unidentified), into the village plaza. Here they 'took a rope and suspended the idol from a coconut tree, so that the people of Mutalau might throw spears at it. They cried out, "If the spears pierce [it], Nemaia . . . can go up to Mutalau, but if they miss he must stay back".' Twenty spears missed. Then Makaea tried, but failed; next, Vihekula, dancing, threw his eighteen-foot spear, 'so heavy that a boy of five years could not carry it', and pierced the idol. But the spear slipped away and nearly went through a person named Apelamo. 'After this they pulled the god about on the top of the line, and sang . . . [Why did the warrior die?]'[8]

Loeb, who interpreted this ritual merely as a 'primitive drama . . . very old and of considerable importance', added that among Aztecs, Greeks and Christians (in miracle plays) drama had started 'in a ceremony in which a chief god was sacrificed, mourned over, then resurrected'; and concluded that 'although the Niue idol was not brought to life again, yet we may be justified in calling the Niue ceremony a primitive drama of the Polynesian people'.[9] That Limaua was believed to return to life, but not as part of the ritual, will be discussed later.

The recurrence of the spear-throwing ritual in a farewell ceremony suggests that it had symbolic values besides that of ritually killing a god who might be reborn. It was, to begin with, a rite of passage to separate in formal farewell two closely affiliated parties. Geographical place and social status as well as allegiance and other sentiments would change. The traveller had to 'kill' the existing affective bond, represented by Limaua, before he could depart to form a new bond (or return to an earlier one) elsewhere. If he failed to destroy that allegiance by a definitive act of symbolic hostility and renunciation he could not leave, for he would then lack justification for going and depriving his people of his social and material contributions to their corporate strength and unity.

The mission teacher, in his symbolic attempt to shift allegiance, had surrogates from his new village to pierce the effigy. He, cast, I believe, in the symbolic role of betraying Tuapa to Mutalau warriors, waited for them to achieve victory in order to 'escape' with them. The anthropologist, having no American surrogates, had himself to throw the spear. White guests, being British and Niue residents, presumably were unacceptable substitutes.

As if to prevent or at least delay his demolishing the bond between himself and his *kaina*, 'hostile warriors', men of his group and their kinsmen, imitated real warfare by rushing out to ambush, surprise and threaten him. They prevented the success of his first hostile act but not his second. Despite absence of reference to

Tuapa men distracting Mutalau men by similar, pretended resistance it was probably present.

Failure to hit the effigy the first time is significant. The overt explanation is distraction caused by actual physical resistance by home villagers acting as warriors. Psychological conflict may also be expressed: unconscious reluctance, by each traveller about leaving and by surrogate spear-throwers about accepting obligations concomitant with success. The missed shots, of course, created dramatic suspense for the crowd. Further, in Niuean custom and myth, the number two has ritual importance. In Nemaia's farewell, the significant throws were not the first twenty but the last two by named men, the first of whom missed and the second succeeded. That the anthropologist's throws numbered two may be coincidental but, again, unconscious factors perhaps functioned, such as knowledge of Nemaia's example and of the number's significance. Besides the number two, Niueans occasionally defer to the widespread Polynesian preference for eight or ten, or their multiples (hence twenty spears), and the Western preference for three.

Throwing the spear may, of course, have been simply a test of skill which the traveller or his defenders had to pass to assure his future protection among strangers. According to tradition, an ancient Niuean warrior, Laufoli, won a series of tests of skill on Tonga after which Tongans permitted him to settle there with a Tongan wife.[10] If Loeb correctly interpreted his crowd's sentiments, 'disappointment' was expressed when he missed and 'joy' when he hit. These obvious responses to hits and misses, as in games or other tests of skill, would be appropriate not only if they related to the spear-thrower's ability to defend himself until established in his new residence but if he symbolized the executioner of the traitor who had betrayed the warrior mentioned in the lament. If he were being symbolically hostile toward his own people, however, the responses would be appropriate only if failure in the ritual unconsciously implied that then only undesired real misbehaviour could sever the friendship.

That the effigy symbolized, in part, the people with their village as well as the sentimental tie is evident from the anthropologist's landlord, his kinsman through his residence in the *kaina*, assuming the role of the pierced effigy. The man lay down on the ground where villagers mourned and chanted over him the same dirge used in 1891. Both anthropologist and mission teacher had now formally disowned the village which equally formally had resisted and mourned its failure objectified by the damaged image and its human substitute, representing a corpse. Every goodbye is a form of death.

These preliminal rites (like those associated in many regions with formal leave-taking) had been prolonged by a grand feast, exchange of gifts, doubtless with the oratory that accompanied such exchanges in Niue, and exhibitions of social dances. These were also part of Niuean welcoming ceremonies,[11] transitional rites of the stranger's entry into the group, but differed in having a climax of ritual aggression between real or putative kinsmen, a feature of another type of farewell—mourning over a prominent dead person.

The liminal stage began with chanting and wailing over the dead. Theoretically the travellers' situation was now delicate. Being on the threshold between old and new statuses and residences they were technically outcasts and potential strangers and enemies. What happened as one waited for a ship and the other to move to Mutalau is not documented. Mutual roles of villager and traveller, however, being now unclear and liminal might lead to erratic, unpredictable behaviour and uncomfortable embarrassment.

Almost as little is known about the stage of incorporation and reintegration after the physical separation. Presumably each traveller participated in welcoming rites of passage at his destination to start a new life or a modified return to the old. Villagers, apparently closing the social gap left by departure, probably anticipated Limaua's reappearance. In fact they claimed to have seen him soon after the 1891 ceremony which had somehow angered him, as will be discussed later.

The former seriousness of separation and change of residence is apparent in the animosity shown, during the early and mid-nineteenth century, toward Niueans returning after an absence caused by no fault of their own. Any Niuean who left on a ship and returned was killed or likely to be killed.[12] Two young men, Uea and Tupuamana, whom the Reverend John Williams carried off in 1830 but returned several months later, 'had trouble in landing, because by the act of leaving the island they had become foreigners, and hence people to be excluded'.[13] In a subsequent battle Tupuamana's relatives defeated his opponents to enable him temporarily and imperfectly to be reincorporated into his village. He later had to flee on a passing ship, however. According to one account, he and Uea were blamed for influenza that broke out after their return.[14] Another account is that Uea introduced a disease resembling syphilis which led to an uprising against him and his family in which he was among the slain.[15] Escaping to Samoa with Tupuamana was Peniamina (Benjamin) Tukai who, on returning in 1842 as a missionary, was so threatened that he left on the ship that had brought him. Returning in 1845, his life and foreign possessions, all regarded as infectious, were endangered by an armed crowd which finally spared him and his objects.[16] He too had to flee the island later, but because of trouble over a woman. Foreign objects continued to be regarded as pollutants even after people became courageous enough to visit passing ships, and foreign gifts were hung in quarantine in the bush for weeks before being used.[17]

Complete strangers, including other Polynesians, were also unwelcome. Castaways from other islands 'were invariably killed'.[18] The menacing reception accorded his expedition led Captain Cook, the European discoverer of Niue in 1774, to call the place 'Savage Island'.

Turner, a medical missionary, and Loeb attributed this attitude to fear of disease being introduced. Thomson, a visiting British Administrator, echoing missionaries from whom his data came, conjectured that castaways whose arrival had led to an epidemic gave rise to the Niuean 'quarantine'.[19] Loeb's similar theory is that pre-European Tongan visitors, perhaps causing the first serious epidemic, inspired the Niuean policy.[20] By using a merely rational explanation, these writers overlooked the possibility that these epidemics merely intensified an older fear, reported elsewhere in Polynesia and other parts of the world, of foreign spirits and foreign magic that belong to strangers and returning residents.[21] Varied misfortunes would afflict land and people because of local magicians' inability to counteract foreign mana. This is suggested by Peniamina protesting to his countrymen that he was a Niuean man like themselves, not a god, and with no control over disease.[22] Introduced objects, believed to share their owners' dangerous, contaminating *tapu*, people wanted destroyed or returned to the ship.

Aboriginally the system of purificatory rites was, I believe, too weakly developed to handle anything newly arrived, whether animate or inanimate, in less stringent ways. The old custom for anything ritually unclean was to destroy it or impose a long *tapu*. Entire plantations and coconut trees were destroyed when their owner died; his fishing area and bush land, like handlers of his corpse, were made *tapu* for over three months. Later, the custom was to put a six-month *tapu* on what formerly had been destroyed.[23] Turner's medical term 'quarantine' surely refers to a ritually neutralizing period for foreign objects to divest them of their foreign sanctity.

Linked to a fear of ritual pollution was anxiety about nonconformity by strangers, particularly Tongan invaders, to custom in Niue, known as Motu-te-fua, 'Island-in-itself', because of its physical isolation—the nearest neighbour was Vava'u, Tonga, three hundred and sixty km westward. A long chant twice expresses concern about nonconformity. First, Tagaloa, the highest god in the pantheon, is invoked to

> Take the stranger to his own island,
> Lest he break the laws of Motu-te-fua.

L

Then, Lava-ki-umata, the god-of-the-eyelid, is asked to

> Come down on the right side,
> Come down and block up the horizon.
> Stop the stranger from coming here,
> Lest he break the laws of Motu-te-fua.[24]

These customs and attitudes about strangers and returning residents suggest the unhappy lot of outcasts and newcomers. The farewell ceremony, emphasizing the serious and sorrowful step— once nearly irrevocable—of leave-taking by respected members of the community, provided a publicly recognized, orderly, and peaceful departure that helped villagers and travellers reconcile themselves to the event. The departure of Uea and others, on the contrary, had been unritualized, with no ceremony latently prophetic of return. But, of course, Western influence eliminated older rites, preliminary to entry, in which an armed challenge from warriors ready to fight to the death was reinforced by a society rallying to close its ranks against the supernaturally malevolent threat of strangers to their cohesion and welfare. Pre-European Tongan invaders are evidence, however, that strangers sometimes passed the preliminary and dangerous Niuean rites, entered the transitional stage of welcoming customs, and finally were adopted and incorporated into the society. Ceremonies to formalize departure from the island or from one part of the island to another were, I believe, unlikely to have existed aboriginally in the war-torn island. Departures tended to be secret escapes into hiding from enemy pursuit or endless feuding.

Limaua's effigy also represented a warrior, perhaps in two aspects—the warrior betrayed, the warrior as traitor. Identification with a warrior is evident from the effigy's martial costume, described later, and the 'very old' lament of unknown origin, with archaic words known only to very few, chanted in 1891 and 1924 over the speared effigy or its human surrogate.

The chant may have been composed for a warrior whom Aliutu people had partially eaten in anger, the only record of Niuean cannibalism except in folk-tales.[25] The song is:

> Why did the *toa* die?
> He died because they ate him bit by bit . . .
> Awake to lament that *toa*.
> Awake to lament that *toa*.
> You are the man who betrayed the *toa* that night.
> Awake to lament that *toa*.
> Awake to lament that *toa*.

Nothing is known of the chant's meaning or significance. However, two different warriors are mentioned—the one eaten and the one betrayed. Whether the wailing is over one or both is unclear. Perhaps the very ambiguity as well as the age of the chant rendered it 'the customary *tagi*', usable by any village. The eaten warrior was an enemy, according to Loeb, but I believe he was such because he was a traitor to a fellow warrior as indicated by the use of the verb 'betrayed' in the song.

Traditions describe betrayal and double betrayal.[26] A woman betrayed her people by pointing out to the enemy the road to the fort; a wife betrayed her husband; and two real traitors with real grudges undid the work of a fellow warrior pretending because of a grudge to betray his side to the enemy and lure them into ambush. A favourite trick was to invite people against whom one had an ancient grudge to a feast and then kill them. A famous example concerns Mutalau people who, while living in a cave, were ambushed. All were killed except for one man, who, a generation later, invited the enemy leader and his relations to a grand feast. While dances and chants were being performed in their honour their weapons were removed and used to kill them.[27] Of special interest is a pretended betrayal of their village by two warriors who pointed out to the enemy a figure sleeping by the fire as that of their leader. When the enemy war party arrived it was ambushed and wiped out. The figure had actually been that of a tapa-clad, wooden image, called generically a *fakatino*.[28]

Conventions of fighting included trickery, duelling, and frightening off the enemy by hideous faces and menacing feints. Battles were often at night. While physical injury and loss of life were ordinarily comparatively light, the constant feuding kept Niue in turmoil. Some people, like the Mutalau band, hoping to live peacefully, moved into isolated caves and bush regions, but war parties had sport in discovering them. Men, seeking to avoid battles, engaged in fearsome boasts and long-winded oratory. Causes of war included hostility between two endogamous moieties which divided the island socially and geographically; jealousy between villages and between families within a village; quarrels over land and women; and desire to avenge insults, taunts, and losses in competitive games of skill. Because of frequent warfare, shifts of residence from one place to another were risky, for new residents were protected neither by former nor new neighbours, if any.

Among its symbolic meanings, Limaua's effigy in the farewell ceremony may have represented a warrior of the village being speared either by a traitor and the enemy warriors he had joined or by a pretended traitor luring the enemy to be ambushed. It may have stood for a captured warrior, a traitor, being executed. Eating the victim represented his literal and symbolic incorporation, or reincorporation, into the village that had suffered, through betrayal, the loss of one or perhaps two warriors and was restored through the communion meal to wholeness. Conceptualizing Limaua

as a warrior introduces pre-Christian belief in warriors as the
strong, brave, and politically powerful members of Niuean society.
To be recognized as a warrior gave a man prestige. One not
recognized was a very poor creature even if people appointed him
king of Niue and guardian of their rainmaking symbol. Martial
metaphors and similes, while not peculiar to Niuean Christianity
or aboriginal culture, have their local twist. Prisoners of war
were taken, metaphorically, in the fish net, and the metaphor, updated, appears in a prayer to Tagaloa, here identified with
Jehovah:

> Blessings, O Tagaloa.
> Bless the proud and wicked people,
> Place thy spirit in their minds that
> They may be caught in the fish net of Jesus.[29]

Despite absence of overt links, the effigy of Limaua and his
drama recall the betrayal of Jesus by Judas Iscariot, the suicide of
Judas by hanging, and such Old World pagan customs reinter-
preted by Christians and introduced into many parts of the world
with Christianity as that of hanging up, on the Saturday before
Easter Sunday, effigies of Judas to be attacked, torn, and later
burned in a bonfire made with sacred and purifying new fire that
symbolized the conquest of evil by good. What happened to the
Tuapa effigy of Limaua is unreported; the Aliutu effigy was taken
to the Bishop Museum, Honolulu, which later destroyed it by
unknown means.

Information about the effigy's appearance is reconstructed
from Loeb's relevant published comments and photograph,[30] two
unpublished photographs he took on Niue to show the ritual,[31]
and a few words in the Museum catalogue and card file which
describe No. B7753 as the figure of 'a god, Limaua . . . made for
Dr Loeb after ancient model', and presented by him in April
1924, to the Museum which in May 1937, 'discarded' it but kept
'4 Ovula shells . . . (turned over to Malcology)'. The catalogue
adds: 'Arms and legs separate; cap of tapa. Human hair and beard;
glass eyes; head and trunk 49".' The word 'monstrosity' written
across the filing card suggests why the image was discarded. The
unidentified writer, seeing perhaps no connection between the
effigy and other Polynesian images, regarded it as of no ethnographical value, whereas the Ovula shells, being pure Polynesian
and uncontaminated by foreign acculturation, were worth saving.

The image presents Limaua 'as an ancient *toa* with the customary flowing beard, decorations of white shells, and *ti* girdle'.[32]
Its construction was hedged with restrictions, for Aliutu craftsmen
allowed no one near when they were 'hewing the model', presumably of wood like that used in 1891. The large long head,

disproportionate to the slender torso, apparently cut from the same piece of wood, had a large nose and closely set eyes carved out and fitted with glass. The face had sideburns, a moustache, and a long beard of very wavy, even curly hair which falling on the chest obscured the neck. Aboriginal warriors when enraged customarily chewed the end of their beards, an act supposed to terrify the enemy, but bound up their long head hair under a cap to prevent the enemy grabbing it. Limaua's image had a pointed tapa cap, *matatua,* one of the types worn by warriors, over his hair which is not visible in photographs but which like his beard, according to Museum records, was of human hair.

The effigy's thick kilt, *titi,* of *ti* leaves (*Dracaena terminalis*), resembled a warrior's. No belt appears in the published photograph, but a photograph at the ritual shows over the effigy's kilt waistband an Ovula-decorated girdle, *fatu-a-kafa,* such as a warrior wore to hold stones for throwing in battle. On the chest hung an open-string necklace with an Ovula shell at each end. The chest, recalling Easter Island wooden images, was apparently very deeply carved. Each arm above the elbow had a string around it with a dangling Ovula shell. The long, skinny, modelled arms, of separately attached wood, were bent at the elbows to form an angle with the body. Hands, somewhat cupped, apparently were carved to show some fingers. The legs, presumably also of wood and separately attached like the arms to the torso, end in feet equipped with what looks like shingle nails inserted to simulate toe nails.

The torso and its apparently inflexible head were slightly over 125 cm long. The added legs would have made the entire effigy at least life-size. As a matter of fact, enlarged photographs of the effigy, suspended and extended at the ceremony, suggest that it was longer than the men raising it.

Whether its legs and arms—the effigy's flexible parts—could be manipulated, and if so, were indeed moved, is uncertain. The effigy as a whole, however, was definitely made to move on its suspension line hung from one tree in 1891 and between two trees in 1924.[33] In 1891 it was pulled about 'on the top of the line', perhaps to dishonour it further as was customary with a slain enemy's body.

A rope is clearly visible in Bishop Museum photograph No. 10096; the main line of horizontal suspension passes behind the vertical image from one coconut tree to the other. It is not possible to determine whether this rope was hitched around the image's neck or, more likely, passed through a perforated knob or a large screw-eye just below the neck. To make the image move 'violently up and down' on the horizontal rope would require the rope to pass through a hole or to be looped around the neck. The rope would then have to be slackened, lifted slightly, swayed, and tightened to get up-and-down bouncing in addition to back-and-forth movement. Judging from Bishop Museum photograph No. 10103, possibly a second, controlling line, or one for each arm, produced up-and-down movement.

In 1891 the effigy carried to the plaza was wrapped in tapa, in 1924, in cloth. Evidently temporary wrapping or veiling was essential. Besides obviously providing drama as it fell away before the crowd when the figure was hung up and the god exposed to view, the covering also protected the sacred object from the profane world as it was carried in procession on men's shoulders from the place of construction to the place of sacrifice.

Images, whether of wood or stone, for secular or sacred use, were uncommon in Niue, as in most of western Polynesia. Except for Limaua's effigy the only Niuean images reported are the *fakatino* of a man used to destroy the enemy, as already mentioned; a stone image of Huanaki, a god some Niueans claimed discovered their island; and an undescribed image of an unnamed god with man-like legs which Niueans broke up during an epidemic attributed to it.[34] As *fakatino* means literally 'made-body' (*faka*, causative; *tino,* body), Limaua's effigy is a *fakatino.*[35]

No evidence exists that Niue ever had a puppet theatre or any drama combining human and puppet actors other than in the Limaua ceremony. As in other Polynesian islands, foreign contact stimulated a latent interest in drama. Loeb remarked, 'In the last few years the Niueans have imported the foreign trait of theater going; but their native plays, called *kifaga,* resemble mildly those of the London music hall'.[36] That Limaua's figure as constructed and operated in 1924 may have been slightly more than a large 'puppet image' or 'movable image'[37] and approximated a marionette may be inferred from the possible use of a control line or lines to manipulate the figure on its horizontal suspension rope.

Limaua, masquerading in effigy as a warrior, appeared in the ocean as 'a kind of merman, with streaming hair, and a fish's tail'.[38] He was probably only a minor local deity, presumably too unimportant for Loeb to list with numerous gods who were localized and less important than Tagaloa whose worship was general.[39] Tagaloa, a sky god with seeming dominion in all departments including war, land, and sea, became identified with Jehovah in the modern era. He therefore remained important whereas other gods, while still believed in, were labelled 'the works of Satan' and demons, and lost most of the former respect paid them such as prayers of supplication and offerings of fish or flower wreaths.[40]

Limaua resided at Houma in Aliutu, or more likely at a dangerous reef near by. Anyone frightened by seeing him or of passing a dangerous reef where he might be, threw him wreaths of flowers or fish. His dominion, it seems, extended beyond Alofi Bay. To make him kindhearted and let them pass, fishing fleets wishing to go to Oneiki, Avatele Bay, and elsewhere gave him a kind of toll offering of taro, coconuts, and papaya on their departure and strings of fish on their return. He was 'an angry god', whose habit was 'to be angry all day long' and thus rule 'mightily upon the sea'.[41] In being angry, that is, high-spirited, quick-tempered, and ever spoiling for a fight he behaved like a warrior.

To those making offerings Limaua provided a large, safe haul of fish. To others who ignored him and his warning shouts of 'Beware'! he let down his long hair, angrily shaking his head to create currents and whirlpools, and paddled, first with one hand and then with the other, to reverse the currents and damage the canoe. Great currents are still attributed to him. He was perhaps the same god as Water-spouting Mouth (Gutu-puhi-peau) who manipulated currents to make them swift around a point at Aliutu.[42]

Warrior-like, Limaua boasted of his power. He told a fellow sea-god, Blowhole, at Aliutu how he would help him trap a thief who had stolen some of that god's fish which it was his duty to feed:

> If the man comes, I will be able to stretch out my hands to the horizon, and to the beach. If he is in their midst, I will move my head from side to side (in order to create a current). If he comes beneath the water, I will paddle with my hands, so that he will be drifted to the horizon. If he comes along the beach I will paddle with my hands so that great waves will roll up to the shore. But if he comes in the midst of the sea, then I will shake up and down with my head, and allow him to sink below and die.[43]

Such is the sea god that Niue ritually killed and mourned. Aliutu and Tuapa villages may have intended either the departing person or his surrogates to bear the onus of the death while they could claim, should he return, that they had vainly defended him and had lamented his death.

It is unknown why Niueans singled out Limaua, such a minor ocean god, for a 'killing the god' ceremony. My conjecture is that he was a special god to a family who to control his exuberance or to punish him instituted the ceremony that subsequently became arbitrarily attached to a farewell ritual. The whole was adopted by other families. If Limaua's custom of creating whirlpools and currents had led to death or damage to the worshipping family's fishermen, a 'betrayal' of them, the family may have sought revenge by casting him off, as Polynesians did with unsatisfactory gods, or 'killing' him. The uncommon Niuean use of images suggests to me that the European custom of hanging Judas in effigy and attacking it may have inspired the most dramatic element of the 'killing' in the 1891 and 1924 performances.

Re-enactment of Limaua's rebirth was not part of the 1891 and 1924 ceremonies. Belief in his return, however, is evident in experiences of Niueans claiming to have seen the god in the ocean and their belief, or hope, widespread in Polynesia, and other parts of the world, of the dead being reborn like the moon. This older belief appears in a Niuean prayer to the Christian Jehovah to whom missionaries assigned the alternate name of Tagaloa. Part of the prayer is

> Blessings, Oh God of the Rainbow, die,
> But die to come to life again:
> Do not die the death of the rat,
> But die like the moon,
> For the moon dies and comes to life again.[44]

Niueans did not, it seems, conceptualize Limaua's eternal return after each death with the relative clarity of Hawaiian belief in the return of the god Lono (Orono), with whom Captain Cook was identified. Beckwith wrote: 'The matter-of-fact way in which the [Hawaiian] multitude regarded the death of a god has curious confirmation in [Captain James] King's statement that after Cook's death the people inquired anxiously of King when "the Orono" would come again.'[45]

Limaua, although ritually slain three times at least, continued to be seen and to affect people's lives on the ocean. Two men, one of them Loeb's principal informant, had together seen the god. The informant had bravely struck the floating god's face with his paddle and forced him below the waves. This man continued in the future to fish in the open sea but his companion never dared to go again. Something in the 1891 ceremony, Niueans claim, so enraged Limaua that 'for three days and three nights he floated on the top of the waters, with his hair floating on the waves'.[46]

That a god could be killed was a common enough idea in Polynesia. Limaua was not the only Niuean god whom people tried to slay or humble. Not all, however, are thought of as being reborn. How established the god-killing practice was may be judged from the resistance by certain Niuean shamans to Christianity after the mid-nineteenth century when Paulo, a Samoan missionary, resided on Niue.

More than one version tells of Mulia, chief shaman of Niue, battling the Christian Trinity.[47] Mulia, 'constantly angry', one account states, desecrated the church by holding a feast there, doing a war dance in the aisles, beating the native drum, performing death magic, and cursing that 'Jesus shall die'. With another very important shaman, says another account, Mulia, one Sabbath, did the war dance, beat the drum while Paulo tolled the church bell, and repeatedly threw spears and stones into the air 'in order to wound the God in the skies, and thus kill him'. Then the two shamans defiantly feasted, cooking being forbidden on the Sabbath. On the journey home the other shaman died; soon after Mulia died, and people said, 'It was the true God who killed them . . . '. Another version has Mulia converted like the Apostle Paul and talking endlessly about the crucifixion of Jesus whom he wished to emulate. But, previously, he had 'knocked down the image' (perhaps a cross) set before him by two converted warriors and had otherwise defied them and the Holy Ghost. Subsequently, angry at the lightning of sky gods, he did the war dance and threw spears upward to kill them. But the lightning intensified; 'the word of God came down in forked flashes' and first blinded, then knocked down Mulia. When he recovered he became a very devout Christian. Thus old and new customs and beliefs united with regard to 'killing the gods'.

Although Niueans do not explain their repeated slaying of Limaua and his reappearance, they had, in the eighteenth century, institutionalized the reason, but not the method, for killing the island king, *patuiki*. The reason was his failure to maintain island well-being, linked to the most sacred object, a rainmaking fetish, the abode of Tagaloa, kept in a sacred house at Fatuana, and constantly warmed by a fire beneath it. Made from the core of the sacred *kafika* tree (unidentified), the *tokamotu*, or fetish, was shaped like the end of a dart or a sharply pointed wooden knob, and covered with tapa secured with dried banana skin. Even chiefs could not, without permission, enter its sacred shelter; unauthorized entry, people believed, produced blindness. Loeb considered as apt S. Percy Smith's comparison of the national fetish to the Ark of the Covenant of the Children of Israel.[48]

The king protected the sacred, rainmaking fetish, 'the core of the island', from getting rough, damp, or covered with spider webs believed to prevent rain. The chief *alaga-vaka-ne-mua*, 'a kind of Prime Minister', questioned him about the state of the treasure to report to the warriors, the real rulers. They, with chiefs, selected a king, often a nonentity willing to risk the position. Warriors manipulated political matters through warfare and other means to put a certain figurehead into this religious office, a kind of high priesthood. Frequently the office went begging.

To Niue, an upraised coral island subject to severe droughts, neglect of the fetish meant famine; to the king, death at the hands of the people. Although four or five kings who died naturally presumably had controlled nature through good care of the fetish, others died violently, and one or two at least through no failure of duty. Fokimata, one such king, was slain, hit in the head by a rock, by warriors during intergroup strife. When selected as king he had first refused because his predecessor and cousin, peace-loving and successful Galiaga, had been assassinated. His hesitation dispelled by appeals to pride and patriotism, Fokimata came to enjoy kingship, for in his death lament he cried:

> I wish that a foreign ship would come,
> That I could give up my kingship.
> I like to be a king,
> But no one else likes me to be king.[49]

The desirability of kingship had declined after Galiaga had been killed by a man who hoped thereby to cause a famine to starve enough people to include a thief who had stolen *talo* from his field. Niueans, instead of punishing the assassin, killed the thief's entire family. Sadly they recalled Galiaga's chant when he was anointed king, perhaps during the last quarter of the eighteenth century. The refrain was:

> The king establishes peace.
> Let there be peace and joy on the island,
> Let there be peace and joy on the island.[50]

In 1845 when the Reverend George Turner visited Niue the position of king was vacant. It had been vacant since Fokimata's successor, king for a year, had been killed because of a famine in which he too had nearly starved to death. The famine, some said, really resulted from Fokimata's assassination and the illegitimate means used to appoint his successor. Turner wrote: 'Of old they had kings, but as they were the high-priests as well, and were supposed to cause the food to grow, the people got angry with them in times of scarcity, and killed them; and as one after another was killed, the end of it was that no one wished to be king.'[51] In 1876, under European missionary control, warfare was abolished and a new order of kings, also with religious functions, was established without the sword of Damocles overhead. The third and last king, anointed in 1898, died in 1917.

When asked why kings were formerly killed, a Niuean replied, 'Why do the people of your country kill your *patuiki* when things are bad?'[52] Niue did not kill chiefs for failure of mana, for they had none. A whole village supported its chief, whereas only his kinsmen supplied the king with his necessities. One king, by abducting his brother's wife, lost his means of support, for his relatives turned against him. Abandoning the sacred fetish, he hid with his wives and children. A famine followed but when the runaway king sent two sons to steal the fetish for him to care for properly, rain fell and Niue prospered. Later the abducted woman gave a feast at which she claimed credit for stealing and saving the fetish.[53]

Other Polynesians with sacred leaders gifted with mana to control nature did not kill them during natural disasters. Easter Island's sacred king, for example, held office from one tern-egg season to the next when he retired in honour to be replaced by another 'bird-man'. Niueans, according to Loeb, added the custom of killing the king when nature failed, a trait absent from the rest of Polynesia and Melanesia.[54]

This 'king complex', combining Tongan and Niuean features, emerged around A.D. 1700 when a Tongan chief named Mutalau (the Niue village where he settled was named for him) went to Niue, his mother's childhood home, with his followers. He conquered it, and created a kingship patterned after the Tongan Tu'i Tonga with himself as the first sacred king. It is unknown when and by whom sacred power became fixed in the fetish as a national treasure to be guarded by the priest-king with his life. Loeb wondered if an obscure chant attributed to Fokimata indicated 'that Mutalau brought over the *tokamotu* in token of the subjection of Niue to Tonga'.[55] More likely, the custom of protecting a family sacred fetish was expanded to the national level. If it was the Tongan who tied rainmaking power to the position he failed to anticipate the possibility of regicide or mistakenly assumed Niuean ecological conditions were as favourable as Tongan. Probably, it was Niueans, strongly democratic, who added belief in the king's power to control weather through the fetish and the custom of regicide for failure, as two checks to prevent an autocracy.

The Tongan innovator was killed by two youths avenging their father's death, thereby, people claimed, establishing on Niue the custom of blood revenge. Apparently Mutalau, although a great warrior, left the office politically too weak to protect his successors. A king, even with a representative in each village, had, it seems, no assured military support. Fokimata, caught in war between north and south, begged for, and received, military protection; then war broke out between east and west, and because he lived in the west, an eastern warrior killed him. Had the position been hereditary, families with an economic and social stake in it would have reinforced it. It was literally a dead-end job for most of the kings. Within a century Mutalau's innovation had died, to be reborn temporarily in modified form under Western influence.

Sir James Frazer ignored local political and historical events operating in each of his examples, including the Niuean, of the custom of a more vigorous successor, or his representatives, killing a weakened king to maintain the sacred spirit, abode of people's well-being, especially as influenced by rain. Kingship to Frazer had evolved from the position of public magician which in turn had evolved from that of rainmaking magician. History on Niue short-circuited this hypothetical, evolutionary sequence. Diffusion from Tonga and local adaptations gave the Niuean sacred kingship its characteristics. Within a century it had ended because the island, already divided by warring factions, had merely acquired a new cause for war, for after a king's natural death, execution, or assassination a new social equilibrium was rarely achieved.

It is not known whether any king was hung and then speared in effigy or reality and whether Limaua was ever slain except through the sympathetic magic of an effigy. No pattern of method appears in the scanty traditions about the deaths of Niuean kings by assassination or authorized execution. Both god and kings, however, were fated for violent death at the hands of the people if they failed in their duties. Their failure was a betrayal, and traitors were punished by a rite of separation, death. The individual king, not being divine, died, but the kingship continued; the god died but eventually reappeared. Each had competitors and fault-finding enemies. The king, although no examples are recorded, competed with shamans who, possessed by gods (the king did not go into trances), claimed among their many skills the ability to bring rain or drought. Niue, while localizing this power outside the king in the *tokamotu*, clearly blamed the king for droughts and not the sacred mechanism—or shamans. Limaua might be denied his offerings by defiant fishermen or hit in the face with their paddles, and form intrigues and pacts with equally minor gods like himself for mutual protection of interests. The king's ritual duties related basically to the land, to the growth of crops, and the rain that made them grow. Limaua's duties related to the sea and the protection of its resources through his manipulation of currents. Such sanctity as the king had came not from birth but from his association with the most sacred of fetishes, the occasional residence of Tagaloa, highest god of land, sea, and sky. Limaua, sacred by birth, gave the mana of a god, albeit a minor one, to his domain.

Loeb remarked, it will be recalled, that the 1924 ceremony was a primitive drama.[56] My discussion thus far has been to demonstrate how much more it was than drama alone; that it was additionally a rite of passage incorporating a complex amalgamation of customs and symbolisms of varied origin, as well as concepts also expressed in orally transmitted traditions of political events and sacred narratives and chants.

Now, however, my focus will be on the more characteristically theatrical aspects of the ceremony as folk drama. It is not possible to attempt any conjecture about the influence, if any, the undescribed nature of the imported 'foreign trait of theater going'[57] had on the 1924 performance to make it different from that in

1891. That Niue had no 'theater going' before this foreign importation is hard to believe because so many Polynesian islands at the time of first Western contact already had elaborate variety shows with singing, dancing, dramatic skits and exhibitions of skill and learning. While islands differed in their degree of professionalism, the strength of the Polynesian bent for theatre is evident also in their ready adoption of foreign props and even plots which they learned about during the increased travel after Western contact.

Characteristics of Niue folk drama or theatre, either explicit or implicit in Loeb's description and photographs of the 1924 event, include the clear separation of the event from ordinary, daily life. This was marked by preliminary mood-creating feasting and dancing; a fixed succession of incidents forming a plot known to all, with a beginning, middle, and end (three-act tragedy); a cast of performers from the local community playing roles in the plot (all male, amateur actors, role-rehearsed); even a stand-in actor (for the puppet); a stage area with actors' positions blocked out for them; a section near by representing off-stage; stage properties (puppet image, ropes for its suspension, two living coconut trees, weapons or simulated weapons); costuming (puppet image and most living actors dressed as traditional warriors); stage hands; an audience (men, women, children), many of them seated, separated from the stage and the actors, and not participating in the action except perhaps at the finale; and a stage director or master of ceremonies. Formal dialogue seemingly was absent; chants, war dances, and pantomime carried the plot forward; no reference occurs to musical accompaniment.

The drama took place in daylight hours. The stage was an outdoor area, of open land except for a background of trees. The stage, or rather its central section, was defined by the two coconut trees between which the effigy was to be suspended. The area behind this section was also part of the stage. The front of the stage area extended forward from the two trees for at least ninety metres or more. No curtains separated stage from audience; the off-stage area serving as wings was probably partly shielded from audience view by the trees. Here two groups waited for their cue to go on stage.

The first act opened when four men entered bearing on their shoulders the heavily wrapped effigy of the god Limaua. I have called them stage hands, for photographs show them wearing white singlets, long pants, and caps or hats; one, however, may have added a warrior's grass kilt around his waist. They might be interpreted as actors playing the roles of bearers and servitors of the mysteriously wrapped god which they held dramatically and conspicuously for all to see. Their next action in elevating the effigy on a rope between the trees was doubtless not intended to be a major feature because as they entered they were immediately followed by a band of warriors who commanded audience attention by their traditional kilts, weapons which they brandished, chants, and war dances. They were the defenders of the god Limaua, who, after his elevation, was manipulated so that his wrappings fell away to expose him to view. The audience now hushed in respect and anticipation. The band of warriors withdrew to their defensive position behind the elevated effigy, whose manipulators now were putting him through lively gyrations to signal that he was a living, defiant god. This, I believe, marked the end of Act I.

Act II began with the entry on stage of the god's attacker, who, unlike the other performers, apparently was relatively unrehearsed and certainly unprepared for an assault from the god's band of warriors. It is not stated whether he entered from the wings or from the audience. Someone who must have served as director handed him his weapon. From a distance of about ninety metres (thus the front boundary of the stage is learned) he was to pierce the actively moving effigy of Limaua. Suspense was great for audience and performers. Just as he was about to hurl his weapon, the defenders of the god rushed forward from behind the effigy at the attacker. They surprised and distracted him so that he missed his aim. He interpreted the audience's response as disappointment. Unstated means having been used to ensure success on his next throw, he struck his spear into the effigy's face. He interpreted the audience's reaction as one of joy. Emphasizing his successful blow, the manipulators let the effigy droop like a slain god. Thus the second act ended.

Perhaps to save time and prevent loss of mood the slain god was not removed from his elevated position. Instead his human stand-in lay down on the stage. Those who wailed in mourning over him chanted the famous dirge for a fallen warrior. Presumably the mourners were his band of unsuccessful defenders. Thus, the third and last act of the tragedy came to an end.

In 1924 the event had, one judges, a greater theatrical clarity and structure than that of 1891, thirty-three years earlier, when the attacker had surrogates acting for him and they repeatedly missed their aim to the point of what may have been weariness and anxiety for all concerned instead of pleasurable suspense. Also in 1891 the effigy was elevated by a rope from a single tree so that if anyone was manipulating it the effect was less visible and dramatic than in 1924. That the ritual significance of the event was still felt too deeply for it to have become even partly play, as in 1924, is evidenced by beliefs that the subsequently resurrected Limaua was angry with the people. During the intervening years old customs and beliefs had weakened enough for the people of Niue to develop a theatrical selectivity and perspective toward the ceremony and to make of it a folk drama, rich in symbolism.

We have come a long way from Nemi, as Frazer might say, and from the farewell ceremony held in Niue in 1924 with its 'puppet image', perhaps actually a marionette, of the god Limaua. The 'monstrosity' has been shown to have reflected many interrelated phases of Niuean culture. Old and new, native and borrowed, Christian and pagan beliefs, myths and customs have combined not just in the figure's construction but in the magic and religion associated with the 1924 and 1891 farewell ceremonies. Violence has been revealed as part of the customs associated with rites of passage, whether in kings being actually killed to end drought and famine, gods symbolically killed to end epidemics and dangers at sea, traitors literally or symbolically killed to end their disloyalty, or bonds of loyalty and affection between friends symbolically killed so that they might go their separate ways relieved of mutual allegiance, privilege, and obligation. By 1924 the event of the farewell rite of passage had been transformed into a theatrical production in which the plot recapitulated, in highly concentrated and intricately symbolic form, many experiences, mythological motifs and customs of past Niue culture, and was directed toward the resolution by artistic means of conflict brought about by a member of the community leaving it. The older ritual quality was retained by having that individual play a leading role in the drama. The most strikingly obvious change in the Niuean ritualized slaying complex is that a wooden puppet-marionette came to be substituted in post-European times for a living human being.

NOTES AND REFERENCES

[1] Research on Polynesian puppets and marionettes was begun when I was Visiting Senior Research Associate at the Smithsonian Institution, Washington, D.C., on a National Science Foundation grant in 1966-67. I regret that my study of Niue was done after the death of my friend and former professor, Dr Loeb, so that I could not discuss it with him. I am grateful to the Social Science Research Institute, University of Hawaii, for typing assistance. This essay has been adapted from my paper 'Return to Nemi via Niue, Polynesia: Drama, Puppet Images, Myths, and Customs in Symbolic Slaying', read in August 1973, at Indiana University, Bloomington, Indiana, at the folk-lore conference connected with the Chicago meetings of the International Congress of Anthropological and Ethnological Sciences.
[2] Frazer 1920:I, 8-9, 354-5; III, 17.
[3] van Gennep 1960.
[4] Loeb 1926:125.
[5] *ibid.*:126; Pl. 1, map of Niue; 14-22, list of place names.
[6] *ibid.*:127.
[7] *idem.*
[8] *ibid.*: 126.

9 *ibid.*:127.
10 *ibid.*:149.
11 *ibid.*:115-16.
12 Turner 1861:524.
13 Loeb 1926:32-3.
14 Turner 1861:471.
15 Loeb 1926:33.
16 Thomson 1902:75-6.
17 Turner 1861:466, 524; 1884:305-6.
18 Turner 1861:523.
19 Thomson 1902:90.
20 Loeb 1926:29-30.
21 Frazer 1920:III, 102ff., 111ff.
22 Turner 1861:466.
23 Loeb 1926:89.
24 *ibid.*:221-3.
25 *ibid.*:175.
26 *ibid.*:139-41.
27 *idem.*
28 *ibid.*:141, 165.
29 *ibid.*:38.
30 *ibid.*:125-7, 93-4, 58, Pl. XIIIc.
31 Bishop Museum negatives Nos 10103 and 10096.
32 Loeb 1926:125.
33 *ibid.*:126, 127.
34 *ibid.*:141, 165.
35 The moon, *mahiva,* is poetically a *fakatino,* idol; *ibid.*:222.
36 *ibid.*:46.
37 Speaight 1955:32-5.
38 Loeb 1926:125.
39 *ibid.*:160-2.
40 *ibid.*:159.
41 *ibid.*:206.
42 *ibid.*:204.
43 *ibid.*:209.
44 *ibid.*:38.
45 Beckwith 1951:24.
46 Loeb 1926:126.
47 *ibid.*:36-7.
48 *ibid.*:167-8.
49 *ibid.*:54.
50 *ibid.*:52-3.
51 Turner 1861:469; 1884:304-5; Frazer 1920:I, 354-5.
52 Loeb 1926:55.
53 *ibid.*:168.
54 *ibid.*:55.
55 *ibid.*:53, fn. 10.
56 *ibid.*:127; and above.
57 *ibid.*:46; and above.

'A happening frightening to both ghosts and men': a case study from Western Samoa

DEREK FREEMAN*

Samoa, as Robert Louis Stevenson once remarked, is a land of 'elaborate courtliness', where chiefs live out their days 'surfeited with lip-honour'.¹ Chieftainship, the Samoans themselves aver, was founded by God (*'o le matai, 'ua fa'avae i le Atua*), and they liken a chief to a banyan tree towering above the surrounding forest. A chief, they say, is one of the elect, and those over whom he has authority are required to show him every respect. Indeed the relationship (*vā*) between a chief and an untitled individual is claimed to be sacrosanct, or *sā*. For Samoans, then, any altercation between an untitled man (*taule'ale'a*) and a chief (*matai*) is untoward and ominous, and actual fighting 'frightening to both ghosts and men'.² It is with just such a happening—a fight between a *taule'ale'a* and a *matai,* and the way in which this 'outrage' was dealt with by the *fono,* or council of chiefs, that I am here concerned. These events (which I witnessed in 1966) are both absorbing in themselves and bear on fundamental aspects of Samoan life and culture.

In 1966 two untitled men of Sa'anapu,³ a village of 940 souls on the south coast of the island of Upolu in Western Samoa, were cultivating immediately adjacent tracts of land, clearing the virgin forest and planting taro in the fertile volcanic soil. They were from different *'āiga,* or extended families, and had long been rivals. To the west lay the plantation of Meatai (aged thirty-two years), and to the east that of Sene (aged thirty-five years). The boundary (*tuā'oi*) between them extended southward from an inland road towards the sea.

* I first met Harry Maude in Fiji in July 1946 when I was returning to Samoa, after a stint in the R.N.Z.N.V.R., to continue my researches in Sa'anapu. We met again in London in October 1947. At that time I was working in the archives of the London Missionary Society at Livingstone House, and Harry and Honor Maude, as my pocket diary reminds me, were staying in South Kensington. We talked at length about the Peruvian labour raids, into which I was delving at the Public Records Office, and the history of the Ellice Islands. Some years later we found ourselves colleagues at the A.N.U. Knowing that Harry has long had an interest in indigenous modes of dispute settlement in the Western Pacific, I offer this depiction of a Samoan *fono mānu*—seen very much from the viewpoint of an insider.

163

M

Early in April 1966 the boundary reached a huge banyan tree, the roots of which straddled parts of the two plantations. Sene was the first to continue felling to the south of this tree. He did this without consulting Meatai who was soon complaining that Sene had veered too far to the west. In such a situation the proper course is to appeal to the *fono* of chiefs for a ruling. Instead, with the knowledge of his *matai*, a fifty-three-year-old talking chief named Volē Toilei'u, Meatai cut across the line of Sene's advance with his bush knife intruding three or four paces into territory that Sene claimed was his.

In Samoa disputes over territory arouse intense feeling; indeed it is said that the invasion of any part of a man's land is experienced as though it were an attack upon his person. 'It is just as though the trespasser had come', one man told me, 'and struck me in the belly' *(tusa 'ua sau tu'i lo'u manava)*. Certainly when Sene discovered Meatai's intrusion he was infuriated, and early on the morning of Wednesday 13 April 1966 he made his way down to the village to air his grievances. He was standing on family land at the edge of the *malae*, or ceremonial ground of Sa'anapu, when to his surprise Volē Toilei'u came walking by.

Sene at once accosted him: 'Volē, as you're the chief, let's go and mark that boundary'.

'Alright, let's go, and if need be we'll fight!', Volē replied in bantering tones.

Irritated, Sene retorted: 'What's that? And you a chief? Are you mad?'

'Mad am I?' exclaimed Volē, 'As I've told you, if it comes to it, we'll fight.'

This further incitement was too much for Sene, and turning on Volē he shouted: 'Is it trouble you're wanting?' (words which, to a Samoan, are a challenge to fight).

Infuriated at being so affronted by a mere *taule'ale'a*, Volē lost control, and lunging forward lashed out at Sene with clenched fists. Both men were by this time incensed and were soon fighting violently. Sene, who was the younger of the two, quickly gained the upper hand and with a heavy blow to his mouth sent Volē sprawling on to the sand of the *malae*.

In Samoa serious fighting between individuals of rival families is much feared, for there is a danger of the conflict spreading until the whole community is ranged in warring factions. Intervention is thus common, and particularly by the women of the families involved. The first woman to arrive on the scene, just as Volē was regaining his feet, was Afega, the twenty-eight-year-old daughter of Sene's eldest sister. She at once sought to interpose herself between the two men.

Afega was soon joined by Poto, the forty-four-year-old sister of

Sene. Dismayed at Sene's rashness Poto laid her hands on his shoulders and, shouting at him to desist, pushed him back towards the territory of the Lea'anā family to which they both belonged. Volē, smarting at the indignity of having been knocked down by Sene, struggled wildly to retaliate, but was impeded by Afega who clung tightly with both hands to his right arm.

At this juncture a *matai* arrived on the scene. He was Volē Na'oia, a fifty-eight-year-old talking chief and related to Volē Toilei'u. As is usual when chiefs intervene in a fight, he was carrying a stout stick. This stick Volē Na'oia used to belabour Sene who was obviously guilty of fighting with a *matai,* and to make it worse, on the ceremonial ground of the village. Intimidated by Volē Na'oia, Sene began to withdraw, while his sister, Poto, continued to push him away from the scene of the fight. Soon after this a senior titular chief, Mati Lua'itaua, sixty-three years of age, laid hold of Volē Toilei'u, and firmly led him away to a near-by house. Determined intervention by two women and two *matai* had brought to an end the clash of Sene the *taule'ale'a,* with Volē Toilei'u, the *tulāfale.*

That it was a serious fight there can be no doubt, for when I saw Volē a few minutes after the struggle was over, he was breathing heavily and trembling with rage as he fingered his split and bleeding lower lip. He was highly indignant at having been struck by an untitled individual.

Sene, for his part, was in a turmoil, elated at having knocked down Volē, but perturbed at the enormity of his actions. I found him back on his own territory, in an agitated state, quite oblivious of a deeply incised wound between the knuckles of the middle and index fingers of his right hand. As he examined this wound, to which I drew his attention, he began to realize how hard he had hit Volē, and was soon expressing fears about the way he would be dealt with by the *fono* and about the possibility that others of the family of Volē Toilei'u might attack him under the cover of darkness. Yet for all his fears Sene remained defiant. What he had done he had done with cause, he said, and he was prepared for whatever the consequences might be. 'If I have to die', he told me, 'then I'll die' (*Tusa pei a oti, oti ai*).

Word of the fight between Volē Toilei'u and Sene soon spread through the village. There was immediate concern by the chiefs. In September 1920, as some of them still recollected, an altercation over land between an untitled man and a chief had ended in tragedy. A *taule'ale'a* named Suluvale, in a fit of ungovernable passion, had murdered the high chief 'Anapu Soa'ai, and then been struck down and killed by several of the *matai* of Sa'anapu.[4]

It was quickly made known that a special *fono mānu*[5] or juridical council to consider the actions of Sene and Volē Toilei'u would be held early the following morning. To deal with more pressing problems two chiefly deputations were formed: one to ensure that no further attack was made on Sene, and the other to inspect the contested boundary. Both of these deputations I was able to accompany.

We found Sene hiding in the bush, his right hand heavily bandaged, fearful of the coming night. His version of where the proper boundary lay, as well as that of Meatai, was listened to, and the disputed ground inspected in detail. Meatai and others of the Volē family were then cautioned most solemnly against attacking Sene, or otherwise taking the law into their own hands.

At this point let me digress briefly to describe the relationship between the *fono* of *matai*, of which Volē Toilei'u was a member, and the *'aumāga* to which Sene belonged. A Samoan *nu'u*, or village, is composed of a series of related *'āiga*, or localized extended families. Traditionally, the members of each *'āiga* lived together in a cluster of houses under the direct authority of their *matai*. After being selected for office by the members of his *'āiga*, a *matai* must have his appointment ratified by the *fono* at a *saofa'iga*, or installation ceremony. This done he is entitled to sit as a member of the *fono*, his position within this body being determined by the rank of his title. In 1966 the average age of a *matai* in Sa'anapu was fifty-three years, with eighty-three per cent of the *fono* of forty-seven members being forty-one years of age or over.

A Samoan *matai* may be either an *ali'i* or a *tulāfale*. *Ali'i* is the designation given to chiefs whose rank is of an exalted kind, the term most commonly used to describe their rank being *pa'ia* or sacred. In ancient Samoa certain of them were believed to be related to the gods. All *ali'i*, or titular chiefs, as I shall call them, possess special rights, as, for example, the right to be addressed in honorific language, the right to a house-site, or *maota*, with a ceremonial name, the right to a kava cup title; and *ali'i* of the highest rank enjoy the right to wear a *tuiga*, a head-dress of bleached human hair, symbolic of the sun, and to have performed elaborate funeral rites, known as *lagi*.

In contradistinction to *ali'i* are the *tulāfale*. It is their responsibility to safeguard (*puipui*) and enhance (*fa'aopoopo*) the sacredness of *ali'i* by performing a wide range of duties, some of them onerous, which are judged to be beneath the dignity of a titular chief. In particular, *tulāfale* are responsible for the sharing out of food and property, and for the making of set orations. In the literature on Samoa they are commonly referred to as talking chiefs.

All of the mature males of a village community who are not *matai* are expected to belong to the *'aumāga*. In Sa'anapu in 1966 there were seventy-five members of the *'aumāga*, their average age being thirty-two years, and eighty-one per cent of them being under forty years of age. Thus, although there are some older men in the *'aumāga,* the average difference in age between members of the *fono* and the *'aumāga* is about twenty-one years. Traditionally, a young man joined the *'aumāga* after he had been tattooed, and he remained a member of it until he became a *matai,* or could no longer work. Under their leader, who is appointed by the *matai,* the members of the *'aumāga* perform all manner of tasks, much of the work they do being at the direct behest of the chiefs; it is usual, for example, for them to provide food for the *fono* when it meets. Most *matai* have themselves been members of the *'aumāga* for twenty years or more, and it is often said that a man's strongest claim to a title is the service *(tautua)* that he has given while in the *'aumāga.* There is thus a sense in which the *'aumāga* provides a training ground for those who aspire to chieftainship. At the same time, however, there is a marked distinction between those who hold titles and those who do not, and the *fono* of *matai* is ever on the alert to ensure that members of the *'aumāga* are diligent and respectful in carrying out their duties. In its full social context then a fight between a *matai* and a member of the *'aumāga* is a flagrant event, directly subversive of the values of the traditional order.

The especially summoned *fono mānu* met early on the morning of Thursday 14 April 1966 in the principal *fale tele,* or round house, of the family of Volē Toilei'u. It was attended by virtually all of the chiefs who happened to be in residence. Soon after 8.30 they were sitting cross-legged in their appointed places, the more important *tulāfale* at the front *(itū)* of the house, the *ali'i* against the posts of its curved sections *(tala)* on either side; while at the back were assembled the lesser *tulāfale* whose task it was to perform the kava *('ava)* ceremony with which the *fono* would begin.

As the kava was being prepared the first set oration of the morning, in which the significance of the *fono mānu* was announced, was made by Lauvī Vela, a senior *tulāfale.* Lauvī, a staid and earnest man, began by reciting the honorific titles *(fa'alupega)* of all Samoa, and then of Sa'anapu, a clear indication of the high importance of the occasion. All of the *matai* of the community were aghast at the incident which had occurred the previous day, said Lauvī, and they were gathered together to seek concord so that the life of the community might continue.

As Lauvī's peroration reached its climax the initial kava ceremony of the morning began, the first cup going to Mulitalo Iuma, the senior titular chief *(ali'i)* present. As he lifted the corner of the mat on which he was sitting and poured a libation on to the pebbles beneath, Mulitalo prayed that peace would indeed be regained. The other senior *matai* present were then served in rank order.[6] Volē Toilei'u, who was sitting at the rear of the house, was wholly omitted from the ceremony—a pointed expression of the disfavour of his fellow *matai*.

Ordinarily, members of the *'aumāga* are encouraged to listen to the deliberations of the chiefs, and it is common to see small groupings of *taulele'a* gathered in the immediate precincts of a *fono*. On this occasion, however, Mulitalo Iuma instructed one of the younger *tulāfale* to drive away the few untitled men who had come to eavesdrop. The condemnation of Volē Toilei'u was to be for the ears of *matai* alone.

As is mandatory in Sa'anapu at all juridical *fono*, it is the *ali'i*, or titular chiefs of the community, who speak first, making known their individual judgments. The first of them to speak was Mulitalo Iuma, a man of sixty-two years, suave of manner and a consummate politician. After dwelling on the great seriousness of the matter under discussion, he launched upon a sustained condemnation of Volē Toilei'u. The action of Volē in instigating the fight with Sene being common knowledge there was no formal calling of evidence. Instead, Mulitalo Iuma concentrated on pointing out to Volē Toilei'u the great impropriety of his behaviour. What he had to say was wholly in moral terms. Volē Toilei'u, Mulitalo declared, had forsaken his duty as a chief *('ua tia'i lou tiute fa'amatai)*, and exercised his will in a most mistaken manner *(fa'aaogā sesē lou loto)*. As a result, all of the *matai* of the village had been put in the wrong, and the peace of the whole community seriously threatened. A *matai*, Mulitalo went on, was expected to show patience *('onosa'i)* in difficult circumstances, and at all costs maintain his dignity. He was appointed not to start quarrels, but to stop them. A *matai* was like God. God does not attack his own people, yet Volē had initiated an attack on a fellow villager. A *matai* ought to live by spiritual values and not be ruled by the promptings of the body, as had Volē. Volē's judgment, Mulitalo concluded, had been defective, he had behaved wildly, transgressing all bounds, and ought to feel nothing but shame at his actions.

As he listened to these words Volē Toilei'u sat cross-legged at the back of the house, his head bowed and his hands clasped. He was obviously under strain at being so severely rebuked in the presence of his fellow chiefs, yet, as is required by Samoan custom, he suffered the opprobrium that was heaped upon him with gestures of submissive forbearance, effectively inhibiting any open expression of the annoyance he felt.

Under Samoan custom a *matai* is held responsible for the actions of all members of his *'āiga*, and it was to Tafili, a senior *matai* of the Lea'anā family and the maternal uncle of Sene, that Mulitalo next turned.[7] Tafili was berated for his carelessness, and adjured to assemble all members of the Lea'anā family and instruct them in the principles of correct behaviour. The relationships between the heads of families must ever be dignified, declared Mulitalo, and he enjoined all *matai*, and especially those immediately concerned with the clash of the day before, to foster the growth of concord. He had been speaking for about nineteen minutes, and the tenor of his remarks set the course of the rest of the *fono*.

Mulitalo Iuma was followed by three other *ali'i*: Mati Lua'itaua, Tuigamala Mafiti and Tafafuna'i Pati, all of whom traversed very much the same ground, roundly condemning the actions of Volē Toilei'u. Mati placed particular emphasis on the need to safeguard the sacredness of *matai*, this sacredness being the creation of God. Tuigamala, speaking forcefully, lamented Volē's limited supply of patience, which was, he said, about a quarter as much as it should be, despite the fact that Volē had been a *matai* for more than twelve years. The unfortunate Volē remained tensely silent, his head still bowed, the thumb of his right hand pressed strongly against the bridge of his nose, as he struggled to contain his feelings. Life was difficult, Tuigamala went on, but all went well if one walked uprightly in obedience to God's will. Tafafuna'i concentrated on Volē's complicity in the actions of Meatai which had precipitated the dispute. Volē had visited the plantations two days previously when there was every opportunity for him to have plotted an agreed boundary in collaboration with Sene. Instead, he had fought with a *taule'ale'a*, which, for a *matai*, was the most improper of actions.

The four titular chiefs Mulitalo, Mati, Tuigamala and Tafafuna'i, whose role it was at this *fono mānu* to point to behaviour that merited punishment, had made it clear that while Volē and Meatai were the principal culprits, Sene and the *matai* of his *'āiga* were also directly culpable. The four *ali'i* had spoken for a total of seventy-four minutes, and Volē had been subjected to a public shaming of a most gruelling kind.

It next fell to the talking chiefs to decide what the punishments should be. The first of them to speak was Lauvī Vela. He began by dwelling on the failings of Volē, and then went on to emphasize the heinous nature of any assault on a *matai*, a *matai* being one whose body is sacred (*'ua pa'ia le tino 'o le matai*). To attack a *matai*, Lauvī asserted, with great vehemence, was to attack the community itself (*'afai 'ua oso 'i le matai 'ua oso 'i le nu'u*). There could be no doubt about the gravity of what had happened and therefore, declared Lauvī, the community must that very day be provided with a supply of food in accordance with custom. Only in this way could the ill-fortune which had come upon them all be cast into the empty wastes of the ocean.

Le Sā Paulia, the next talking chief to speak, pleaded with Volē to look on the reprimands he was receiving as expressions of concern for his welfare. A duly appointed *matai*, Le Sā went on, is a representative of God (*'o le sui 'o le Atua*); thus, Volē could be said to be a God of this world (*'o se Atua 'o le lalolagi*) as were all *matai*. This being so it was surely most wrong for Volē to have incited trouble as he had done. The penalty nominated by Lauvī, Le Sā concluded, was fully deserved.

The third talking chief to address the *fono* was Alo To'alima, a sagacious man of seventy-two years, who had held his *tulāfale* title for over thirty years. The main thrust of Alo's speech was that the relationship between the chiefs of a community and those who serve them was of a sacred kind (*'ua sa le vā 'o matai ma tagata tautua*). This solemn principle, Alo went on, had been desecrated by Volē as also by Sene. Alo then remarked on Volē's predeliction for rushing headlong into disreputable actions, and charged him to change his ways forthwith. Talifi, Sene's *matai*, also came in for special notice. He was berated by Alo for having once shown an interest in the Mormon religion, and was told not to hanker after novelties, but to live in accord with long established tradition. Then, as was his right, Alo To'alima announced the fines imposed by the *fono*: both Volē and Tafili were to provide a baked pig of maximum size, together with taro, *palusami* (a favourite relish made from young taro leaves, coconut cream and sea water), and coconuts; and, in addition, provide a light repast (*tī*) for the assembled *matai*.

The three *tulāfale*, Lauvī Vela, Le Sā Paulia and Alo To'alima, had spoken for almost forty minutes, little more than half as long as the titular chiefs. The wrongdoing of Sene and Volē had been rehearsed and penalties imposed. It was now for the *'āiga* of the culprits to respond.

The first to make a move was Volē Na'oia, seeking to speak on behalf of his fellow *tulāfale*, Volē Toilei'u. He was at once interrupted by Lea'anā Satini, who, as a titular chief, insisted that he should have pride of place in reply. Speaking for the members of the *'āiga* to which Sene belonged, Lea'anā Satini fully accepted the decisions that had been reached. Humbling himself before the *fono*, he apologized for Sene's failure to comprehend the nature of the relationship of respect (*vā fealoa'i*) that ruled between *matai*, and asked for forgiveness. Tafili, Sene's uncle and immediate *matai*, responded in similar vein, thanking the *ali'i* for their vigilance in safeguarding the welfare of the village. To show that all dissension was at an end he would, he said, offer his hand in reconciliation. He then rose to his feet and crossing the floor of the *fono* shook hands with Volē Toilei'u, Volē Na'oia and Tuigamala Liuliu. It was a tense moment, for feelings were still running high, and, as they clasped hands, the four chiefs did not look at one another.

It was next the turn of Volē Na'oia and Tuigamala Liuliu. Each of them freely admitted the misbehaviour of Volē Toilei'u, who, said Tuigamala, had abandoned his duty as a *matai* in initiating an attack on one of the Lea'anā family, and on their own territory. They fully accepted the fine which the *fono* had imposed.

By this time the *fono* had been sitting for over three hours. It had been a not unsuccessful session during which a potentially disruptive situation had been contained—at least among the *matai* of the village. To mark this accomplishment Mulitalo Iuma called for another kava ceremony to be held. As the kava was distributed to the leading *matai* present, the rank order of the village, so basic to the structure of the *fono*, was yet again reaffirmed.[8]

As noon approached a repast of boiled rice and tea was served to all of the *matai*. The tea of the titular chiefs, in accord with present-day custom, was served in china cups and saucers, while the talking chiefs, as a mark of their lower rank, received their share in enamel mugs.

Soon after midday Tafili returned to display the food which his *'āiga* was proposing to offer the *fono*. It consisted of a large pig (as yet uncooked) and two huge baskets of taro. Alo To'alima, on behalf of the *fono*, signified acceptance and the food was taken away to be baked. Having made his peace with Volē, and provided the stipulated fine, Tafili went on to appeal to the *fono* to take note of what he claimed were continuing threats by Meatai and the others of his *'āiga*. This appeal met with an immediate response from Lea'anā Poliko, a proud old titular chief of eighty-two years. In Sa'anapu the Lea'anā *'āiga* is divided into three major branches, each branch having its own territory and managing its own affairs. What Lea'anā Poliko assured Tafili before the entire *fono*, with intense emotion, his voice and his hands trembling, was that if any hurt were to come to Sene, then the other branches of the *'āiga* would not stand by (*e lē nofo Lea'anā ma Lea'anā*). In these words Lea'anā Poliko was declaring that his extended family (of forty-nine members) and that of Lea'anā Satini (of forty-four members) would most certainly come to the aid of Tafili's family (of seventy members) if Sene were in any way molested.[9] With this show of solidarity the situation suddenly became more tense, and the *fono*, after being reminded by Lauvī Vela that 'the devil never sleeps', went on to declare that anyone renewing the fight would be banished from the community.

The deliberations of the *matai* having reached this critical juncture Mulitalo Iuma called on three low-ranking *tulāfale* to seek out Sene and Meatai and bring them before the *fono*. The first to arrive was Sene, accompanied by his first cousin Fa'i, a man of thirty-four years and his partner in working the land. Their entry to the *fono* was entirely without ceremony, and they were made to sit on the pebbled floor without the mat that is ordinarily offered to visitors. Almost at once Lauvī Vela, speaking on behalf of the assembled *ali'i*, began to rebuke Sene in the harsh tones of a disapproving father. Sene's fault, said Lauvī, was that he had dared to lay hand on a *matai*. Volē, Lauvī went on, was the brother (*uso*) of all the other *matai* of the community, including Sene's ailing father Lea'anā Fa'alolo, his uncle Tafili, and his brother Leao. To attack Volē was to attack all *matai*, and the most serious of offences deserving the penalty of banishment. Never forget, Lauvī told Sene, that the laying of a hand upon a *matai* is utterly prohibited (*sā lava*) and that even if an untitled individual is struck by a *matai* he must never retaliate.

Lauvī next turned to Meatai who was sitting, as directed, a few paces away from Sene. He too was sharply scolded, and, like Sene, threatened with expulsion from the village. An untitled man, said Lauvī, was esteemed most of all for his humble heart (*loto maulalo*), and good fortune came only to those who gave good service (*tautua lelei*) to their *matai*. In contrast, Lauvī went on, Meatai's action in cutting into the territory of another *'āiga* was wantonly provocative. Fixing Meatai with angry eyes, Lauvī exclaimed passionately: 'Have done! Have done! Live peaceably! Peaceably! As would a well-intentioned man!' (*'Uma! 'Uma! Nofo! Nofo! 'O le tagata manuia lea!*)

Stirred by these words Meatai sprang to his feet and moved towards Sene. Sene too leapt up, and there, before all of the *matai*, the two men, who had not long before been suffused with hatred, were clasping one another by the hand and pressing together the sides of their faces as do devoted friends.

This sight—an unexpected and highly emotional culmination to Lauvī's oratory—was deeply moving to all of the *matai* present, and not a few of them, including several high-ranking *ali'i* wept openly. There could be no doubt, I was told afterwards, that this particular *fono mānu* had been blest with great good fortune.

The mood of the *fono* was now euphoric, for a situation which earlier had been 'frightening to both ghosts and men' had given way to feelings of reconciliation and amity. It was Lea'anā Satini, a much respected titular chief, who, sensing this changed mood, uttered the words which brought the *fono* to its peak: 'We are of one village!' he proclaimed, 'And all brothers! All brothers!' (*'Ua tasi lava le nu'u! 'Ua uso 'uma! 'Ua uso 'uma!*)

Soon after this Sene, Fa'i and Meatai departed, but the *matai* stayed on, waiting for the pork and other food to be shared out. Before they dispersed there was a third and final kava ceremony to mark the conclusion of a memorable *fono*.[10] It had lasted for nearly seven hours, but the time had not dragged, and at its climax the censorious chiefs who had assembled in the early morning found themselves, of a sudden, exhilarated and inspired. As the ancient phrases of the kava ceremony rang out there was a fresh realization of how precious were the stern values and the 'elaborate court-liness' which lie at the heart of the *fa'aSāmoa*.

NOTES AND REFERENCES

1 Stevenson 1892:2-4.
2 The expression 'frightening to both ghosts and men' (*fefefe aitu ma tagata*) was used by the talking chief Lauvī Vela during his opening oration at the *fono mānu* held in Sa'anapu on 14 April 1966.
3 In this paper I have elected to use the actual names of individuals. I have done this in the interests of authenticity, and because, in a sequence of most testing situations, all of those involved, at one time or another, be-haved so well.
4 An account of these events is given in *Samoa Times*, 18 September 1920.
5 *Mānu* means to proclaim or announce; a *fono mānu* is a *fono* especially summoned at the direction of the *ali'i* of a community. In former times a *tulāfale* would walk through the village at dawn blowing a conch shell and announcing the holding of the *fono mānu*.
6 The order of distribution at this first kava ceremony was: *Mulitalo Iuma*, Lauvī Vela, Le Sā Paulia, *Mati Lua'itaua, Mati Nei, Tuigamala Mafiti, Tuigamala Liuliu, Tafafuna'i Pati, Lea'anā Poliko*, Luamata, Lalogafau, Tafili, Volē Na'oia, Lauvī Taipisia. (The names of the *ali'i* are in italics.)
7 The senior *matai* of Sene's *'āiga* was, in fact, his 77-year-old father, Lea'anā Fa'alolo. However, because of an incapacitating illness Lea'anā Fa'alolo was in no way held responsible for the behaviour of his son. Instead, it was Lea'anā Fa'alolo's 58-year-old brother-in-law, Tafili, the holder of a *tulāfale* title within the same *'āiga*, who was taken to task by the *fono mānu*.
8 The order of distribution at this second kava ceremony was: *Mulitalo Iuma*, Lauvī Vela, *Mati Lua'itaua, Mati Nei*, Le Sā Paulia, *Lea'anā Satini, Lea'anā Poliko*, Alo To'alima, *Tuigamala Mafiti, Tuigamala Liuliu*, Volē Na'oia, *Tafafuna'i Pati*. (The names of the *ali'i* are in italics.)
9 This incident bears on a principal issue in Samoan studies during recent years. In 1962 Ember (1962:968) expressed the view that when *'āiga* seg-mentation occurs in Samoa, the segment breaking away, 'instead of con-tinuing to acknowledge common ancestry' with the descent group it was leaving, would consider itself to be a new localized unit. The three branches of the Lea'anā *'āiga* emerged at the beginning of the present century. At the *fono mānu* held in Sa'anapu on 14 April 1966 these branches exhibited a solidarity which made it plain that they still recognized a common ancestry, and were prepared to stand together, and, if necessary, fight together in a crisis.
10 The order of distribution at this third kava ceremony was: *Mati Lua'itaua, Mati Nei, Lea'anā Satini, Lea'anā Poliko, Tuigamala Mafiti, Tuigamala Liuliu*, Alo To'alima, Le Sā Paulia, *Tafafuna'i Pati*, Luamata, Lauvī Taipisia, Tafili, *Mulitalo Iuma*. (The names of the *ali'i* are in italics.)

Me'a faka'eiki: Tongan funerals in a changing society

ADRIENNE L. KAEPPLER

'Oku 'eiki 'ae tangata he'ene mate.
A man becomes a chief when he dies.

TONGAN PROVERB

Me'a faka'eiki, 'chiefly things', aptly conveys the attitude of Tongans to their funeral ceremonies.[1] Although the dictionary defines *me'a faka'eiki* as the honorific term for *putu* or funeral rites,[2] it may conceptually be extended to all levels of Tongan society for, as the proverb says, a man becomes a chief when he dies. An individual's funeral is probably his most important *rite de passage,* for at this time are recorded for all to see and to pass down through oral tradition how the individual was related to others, his dignity, rank, and how much and by whom he was beloved. Funerals are also the most important societal occasions, for here can best be seen how the various elements of Tongan society fit together and it is here that much of the enculturation of the young in Tongan traditions takes place.

In contrast to one's day-to-day existence, especially in modern times, when status and rank are largely put aside in order to cope with the exigencies of the Western overlay which has significantly changed the surface manifestations of Tongan society and culture, funerals are the occasions *par excellence* when status and rank prescribe the actions of all concerned. Indeed, it does little good for an individual or family group to not attend or to pretend to be culture free, because it will only draw attention to the role they should have played. This analysis attempts to demonstrate the importance of funerals in the perpetuation and evolution of Tongan social and cultural traditions, and to show how funeral ceremonies have been altered in recent years to complement the nuclearization of the family. In effect, this essay illustrates some of the concepts set forth in an earlier paper[3] which delineated categories and principles of status and rank that a Tongan must understand in order to decide if another individual outranks him on a particular occasion, and thus know how to interact with him. Neither that paper nor this are ethnohistoric, or attempt to explain the past. Rather, the focus is ethnographic, by which I mean that the traditions recorded here are those by which Tongans today view their past, and that they use to organize and manipulate the present and the future. Although it may be true that much of this has little relevance in a Tongan's everyday life in village or urban centre, it is equally true that without such knowledge a Tongan cannot operate as a full member of his society during special occasions such as funerals or *kātoanga* (public festivals).

A certain amount of ethnographic data will be presented in the course of the analysis in order to put on record some of the traditions that are rapidly disappearing and virtually unknown to many Tongans today. Much of the analysis will be expressed in terms of the funeral ceremonies of Queen Sālote Tupou III which was one of the most important *me'a faka'eiki* in living memory and will serve as a model for future funerals carried out in the 'traditional' manner. In the course of the analysis it will be pointed out how Sālote's funeral rites differed from the more usual *me'a faka'eiki* and it is hoped that this account will illuminate the rather sketchy information on funerals hitherto available.

The most important organizing principle in ordering social relationships on special occasions such as funerals is that of hierarchical ranking.[4] This social principle is visually reinforced by material culture and linguistically reinforced by honorific language and poetic allusion. The principles consistently expressed during funeral ceremonies are those of who is high (*'eiki*) and who is low (*tu'a*) among *kāinga* (bilateral kinsmen) and within the class ranking system (that is, the personal class rank of the individuals concerned) with *kāinga* status taking precedence. Little attention seems to be paid to *ha'a* rank (that is, the abstract ranking of titles that derived through collateral segmentation within the societal structure, which emphasizes patrilineality) except as this is manifested in an individual's personal class rank or 'blood' (which emphasizes bilineality). The relationships expressed are preeminently those of prestige rather than those of power (although the prestige acquired may be useful later in realignments of power).

The elemental principles brought into play are that, in the generation above ego, father's side is *'eiki* while mother's side is *tu'a;* that in ego's own generation, sisters and their descendants are *'eiki* to brothers and their descendants; that personal rank acquired through the mother is equally or even more important than that acquired through the father; that husbands and wives have a certain equality expressed by the surviving spouse in *tu'a*ness in order to give 'dignity' to the beloved dead one; that children are *tu'a* if the deceased is male while they are not *tu'a* if the deceased is female; and that grandchildren are not *tu'a*, but the amount of their elevation depends on their personal rank acquired through *kāinga* and class ranking principles.

It follows then that at the funeral of Queen Sālote those in generations above her related through her father should be *'eiki* (and especially her father's sisters and their children, or the father's father's sister's daughters, or anyone who stands in the relationship of *mehikitanga* to the dead person, and their children) while those related through her mother should be *tu'a;* that her brothers and their children should be *tu'a;* that her personal class rank acquired through her mother is equal or more important than that acquired through her father (in contrast to her right to reign which was inherited through her father); that her husband would express his feelings for his beloved by making himself *tu'a;* that her children would not display *tu'a*ness; and that her grandchildren would display their *'eiki*ness, especially the eldest son and daughter of her eldest son. Let us analyse, then, what individuals and segments of society were *'eiki* and *tu'a* during the funeral ceremonies of Queen Sālote.

If one does not know the genealogical relationships of individuals interacting during funeral ceremonies, a first step is to distinguish what type of matted garment is worn around the waist in place of the usual *ta'ovala*. The individuals who are most *tu'a* will wear huge ragged mats which nearly cover all of their black clothing, and may even extend above the head. These large ragged mats are worn by those known as *liongi* (those who are the most *tu'a* to the dead person). For a dead man the *liongi* are those related through the dead man's mother; for a dead woman the *liongi* are those related through the dead woman's mother as well as the dead woman's brothers and their children. Also considered *tu'a,* but not *liongi,* are a dead man's parallel cousins related through his father's younger brothers, that is, the children of a father's *tehina* (younger sibling of the same sex).

Those most in evidence wearing the largest most ragged mats at Sālote's funeral were the nobles Kalanivalu (the ranking chief of the Tu'i Tonga line) and Vaea (by title a chief of the Ha'a Havea) as well as the Fijian chief, Ratu Edward Cakobau. An analysis of the genealogical relationships of these three men reveals that, although they are not closely related to each other, they are in fact the 'correct' *liongi* to Sālote. The Kalanivalu in 1965 (now dead) was Sālote's *fa'e tangata* (mother's brothers and all male kinsmen one generation above ego related through the mother)—Kalanivalu was Sālote's mother's father's mother's brother's daughter's son.[5]

Vaea is Queen Sālote's *fakafotu* (a female's brother's children)—Sālote's father (Tupou II) had a son (Vilai) by Tupou Moheofo (of the Tu'i Tonga line); Vilai was Sālote's (half) brother and his son (Vaea) is Sālote's *fakafotu*.[6]

Ratu Edward Cakobau is also Sālote's half brother—the son of Tupou II and a Fijian chief. Thus, these three high-ranking men and their children were the *liongi* and thus *tu'a* at Sālote's funeral in spite of the fact that they are of very high *ha'a* and personal class rank, illustrating that in funerals *kāinga* status takes precedence over class and *ha'a* rank. Probably the lowest *liongi* of all, however, was Lepa, the brother of Sālote's mother and thus her closest *fa'e tangata*[7] and from the Tongan point of view her closest living *tu'a* relative at the time she died.

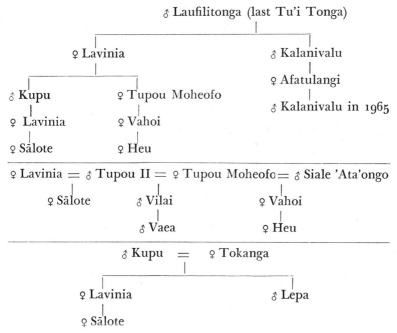

♂ Laufilitonga (last Tu'i Tonga)

♀ Lavinia   ♂ Kalanivalu

                             ♀ Afatulangi

♂ Kupu   ♀ Tupou Moheofo   ♂ Kalanivalu in 1965

♀ Lavinia   ♀ Vahoi

♀ Sālote   ♀ Heu

♀ Lavinia = ♂ Tupou II = ♀ Tupou Moheofo = ♂ Siale 'Ata'ongo

   ♀ Sālote   ♂ Vilai   ♀ Vahoi

                 ♂ Vaea   ♀ Heu

         ♂ Kupu = ♀ Tokanga

      ♀ Lavinia   ♂ Lepa

      ♀ Sālote

Fig. 6   *Tu'a*—'those who are low'—in relation to Queen Sālote

Lepa accompanied Sālote on her last trip to New Zealand in order to symbolically fulfil his duties to her at her death. Lepa, however, was not as conspicuous during the funeral ceremonies as Kalanivalu and Vaea, because in addition to the fact that he was quite old, his personal class rank was not as high as theirs, having descended in a younger and less distinguished line, and he would not benefit from any power play that would be advanced during the funeral ceremonies.

Those who are *tu'a* or low to a dead person are called *liongi*. When alive the individual was *fahu* and could 'please herself' with those *tu'a* people and one might suggest that *liongi* is a reciprocal term for *fahu* that implies a relationship which will be activated only at the *fahu*'s death.

The people who are *'eiki* at a funeral have no collective term corresponding to *liongi*. It is important to remember that those who are *'eiki* at a funeral are not *'eiki* to the *liongi—'eiki*ness and *tu'a*ness is only a relationship to the deceased, not to each other.[8] Those who are *'eiki* and those who are *tu'a* have certain rights and duties to the deceased which are activated at certain *rites de passage* in relation to that individual. This same group may have never assembled before, except perhaps (for those who were alive at the time) at the deceased's wedding. The people who assemble at a funeral are in no way a corporate group, but pre-eminently the *kāinga* of the dead person and the *kāinga* of his spouse. This also tells us something about the term *kāinga* in its traditional sense. The more modern concept of *famili* (which emphasizes the nuclear family) as it is used today makes little sense in traditional funeral rites and indeed has little place in the traditional social system. Tongan social organization was not based primarily on corporate groups, lineality, or locality, but rather on the concept of *kāinga* (consanguineal relationship) and the social status derived from Tongan principles of *'eiki* and *tu'a*.

Kinsmen who are *'eiki* to a dead woman are those related through the father—the dead woman's father's 'sisters' (that is, *tuofefine,* all female kinsmen of his generation), and his older brothers (*ta'okete*). These individuals would be *mehikitanga* and *tamai* to the dead woman (as would her father's father's sister's children). Apparently there were no appropriate individuals of these kinship categories to Sālote, for no one acted as *fahu* at her funeral. Theoretically a chief of higher class rank (as derived from *ha'a* rank) could serve as *fahu,* but given Sālote's genealogy this was impossible. Someone of the Tu'i Tonga line or the Tu'i Ha'a Takalaua line might have done this; however, the Tu'i Tonga line was *tu'a* because it was the line of Sālote's mother, and the Ha'a Takalaua could not be so elevated because it was the line of Sālote's husband. It is also possible for a chief to be outranked within his own *ha'a* derived from descent from a brother and sister sibling pair, but this was effectively prevented two generations earlier by a strategic cross-cousin marriage between the grandchildren of Tupou I.[9] If Tupou II (or his father, or father's father) had had a sister, she or her children might have been *fahu* at Sālote's funeral (depending on their marriages) and could have taken the best of the *koloa* (mats and bark cloth), directed the distribution if she pleased, and would have been given the back section of certain pigs as her right. As it was, there was no proper *fahu*. Probably the individual with the closest right was Heu because some of Heu's genealogical connections to Sālote are slightly higher, but not of the right order to be *fahu*.[10]

PLATE 1 (*above*) Communal distribution of papayas at Napuka Atoll,
Tuamotu Archipelago, 12 June 1934
(*below*) Distribution of fish at the Men's House, Touhou, Kapingamarangi,
17 July 1950

PLATE 2 The symbolic slaying of Limaua (*above*) He is hoisted on a rope by two men (*below*) The plaza is cleared for the drama

It is significant to note that Sālote's class rank as derived from her mother was acknowledged, in that the ceremonies of *faka-pō-teau* observing the hundredth night after her death were essentially those accorded only to the Tu'i Tonga. Although this was usually explained by stating that the Tu'i Kanokupolu line had 'taken over' prerogatives of the Tu'i Tonga line, in reality it was an accepted way to transfer prerogatives from the Tu'i Tonga line to the Tu'i Kanokupolu line by the means of Sālote's Tu'i Tonga blood. Indeed, the prerogatives of the Tu'i Tonga line that have been absorbed were not simply 'taken over' but appear to have been transferred by the traditional Tongan method of using class rank to reinforce *ha'a* position by the time-honoured means of *moheofo* (the 'spouse takers' line being elevated by the rank of the 'spouse givers' line). Lavinia of the Tu'i Tonga line was given as *moheofo* to Tupou II of the Tu'i Kanokupolu line thereby elevating the class rank of Tupou II's descendant Sālote and thus acquiring for the Kanokupolu line prerogatives of the Tu'i Tonga line, exemplified by *faka-pō-teau* of Sālote's funeral rites.

Sālote's consort had died first so we could not observe how his behaviour might have expressed the principle of relative equality between spouses, but it is perhaps significant that the chiefs and people of Sālote's late husband's line (Ha'a Takalaua) prepared one of the three major *'umu* (earth ovens) of food during the first ten days of mourning. The three *'umu* came from kinsmen of father, mother, and spouse—the fact that the lineages of these three groups correspond to the major societal lines was in this case only coincidental, for at this time *kāinga* relationships were being activated (societal relationships were being separately activated during the four *pongipongi* as will be seen below).

The last *'eiki-tu'a* principles in evidence at Sālote's funeral were those activated by Sālote's children and grandchildren. Ideally a woman's children are not *tu'a* to her during her funeral rites and her grandchildren have a certain freedom of action. This is indeed what happened in spite of her position as sovereign of the Kingdom. Sālote's two sons (Tupou IV and Prince Tu'i Pelehake) wore neutral mourning mats without ragged fringes. The grandchildren through Tu'i Pelehake also wore neutral mats, but the children of Tupou IV wore mats that indicated that they were *'eiki* to the deceased—his eldest daughter Pilolevu wearing a mat that indicated she could 'please herself' in what she wore. This was appropriate not only because of the lack of restraint between grandparent and grandchild, but also because of her position among her *kāinga* (eldest daughter of Sālote's eldest offspring) and her personal class rank derived from her various ancestors particularly her father's father (Sālote's husband) who was

N

higher in class rank that Sālote, giving Pilolevu the status of *mokopuna 'eiki* (chiefly grandchild) in relationship to Sālote.

In order to illustrate how these *'eiki-tu'a* principles were manifested the main events of Sālote's funeral will be summarized. Queen Sālote left for New Zealand on 4 November 1965 to receive medical treatment and she was not expected to return alive. People were discouraged from coming to see her off and there was no dancing (as there often was on royal departures). Girls of Queen Sālote College lined the road and all was silence as she drove past. On 13 December there was a rumour that the Queen had died, which spread rapidly along with accounts of supernatural signs of her death—the sun had set very red during the past week (always a bad sign), and the white bat which only appears when the sovereign's death is imminent had appeared in Nuku'alofa accompanied by two black bats.[11] On the thirteenth it was raining, but strangely there was no thunder, which there should have been if the Queen was dead. The rumours were premature, but on 16 December she did pass away. Sālote's younger son, Prince Tu'i Pelehake, had accompanied her to New Zealand, and the Prince Regent arrived shortly after her death. The first public announcement in Tonga was on the 7 a.m. B.B.C. news broadcast, and an official announcement on the Tongan radio station followed shortly after. In Tongan it was phrased as *'Kuo tō 'a e La'a 'o Tonga'* (the sun of Tonga has fallen). In accordance with the decision of the Privy Council which had met on 14 December, a meeting of the nobles was called and the Prince Regent Tupouto'a-Tungī was declared King of Tonga, and a six-month period of mourning was to be observed.

Ordinarily when a chief dies mourning *tapu* are observed mainly by his *kāinga* and those who live on his *tofi'a* or hereditary land. When the sovereign dies the whole kingdom mourns. It is said that the new King wanted only a three-month mourning period, but Kalanivalu and some of the other chiefs insisted that six months was proper to uphold Sālote's dignity. The death of Sālote and the succession of the Tupou dynasty was characterized poetically: *'Punakaki e Fā ka 'oku kei 'alaha hono tu'unga'*, the flower of the pandanus has fallen but its sweet smell lingers on.

The shops were in chaos with the frantic buying of black cloth which everyone would have to wear. Flags were flown as low as possible and store windows and buildings were draped in black. Huge mourning mats soon appeared, some reaching to the ground and up to the head. Anyone having even a remote ancestor in common with Sālote wished to make it publicly known by wearing a *liongi* mat, but many were quickly discarded, when public opinion declared them *fie 'eiki* (pretending to be a chief). Mourning restrictions prescribed no noise or gaiety and specifically no bark cloth making, no dancing, no Tongan music (except Christian hymns), no moving pictures, and no parties. Black mourning clothing and appropriate waist mats were prescribed.

It is not known how Sālote's body was prepared for burial, presumably it was embalmed or treated in accordance with New Zealand law. Tongan custom prescribes that a dead female have her body prepared by her father's sister's children or someone higher in *kāinga* rank who will not be harmed by the spirit of the dead person. The body of a male should be prepared by his sister's children or his father's sister's children. Preparation usually includes closing the eyes, putting the limbs straight, and washing the body. As we have seen above, no one stood in this relationship to Sālote. Her death in New Zealand made this step unnecessary, but it probably would have been carried out by Princess Pilolevu (eldest daughter of the new King) or someone on her behalf. The body should then be wrapped in oiled bark cloth of a specific size.[12] After the body of a chief is washed and dressed, it is taken over by the chiefly undertakers, Ha'atufunga. Commoners are attended by the *fahu*.

In the interim the new King arrived and each of the nobles declared individual allegiance to him. On Sunday 19 December commemorative church services were held and the entire day was one of prayer. When the remains of Sālote were returned to Tonga on the twentieth the Ha'atufunga met the plane along with the royal family, government officers, and others. The casket was carried from the plane by officers of the Tonga Defence Force along a bark cloth pathway and placed in the hearse accompanied by a Ha'atufunga. The entire route from airport to the royal chapel inside the palace compound was lined by school children and adults who sat in tearful bowed silence as the hearse passed. In places the road was covered with mats and bark cloth and all persons wore black[13] with large waist mats—the size, type, and raggedness depending on any relationship to the Queen. Those not claiming relationship wore mats that were not ragged or overwhelmingly large. Only *liongi* wore large mats. Among the largest was that worn by the daughter of Kalanivalu (by traditional reckoning one of the highest individuals in the land) that reached the ground and extended up to her head, and her hair was down and dishevelled. When the hearse reached Mala'ekula, the royal cemetery where Sālote would be laid to rest, a twenty-one-gun salute commenced and finished as the hearse reached Pangai, the palace green. The casket, draped with the sovereign's flag, was carried into the royal chapel to lie in state on a platform of mats and bark cloth. She was attended by the ranking Ha'atufunga and four members of the Tonga Defence Force who stood at each corner with their backs to the casket in British fashion. Contrary to European tradition, however, no one was allowed in the chapel except her very close family, primarily her children and grand-children, in spite of the fact that she had lain in state in Government House in New Zealand and thousands had filed past her bier.

Meanwhile temporary houses were constructed behind the palace and at the homes of several chiefs. Those at the rear of the palace would house the Ha'atufunga while the latter would house the chief's *'kāinga'* or people who would come to help with the preparation of the food that would be given in great quantities to the palace. Heads of state and others arrived including Ratu Edward Cakobau. The formal ceremonies of Sālote's last *rite de passage* were ready to begin. That night there commenced a three-night watch or *takipō* (regal for *'apō*) during which the palace compound was completely surrounded by burning torches from sundown to sunrise. On the sacred ocean side of the palace the fires were those of Tāufa'āhau, the new Crown Prince and *mokopuna 'eiki* of Sālote. On the other three sides outside the palace wall were some hundred fires representing various villages and islands as well as secondary schools, churches, Girl Guides, and other associations. The side of the fire facing the body was *tapu* and no one could walk there (save the *fahu* and grandchildren who might take such liberties but did not). Each coconut spathe torch was attended by three people who sat on the other three sides and changed periodically (about every half-hour). A person of rank, for example, the village chief's daughter, sat at the centre facing the corpse and held the torch while the two others attended to the falling ashes by covering them with sand. At sunrise the fires must be extinguished by command of someone *'eiki* to the deceased who either extinguishes the fire or calls out for them to be extinguished. At Sālote's funeral this was done by Princess Pilolevu.[14]

Ordinarily during the watch for a chief the *fahu* sits at the head of the deceased and one or two Ha'atufunga sit at the sides. Loud lamenting at the death of a chief is forbidden in the house in which he lies, except for those who are *'eiki* to him and par-ticularly the *fahu* who is allowed to lament as loudly as she pleases.[15] In the absence of embalming, body fluids may escape and those who prepared the body are summoned by the Ha'atu-funga to bring unpainted bark cloth to clean any mess. Anything used on such occasions will be wrapped and buried with the corpse. Near the head of the deceased the *fahu* would have a *kato alu* (ceremonial basket) lined with a mat and containing scented Tongan oil, perfume, or powder to apply to the face at appropriate intervals. The dead person's face is usually covered with a thin cloth (to keep away flies) and each time someone new comes into the room the *fahu* removes the cloth and applies oil or perfume so the newcomer may kiss the dead and then retire to his prescribed station. The Ha'atufunga or *fahu* uses a fly whisk or a piece of cloth to keep the flies from the dead.

Beginning on 21 December (the day following the return of Sālote's remains to Tonga) daily ceremonial presentations of food were made. The chiefs asked their people to contribute food[16] and most did so willingly for their beloved Queen, even if they might have only tapioca and bananas (the two lowest foods) left to eat for themselves. Pigs, *'ufi,* and *kape* (the highest foods) were the main food gifts. Presentation, enumeration, and acceptance, were done in the stylized ceremonial manner. The food would be used to feed Ha'atufunga and all those who had come to mourn —mainly those who were staying at the palace and the homes of chiefs. High-ranking females stayed with Princess Pilolevu 'to look after her'. Those not related to Sālote activated relationships with those who were. Former liaisons that had resulted in illegitimate (by Christian standards) children were openly acknowledged in an effort to claim relationships to Sālote or her *kāinga.* Everyone wanted to take part in this important occasion in as close a way as he could. It was truly national in scope—those who could not attend the burial were still part of the proceedings, at least in giving and mourning. Thousands of others would come to Nuku'alofa during the following six months to represent their home areas at other parts of the ceremony.

A special funeral bier, *kauala* (regal for *fata*), was constructed at Pangai (in view of anyone who cared to watch) consisting of a square wood platform with long timbers extending on its four sides to enable many men to carry it on their shoulders. The platform was surmounted by upright and cross-timbers that were covered with black cloth to form a canopy. On the morning of 23 December, the day of Sālote's interment, the bier was carried to a place near the royal chapel and the two hundred men from Kolofo'ou and Kolomotu'a sat patiently waiting to carry it to the tomb. They were dressed in black clothes and large mats, the size and raggedness depending on any relationship to Sālote. Before a body is interred there is a final gathering of the close *kāinga* and final preparation called *teu* which consists of wrapping the body in mats and bark cloth. At Sālote's *teu* it is said that the casket was opened in the presence of the royal family. By this time Hala Tu'i (the street that joins the palace to Mala'ekula) was lined with seated people and thousands were already seated in Mala'ekula. Huge ceremonial bark cloths and mats were carried via Hala Tu'i from the palace to the royal tombs on the shoulders of several men. Precisely at 10 a.m. the salute cannon near the waterfront was fired, then the bell from the Wesleyan Centenary Church was rung. Cannon fire and church chime alternated until the funeral cortège reached Mala'ekula. The two hundred carriers brought the *kauala* surmounted by a pile of bark cloth and mats to the doorway of the royal chapel and again sat down. The casket was carried from the chapel by officers of the Tonga Defence Force, preceded and followed by the two ranking Ha'atufunga, and placed on the *kauala*. Takapu sat down on the left side of the casket and Lauaki stood at the right rear corner, both wearing huge ragged mourning mats. The two hundred carriers lifted the *kauala* bearing Sālote in her flag-draped casket and the two Ha'atufunga to their shoulders and proceeded to Hala Tu'i on a bark cloth pathway.

The procession was led by a guard of honour including the Royal Guard in their white uniforms and black arm bands, a detachment of the Tonga Defence Force marching with reversed rifles, the Police band playing funeral marches, and the officiating clergy—the European accoutrements of a state funeral. The Tongan part of the procession began with two chiefs preceding the *kauala* and Kalanivalu walked at the rear right corner. The seated Takapu waved a fly whisk in a stylized manner over the casket while the still standing Lauaki whisked nonexistent flies with a piece of coloured silk. About twenty chiefs followed and then came the royal mourners. The latter were led by the elder sons of Sālote's two sons carrying Sālote's royal orders and medals on velvet pillows. The new King and Queen followed, closely accompanied by Ngalumoetutulu in the largest mourning mat of all. Ngalu, the aide-de-camp, was the oldest son of Kalanivalu—Sālote's *fakafotu* and thus among the most *tu'a* of the *liongi*. Had he not been the King's aide-de-camp he would have been far removed from this *'eiki* group. Tu'i Pelehake and his wife Melanaite (the latter wearing a relatively low mat) followed and then came Sālote's other royal grandchildren. Princess Pilolevu wore a mat that demonstrated she was the *'eiki* of the funeral. The procession was completed with overseas dignitaries, Ministers of the Tongan Crown, representatives of all the churches in Tonga, foreign and Tongan parliamentary representatives, chiefs of Fiji and Samoa, Tongan nobles, heads of Tongan government departments, and finally more than one hundred girls from Queen Sālote College carrying the floral tributes (*pale*).

Reaching Mala'ekula the guard of honour took its place at the right while the royal family and official visitors took their places in the temporary buildings on the left. The clergy climbed the *mā'olunga*, or tomb proper,[17] and the *kauala* was carried into position. The two Ha'atufunga were joined by two others and each sat at a corner of the casket and continued to whisk. The Christian service was then carried out led by the Reverend G. C. Harris of the Centenary Wesleyan Church and the eulogy was delivered by the Reverend Dr A. H. Wood who for many years was the ranking missionary in Tonga and came from Australia for this occasion. This ended the Christian part of the ceremony and the four ministers (including two ranking Tongan ministers, the Reverend Dr 'Amanaki Havea and the Reverend S. T. Simiki) descended from the *mā'olunga* and the Tongan service commenced.

A large number of women, who had been seated on the ground at the foot of the *mā'olunga*, now arose and proceeded with the help of several men to unroll a very large mat. With it they formed a large circle or screen called *kolohiki*, or simply *kolo*, around the tomb in which Sālote was to be placed. The women stood with their backs to the mat and held it in place with their arms above their heads. A huge bark cloth was then unfurled and used to encircle the entire tomb area and *kauala* in another *kolohiki*, held in the same way. This effectively shielded the most important part of the ceremony from all save the Ha'atufunga.[18] As related to me by one who was inside the inner *kolohiki*, the men of the Ha'atufunga lines began their work by removing the three pieces of the vault cover, to an old chant under the direction of Lauaki. Inside the vault was the casket of Sālote's consort, Tungī Mailefihi, who died in 1941. One of the young men went down into the tomb and covered Tungī's casket with a mat. During this time all that could be seen from the outside was the movements of the top of a ladder, and a final European tribute was fired by a party of the Tonga Defence Force near the tomb. A three-foot 'bed' of bark cloth and mats was put down and the casket was moved from the *kauala* into the tomb. The cover of the vault was then replaced and the *kauala* was sprinkled (*luluku*) with a solution with *uhi* leaves to chase away any *fa'ahikehe* or malevolent spirits (known today as *tēvolo*, devils). These are believed to be spirits of the dead who can harm the living, especially those who are *tu'a* to them.

In the meantime the two pillows holding the royal orders and medals had been taken inside the *kolohiki* and were returned to their bearers. The large bark cloth was lowered and taken away and somewhat later the mat was lowered and placed in the *kauala*. The flag that had covered the casket was folded and taken away by the police. The women sat down and the men carried the *kauala* to the left side. The men of the Ha'atufunga lines formed a sandbag brigade and the vault was heaped with a truncated pyramid of sand. By tradition, commoners may not leave the graveyard before the chiefs, and the King left promptly in his limousine with the Queen and his aide-de-camp—almost concealed in his huge mat. Some of the others also left in limousines and the crowds dispersed.[19]

The actual interment over, attention was focused on the temporal divisions of mourning and the associated ceremonies, especially in relation to the Ha'atufunga, who claim special rights and duties. According to Tongan tradition the line of Lauaki descended from the *falefā matāpule* Maliepō of celestial origin. The lines of Takapu and Hautaulu originated from twins born of a chief that came from Samoa. Before he died he instructed his sons to keep his body for several days and how to look after it.[20] According to the Tongan ranking system dead chiefs must be looked after by someone *'eiki* to the dead or by someone unrelated, thus those of celestial or foreign origin serve the purpose admirably and the descendants of these individuals are still the chiefly undertakers. For the first ten days after the burial of a high chief the Ha'atufunga who looked after the body during the *takipō* are under the *nima tapu* (sacred or *tapu* hands) and cannot feed themselves. Further, they cannot engage in any work for one hundred nights and in effect become *'eiki* to the *'eiki* who must furnish them with food and drink for six months.[21] The Ha'atufunga will take the chiefly positions in the kava ring and the chiefs will mix and serve their kava.

During the funeral rites of Sālote the Ha'atufunga lived in a temporary house behind the palace for six months. For the first hundred days all thirty-one Ha'atufunga stayed in the house, as well as some of their families. Lauaki and Takapu remained the entire six months and there were always at least four others but these changed during the course of the six months (usually each weekend) and the various *ha'a* took turns feeding them. For the first ten days those with the *nima tapu* were fed and their kava had to be poured into their own personal cups. Their duties were mainly to look after the grave—making sure the sand was clean and piled properly. Others who remained to mourn for the first ten days stayed in the temporary houses built at the homes of Kalanivalu, Tu'i Pelehake, and other chiefs, going to Mala'ekula morning and evening and eating food provided by the various chiefs. It is the preparation and ceremonial presentation of food that occupied much of these first ten days. Each day trucks were sent by the various chiefs to their villages for pigs and other food which was taken to the chiefs' houses, mainly in Nuku'alofa, and prepared in large earth ovens *('umu)*. The food was provided by chiefs, *matāpule,* and people who held land allotments from them. If the latter did not raise such food themselves they had to get it from relatives who did, or buy it. During the first ten days the three major *'umu* were those of the lines of Sālote's mother, Sālote's father, and Sālote's husband. The cooked food was taken to Pangai usually on trucks that parked near the ocean. The food was carried in coconut-leaf baskets hung over poles resting on the shoulders of men and women. The baskets were placed in rows, and then the large green kava roots and pigs would be placed in front of the baskets. The presenting chief often accompanied the largest pig and would then go to join the *matāpule* and other chiefs who sat facing the food. The people sat under the trees, the men together and the women together. The *matāpule* would then divide the food and the men and women would again put it on the poles to carry it to the palace and other places, the best going to the Ha'atufunga. This presentation at Pangai took place after the food had first been assembled at some other place; for example, the Ha'a Takalaua (now called Ha'a Vaea) villages assembled at the house where Sālote's husband lived before he lived in the palace (that is, the first house behind the present Dateline Hotel now belonging to Halaevalu Maile). In this case the noble Luani was in charge and the food arrived (already cooked) between 11 and 12 and a ceremonial presentation took place. At about 12.30 the food was taken to Pangai.

Besides these daily food presentations at Pangai, there were also four ritual kava ceremonies, *pongipongi,* in which the ceremonial presentation of food was an accompaniment to royal kava drinking during which the new King was called by his new name, Tupou. The presiding *matāpule* was Lauaki or the *matāpule* seated on the King's left (Lauaki's usual place), rather than Motu'apuaka or the *matāpule* seated at the King's right, who usually presides at formal kava ceremonies. These four *pongipongi,* held every third day in the open space behind the palace (Loto'ā),[22] by four societal groupings were ostensibly to honour the dead Queen, affirm allegiance to the new King, and above all to acknowledge the rights and duties of the Ha'atufunga. In addition, however, they also implicitly reinforced and assisted in the legitimization of the participating lines of chiefs.

These *pongipongi* focused the attention of the public on the four major societal divisions as they are presently constituted, that is, the grouping of title holders under the Ha'a Ngata, Ha'a Havea, Ha'a Vaea/Ha'a Latuhifo, and Kauhala'uta. Besides demonstrating that all lines were now subservient to the King and his government, in effect this gave the appearance that the four groupings had a kind of ceremonial equality, and their ordering implied successive ranking. It is instructive to note how the older ritual ordering was altered to suit the occasion and how traditional prestige became subservient to power in the reordering of traditional ranking of societal groupings vis-à-vis each other. A more traditional division of *pongipongi* among societal groups (although we do not know how old this rationalized order is) would have been among the so-called three lines of kings—the Tu'i Tonga line and his chiefs of the Kauhala'uta, the Tu'i Ha'a Takalaua line (which would

include Ha'a Vaea and Ha'a Latuhifo), and the Tu'i Kanokupolu
line (which is the ranking line of the Ha'a Ngata and includes
the Ha'a Havea). The new ordering in which Ha'a Havea has an
equal place actually accords Ha'a Ngata one half of 'traditional'
power instead of one third. One could suggest that the Ha'a
Havea line is rising because of its inclusion of Vaea, a strong and
important chief because of his personal class rank.[23] The new
ordering also effectively eliminates the Tu'i Tonga and Tu'i Ha'a
Takalaua lines because their titles have been dropped—Tu'i Tonga
duties being fulfilled by Tu'i Pelehake and Kalanivalu and the
Tu'i Ha'a Takalaua duties being fulfilled by Tungī (when one is
appointed) and by the chiefs of Ha'a Vaea[24] and Ha'a Latuhifo.
Such lineage reshuffling and the rise and fall of chiefly titles is characteristic of Polynesian political systems and demonstrates that the
Tongan social system is still viable within its endemic Polynesian
parameters. In the past, one Tongan form of political redundancy
was to give an unwanted title an aura of sanctity and thereby prevent its holder from participating in power play such as the
sanctification of the Tu'i Tonga and Tu'i Ha'a Takalaua. Today
power is aligned mainly by strategic marriages and selective appointment of titles. In spite of the European influence in politics
and ceremony that is superficially observable, the traditional
Tongan system of political power play among chiefs is still very
much alive and Tonga can justifiably claim that it is one of the
last strongholds of Polynesian social systems.

During the four *pongipongi,* and indeed throughout the ceremonies of Sālote's *me'a faka'eiki,* it was quite apparent that the
lines of the Tu'i Tonga and the Tu'i Ha'a Takalaua have been
almost totally eclipsed by the Ha'a Ngata and its subdivision Ha'a
Havea, not only in power, but in status and prestige as well.
There has been little question about the lines of power since the
rise of the Tupou dynasty, when power was gained by force of
arms. Additional status and prestige of this line have been acquired
through the generations by strategic marriages, which is also part
of the traditional system. Today in a world not quite so attuned
to questioning which parental line is being activated on a particular occasion the prerogatives of one line can easily be absorbed
by another and people tend to overlook sidestepping. For example,
the present Kalanivalu is married to a daughter of Tu'i Pelehake
and their children will be entitled to the prerogatives of the
exalted Tu'i Tonga line (Kalanivalu being the ranking descendant
of this line). Tu'i Pelehake, however, is a stronger chief (being the
brother of the King) and in the next generation it is unlikely that
many will question from which parent certain prerogatives came
(except for knowledgeable members of the Tu'i Tonga line itself).

The rise and fall of chiefs by power and marriage may continue as in the past.

In the four *pongipongi* personal class rank and *kāinga* status were also acknowledged. The four women who served the kava to the new King, for example, were four of the high-ranking females of the kingdom (within the appropriate age group). Serving kava to the King acknowledged their high rank, but also demonstrated that in this societal context they were subservient to the King. During the ritual sharing of a pig among the assembled chiefs and *matāpule* of the *kai fono* (or relish) for the ceremony, the shares of food presented to the individual participants were ceremonially taken away by someone who individually outranked these high-ranking men within their *kāinga*. The fact that the King's *kai fono* was taken each time by a foreigner visually acknowledged that no Tongan can 'please himself' in regard to the King.

The preparation, ceremonial presentation, and acceptance of food at Pangai and Loto'ā during the first ten days of mourning were some of the most important aspects of Sālote's funeral. At funerals of chiefs tradition prescribes that mourners stay together for ten nights. During this period the people and Ha'atufunga must be fed and there should also be a distribution of food called *feipulua* in which the food is prepared and presented by the various *ha'a* and must include a large number of pigs. The *'umu* are prepared at the homes of the various relatives, brought together by *ha'a*, presented by the *ha'a* head, and then redistributed according to *ha'a*. The *feipulua* may be one, five, or ten days after burial and is more prestigious than the alternative food distribution, *feitu'uaki*, which is prepared in one community *'umu* near the place of the funeral and usually distributed the same day to the individuals attending the funeral.[25] *Feitu'uaki* is usually sufficient for funerals of commoners, but today some chiefs are beginning to use this form of food distribution. At Sālote's funeral food was prepared and presented from all the chiefly lines. Presentation of prepared food implies that the receiver is higher than the giver and is evidence of humility. The father's line being *'eiki* need only bring *tokonaki* (food that is not prepared). It is possible that the line of the Ha'a Takalaua might have been exempt from bringing prepared food, but Sālote's marriage into this line prescribed that it, too, bring food.[26]

The preparation and presentation of ceremonial food also serves an important educational function. Before the food and kava are presented at the palace, they have been presented one or more times previously—first on the village level, then to a chief more senior in the *ha'a* hierarchy and possibly again to the head of the societal division. Each time it is ceremonially presented and enumerated and then divided—a portion going to an appropriate person in that chief's *kāinga,* and only then is the rest given to the palace. At each level the presentation must be done in the proper way and there is no lack of *matāpule* to tell the unwary how to do it, or that they have done it wrong and to do it over again. Each level emulates what they have seen at similar presentations at a more *'eiki* level of the society. At Sālote's funeral there was a great lack of detailed knowledge among the ordinary people of what was going on. They knew what was to be done in their village as told to them by the chief or *matāpule,* but few knew how it all fitted together.

The next major temporal division was the period of time between the ten nights of intensive mourning *(faka-pō-hongofulu)* and the ceremonial observing of *faka-pō-teau* or hundred nights. During this period much time and creative energy was expended in making decorations for Sālote's grave. At the time of burial the grave was decorated with floral wreaths and shortly afterwards an extensive scaffolding of upright posts and cross-pieces to hold grave decorations called *tapu* was erected. The first several sets of *tapu* were made of flowers chosen primarily for their good smell and were changed on 30 December and periodically thereafter. These *tapu* were meant to be decorative but also meant to send a sweet smell to the grave. Meanwhile more elaborate *tapu* (mainly of *fau*) were being prepared for special presentations to the palace which would be accompanied by presentations of food. Within this temporal division, on 1 February, the Tongan radio station began again to play Tongan music, but only the compositions of Queen Sālote, which were meant to remind the people of Tonga of her good works. Because Tongan music expresses joy it was prohibited during mourning.[27]

The *faka-pō-teau* ceremony was held on 2 April. It, too, included extensive presentations of food, but differed from other such presentations. The main element of the ceremony, which took place at Loto'ā where the four *pongipongi* had been held, was the individual presentation of kava roots by the nobles to the King as a sign of their individual allegiance. Food and *tapu* were also presented but kava drinking was not part of the ceremony. The procession of some three hundred people from Fatai (the home of Tu'i Pelehake) to the palace was led by Vaea, each person bearing kava or food. Unlike a kava drinking ceremony where all partake, *faka-pō-teau* is characterized by giving without return. Following the presentation the coarse ragged mourning mats could be discarded. Some of the chiefs of outlying islands who were not able to attend the *faka-pō-teau* held separate presentations of food and *tapu* and pledged their allegiance to the new King.

Preparations continued for the final ceremony *hifo kilikili* which would take place on 14 June. The main element of this ceremony consisted of decorating Sālote's grave with oiled volcanic stones which would signify the end of mourning and the end of the Ha'atufunga's work. The appropriate *kilikili* stones are found only on the island of Tofua in the Ha'apai group and Vaea, in his position of Governor of Ha'apai, travelled in January to Tofua to organize the gathering of the *kilikili* stones. The five hundred sacks of *kilikili* were then personally called for by the King in February, taken to Tongatapu, and the task of sorting began.

The *kilikili* stones were sorted by size, the work done mainly by women who took part one or two days per week as members of their villages or as members of women's organizations such as Langa Fonua. *Hifo kilikili* was associated with the last series of presentations in conjunction with Sālote's funeral. The ostensible reason for the presentations was ceremonially to present oil to anoint the *kilikili* stones before they were placed on the grave. The oil was contained in glass bottles and decanters (traditionally gourds were used) and the bottles presented in ceremonial baskets of *kato alu* type, lined with a fine mat. The presentations of the oil to the palace were accompanied by food, kava, and sometimes by more *tapu* grave decorations. The presentation from Ha'apai through Vaea, for example, included, among other things, a truck-load of *'ufi* (yams), a huge turtle, a special funeral mat nine metres long and 2.4 metres wide of a type called *efu,* and a spectacular *tapu* of natural and royal purple *fau* ribbons made by Pilolevu College in Ha'apai. The presentation of the women's organization, Langa Fonua, included eighty baskets of bread (each of twelve loaves), four huge bags of sugar, eleven boxes of twelve bottles of oil, a *kato alu,* a large bark cloth, mats, and a *tapu* to decorate the gate of Mala'ekula.

Hifo kilikili itself took place on Mala'ekula beginning at 4 a.m. on 14 June when the Ha'atufunga assisted by their sons and male relatives began washing the *kilikili* stones in sea water in huge wooden bowls of the *sene* type. The clean *kilikili* were then placed on thick layers of black bark cloth and oil was poured on them. About 10 a.m. a ceremonial oil-bearing procession from the palace began bringing the oil that had previously been presented. The procession consisted of more than three hundred high-ranking females, many carrying a *kato alu* lined with a fine mat and containing decanters of oil. Other women (and a few men) carried more oil, mats, and black bark cloth. One of the ranking women was the eldest daughter of Kalanivalu, who wore a huge shredded mourning mat reaching from the ground to her head and carried a very large *kato alu* which had been presented at the palace the previous day by her younger sister. The last was a *kato alu toho,* a basket of such large size that it was pulled on a sledge. A further group in the procession consisted of a large number of women carrying *tapu* of brightly coloured European cloth attached in decorative ways to long poles. These, a gift of Tu'i Pelehake sent by his eldest daughter from Auckland, surrounded the perimeter of the entire area held by their female carriers for the duration of the ceremony. The decanters and bottles of oil in their decorated baskets were placed in front of the temporary shelter in which the King was seated. The oil decanters were carried to the area where the oiling of the stones was proceeding by members of the Ha'atufunga lines, assisted by the younger daughters of Tu'i Pelehake. The stones were then placed in specially made coconut-leaf baskets of the *'oa* type and carried to the bottom of the *mā'olunga* (tomb) where Ha'atufunga sat on the sides of each step leading up to the truncated sand pyramid on top of Sālote's vault. The baskets were handed up from one to the other to those at the top who placed the stones on the lower section of the pyramid while Ha'atufunga Lauaki stood at the top and directed the work. Other graves on Mala'ekula also received a new layer of *kilikili*. Wreaths were then placed on the various graves and flowers inside glass bowls were placed on Sālote's grave. The Ha'atufunga descended and Lauaki reported to the King that the work of the Ha'atufunga was completed. The King's *matāpule* Kioa acknowledged Lauaki's speech and the ceremony shifted its venue to the palace grounds where in the afternoon a large ceremonial presentation of food was to be made to the Ha'atufunga. There were left, however, baskets of pieces of red coral called *kilikili kula* which would be used later to further decorate the grave. At least some of these had been given by 'Eua during their presentation for the *faka-pō-teau*.

In the open space behind the palace (Loto'ā) a large number of people were seated and *matāpule* quietly took their places on the veranda. A procession of chiefs entered through the side gate of the palace grounds and included not only the nobles, but all the high chiefs, their sons, and grandsons, each carrying a kava root. The kava was deposited and then the larger kava roots were brought in, including twenty-seven *kava toho* many of which were pulled in on forked sledges, and lastly came one huge *kava toho tefisi*. More than nine hundred baskets of food were then carried in by men and women on carrying poles. Finally the cooked pigs were brought in including twenty-seven *puaka toho* of the largest size, many on high platforms dragged by twenty or more people. In contrast to usual presentations, the chiefs helped to bring in the food; Vaea, for example, brought in food four or five times. The King then took his place at the doorway at the centre of the veranda. The Ha'atufunga led by Lauaki then walked in a slow steady pace from their living quarters at the back of the palace grounds to the veranda. Some of the *matāpule* seated at the left side of the King arose so that Lauaki and some of the others could take their proper places. The seating of Lauaki in his place at the left of the King signified that his duties for Sālote's funeral were over and he could now proceed with his usual duties for the King. The ceremonial counting of the food from smallest to largest was then carried out with Lauaki participating in the recapitulation of the totals. After the two speeches by the *matāpule* Ma'umatāpule and Kioa, the chiefs filed out and the King left the doorway. As in the *faka-pō-teau* ceremony, kava was not drunk—the emphasis was not on sharing, but on giving.

Mourning officially ended at midnight on 15 June when a band played at the palace. On 16 June the *tukipotu* ceremony began at 8 a.m. when four grandchildren of Sālote ceremonially beat bark cloth to signify the lifting of the restrictions on making bark cloth and making noise. The *tukipotu* should be done by the *fahu* of the deceased, but as Sālote had no *fahu* the closest were her *mokopuna 'eiki*, grandchildren. After this ritual beating at the palace the women of Kautaha Fanamaka (a bark cloth making women's group) continued the *tukipotu* on the top of Sia-ko-Veiongo, an elevated rise in Nuku'alofa, and finally retired to their work house to finish.

In pre-Christian times the lifting of the mourning restrictions (*fakamalele*) for the Tu'i Tonga was the prerogative of two *falefā matāpule* Fakahafua and Tu'iloloko (now Malupō). This consisted of Fakahafua imitating a bustard-quail and Tu'iloloko presenting his bare bottom to the individual chiefs and *matāpule* who were assembled at the final ceremony. For this performance Tu'iloloko could claim for himself some of the *koloa* brought as gifts to the deceased.

The mourning was over. The bark cloths were laid out to dry the oil. The mats and bark cloth kept in the octagonal building on the palace grounds were sorted, refolded, and put away. The houses where the Ha'atufunga and *matāpule* had been living since Sālote's death were taken down. The children began to wear coloured clothes again. But the deathly silence remained. Bark cloth was not beaten,[28] black mourning clothes were still worn, large mats were still in evidence, and for many (especially the *liongi*) the mourning continued for another six months. Ha'atu-funga would continue to look after the grave and no one else was allowed to climb the tomb except for Sālote's two sons and her *mokopuna 'eiki* (grandchildren).[29]

Queen Sālote's funeral was in some ways atypical of *me'a faka'eiki* because Sālote's ancestry had been artificially skewed by cross-cousin marriage to prevent her line being outranked. Indeed, in the Tongan view a main reason for not marrying a relative is that on ceremonial occasions, and especially funerals, family relationships will not operate properly. A more typical funeral, in which the family relationships could operate properly, was the *me'a faka'eiki* of Hopoate who died on 10 July 1966, aged eighty-nine. Hopoate was the last person who stood in relation to the late Queen Sālote as *tamai* (father and male kinsman of his generation). A son of Wellington Ngu and a direct descendant of Tupou I, Hopoate was illegitimate by Tonga's Christian law and thus could not ascend the throne had the chance arisen, but his father's sister was the mother of Tupou II, making Hopoate a *tokoua* (kinsman of the same sex and same generation) of Tupou II, *tamai* of Sālote, and *kui* (kinsman of the grandparental generation) of the present King. Tupou IV because of his personal rank[30] was thus *mokopuna 'eiki* to Hopoate.

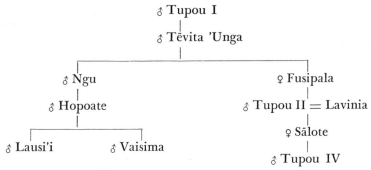

Fig. 7 *'Eiki*—'those who are high'—in relation to Hopoate

At the *me'a faka'eiki* of Hopoate kinsmen brought uncooked food and the *'umu* was prepared by those who were *tu'a* to Hopoate, the most conspicuous of whom was his son Vaisima, one of the most respected dance leaders of the kingdom who instructed the *lakalaka* dances of the sovereign's village Kanokupolu. Hopoate had died in the hospital and the doctor had prepared the body. The wake lasted only one night. The body was attended by four Ha'atufunga and Heu, who sat near the head. The *fahu,* however, was King Tupou IV and he came from Nuku'alofa to Lapaha to kiss the dead man. Before the King arrived the house was cleared of most of the people and a bark cloth pathway was laid from the dead Hopoate to the King's car. After kissing Hopoate the King left immediately and Heu, whose relationship to Hopoate goes back to Tupou I, continued to distribute the *koloa* as she wished.

Near the time for the final preparation for burial, which includes the wrapping of the dead person and placing him in his

PLATE 3   A happening frightening to both ghosts and men (*above*) The 'fight' between Volē Toilei'u and Sene (*below*) Lauvī Vela, the influential talking chief of Sa'anapu

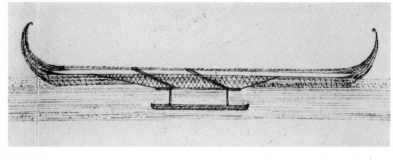

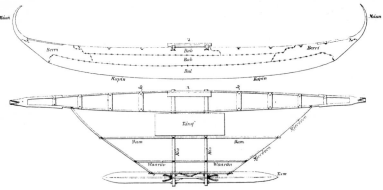

PLATE 4   Canoes from Mapia (*above*) A sketch by Samuel Hill 1816
(*below*) A sketch by J. S. Kubary

coffin, if one is used, there is a final period of wailing. This *tangi* is done mainly by the close female *kāinga* of the deceased, lasting for about half an hour, and the close male relatives come in to kiss the deceased for the last time. The women and girls are then sent away and the men do the final wrapping directed by the *fahu*. The deceased is then carried in a procession to the place of burial, which today is in one of the cemeteries established for the purpose in the villages, often associated with a church.

If the deceased was important in life, the procession may be led by the police band playing dirges and hymns while the church bells chime their most mournful sound. The funeral bier is usually carried by some twenty men[31] closely followed by several ministers of the church of the deceased. *'Eiki* mourners follow, then *tu'a* mourners, then secondary school children carrying the floral offerings. Individuals not related to the deceased, but belonging to an association of which he was a member, will walk as a group. The balance of the procession is made up of men and then women. If the deceased had chiefly connections, some of the high-ranking men and women may be waiting at the cemetery. A Christian service is held which includes the singing of hymns, and each of the ministers delivers a short remembrance. After this a high-ranking man (not necessarily closely related) will give a speech to thank people for coming. The wrapped or coffined deceased is placed in the ground with his head toward the sunrise, or into a vault on a mat and covered with sand, or the vault cover which may be cemented. If someone is already interred in the vault it must be shielded from the eyes of the populace. It may be surrounded with a large piece of bark cloth while the people are waiting or prepared before the procession arrives either by Ha'atufunga or, if the person is not of high enough rank to rate a Ha'atufunga, by the *fahu* or other persons who are *'eiki* to the deceased or by persons unrelated to him. The preparation consists of rewrapping the bones of previous occupants in bark cloth or covering the casket with a mat so the new individual can be laid on top. If the remains of the individuals already buried are *'eiki* to the new dead person, they may be placed on top of the newly interred. The gathered people all return to the home of the deceased for their share of the feast food if the distribution is a *feitu'uaki* and some will remain for five or ten days. During this time families or other groups will come with *hala* or *feitu'ui* (kava and bread or other food) to pay their respects to the dead person or the bereaved. Kava may be made and served and cooked food, along with mats and bark cloth, will be given in return. What is given in return is often of more value than what was brought.

After Hopoate's burial many remained at the house to mourn. The following day the Ha'atufunga lifted the *tapu* from the house

O

where the dead man lay with a *luluku* ceremony. The *luluku* liquid, composed of the juice of two green coconuts, a bottle of sea water, a bottle of Tongan oil, and pulverized *uhi* leaves, was sprinkled about the house and on its occupants with a tree branch. This rid the house of the *fa'ahikehe* spirits and it could be again used for eating and smoking. At the funeral of a commoner when there is no Ha'atufunga, the *luluku* is done by the *fahu*.

After the burial three *puako toho* were taken to the King, the King's brother, and the Bishop (Hopoate and his family are Catholic). The back portions of other large pigs were taken to Kalanivalu (the noble of Hopoate's village Lapaha) and other chiefs who attended.[32] The following day another *puaka toho* was similarly distributed, and another on the tenth day. Each of the other days *'umu* food was prepared and divided to feed the mourners. The three *puaka toho* distributed on the day of the burial were furnished by Hopoate's two sons and a nephew. The next day the *puaka toho* came from the eldest son, Lausi'i, and on the tenth day from Vaisima. The husbands of Hopoate's two daughters should have also contributed pigs, but extenuating circumstances prevented this. The food for the ten days was furnished by Hopoate's *kāinga* and *matakali,* that is, individuals related to him in any way, not just *kāinga,* including those related through his wife and the spouses of his children and grandchildren (and could include the legitimate descendants of Hopoate's father).[33] The use of the term *matakali* at a funeral implies that the individual is not acting in an *'eiki* or *tu'a* relationship of his own to the dead person, but rather is activating a *kāinga* or affinal relationship to some intervening person. It is mainly at a person's funeral that his whole *matakali* is activated. At Sālote's funeral if one were not *kāinga,* he might be *matakali,* but such relationships are easier to distinguish at the funerals of others.

Unlike the funeral of Sālote, in most cases everyone who comes to a funeral is permitted to enter the room. Each family comes as a group (mainly women) bringing food, mats, bark cloth or European substitutes and floral tributes. Before the flowers and *koloa* are taken to the room with the dead person and the *fahu,* they are first presented to a representative of the spouse or to someone of the line of the deceased's mother or father. The gifts are then taken to the room with the corpse and placed on the floor. Each person of the new group kisses the dead and either sits in the room with him and those *'eiki* to him, or goes outside to share in the work of those who are *tu'a*. The men who are *'eiki* usually form a circle outside and drink kava. If one is related in two ways, presentations must be made twice: one might go with the family of one's spouse and also with one's own family; or an individual may be related to the deceased through both his father and mother and each relationship must be acknowledged. It is during the wake that information about genealogical relationships is passed on to the following generations. And it is here that the food for gossip often originates. For example, the individual called to be *fahu* should go back in the ancestry of the father of the deceased to a brother and sister. Ideally this brother and sister should have chiefly blood, or in the case of a dead chief, it should go back to the highest chief possible.[34] The descendants of the sister of this sibling pair will provide the *fahu*. Today, however, with the progressive nuclearization of the family, the *fahu* called is often taken from only one generation back—the father's sister or her descendants, or even the descendants of a dead man's sister. For example, at Hopoate's funeral, his sister's child might have been *fahu*, but this did not occur—there was no gossip engendered by Hopoate's funeral. This proper way of choosing a *fahu* is characterized as *lohuloa*—that the *fahu* should descend through a brother-sister pair on the father's side no matter how far back.

Other funerals might have the opposite effect. For example, a young boy whose father's father was a noble (but his father was not) was accidentally killed. Instead of bringing the *fahu* from the line of the grandfather's sister or the great grandfather's sister, the *fahu* was the dead boy's father's sister (his *mehikitanga*). This improper way of choosing a *fahu* is characterized as *humataniu,* which implies family selfishness in that love is restricted to a few special people. This family was already in the local gossip for several other reasons and the closeness of the *fahu* furnished another reason to ostracize them for it reinforced a funeral *tapu* that they had broken a few months previously. On that occasion the family should have been *liongi,* but the eldest daughter of the family wore a small *ta'ovala* instead of a ragged mourning mat and sat close to the dead person instead of leaving the room and plaiting baskets outside as the *tu'a* people should do. It is likely, however, that families who fly in the face of tradition by choosing a close *fahu* or refusing to act as *liongi* do so deliberately in order to emphasize a choice which they as a family have consciously made. Usually such families are those oriented toward Western education or those who wish to de-emphasize the role of chiefs in Tongan society. By decreasing the role of more distant *kāinga* and increasing the role of the nuclear family, they remove themselves from the traditional social structure and must be prepared to go it alone at times of crisis, both materially and psychologically. In the instance cited above, there were both Western education and European friends from whom money was borrowed.

In 1975 it was apparent that such family nuclearization was increasing, often exemplified by the choice of close *fahu* for a funeral or improper behaviour of *liongi* (and in some cases no

one acting as *liongi* at all). Another way in which this tightening
of the family circle is seen is in the prior presentation of the
funeral gifts before they are taken to the *fahu*. Instead of the more
traditional three groupings of individuals related through the
kāinga of mother, father, and spouse, with a place provided for
each group for the presentation and recording of gifts, the *kāinga*
of mother and father may be collapsed artificially into one group
headed by a sister emphasizing the unity of the nuclear family.
Or if the deceased was not married, they might simply present all
the *koloa* to the *fahu* without prior presentation.

It is unlikely that gossip will be powerful enough to reverse
the trend toward attenuation of traditional kinship obligations.
Many have found that a money economy and traditional Tongan
values are not particularly compatible and that the Western idea
of individual achievement irrespective of chiefly birth is difficult
to reconcile with the retention of Polynesian values in everyday
life. Western educated, tightly knit nuclear families have found
funerals an avenue to resolve some of the inconsistencies. If a
family wants to change its interaction patterns to stress friendships
and associations instead of distant kinship obligations, a funeral
is an obvious occasion to do so. Today non-traditional funerals
are a consciously perceived alternate—the family will decide if the
funeral will be *tuku koloa* (*koloa* is brought and a return is expected) or *fakapalangi* (one may take a gift but a return is not
expected). It has been suggested above that the funerals of commoners are for the most part simply less grandiose versions of
me'a faka'eiki in which men's actions are prescribed by Tongan
principles derived from *kāinga* status. Indeed, the disregarding of
distant chiefly ancestors in favour of closely related kin is consistent with the apparent disregard of *ha'a* filiation by all except
those who might benefit by power play at high societal levels.
Funerals of the *'eiki* will doubtless continue to serve as a medium
for reconstituting chiefly alliances and assisting in the rise and fall
of chiefly lines, while funerals of commoners are likely to assist
in the nuclearization of the family.

The emphasis on *famili* and one's domestic group at the expense of the sublimation of *kāinga* in its traditional wider sense
is responsible for the 'new' social organization of Tonga as described by Decktor-Korn, Aoyagi, and others.[35] The 'traditional'
and the 'new' are nowhere better demonstrated than at funerals.
Traditionally one attended a funeral primarily because of one's
relationship to the deceased, and one's actions were prescribed by
this relationship. A funeral summarized the dead person's life
including the station of his birth in societal terms, his status among
his *kāinga*, and his personal achievements. The dead was the
focus of the recalled genealogical information, which recounted

his ancestry, his descendants, his *kāinga* and his *matakali*. Funerals demonstrated the social unity of Tongan society—for even the most humble of men there were *liongi* to mourn and cook, there were fine mats brought on their behalf, and others to take them. He was *'eiki* on this day if on no other.

According to Decktor-Korn,[36] who worked in Tonga mainly on a village level, *kāinga* attend funerals because of their relationships to the bereaved. In my view this can only be the case in the most Westernized of Tongan families, for where this happens Tongan kinship principles can no longer operate. Even in families that emphasize *famili* over *kāinga* it is primarily the relationship to the deceased that is activated and roles played at funerals often foretell future relationships to the deceased—for example, a girl may attend the funeral of the father of her fiancé, but her actions will be appropriate to her future family status. Even terms used for funeral gifts indicate relationship to the deceased. *Hala* are gifts that are the duty of those related as *kāinga* to the deceased, and a subdivision of this is *tuku fatongia,* which are gifts required of certain categories of blood relatives (that is, a man's real brother and *mehikitanga*). *Tuku ofo,* on the other hand, are given by those who are not *kāinga* to the deceased but who are activating a relationship to one of the bereaved, and may be friends, helpmates, or others, such as fiancé. It may be that *feitu'ui,* gifts of sympathy, are a response to this rather new concept of activating relationships to the bereaved rather than the deceased, or that a traditional concept has been extended to include gifts to the bereaved.

Traditionally funerals have been the time for *kāinga* to mend quarrels and broken relationships. They have been times for redistribution of *koloa* and food in which indirect reciprocity is activated by relationship to the deceased.[37] Individuals are alternately high and low depending on traditional kinship principles and a series of funerals will enculturate the participant into the intricacies of multidimensional ranking. Funerals activate rights, privileges, and duties within the traditional social system and constitute, perhaps, the last stronghold for its perpetuation. The evolving *famili*-dominated social system, which emphasizes the nuclear family, departs from tradition in several ways that are crucial for the retention of Tongan cultural identity as a Polynesian society. The concept of *kāinga* and its hierarchial ramifications is the substratum on which the Tongan social system is predicated. Continued attenuation of the *kāinga* concept must inevitably result in a society in which tradition-minded aristocrats are separated from others who no longer activate their distant relationships with the chiefs and look upon tradition as a quaint remnant of the past. Or a society may evolve in which the values are entirely those adapted from the Western world while 'tradition' in rather spurious forms is conjured up for tourists.

NOTES AND REFERENCES

1 The data used in this analysis were collected during one-and-a-half years of field work from 1964 to 1967 which included the entire funeral and mourning ceremonies of Queen Sālote from the time of her death through the end of the six-month mourning period. The data were checked during a further month of research in 1975. Field work was supported by Public Health Service Fellowship No. 5-F1-MH-25,984-02 from the National Institute of Mental Health, and by the Wenner-Gren Foundation for Anthropological Research to whom I wish to express my warmest appreciation. I also wish to thank the Government of Tonga under their majesties the late Queen Sālote Tupou III and the present King Tāufa'āhau Tupou IV, as well as the many Tongans who helped me in my work especially Sister Tuifua, Tupou Posesi Fanua, the Honourable Ve'ehala, Vaisima Hopoate, Nanisi Helu, Halaevalu Maile and Ana Tupou.

2 Churchward 1959:130.

3 Kaeppler 1971.

4 see *ibid.*:174.

5 The important factor being that descendants of a brother are *tu'a* to descendants of a sister, and thus *liongi*.

6 The important factor being that Vaea is Sālote's brother's son and thus *liongi*. Vaea is also 'low as related to Sālote through her mother but the relationship is not as close as through her father. Vaea is thus *tu'aua*, low to Sālote through both her mother and her father.

7 The mother of Lavinia (Sālote's mother) and Lepa was Tokanga, a chief from Niuafo'ou, in addition to the fact that Kalanivalu's second title was Fotofili (a title from Niuafo'ou), giving all the people of Niuafo'ou the status of 'diluted' *liongi*. Kalanivalu was also a *fa'e tangata*, but not so close as Lepa.

8 The *fahu*, however, might cut the hair of the *liongi* as an additional outward sign of their *tu'a*ness to the deceased.

9 See Kaeppler 1971:186 for genealogy.

10 See genealogy, p. 177. Incidentally Heu is the mother of the present Queen Mata'aho but this was not important at Sālote's funeral.

11 In some families the appearance of a white lizard is an omen of death.

12 Details on the appropriate material culture will be included in my forthcoming publication, *Material Culture in a Stratified Society: Tonga.*

13 Except school children who wore their school uniforms.

14 During the first two nights of *takipō* hundreds of people were milling around making quiet noise, mainly renewing friendships and not paying attention to the police who tried to keep the area clear and quiet. On the third night, after an announcement on the radio, all was quiet and everyone sat down. Traditionally funerals are held about 24 hours after death. As the Queen was embalmed it was possible to postpone her burial until overseas visitors arrived (although the burial of Tupou II was also left for more than one day). A recent innovation is to place the dead bodies in a refrigerated room at the hospital until relatives arrive from overseas.

15 During wakes there is usually much singing of hymns and sometimes special choirs or brass bands are brought in.

16 Besides food, money was also needed. For example, in the village of Ma'ufanga each individual was required to give £1.

17 *Langi* is only used for tombs of the Tu'i Tonga line. *Mala'e* is used for burial places of the Tu'i Kanokupolu line: *fa'itoka* is for commoners. This terminology may be relatively recent as it was not recorded by eighteenth-century visitors. Mala'ekula, the location of the royal tombs of the present dynasty, is in Nuku'alofa. Before its use as a tomb, it was an open space for celebrations, particularly a famous one at which everyone wore red, hence its name—*kula* meaning 'red'.

18 Some of the Ha'atufunga were also related to Sālote as *liongi* and thus should not have taken part as Ha'atufunga. It is said, however, that some in fact did take part, preferring to activate their Ha'atufunga prerogatives rather than act as prescribed by their *kāinga* relationships. It is also said

that these individuals sneaked down the back of the tomb so they would not be seen.

19 At this point in a funeral it is usual for a man who is *'eiki* to the deceased to extend his gratitude to the people and to detail the activities that remain to be executed in connection with the funeral, particularly the preparation and distribution of the food. Also, at this time the mats and bark cloth that had covered the corpse are gathered up and taken back to the house, where the corpse had been lying, for further distribution. It is said that the keeper of the graveyard can do what he pleases with the *kauala* or *fata*. At Sālote's funeral the *kauala* probably went to the Ha'atufunga who are the keepers of Mala'ekula.

20 According to the nineteenth-century literature, bodies were occasionally kept for some time before interment, including one example in which a child was not interred for seven years.

21 These rites are not reserved strictly for the sovereign. When Kalanivalu's wife died, he declared a six-month mourning period. The two high Ha'atufunga Lauaki and Takapu were brought in and had *nima tapu* for ten days and were fed for six months. It is said that the funeral of Ulakalala-Ata was even more 'spectacular' than Sālote's because Sālote directed it.

22 In contrast to the ordinary *'umu* presentations which were held at Pangai.

23 Were it not for the Christian concept of illegitimacy, Vaea would have a claim for being king today, see genealogy, p. 177. It is possible that Vaea's daughter will be the next Queen.

24 Ha'a Vaea does not include the title Vaea, which is included in Ha'a Havea.

25 It is said that Tungī Mailefihi instituted the *feitu'uaki* for more equitable distribution of food regardless of the presentations by *ha'a*. For 'less important funerals *feitu'uaki* is often preferred today because everyone receives a share of the food; whereas, because the *feipulua* is distributed according to *ha'a*, some of the food must be presented to individuals of status within the *ha'a* even though they did not attend the funeral.

26 Ha'a Takalaua is the line of the present King's father and they will be *'eiki* at the present King's funeral. It will be interesting to see how the *fahu* position will be dealt with at that time, especially in regard to the distribution of food, mats, and bark cloth.

27 European music was permitted. Non-Tongan noise was also permitted, such as blasting for the construction of the new wharf.

28 It was said that no woman wanted to be the first to beat bark cloth for fear of being the target of gossip—that she was a no-good woman who did not really feel the death of Sālote, that she was greedy, and did not have enough bark cloth on hand.

29 During the ceremony associated with the unveiling of a statue of Queen Sālote at Mala'ekula in conjunction with the Centenary celebration of the Constitution in November 1975, wreaths were laid by the King's eldest daughter and the Crown Prince accompanied by Ha'atufunga.

30 The important factors of his personal rank in this case is that Tupou IV's maternal great grandmother was the sister (and thus higher) of Hopoate's father; and that Tupou IV's father descends through higher lines than his mother—his connecting link to Hopoate.

31 Occasionally today a flat open truck is used (which saves constructing a *fata*).

32 A piece was also brought to me because I had been a frequent visitor at Hopoate's house because his son, Vaisima, was teaching me dances he had learned from Hopoate.

33 *Matakali* include people who are 'related' but not necessarily by blood and might also include, for example, the real parents of an individual's adopted children.

34 If there is no proper *fahu* the family should ask the chief of the village or the sovereign to send a *fahu* to the funeral. For example, in the funeral of a man whose father's father was a European, Queen Sālote sent a *fahu* because she had given them their land. The Queen sent the appropriate *koloa* and food to the funeral. At a chief's funeral, if the proper *fahu* has married a commoner, she may be replaced by someone more elevated.

35 Decktor-Korn 1974: Aoyagi 1966. The 'new' social organization was charac-

terized by my informants as the restriction of *kāinga* terms to close relatives. Whereas in the past the terms for siblings were extended to at least third cousins, today sibling terminology is usually used only for siblings and first cousins, and more distant cousins are referred to descriptively. This restricted use of *kāinga* terms is also spreading in the parental generation—the specific *kāinga* terms being applied only to parents and their siblings while those more distant are simply referred to as *kāinga*. Sometimes they are even called *matakali*, but this usually implies that they do not play an active part in the *'eiki-tu'a* duties and obligations.

36 Decktor-Korn 1974:9.

37 In *famili*-oriented funerals the more traditional idea of exchange has been changed to the idea that everything given to the *famili* must be repaid with something of equal value. Also they may not have the proper gifts to give in return (such as mats and bark cloth) and may give European gifts in their place (such as lengths of cloth).

First-child ceremonies and male prestige in the changing Kove society

ANN CHOWNING

The Kove or Kombe of West New Britain[1] have long been the subjects of as much fiction as verifiable, or even simply plausible, description. Some of the fiction—for example, that they make no gardens—is largely the result of careless observation; most Kove villages are now located on tiny offshore islets, while the gardens, on the mainland of New Britain, are hidden from view by a belt of mangrove swamps. But this accusation, along with others (as that they poison their enemies by putting battery acid into their food[2]) also owes something to the dislike in which they are held by the neighbours whom they try to dominate, and by the government and missions, whose influence they have resisted to a notable degree. Their poor relations with outsiders, and their insistence that they are maintaining traditional ways, reflect their self-image. They assert, first, that they are inherently superior to most if not all other human beings, and second, that the only way to prove oneself a proper Kove, a 'true man', is by conforming to the rules laid down by the elders and enforced by most villagers of both sexes. In explaining their culture the Kove constantly state that they do everything exactly as their ancestors did; innovation would produce failure. It comes as a shock to discover that their conservatism is as much a fiction as anything invented by outsiders.

A Kove village, at first sight, does indeed seem more 'traditional' than would be expected after more than sixty years of contact. Admittedly the clothing comes from trade stores, the children are playing hopscotch and marbles, and even the old women speak Pidgin English. But the women also spend all their spare time manufacturing pandanus mats and shell beads, the central items of the exchange system, while endless conferences are held in the elaborately decorated men's houses concerning the ceremonies at which the exchanges will take place. Each village is dotted with carved posts, planks, and platforms commemorating earlier ceremonies, and expert carvers are working on pieces to be used in the future. When the Kove say that they neglect commercial enterprises to engage in *wok tumbuna*, Pidgin for 'the work of the ancestors', one might reasonably assume that they refer to their own ancestors, and indeed they frequently say as much. Their statements are true, however, only if we interpret 'ancestors' as being no more remote than grandparents. The more distant ancestors were those of the inhabitants of other parts of New Britain with which the Kove first began intensive interaction after, and partly as a consequence of, the entry of Europeans into the region. In north-western New Britain, the early phases of European contact facilitated the development of richer art and ceremonies, and at least in the case of the Kove, much of this richness persists. As is usual in Melanesia, the present culture differs notably from that of pre-contact times, but only a portion of the changes has been in the direction of increasing Westernization. Along with some Western traits, the Kove have also adopted a considerable number from other indigenous cultures and have shifted their previous residence patterns and interests to create a new and unique amalgam, which they now present as largely traditional.

It is too late to reconstruct the early history of the Kove with any accuracy. Not only does it soon enter the realm of myth, but the myth itself has been greatly affected by the doctrines of a cargo cult that began shortly after the Second World War. Comparative linguistics indicates that the Kove are most closely related to other coastal dwellers to the west of them: speakers of Kaliai or Lusi (a dialect of Kove), Bariai, and the various dialects labelled Kilenge, which occupy the western tip of New Britain. Beyond New Britain, there are strong links between Kove and some languages of the Siassi Islands and of the north coast of New Guinea, but not with languages spoken farther east in New Britain.[3] It seems probable that the ancestors of the Kove were relatively late comers to New Britain, who entered by sea from the west and never moved far inland. In contrast to some of their neighbours, however, the Kove have no traditions of foreign origins; they think of themselves as having always lived where they are now, with the earliest settlements having been in the centre of the area, while the rest of it was uninhabited. According to some versions of the myth, they were created there. Contradictory versions exist regarding which places were inhabited while either of their two culture heroes, a father and son, was still around, just as the names and deeds of the two are hopelessly confused with each other.[4] Some sites associated with the myths are located a short distance from the sea, but only Vokumu, which extends to the beach, is thought to have been occupied after the culture heroes had departed the Kove area. The names of the culture heroes, Aragasi and Moro, are both translated into Pidgin as 'God', and Vokumu is often called 'God's place' and its inhabitants 'God's men'. Four or five generations before the birth of men who are now middle-aged, Vokumu broke up because of a quarrel, and each married man is believed to have settled in a new site, either offshore or on the mainland, his descendants becoming the senior and dominant patrilineage of the village he founded. Later many of these original villages were abandoned temporarily or permanently by some or all of their residents because of enemy attacks or internal troubles. If the senior patrilineage moved away and subsequently returned, its claims to dominance might be disputed by those who remained.

Prior to the coming of the Germans, incessant warfare—sometimes involving members of neighbouring linguistic groups, but often between different Kove villages—made it dangerous to live on the exposed islands, often little more than sandbars, that otherwise offered a welcome refuge from the mosquito-infested mainland. A few of the islands were originally settled from Vokumu and were occupied fairly continuously thereafter, but what now appears the typical Kove pattern, in which almost everyone lives offshore, is very recent, and a direct result of pacification. Considerable adjustment of traditional land claims was necessary before they all could find satisfactory dwelling sites within reasonable travelling distance of garden sites. The Kove now say that they would feel unhappy out of sight of the sea (only one present-day village is in the bush), but this attitude seems to have postdated their shift in residence. The strong maritime orientation on which they pride themselves is certainly relatively modern.

In the past warfare also inhibited travel. Today the Kove are renowned as traders, middlemen in a set of systems that once extended from New Ireland along the north coast of New Britain, on the one hand, and from western New Britain across the Vitiaz Strait to New Guinea, on the other.[5] According to several informants, however, it was only well after the exodus from Vokumu that the Kove became aware of the existence of any other people except the Kaliai and the inhabitants of the interior. One lineage claims that its members were the first to make contact with the Bakovi or Bola of the Willaumez Peninsula, the people of the French Islands (Bali-Vitu), and the Kilenge. The legends recounting the discovery of these new groups are suspiciously similar and full of improbable details, such as immediate ease of communication with the foreigners. It seems unlikely that they are trustworthy, and particularly unlikely that first encounters with all these groups were as recent as they suggest, given that other lineages believe that some of their distant ancestors came from Bakovi. But the evidence does suggest that voyages as far west as Kilenge date back

only to the time of partial pacification and the introduction of
cloth sails. Though there is some uncertainty, it seems likely that
the Kove did not ordinarily use pandanus sails; undoubtedly they
only used paddles, even a few years ago, to travel to Bali-Vitu.
Cloth sails, which are agreed to have facilitated long-distance travel,
are said to have been introduced by a man who worked for the
Germans in Micronesia.

By far the most important consequences of the new ease of
travel were direct contacts between the Kove and the Kilenge and
Bariai. The later groups are seen as the source of almost all present-day Kove art and ritual, and Kilenge still serves as the language in which songs should be composed. The Kove say that when
their grandfathers visited the Kilenge and Bariai, they saw and
learned from them how to make masks, to build decorated houses
in which pubescent girls are incarcerated, to manufacture elaborate
earrings in a variety of designs, and to carry out the many rituals
associated with men's houses, such as initiation ceremonies and the
use of different noise-makers to represent the voices of the spirits.
A Kove leader would buy the rights to the new paraphernalia,
dances, and ceremonies, often bringing a local expert back to teach
his lineage-mates the correct procedures. The innovations would
eventually be considered the property of the lineage and men's
house of the man who introduced them.

Most present-day Kove villages have several men's houses.
Some of these represent separate migrations to the village, and
others have resulted from splits, either because of quarrels or because an ambitious man wanted to lead his own group. In theory
it is bad to have two important men in the same men's house,
though in fact it is not uncommon for a set of brothers all to be
considered big men. When men's houses have separate origins
they also differ in the details of ritual, dances, mask designs, and
types of carvings that can be made by their members, while those
that have recently split may still share these and co-operate on
ceremonial occasions. Still, the proliferation of men's houses may
explain the fact that dances from the interior and the east, and
rituals from Bali-Vitu, were also borrowed along with those from
the west.

Each men's house is supposed to contain a single exogamous
lineage, but a man who has quarrelled with his brothers, or the
son of a widow or divorcee, may join his mother's brother or
brother-in-law, and consequently a few men's houses contain two
or more lineages, which may intermarry. In the past the members
of the senior lineage of the village, under the leadership of their
senior man, claimed authority over other village residents; they
could order their juniors to work, demand compensation for disrespect, and, they say, not risk retaliation by killing a man who

seduced one of their women. Nowadays, with such authority as exists largely in the hands of government-appointed officials,[6] relatively little attention is paid to the ranking of lineages, but enough prestige is attached to seniority for people to argue about whose ancestor was the first to reach the village.

Founders of men's houses are and were outstanding men, *mahoni*, a term the Kove usually translate as 'rich man' rather than just 'big man'. Distinctions are made between the closest kin of a *mahoni* (son, grandson, or nephew) and all other men, with the intention of discouraging aspirations to a position to which one has no hereditary right. If a man whose father was unimportant decides to build his own men's house, take a second wife, or sponsor a major ceremony, others are likely to ask, loudly and publicly, 'Who was your father? Did he make feasts and lead war parties? Did he make ceremonies honouring you? No, he was nothing, and you are the son of nothing.' If shaming does not discourage presumption, sorcery may be threatened. It is not impossible for a man from an insignificant family to become a *mahoni*, but it is difficult. It is said that in the past each village would only contain two or three *mahoni*, one to each men's house, with the head of the senior one superior to the others. They competed with each other and with the *mahoni* of other villages over the sizes of their men's houses, of marriage payments, and of ceremonies honouring their children, but apparently ordinary men made no effort to act similarly. Only the *mahoni* undertook major ceremonies, so that these were comparatively rare.

Nowadays, however, the majority of men wish to try to make a name for themselves. With the abolition of warfare, the only road to prestige is the sponsoring of ceremonies and the distribution of payments associated with them. Not only has the number of ceremonies increased dramatically, so that problems of scheduling arise within a single village, but the size of the payments that the sponsor is expected to dispense has become enormously inflated. Even if a man does not aspire to become a *mahoni*, he must now put a great amount of effort into simply earning and maintaining respect as a 'true man'. The need to acquire enough shell money to satisfy the expanded system of obligations is largely responsible for the picture the Kove present to outsiders of themselves as ceaseless travellers who are unable to raise enough food for themselves and so live off others and as inveterate opponents of attempts to 'bring them into the twentieth century'.

The basis of the whole exchange system is marriage. The initial payments are usually given by the groom's father and other senior kinsmen to the bride's parents, since young men control too little wealth to finance their own marriages. Once a child is born, however, its father must assume the responsibility of marking each stage in the development of the first-born, regardless of sex, by making a feast and distributing shell money to his wife's kin. The principal recipient should be the wife's oldest brother. Feasts should be made, and payments given, every time a first-born does anything for the first time—goes to the gardens, visits a strange village, has a haircut, learns to make sago—and also every time he is injured or sick. Among the Kaliai, similar payments are said to give the patriline rights over the child that would otherwise be shared by its mother's family, and also to compensate the latter if the child is harmed.[7]. Although such an interpretation would seem plausible for the Kove, they themselves insist that all the payments are really for the child's mother, part of the original marriage payments, even though they reach their culmination at what might be considered a puberty rite for the first-born child.

The sequence begins when a man gives his sister a preliminary gift of a valued item, which may be a dog, a wooden bowl, or a bag of rice. When he wishes to make a feast, he then requests repayment in shell money, which she obtains with the aid of her husband. A true sister receives the largest gifts and should contribute the most, but female cousins may be called upon in the same way. Additional funds are obtained by lending to other men who are making feasts; they should return the loan on demand, at one hundred per cent interest. When the man gives the shell money to his wife's kin (with due attention to repaying their gifts to his wife), they should return pandanus mats, at the rate of a pair for each fathom of shell money, and these are passed on to the women who contributed the shell money in the first place. Both men and women are likely to have many sets of debts, and are almost never in a position to satisfy all of their creditors at once. It is the mark of a successful man that he can collect enough to placate his wife's kin, who would otherwise scold and shame him, or even threaten to take back his wife or to kill him by sorcery. The wife is expected to range herself with her brothers, and Kove men say: 'It is hard to be married to a Kove woman; only a true man can manage it'. To go beyond preserving one's marriage, self-esteem, and life, to be able to give so much that one is acknowledged to be a *mahoni*, requires quite exceptional efforts and ability to influence and command others.

All fathers should sponsor one particularly large feast at the time when a first-born has his ears slit or, in the case of a boy, his penis superincised. In the past both sexes had their ears slit, and the penile incision was done at the same time, but pressures from the schools, which boys began attending earlier and in larger numbers than girls, led to ear-slitting being restricted to girls. While it is considered desirable, at least by the older generation, that all girls have their ears slit, it is not essential; even in the past, if a man died young, his younger daughters might not have the operation. Superincision, by contrast, is a necessity; the worst insult is to be addressed as 'stinking penis', and almost always another male kinsman will sponsor a boy whose father is dead. Although in theory a child is not marriageable until the operations have been carried out, they are often done when the child is so young that they can hardly be called true puberty rites.

The basic operations need not be major ceremonial occasions. These latter tend to be reserved for the time when a girl, her ears healed and stretched, first appears wearing the earrings of her patrilineage, following a long period in which she has been secluded in a tiny raised ornamented house, the *luma-galiki*.[8] While she is in seclusion, her father calls in debts, has masks manufactured, and sponsors the numerous preliminary dances and feasts that precede the climax at which the girl emerges. His wife's kin, the ultimate recipients of the shell money, must act as his 'labourers' during this period, collecting and preparing food for the feasts, drumming and singing at the dances, and above all travelling to distant villages to put pressure on the debtors. The sponsor's delight in ordering about his affines during this period balances his fear of their retaliation if he does not eventually satisfy them.

If the sponsor is himself an artist, he will do much of the work of carving the posts supporting the display platforms and the *luma-galiki*, and the planks and other adornments on the *luma-galiki*, with designs associated with his own and his wife's lineages, and others that he may invent for the occasion. Otherwise he hires another artist to prepare these. (The planks will eventually adorn his men's house or dwelling house, while the posts are simply left standing until they decay.) Meanwhile the men of his lineage, in great secrecy, produce pairs of masks in designs belonging to them or, if their ritual is different, prepare the headdresses associated with their special dances, the *sia* (originally from the Siassi Islands) or the *baruku* (originally from the Willaumez Peninsula). A rich man will pay for additional masks to be made by his wife's lineage and other more remote kinsmen of his child. The masks are displayed at a series of all-night dances followed by distributions of food, partly as a means of attracting the debtors and collecting from them. During this period the girl, who may be accompanied by younger sisters, is in theory completely hidden, only coming out under a mat or entering her parents' house after dark. In fact, if the emergence ceremony is long delayed or the girl is very young, she may be permitted to walk around the village during the night or even paddle off during the day, again hidden under a mat. Girls say that the acclaim they receive when they emerge, and the prestige of being the object of such a ceremony, amply compensate for the tedium of the time spent in seclusion.

The emergence follows an all-night parade of maskers, and is an elaborate affair in which the girl, heavily adorned in a distinctive fashion, is escorted from the house and around the village by masked figures, dancers, drummers, and other rejoicing kin. She is then displayed on an ornamented platform, often in the company of younger siblings who may then have their ears or penes slit. Goods such as baskets and food are distributed to everyone present, and finally the shell money is paid to the girl's maternal kin. Pay may be higher if more than one child is involved, but not as high as if each were done separately. The first-born son of a leading *mahoni* told me that his father held separate ceremonies for each of his ears, slitting and placing earrings in them one at a time in order to maximize the display involved. (The same *mahoni*, in 1972, distributed 1,844 fathoms of shell money when his first-born daughter by another wife emerged from seclusion. The sum, at that time the equivalent of an equal number of Australian dollars, is said to have been the largest ever distributed in north-western New Britain.)

In the past the first-born daughter of a *mahoni* might also be given special treatment of other sorts. She might go naked until adulthood, and not be taught any female tasks, but be served by other girls. Such treatment suggests partial assimilation of her role to a man's, in a society that normally insists on strict segregation of male and female roles, and she might also be permitted to enter the men's house and learn some of its secrets, both of which actions are forbidden to ordinary women. The extreme cases of honouring such a woman included teaching her sorcery and all of the ritual associated with the men's house, so that she might act as a *mahoni* in her own right.

Nothing comparable is reported for boys. In some cases a boy might be placed in a *luma-galiki*, in a separate room from any sisters, rather than following the more common practice of staying out of sight in the men's house until he appeared wearing earrings. One elderly woman whose first-born son was put in a *luma-galiki* says that this was commonly done to boys, but her statement is contradicted by other information; if the practice once was common, it seems to have died out long before boys stopped having their ears slit.[9] It does seem that the son of a *mahoni*, especially a first-born, might be kept in seclusion for a long time, but there is no suggestion that he departed dramatically from the normal male role.[10] Only girls were truly set apart. The fact that girls receive more attention than boys in this patrilineal society[11] does not seem to reflect any mystical notions about female powers or fertility;[12] rather a daughter—particularly a first-born daughter, but any daughter if the first-born is a son—gives the present-day father an opportunity to make a greater name for himself than he can by honouring his son.

It is not clear to what extent the Kove may have altered the ceremonies since they first acquired them, nor whether the Kilenge paid more attention to girls than to boys.[13] The Kove still carry on some ceremonies which the Kilenge have abandoned, but the form may have been changed.[14] Today's ceremonies do fit into a complex of traits which certainly have changed through time. Although adolescent girls now have a measure of freedom, particularly to choose their husbands, they are still much more under parental control than boys, and can better serve as objects of their fathers' ambitions. In theory, after marriage they remain at the mercy of their brothers, but in fact the situation alters radically when a woman begins to participate in exchanges herself. Originally, it is said, the mere fact that the woman was given in marriage provided the stimulus for her husband's subsequent payments, and only men were involved in the transactions, using shell money that they obtained initially from trade, inheritance, or previous payments. Now a man concentrates his attention on his true sisters and other women in the sister category, constantly giving presents in the hope of receiving shell money when he needs it to pay his wife's family. The money itself is no longer manufactured in the places from which it once came, and the Kove now make it themselves, with the work increasingly being done by women. Men are turning from traditional crafts, such as carving betel-mortars and pudding stirrers (so-called 'taro spoons') and from trading expeditions to Kilenge to get pots and wooden bowls of foreign manufacture, to producing a new type of carving for sale to tourists. They then use the proceeds to buy trade-store goods for their sisters,[15] who may also receive direct donations of cash, as well as beer with which to ply their debtors. Except for the beer, which they rarely drink, women now benefit from the cash economy at least as much as men do.

Women also participate equally with men in scolding and shaming those who do not fulfil their exchange obligations, and although it is true that only men threaten sorcery,[16] shame seems to be almost as powerful a sanction in forcing conformity. Women acquire some prestige both as daughters honoured by ceremonies and, when they help their husbands repeat the process for their children, as mothers, but it is through the transactions that occupy so much of their time as wives and sisters that they have the greatest opportunity to act independently and to affect the statuses of both their husbands and their brothers. However often Kove men assert that men are superior and women must listen to what they say, male prestige is only maintained by constant attention to the demands of kin of both sexes.

P

Comparative data from other parts of West New Britain[17] suggest that even before they started visiting Kilenge, the Kove had first-child ceremonies of some sort, just as they had men's houses and affinal exchanges. But all of these seem to have been relatively simple affairs, of slight concern to the average man, who could achieve respect without a great deal of effort. It is easy to see why the Kilenge ceremonies appealed to the *mahoni* as a new route to prestige; it is less clear why almost everyone in the society became and remained involved in using the ceremonies and the associated exchanges for personal ends. The Kove, well aware of how they contrast with their neighbours in their focus on these activities, often express bafflement about their devotion to what they call 'rubbish', shell money and the reputation it buys. Equally often, they express a desire to discard the whole system and devote themselves to 'business', but they tend to agree that unless everyone consents to its abolition, the pressures on the individual to conform are too great to resist. At present the system is still expanding. Possibly because people have not accumulated much wealth when their first-born children are growing up, they now tend to hold equally or even more impressive ceremonies for subsequent children, and men often speak of hoping to dispense more shell money than anyone in their village or in all of Kove has given before. Certainly the system has it positive features. Though quarrels rage incessantly over gift and counter-gift, the art, dances, feasts and ceremonies associated with the process of acquiring a reputation afford a great deal of pleasure not only to the Kove but to their immediate neighbours, who also participate. One man also pointed out that the modern extension of 'gifts' and loans to distant kin in remote villages is the single factor that has overcome traditional rivalries and hostilities that so often led to inter-village fighting in the past. The involvement of an increasing number of individuals in competition for prestige, while divisive on one level, has equally served to unify the Kove, who are bound together in an intricate network of debt. The interdependence has also heightened awareness of what is distinctively Kove about the present culture.

At the same time their boasting about both individual achievements and the supposed retention of traditional ways often sounds defensive. One young would-be reformer said to me, 'They don't realize that the things they're so proud of don't impress anyone outside of Kove'. But in fact their ambivalence is quite openly expressed. At the end of 1975 it was proposed that all the Kove appoint officials to enforce a drastic limit on the amount of time that could be spent on a single ceremony, so that they can avoid the present delays of weeks or even months during which the sponsor tries to collect debts and his wife's kin stay in a foreign village waiting for the final distribution. The time saved is to be devoted to earning cash and to community enterprises such as schools. The compromise sounds ideal; the Kove can continue to hold the ceremonies that have come to mean so much, but the steady acceleration would be braked, and so would their increasing divergence from other New Britain societies. But although people express enthusiasm for the idea in the abstract, within the same day they are complaining of the inadequate sum just received from a debtor and laying plans to acquire much more at the next transaction. For the large majority of the Kove, the rewards of the present system, and the penalties for abandoning it, will probably outweigh the opinion of the outside world for a con-siderable time to come.

NOTES AND REFERENCES

1 The Kove, known to outsiders as Kombe, occupy the Kombe Census Division on the north coast of New Britain immediately to the west of the Willaumez Peninsula. One breakaway village, Tamoniai, is situated far to the west in the Bariai Census Division. Field work carried out between 1966 and 1969 was supported by the Australian National University, and that between 1971 and 1976 by the University of Papua New Guinea. Some of the material in this paper was included in an earlier article, Chowning 1972.
2 I assume that this is fiction because of the unlikelihood that any substantial amount of battery acid could be ingested in the bland local food without detection.
3 See Chowning 1973.
4 Riesenfeld 1950:273-4 cites a version that differs considerably from any that I have collected. His reference is confused, and I have not been able to consult the original.
5 For the latter, see Counts 1970; Harding 1967.
6 One of the results of Kove resistance to government influence is their refusal to join a local government council. As of 1976 they still retain the luluai system instituted by the Germans.
7 Counts 1970:92-3.
8 *Galiki* is the nickname for all girls in seclusion. In fiction, it is also the standard name for an unmarried heroine, a fact that suggests that the seclusion was once more closely connected with marriageability.
9 The first-born son of the old woman is estimated to be in his 50s; the youngest men with slit ears seem to be in their 30s.
10 Possibly because they found the male role too rigid to accept, at least two Kove men have become transvestites, but they are regarded with derision.
11 In some matrilineal societies in New Ireland (see, e.g., Neuhaus 1962:305ff.), pubescent girls were incarcerated for a considerable period, but we have no evidence of diffusion between these areas, though there are suggestive similarities in some of the myths (see Riesenfeld 1950:245, 247).
12 Cf. Salisbury 1965:72.
13 See Dark 1974:48.
14 Kove attitudes towards the symbolic aspects of masks and other ritual paraphernalia differ notably from those reported by Dark and Gerbrands for the same materials in Kilenge.
15 Even during the food shortage caused by the 1972 drought, women com-plained that their husbands used most of their cash to buy rice and flour for their sisters, in hopes of receiving shell money in exchange, and brought only a little back for their own families.
16 A woman may help her brother sorcerize her husband, but she also fears being sorcerized by her brother if she does not pay her debts to him.
17 Chowning and Goodenough 1971:146-7; Laufer 1951.

An Australian moving frontier in New Guinea

FRANCIS WEST

A moving frontier, in Frederick Jackson Turner's sense of a belt of free land at the edge of settlement which lures successive waves of people who there forge a society different from that of their origins, has found little favour with historians of Australia. Despite the similarities between Australia and North America, Turner's thesis has never seemed an adequate explanation of the history of European settlement within the Australian continent. Nor, although until the last quarter of the nineteenth century there was a belt of free land in the islands of the south-west Pacific, have Pacific historians found much use for Turner's moving frontier, except perhaps in the case of Hawaii and the American frontier which moved beyond the west coast into the North Pacific. One American historian, D. C. Gordon, indeed called his book *The Australian Frontier in New Guinea 1870-85* and made his reverence to Turner in a chapter entitled 'The Missionaries Open the New Guinea Frontier'. Gordon distinguished between frontiers which were political boundaries and those which were the border between settlement and wilderness. Having done so, he then concerned himself with the Australian frontier in the political, European sense of Sir Keith Hancock: a frontier was 'something fixed. It is the sharp edge of a sovereign state. In books dealing with American history the frontier is something moving. It is the advancing fringe of a dynamic society'. Such a fringe did indeed advance, from Australia and New Zealand, into the South Pacific Islands during the nineteenth century, but it was not really a frontier in Turner's sense. For the dynamic of his moving frontier was land and then settlement upon it, and the South Pacific Islands have been, to use a French distinction, not colonies of settlement but colonies of exploitation.

That distinction was not always obvious to men in the 1870s. When the Reverend James Chalmers and his wife joined the Reverend W. G. and Mrs Lawes on the London Missionary Society frontier in New Guinea in 1877, he at least found it necessary to discourage the idea of a settlers' frontier. Speaking to the Royal Colonial Institute at the meeting of 11 January 1887, he said:

nowhere have I seen our boasted civilisation civilising, but everywhere have I seen Christianity acting as the true civilisor . . . We need no more territory whilst Australia with its wide acres is still unoccupied, and will be so for another century. Moreover, New Guinea is never likely to become a land fit for colonising. Its position and climate are both against it . . . the young, pushing, daring Anglo-Saxon colonist would look upon the 'nigger' as something to be got rid of, at all events as a nuisance in his way.[1]

By colonization, Chalmers understood European settlement, not the transient activity of gold prospectors, traders, labour recruiters; and in this belief he opposed the annexation of New Guinea which he believed would encourage such settlement. In fact the British annexation in 1888 did not produce a colony of settlement any more than did the German to the north, nor yet Australian control in Papua in 1906. Those Europeans who settled on land were either the employees of large companies or individuals who had little thought of remaining as permanent residents. New Guinea was not 'a land fit for colonising'.

Or, at least, it did not seem so until the discovery of the grass plateaux of the central highlands. After the initial discovery by missionaries and prospectors of the grass valleys behind the high mountain ranges of the interior, the first systematic examination of the highlands by the patrol of J. L. Taylor and the Leahy brothers in 1933 produced such statements as:

a fine grass upland region, which may prove to be the best and most important part of the New Guinea of the future,[2]

and, after Taylor's and J. Black's Hagen-Sepik patrol of 1938:

I think we should adopt the policy of the government of Kenya and reserve the highlands of New Guinea for Europeans . . . the existence of these highland areas make New Guinea . . . something between a second Java and a second New Zealand.[3]

Taylor had a vision, in detail, of the kind of settlement which ought to happen: European farms and townships offering work to the natives who should also be encouraged to develop their own land for productive crops. He assumed, as did many of the early entrants into the highland valleys, that the indigenous settlement on spurs and ridges separated by unused or unoccupied land left large areas of this temperate, green and fertile grassland available for European settlement. In the six years between the 1933 patrol and the outbreak of the European war unofficial voices raised the same point, usually in the context of lack of any government policy about settlement, culminating with criticism of Taylor's 1938 patrol for its high cost (about £40,000) and lack of any expert survey of settlement potential.[4] The valleys of the Central Highlands were, in short, to both official and unofficial observers, a free belt of land at the edge of settlement in New Guinea.

That belt of land certainly lured gold prospectors and missionaries. After the good claims at the Edie Creek gold strike had been exhausted by 1928, a number of prospectors penetrated over the Ramu-Markham fall into the Eastern Highlands. Rowlands, Ubank and the Peadons were working claims before the Leahy brothers publicly revealed the extensive grass uplands in the mountainous interior after their 1930 journey across the Eastern Highlands. The Lutheran missionaries at Lihona, on the northern, coastal slope of the Bismarck Range, who had described the grass lands to Hauptmann Detzner during the First World War,[5] and from whose station the Leahys set off in 1930,[6] themselves followed the prospectors into the grasslands to establish their own stations. In 1934 Catholic missionaries of the Society of the Divine Word, who in 1932 had heard at their Bundi station on the northern face of the Bismarcks of the big valley over the range, penetrated into the highlands down the Chimbu valley.[7] This history of discovery is well known, if only because the question 'Who was the first?' has been answered and argued over by the early entrants to the valleys and by later writers.[8] The material and spiritual gold rush into the highlands which occurred between 1930 and 1935 was followed at the time by a literary gold rush,[9] and since 1950 by an academic, primarily an anthropological, one.

The miners' and the missionaries' frontiers were of different kinds. A gold prospector worked a creek or river-bed until he found payable gold and then exhausted it before moving on to another claim, or he failed to find gold and moved on; such a man was a transient not a permanent settler. A missionary seeking to lay up treasure in heaven might, as an individual, move from one station to another after a few years, but his relief or replacement nevertheless meant a permanent, not a transient mission settlement. But permanent or transient, both frontiers involved land. A miner, with his 'line' of at least a score of workers, obviously needed land for his camp and might, if the locals could not or would not supply food, need land for gardens. A missionary needed land for his house, quarters, church, school and gardens. In the highlands, because of the difficulty and the slowness of land communications, both miners and missionaries needed land for temporary or permanent airstrips. Of course this demand for land was not on the scale required by European plantation settlement, but that is a European statistic. To any local community, a miner's camp, a missionary's station, and the airstrips of both might amount to a considerable demand upon land. For example, in 1934 the Catholic mission entered the Chimbu valley from Bundi and walked along the Wahgi valley to Mount Hagen, marking sites for mission stations along the way. On Father Ross' count, nine such sites were then marked, and a tenth in 1935; two of them, at Mingende and Wilya, were intended to be central stations.[10] The latter began to be removed in 1935 to Rebiamul and for this station the area of land involved was two hundred acres. From Wilya, between June and September 1934, nine further outstations had been established; this was the land settlement, within a few months in 1934, of a single central mission station.[11] The Lutheran missionaries, moving into the highland valleys from the east in the track of the Leahys' 1930 expedition from Lihona, also established two central stations and placed catechists in at least as great a number of sites as the Catholics, and usually not far distant from them. Indeed, the two missions leap-frogged along the highlands all the way to Mount Hagen; by 1935 there were ten European missionaries and seventy-four helpers.[12] One contemporary observer thought that all the dispositions were made for a great inter-mission battle, which took the form of placing native catechists and teachers in as many highland communities as there were available personnel to peg out a spiritual claim.[13] Each such outstation required land. The total acreage was not extensive but in the case of any particular highland group it might represent a significant fraction of garden land, land occupied and used by European and non-European strangers who, whether they regarded themselves as permanent or transient, must nevertheless have seemed permanent to the communities in which they settled until such time as they actually left, as unpredictably as they had come.

That unpredictability of European arrival and departure was not the only unpredictable aspect of land settlement. Because the miners' and the missionaries' frontier moved ahead of the government's frontier, there could be no land purchase under the Land Ordinance which required government officers to survey the land, buy it from the owners and then make it available as leasehold to the European settlers.[14] In an uncontrolled area, this procedure could not be followed. What happened in the highlands was unofficial. The Catholic missionaries, for instance, tried to find out in which groups they would be welcomed or invited to stay and land made available; then they marked out the site and bought it from the owners for payment in European steel tools, cloth and 'traditional' shell currency and valuables.[15] In the missionaries' view they became what Father Nilles called the 'natural' owners of the land.[16] At Mount Hagen, when Father Ross moved the mission site from Wilya to Rebiamul, the original land 'returned to the former native owners' and the owners of the new site were 'very well paid in axes, spades, knives, cloth and shells, so that to this day there have never been any complaints or repercussions'.[17] Father Ross' account of the Wilya-Rebiamul land purchase differs from the practice of his colleagues in the Chimbu. There, when a mission station was moved, ownership of the land originally purchased did not return to the former owners, although they might be allowed to use such land.[18] Nor does Father Ross mention that he received any payment from those original owners who reoccupied the Wilya land.

Leaving aside the notoriously difficult question of applying European concepts of land ownership and tenure to indigenous land custom, this early mission settlement in the highlands produced the confusion involved in moving mission sites and the further confusion that, in the absence of administration officers, 'natural' ownership or title was not recognized by the government until, at a later date, its officers went through the procedure established by the Ordinance of surveying the land which had been unofficially 'bought' by missionaries and miners, determining whether the natives were willing to sell, whether the land was surplus to their present and future needs, and then obtaining from the European 'natural' owner the price of the land, at an official rate, to be passed on to the native owners.[19] So the European paid twice for each of those early land transactions, and the owners were twice paid. The native owners, in Father Nilles' opinion, concluded that the Europeans were fools.[20] Some missionaries retained a bitterness against the government on this score which was intensified by other aspects of the frontier as it moved into the highlands.

The miners' and missionaries' frontiers ceased to move in 1935. The immediate cause of this was the Catholic settlement in the Chimbu. One of the outstations was built on land at Womkana. In December 1934 Father Cornelius van Baar discovered that the mission house had been burned down.[21] He told the Womkana people to rebuild it or, on his next visit, he would shoot three of their pigs by way of compensation. When the house was not rebuilt, Father van Baar, en route with Father Morscheuser for Bundi, together with a mission helper shot three pigs. The mission party, on its way from Womkana, was then attacked and Father Morscheuser killed. In January 1935 Brother Eugene, on his way through the Chimbu valley, was attacked at Gogolme and later died of his wounds in the hospital at Salamaua. These two murders of missionaries, men who in the eyes of the Australian press were men of peace and goodwill, obliged the government to act to protect the unofficial Europeans in the uncontrolled area. Since 1925 there had been an Uncontrolled Areas Ordinance upon the statute book of the Mandated Territory of New Guinea which required entrants to such areas to have a permit to enter.[22] Those permits were intended to ensure that any unofficial European should be properly equipped to enter new country, a criterion which in theory required of the European four years experience with coastal natives and an escorting party which carried four rifles and was experienced in their use.[23] In practice, especially at the time of the Edie Creek gold rush, this requirement could not be strictly enforced, nor could unofficial people who were not properly equipped to that standard in practice be prevented from entering new territory. Nor were they. There were complaints from prospectors in the Eastern Highlands in the early 1930s about the presence of inexperienced miners;[24] the murder of Captain Bernard McGrath in the Eastern Highlands in 1933 was the occasion of one such complaint, coming as it did after numerous thefts from and attacks upon miners working in what was called the Upper Ramu and Purari area,[25] and the killing of Assistant District Officer Ian Mack by highlanders at Aimontina, two miles walk from one of the two government stations in the highlands in June 1933. Still, miners and government officers were presumed, in their public and press image, to be able to look after themselves. Missionaries, men of peace even if, like Father Ross, they carried a .38 calibre revolver rather than a crucifix to show highland natives he met during his journeys near Mount Hagen,[26] were believed to need government protection.

In 1935, under the Uncontrolled Areas Ordinance, the Administrator exercised his power to regulate entry. No new unofficial entry was permitted, but miners and missionaries already established in the highlands were allowed to remain under restrictions upon their movements which confined them to the immediate vicinity of their camps or posts.[27] A missionary's permit was endorsed with the names of the groups he was allowed to visit. That caused some anger. In February 1938, for example, the Lutheran missionary G. F. Vicedom's permit allowed him to visit the whole of the groups endorsed on Father Ross' permit but not vice versa. The patrol officer then stationed at the Mount Hagen police post suggested that Vicedom's permit should be re-endorsed to restrict him to an area mutually agreed with the Catholic missionary.[28] This was in effect a 'zoning' arrangement which neither mission liked. Vicedom, in particular, protested that this worked in favour of the Catholics and against the Lutherans;[29] and in the face of this argument, the patrol officer suggested that all groups should be included on both permits, because 'zoning' could not officially be enforced.[30] Vicedom, however, had another ground for complaint. The Lutherans made more extensive use than the Catholics of catechists living with highland groups and not immediately under European supervision. The government's restrictions under the Ordinance required the removal of such unsupervised catechists and teachers from any area which could not be visited by a European clergyman. And this, in Vicedom's view, penalized the

Lutheran mission to the gain of the Catholics.[31] He made no impression upon the local government officers, one of whom in response to his arguments in September 1938 and again in January 1939 that areas close to Mount Hagen were safe enough for tribesmen to walk to dance grounds without weapons, simply reported that the time was far from ripe for any relaxation of the restrictions upon European movements.[32] Indeed in October 1939 the Director of District Services and Native Affairs recommended that fifty per cent of the Lutheran mission teachers and helpers at the main Ogelbeng station should be removed from the highlands.[33] A year later he repeated that the government had no intention of relaxing the restrictions on native teachers which prevented the kind of movement by European missionaries that had led to the killing of Father Morscheuser and Brother Eugene in 1934 and 1935.[34] Indeed in July 1940 a government officer, George Greathead, had gone further and removed two Catholic missionaries, because one priest had infringed his entry permit by taking another unauthorized priest with him on a visit and concealing the fact.[35] That particular incident caused some bitterness in government-mission relations because, in Greathead's opinion, one Catholic priest had tried to influence him on the grounds of their common religion, a bond which was always doubtful in the Mandated Territory where co-religion was apt to be overtaken by anti-German sentiment against both Catholic and Lutheran missionaries.[36]

These tensions between government and missions obviously arose after the official frontier of law and order caught up with the unofficial one of missionary and miner enterprise. When the Upper Ramu valleys were officially discovered in 1930-31, they came within the district whose headquarters were at Madang on the north coast of New Guinea, but with the discovery of gold on the headwaters of the Purari in 1932-33 the Eastern Highlands region was transferred to the district with headquarters at Morobe, also on the coast to the south-west of Madang and close to the northern border of Papua, until, in 1937, the highlands reverted to Madang district. Within the highland region administration was conducted from a series of base camps which were not continuously manned by European officers. In September 1932 the first such camp was established in the Upper Ramu, followed by a second in the Purari headwaters.[37] After McGrath's murder, an advance post was set up at Finintegu in the area known as Bena Bena.[38] In 1933 the patrol which penetrated through the Chimbu into the Wahgi valley and west to Mount Hagen, set up a fourth base camp, the Gormis post, near the mountain.[39] None of these posts was continuously manned; they were used as bases for patrol work in the surrounding areas as need arose: for patrols following Mack's and McGrath's deaths, and for the exploration around

Mount Hagen. After the missionaries' deaths in the Chimbu, two further base camps were established: one at Kundiawa, near the Ege station of the Lutheran mission, the other in the middle valley at Goromei (Gogme or Gogolme) close to the scene of the killings.[40] In 1938 a base camp was established at Wabag, to the west of Mount Hagen, during the Hagen-Sepik patrol.[41]

The methods which the government used to push forward the frontier of law and order were those already used in New Guinea before the discovery of the highlands. From the base camps a European officer with an escort of armed native police patrolled within an accessible radius, walking from village to village, at first making contact and distributing small gifts, on later visits explaining and finally enforcing the government's rules relating to fighting, murder, sanitation and so on. To maintain and extend the influence gained by a patrol, the government appointed in each group a headman, a luluai, to secure compliance with its rules and to report offences. Occasionally an unsupervised detachment of the police or even a single policeman was stationed in an area,[42] and obviously when a European officer was on patrol, his base camp might be staffed only by a few police. That in outline was the system of native administration already in being in the Mandated Territory and applied to the newly discovered areas. In practice, however, it had to be applied with a difference. Where, for example, in other parts of New Guinea or Papua, a post or base camp was generally sited for convenience of access to concentrations of population and ease of access to neighbouring settlements, in the highlands the use of aircraft necessarily meant that a station was sited rather with reference to suitable ground for an airstrip than to the density of indigenous population. Because among highland societies warfare and fighting were major features of life and indigenous settlements were sited for defensive purposes on spurs and ridges, available and suitable ground for an airstrip tended to be, like the land 'sold' to missions, in the no-man's-land which separated groups from each other and therefore, incidentally, the government airstrip and station from them. Where a mission had established a station with an airstrip, exactly the same conditions applied. Hence, as in the Chimbu valley, the proximity of government to mission station. Hence, too, the complaint of the government officer stationed in the Chimbu about the arduous nature of patrol work from Kundiawa;[43] he had to walk considerable distances from the station to reach the people he was administering. Exactly the same situation arose in Papua with the discovery of the southern highlands, because the lake provided a suitable landing place for a seaplane;[44] they were initially administered from the post at Lake Kutubu, from which access to the large population was difficult.

Still, allowing for such variations, the government's methods in the highlands were not essentially different from native administration elsewhere in the Territory, except in one important particular: the government frontier caught up not only with that of the miners and the missionaries but also with that of social anthropology. In the last third of the nineteenth century, one might be forgiven for concluding that the South Pacific Islands were full of governors and potential governors who were all forerunners of social anthropology. This, as least, is the claim made in colonial hagiography.[45] It rests primarily upon ignorance of nineteenth century European intellectual history. Whatever the roots of ideas about social evolution—derived, incidentally, not so much from Darwin as from the utilitarians and Sir Henry Maine[46]—anthropology, when E. B. Tylor wrote in the 1860s, was concerned with survivals in the process of evolution and thereafter with the study of primitive religion, with origins which were the chief concern of Frazer in *Pausanias* and *The Golden Bough*.[47] It was precisely this theory of 'survivals' that Bronislaw Malinowski attacked in the 1920s because it inhibited 'the study of social facts as living items of a culture', because it was the mark of an antiquarian interest in primitive society, not a sociological one.[48] Malinowski's first major work in the Trobriands was published in 1922. So was A. R. Radcliffe-Brown's on the Andaman Islanders. These two men, rather than nineteenth-century colonial governors in the Pacific, made social anthropology relevant to colonial administration. Radcliffe-Brown, in particular, had a direct influence upon New Guinea, for as the first holder of the Chair of Anthropology at the University of Sydney he was responsible for training cadets for the Mandated Territory field staff who actually carried out the extension of government control over the central highlands.[49]

In 1924 E. W. P. Chinnery, who had been an officer in the Papuan service and then labour organizer for New Guinea Copper Mines Pty before the First World War, and then for two academic years a student at Cambridge under A. C. Haddon, was appointed Government Anthropologist in the Mandated Territory.[50] In the same year six young men recruited to the New Guinea field staff served in the field for two years and were then sent to the University of Sydney for one year where Radcliffe-Brown taught them social anthropology. By the time of the discovery of the highland valleys fourteen officers had been recruited in this way and four of them—A. A. Roberts, I. Downs, G. Greathead and T. Aitchison—carried out the major part of the early patrol work. In 1932 Chinnery, retaining the post of Government Anthropologist, was appointed the first Director of District Services and Native Affairs under the government reorganization recommended by P. E.

Walcott.[51] Apart from Chinnery, none of this training made the officers into professional anthropologists. Neither Chinnery nor they, in the midst of other duties, had the time for intensive anthropological field work.[52] But when they confronted the enormous task, within their existing resources, of trying to bring under control a population perhaps double the enumerated one,[53] they were at least aware of the complexities of culture-contact, of the range of possibilities which lay behind the appearance of the native situation. The government officers might not be able to grasp the complexities of any particular situation, if only by reason of available time, but they had an awareness of the complexity of the impact of European society upon the highland peoples.

In one sense this awareness sharpened the edge of dislike between government and missions. Chinnery, believing that native culture was a 'functioning' whole, saw the early stage of government contact as one in which the only things that disappeared were those involving homicide, because the government interfered only with offences against criminal law and 'outstanding abominations'.[54] The missions, by contrast, in Chinnery's view, struck 'killing blows at the very root of native culture'. Chinnery did not disagree with the ultimate aim of mission activity, for he did not see how native culture could survive in the modern world, but he and the officers under his control disagreed with the immediate aims of mission activity because of the complications they caused the government. Hence the administration's caution in the matter of mission land purchase. Hence, in particular, their suspicion of mission teachers and helpers. For such men had a local influence which the government could not easily match. A mission station under a European clergyman, a government post under a European officer; both of these exerted much the same kind of influence over the neighbouring area when highlanders who had heard of the white man came to visit.[55] A missionary travelling to visit his outstations, a European officer on patrol: both were temporary visitors to any particular group. But a mission helper or catechist, not being a European, lived with a local community as an agent of deliberate change, whereas the government-appointed headman or boss-boy was part of the community the mission intended to influence and to change in ways the government believed undesirable. The differing policy over polygamy is a case in point, but there was a general difference of approach between the government which, other than in criminal offences and 'outstanding abominations', wished not to interfere with native customs, and a mission which, like the Lutherans, discouraged dances on the ground that sexual immorality might follow or the Seventh Day Adventists, the third mission to enter the highlands in the early

1930s, who forbade the eating of pork in highland societies whose ceremonial and diet depended upon the pig.[56] The mission helpers tried to police such prohibitions which were no part of the government's law, and the attempt to do so in communities where there was a luluai or boss-boy made that official's life even more difficult than the conflicting pressures government demands and his own community's demands usually made upon him.[57]

There is, of course, an extensive anthropological literature on leadership and the effects upon it of government office as a headman, although in the case of the highlands this discussion is some twenty-five years after the first appointments of headmen by the government officers who began to establish law and order. In 1933, close to Aimontina where Ian Mack was killed, luluais were appointed in neighbouring villages.[58] In 1939 Ian Downs in the Chimbu valley could talk of the three hundred headmen who had been appointed, twenty of whom he then recommended for formal appointment as luluais.[59] Downs' criterion for such a formal appointment by the Administrator was that the hitherto informally appointed headmen or boss-boys could 'dominate' other headmen in the clan. Those luluais were then called in for conferences at the government post, were taken on tour with patrols, were treated with respect, were told they were responsible to His Honour the Administrator so that loyalty to the Administration overrode clan boundaries, and clan loyalties were emphasized over group loyalties. Downs tested the success of this policy by the fact that eighty-five per cent of the information laid in charges before the Court of Native Affairs came from headmen and ninety per cent of the prisoners brought in for offences were brought in by headmen. To Downs that was a demonstration that the 'big men' had indeed been selected to be headmen, that their influence was enlisted for the government. To later anthropologists, for example Dr Paula Brown, this seemed rather a demonstration that government officers led highland society from anarchy to satrapy, from leadership by techniques of management and consent—how to win friends and influence people—to a formal office backed by legal sanctions that did not constitute consensus but despotism.[60] She cited the case of Kondom, a man less than thirty years old in 1950 when appointed luluai of Naregu, whom the government backed in his quite unprecedented power, and whom—by analogy with other appointed officials both in New Guinea and in parts of Africa who 'became rank exploiters of their fellows'—Dr Brown called 'domineering' and 'untraditional'.[61]

With the word 'traditional', however, complications begin to set in, because it implies that there was no counterpart in indigenous society for the luluai who acted as a despot. But R. F. Salisbury, for instance, has pointed out that in the Chimbu this was not necessarily so.[62] The man, Kauwagl or Kavagl, who led the Catholic missionaries into the Chimbu and Wahgi valleys in 1934, was a Chimbu 'big-man', described by Father Schaefer four years after their mission journey.[63] Kavagl had killed two of his wives in fits of anger, had attacked with a club (and sometimes killed) any of his supporters who disagreed with him or who possessed wealth he coveted: he felt in Father Schaefer's words *er sei massgebend*: 'he makes the rules'. Plainly Kavagl was not controlled by consensus and, as Salisbury points out, his career as a despot had already lasted twenty years before the mission and government arrived.[64] When such a man was appointed luluai his authority tended to decrease, not to increase, for in government office he would be dismissed if he used violence and those within his group who opposed him could secure his dismissal by their failure to satisfy a patrol officer: failure to carry, untended roads or gardens, poor houses or sanitation, these led to a luluai's removal for lack of influence or inefficiency.[65] The arrival of the government, in short, could put into the hands of a community sanctions against an arbitrary big man of the 'traditional' kind.

Two such results of the luluai system show some of the range of possibilities. Because particular individuals within highland groups and all or part of the group itself were not passive in the face of government activity, because individuals or groups could and did manipulate the government's administrative system to their own advantage, the perception and judgement of particular government officers counted for more than usual. The appointed headmen were the chief point of contact between the government and the highlanders; they were the 'bearings' upon which the frontier of law and order moved. The importance of the appointed headmen was clearly understood by the government officers who did the early patrol work; that was why they were particularly sensitive to the rivalry and confusion which came from the presence of mission helpers and catechists. They understood sufficient of the complexities of introducing an appointed headman system to a society with no chieftainship to be cautious. So the identification of men of influence, the selection of a boss-boy from among them and then his formal appointment as luluai, was one of the first duties of an officer on patrol. In the highlands, given the obvious prevalence of and emphasis upon fighting, the fight leaders were obvious candidates. In the Chimbu most of Ian Downs' three hundred headmen in 1939 were former fight leaders; they were the obviously influential men in that frontier stage.[66]

Then the frontier stopped moving. When the Second World War came to New Guinea in 1942, civil government was first reduced and then suspended. In the highlands, where a major dysentery epidemic preoccupied A.N.G.A.U. officers, the most that could be done was to maintain existing influence and even then many previously patrolled highland groups were neglected.[67] The mission influence was largely withdrawn.[68] When active civil administration resumed in 1948, those headmen and luluais of prewar days were overtaken by a generation of leaders appointed not so much by the old criteria of influence as by the new criteria of familiarity with European ways, and the term 'prewar official' was used by a new generation of patrol officers with some degree of contempt.[69] The frontier which had started to move into the highlands in the early 1930s nevertheless left a legacy of policies and attitudes in postwar administration which, although overlaid by the new frontiers of labour recruitment, land settlement, development and local government, still regulated the policy which came to be called 'uniform development'.[70] The speed of postwar development was very much the speed at which the frontier of initial contact, of law and order moved.

NOTES AND REFERENCES

1 Chalmers 1886-87:104-5.
2 *Report to the Council of the League of Nations on the Administration of the Territory of New Guinea 1933-34*:117.
3 *Report . . . 1938-39*:119
4 *P.I.M.*, January 1939:16.
5 Biskup 1968.
6 National Library of Australia, Leahy Papers, Diary 24 May 1930: 'Misson [*sic*] endeavouring by hair raising tales to dissuade us from going on'.
7 Ross 1969:320-1.
8 Willis 1969; Radford 1972.
9 e.g. Leahy and Crain 1937; Hides 1935, 1936; Champion 1932.
10 Ross 1969:321.
11 *ibid.*:322.
12 *Report . . . 1935-36*:25.
13 E. W. P. Chinnery, pers. comm.
14 *Laws of the Territory of New Guinea 1921-1945*, Sydney 1947:III, 2649-2720.
15 Nilles 1953:10.
16 *idem.*
17 Ross 1969:325.
18 Nilles 1953:10.
19 *idem.*
20 *idem.*
21 Simpson 1954:83-4.
22 *Laws of the Territory of New Guinea 1921-1945*:IV, 4559-70.
23 Ross 1969:324.
24 *P.I.M.*, July 1934:24.
25 *Report . . . 1932-33*:30.
26 Souter 1963:183.
27 *Report . . . 1934-35*:22.
28 P.O. (Mt Hagen Police Post) to D.O. (Madang), 2 Feb. 1938.
29 G. F. Vicedom to P.O. (Mt Hagen), 2 April 1938.
30 P.O. (Mt Hagen) to D.O. (Madang), 9 March 1938.
31 Vicedom to P.O. (Mt Hagen), 2 April 1938.
32 O/ic (Mt Hagen) to D.O. (Madang), 19 July 1939.
33 D.D.S. to G.S., 23 Oct. 1939.
34 D.D.S. to O/ic (Mt Hagen), 15 Dec. 1940.
35 O/ic (Mt Hagen) to D.O. (Madang), 18 July 1940.

36 West 1968:198-200.
37 *Report . . . 1932-33*:30.
38 *Report . . . 1933-34*:28.
39 *ibid.*:115.
40 *Report . . . 1934-35*:21.
41 *Report . . . 1938-39*:145.
42 e.g. Upper Ramu Post, Patrol Report (P.O. Aitchison), 9-20 Jan., 31 Jan.-14 Feb. and 22 Sept.-7 Oct. 1936.
43 *Report . . . 1934-35*:23.
44 Territory of Papua, *Annual Report 1938-39*:19.
45 e.g. Legge 1958:167, 208; Joyce 1971:xiv.
46 Burrow 1966:18-21.
47 Guthrie 1950:10-15.
48 Malinowski 1944:31.
49 *Report . . . 1932-33*:155-6.
50 *ibid.*:153.
51 *ibid.*:12.
52 e.g. *Report . . . 1930-31*:19 lists three anthropological reports by Chinnery on three separate districts, Morobe, New Ireland and Kieta; in 1931-32 he completed a demographic survey of the east coast of New Ireland, began to investigate a population decrease in New Hanover and made a 'sociological census' in preparation for that investigation, and ethnographic surveys in Aitape, Wewak and the Schouten islands. *Report . . . 1931-32*:10-11.
53 *ibid.*:20, 100-2.
54 *Report . . . 1932-33*:158.
55 Reay 1964:247.
56 O/ic (Mt Hagen) to D.O. (Madang), 18 July 1940.
57 e.g. Salisbury 1964:228-9, 232.
58 *Report . . . 1933-34*:27.
59 Annual Report (Chimbu 1939-40 by P.O. to D.O. (Madang)).
60 Brown 1963:10.
61 *ibid.*:12-13.
62 Salisbury 1964:227.
63 Schaefer 1938:107.
64 Salisbury 1964:227.
65 Upper Ramu Post, Patrol Report (C. P. O. Elliott), 2-21 Nov. 1936.
66 Chimbu Post, Annual Report (P.O. Downs) 1939-40; see also Brown 1963:8.
67 A.N.G.A.U. administered the highlands from Mount Hagen District Office. From the Sub-District Office at Chimbu, for example, in 1945 many groups mentioned in patrol reports had not then been visited for two years, e.g. Patrol Report (Chimbu) no. 9 of 1944-45.
68 Ross 1969:326.
69 Brown 1963:8.
70 West 1956, 1958, 1972.

The Mapia Islands and their affinities

WILLIAM A. LESSA

Surprisingly little is known anthropologically about the Mapia Islands, there being some difference of opinion as to whether the imported Micronesians and their successors who lived there until their recent repatriation were preceded by Melanesian, Polynesian, or Indonesian peoples, or whether these predecessors were themselves Micronesians as far back as can be ascertained.[1]

The islands are located at 0°49'N, 134°17'E, which places them about ninety-five sea miles north-northwestward of Tanjong Saweba, a point on the north coast of the Vogelkop peninsula of New Guinea. The group consists of three low coral islands, Pegun, Bras, and Fanildo, lying on the reef of an oval-shaped atoll that is nine miles long from north to south. Mapia has been variously called St David's Islands, the Freewill Islands, Bunaj (Bunai), and Burat, but Mapia is its designation on current charts.

There are some who assert or at least consider it possible that Hernando de Grijalva's ship, the *Santiago*, in 1537 was the first to reach Mapia, thus equating it with the islands called the Gelles in the accounts of that trans-Pacific voyage.[2] I cannot find any real verification that the Gelles, or Gueles, were indeed the Mapia Islands. Even the editors of the fine third edition of Antonio Galvão's *Tratado*, which gives the most-used account of Grijalva's voyage, state that they cannot identify the Gueles,[3] and Andrew Sharp thinks that they were the Asia (Pasei) Islands located east of Halmahera at 1°03'N, 131°15'E.[4]

What appears to have been the first European discovery of Mapia was that of William Funnell on 7 May 1705. He tells how while en route to India from America he came upon three very low, small islands at 0°50'N. The easternmost (Bras?) was at 0°42'N. The details he furnishes indicate that the northernmost island, which he called the Island of Deceit, was Fanildo, the largest, which he called the Island of Disappointment, was Pegun. His book provides us with the first account of the native population.[5]

The next European sighting of the islands was made on 1 March 1761 by Captain James Dewar in the East India Company ship, the *Warwick*, while en route to China. Dewar named them the St David's Islands in honour of the saint whose feast day it was.[6] Philip Carteret on the *Swallow* next reached the atoll on 25

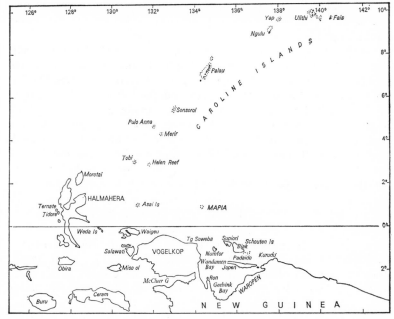

Fig. 8 The Mapia Islands

September 1767 and called it the Joseph Freewill Islands after
the name he had bestowed upon one of the eager islanders who
of his own free will joined the ship as a seaman.[7]

Subsequent visits, some of them no more than mere sightings,
were made by the following: Captain John Meares in the *Felice,*
1788; Captain John McCluer in the *Panther,* 1791; Captain Robert
Williams in the *Thames* together with Captain James Jackson in
the *Carnatic,* 1797; Captain J. Salkeld in the *Minerva,* 1800;
Captain Andrew Barclay in the *Mangles,* 1806; Captain John Tate
in the *Cumbrian,* 1809; Captain Samuel Hill in the *Ophelia,* 1816;
Captain C. Eeg in the *Pollux,* 1825; Captain Gibson in the *Gypsy,*
1840; and Captain Edward Woodin in the *Eleanor,* 1852. The list
is not complete.

The year 1859 marks the dividing line between these visitors
and the subsequent plantation period, which was initiated when
an English captain, C. de Crespigny, arrived and left behind some
sailors to establish a copra industry. He did so in connection with
a Dutch company in Ternate called M. D. Rennesse van Duiven-
bode, which that year had entered into an agreement with the
sultan of Tidore, whereby the latter acquired Mapia (as the
Indonesians called the atoll) as part of his territory and was made
responsible for the protection of the enterprise. Although the contract was for twenty years, and 100,000 florins worth of machinery

for the oil factory was ordered from Europe, the entire project fell through the following year, apparently before the machinery could be delivered.[8]

If the Dutch venture was a failure, that of David Dean O'Keefe, the self-styled 'King of Yap, Sovereign of Sonsorol, and Monarch of Mapia', was not. In a lengthy legal statement to a British court on Yap on 19 August 1883 he provided the following information: he first visited St David's in 1878 and made a lease with King Marawithi for five years for the whole group of islands. At that time there were only fifteen inhabitants, but formerly the islands had been well populated. There was an immense number of graves. The natives of Ternate and New Guinea had killed almost all the people. No lease had been made before he went to St David's, but after he had made his own, another lease was made or an agreement entered into with A. Capelle & Company, a German firm. O'Keefe imported labourers from Yap, as well as men from the New Hebridean island of Tana who had been living in Palau.[9] When he went to St David's he found a man named Harry Terry who had been left there by the Capelle firm. Terry had a Pleasant Island (Nauru) 'woman' and a large family. There were other Pleasant Islanders who had come with him from Kusaie, twenty-eight or thirty in all. The fifteen St David's Islanders lived on Bras and had nothing to do with Terry. O'Keefe made subsequent visits to St Davids prior to 1883, one of them being in July 1880.[10]

The Capelle company's factory at Mapia apparently antedated that of O'Keefe and had been in the hands locally of Terry and, later, August Mertens; but it was a failure. Of interest to us is the fact that the Capelle firm had introduced workers from Pleasant Island, or Nauru, while O'Keefe had brought them in from Yap, Sonsorol, and Tana.

Irrelevant as they may seem, the preceding historical facts have a strong bearing on the question of the cultural identity of Mapia, for they establish 1859 as the real dividing line between indigenous and alien ethnic elements introduced by plantation workers, and thus furnish us the proper background for understanding the only anthropological field work ever done on the atoll—that by Jan Stanislaw Kubary in 1885.[11]

Those who have previously studied Mapia have not seen any problem in its cultural affinities; consequently, they have taken low-keyed stances on the matter. Although the range of their opinions is wide, it is at the same time unsupported by deep argumentation, except for Kubary.

Thus, the distinguished geographer Helen Wallis, in an effort to explain why all of Captain Philip Carteret's encounters with Melanesians ended in bloodshed, and why he was not able to establish good relations with a group of Pacific islanders until he reached the Joseph Freewill Islands (in 1767), says that the reason was this: 'Their inhabitants, a more sophisticated people, Indonesian in origin, came within the range of his understanding, as the Polynesians would have done; the Melanesians clearly did not'.[12]

She is not the only one to speak of Mapians as Indonesians. A mild suggestion along these lines was made at the turn of this century by a Dutch writer, who on the basis of government publications said that the people of Mapia resemble the 'Malayan type more than the Papuan type' but that there were too few people, thirteen, to determine this for a certainty.[13]

A Japanese anthropologist embraces a rival Melanesian hypothesis when he writes: 'Mapia, south of Helen Reef, belonging to the Dutch territory, became a settlement of the Papuan people'.[14] But he gives no justification for his statement. On the other hand, in a later publication he refers to Mapia as being one of the six islands of a Paramicronesian group, the inhabitants of which 'bear a close resemblance to the Micronesians',[15] but he does not elaborate on this assertion and makes no further reference to Mapia. A similarly unsupported position is taken by an anonymous writer, who says that 'Mapia . . . apparently was originally populated by the same stock as the New Guinea mainland'.[16] Along these lines there is a provocative statement made by 'King' Marravidi of Mapia expressing the belief that at least some of the original inhabitants of the atoll were driven to it from Melanesia by winds.[17]

At variance with both the Indonesian and Melanesian hypotheses is the opinion of H. C. Davenport, whose father was captain of one of O'Keefe's schooners. He states that the natives of Mapia, where he apparently lived for some time, had no affinity with either the people of the East Indies or Melanesia, and that the original people were Polynesian.[18] Much earlier than this, Captain Meares of the *Felice* had said that, based on his observations on the canoes, language, and appearance of the Freewills he had a conjecture, 'amounting almost to a firm belief', that the natives of the islands were of the same race as that of the Sandwich Islands.[19] Another champion of the Polynesian hypothesis is the *Pacific Islands Monthly*, which despite its previous advocacy of a Melanesian position maintains that the large flat tombstones on the islets seem to prove that Polynesians lived on Mapia before O'Keefe first anchored his ship there, because 'Papuans and Micronesians have never used such stones for their graves'.[20]

Representing a wholly different opinion is J. A. Jungmichel who says that the people can be compared in physique and clothing, as well as language, to Caroline Islanders, although they themselves do not know where they came from.[21] He is the forerunner of others who have similarly selected Micronesia.[22]

Now that the four conflicting opinions—Indonesian, Melanesian, Polynesian, and Micronesian—have been presented, it remains to examine the evidence provided by observers who have given us something tangible for dealing with the problem. The most valuable of the early accounts of the islanders is that contained in Carteret's journal, here reproduced verbatim as a base from which to ascertain and evaluate clues. Other early accounts will be used when they seem appropriate for making a determination.

25th Sept. we got near three small Islands from which came several Canoes these People radly came on board they had a few Coco Nutts which we got for pieces of Iron hoops, I realy believe for Iron tools we might have bough[t] most everything they had in their Islands, it is amazing to see how immoditrately found they are of Iron which they called Parram, I thought one of them would have gon mad on my giving him three pieces of an old Iron hoop, each piece abt. 4 Inches long I suppose he thought himself as rich as any body in the world, he jumped abt. and laught so very hearty with such a happy Countenance, that I could not but scympathize with him, in his joy and I took a greadell of pleasure in observing the strong emotions of his contenance particularly when any body offer'd to take it away from him.

These Peop[l]e were of a free opend disposition, not mistrustfull, went about in all parts of the ship eating and drinking what ever was given them, where as merry and familiar with our people as if they had been of a long acquaintance, wanting some to go onshore offring to leave others onbd. in lieu, I intended to have stoped at these Islds. if there had been anchorage but the strong westerly current could not fetch them and night comming on, we keep on our Course, two of these Ids. are scarce better than Rocks it is surprising how so many people can find subsistence on such small Ids. they can have no fresh water but what they get by ye Showers of Rain, for their can be no spring in so low land, they lie in 50 minits to ye Northwd. of ye line 12° 06′ Wt. of New Hanover or 136° 30′Et. of London, and called by ye Inhabitent Piggan.

These People are Indian Copper Colour'd (first of the Kind we have seen in these parts) fine long black hair, little beards which they pull out by the roots, have fine white Teeth, go naked except the Privy parts they cover slightly with a narrow piece of fine matting, well made & featured of ye common stature, very neeble and active, many of them went up to our masthead faster and neebler then our people could do, their Canoes well & neatly made fine matts for sails, their rope & fishing Netts well made, one of their People would need stay with us notwithstanding all we & his Cammarades could persuede him to the Contrary, I therefor keept him as it was a free Act of his & called him Joseph Freewill I was in hopes some thing servicable might have been discoverd by him, but he afterwards grue sickly from being so long at sea and died at the Isld. of Celebes, I suppose they must have on those Isld. besides ye Coco Nutts & Palm Trees, Beedle Nutt tree, Bread Fruit and lyme trees from his knowing of

these fruits when he saw them at Celebes and the instant he got ye
bread fruit went and rosted it in the Embers, he seemed to make us
understand that they had plenty of Fish and Turtle in ye Season
and that a Ship & People like us at times one a year or one in 2
years on her way to ye Wward tuch'd at their Ild. for refreshments,
and that there was some more Isld. to the Northwd. of them the
People of which had Iron and were very treatorious to them[.][23]

The traits of culture and physique mentioned above by Carteret as well as other early visitors must be evaluated by referring
them to some sort of standard by which a possible Micronesian
relationship can be established or rejected. In these pages, Mapia
will be compared mostly with its four nearest Carolinian neighbours—Tobi, Merir, Pulo Anna, Sonsorol—and to a lesser extent
with Ulithi, which apparently is the original homeland of the
people of these four places.[24] There are good reasons for regarding
Tobi, Merir, Pulo Anna, and Sonsorol as a virtual unit. Not only
were they originally populated from Ulithi (via Yap), but they
replenished one another's ranks when they were either decimated
or eradicated through typhoons, famines, and raids by Papuans
and Indonesians. Moreover, there has long been regular communication and intermarriage among the four islands. As a convenient way of designating this ensemble, I refer to them as the
'westernmost Carolines'. There is good reason to believe that there
was some interaction between them and Mapia at least as early as
the beginning of the seventeenth century.[25]

In view of other theories of relationship, Mapia will also be
compared with Indonesia and Polynesia, and even more with
Melanesia, especially north-western New Guinea, Numfor, and the
Schouten Islands of Supiori, Biak, and Padaido, whose inhabitants
were daring seafarers who traded not only along the entire north
coast of western New Guinea but far into eastern Indonesia as
well. Of interest also will be the Waropen peoples along the coast
of Geelvink Bay because they too were seafarers and had a reputation for bellicosity, head-hunting, and slave raiding, and had
contact with the world of the Moluccan islands.

In making comparisons every effort will be made, at least for
the present, to use only those traits of Mapian culture and physique
that were reported prior to the plantation period. Only after
making all possible inferences from this approach will it be per-
missible to consider the ethnographic report bequeathed to us by
Kubary as the result of his 1885 field work.

One of the problems confronting the investigator is that rapid
depopulation, threatening extinction, set in after the islands came
to be known to the outside world. Funnell says that in 1705 he
was greeted by forty or fifty flying proas. Allowing ten to each
proa, he estimated that there were about 450 men in the canoes,

with 'multitudes' of people upon the shore.[26] One might be inclined to doubt Funnell's report were it not for Meares' statement
that when the *Felice* visited Mapia in 1788, 'at least five hundred
natives, all men', came out in canoes.[27] When the *Ophelia* arrived
in 1816 it was observed that, 'The inhabitants were numerous'.[28]
The subsequent spectacular decline in population cannot be attributed to anything other than disease and genocide, ugly by-
products of the cupidity of invaders.

The rapid decimation of the pre-colonial population by
slavers has been attested to by D. Parker Wilson, the ship's doctor
who kept the journal of Captain Gibson's *Gypsy*. Two boats that
were sent ashore from the vessel to trade on 23 November 1840
found 'but 8 men and 2 decrepit old women, and they almost
frightened out of their senses'. It was learned from one of the
natives, who spoke a little English, that apparently the people
were being taken into slavery by proas from New Guinea or the
Moluccas and became the property of the Papuans or the Dutch.
The invaders were said to seize and make them fast with thongs
like pigs, stow them in their rickety vessels, and massacre those
who resisted, striking with arrows those who attempted to escape.
The present inhabitants had fled in a canoe but returned again.
The islands, says Wilson, were formerly thickly inhabited.[29]

Further evidence of depopulation may be seen in an ominous
entry in the logbook of the brig, *Eleanor*, Captain Edward
Woodin: 'April 30, 1852. At St. Davids Island. No natives there.'[30]
Undoubtedly, the few islanders who were still left at the time of
Gibson's visit twelve years before had either hidden in terror on
one of the several islands of the atoll or taken off in canoes as
soon as they sighted the visitors. That the islanders had not become extinct is proven by the subsequent assertion of a member
of the earlier mentioned Dutch firm, M. D. Rennesse van Duiven-
bode of Ternate, that, in January 1860, the population consisted
of two men, two youths between the ages of fifteen and eighteen,
two old and one young woman, and two children.[31]

Before beginning a systematic comparison of Mapia traits of
physique and culture with those of other islanders in the Pacific,
I would like to dispose of two imponderables—'emotion' and 'behaviour'—because it might appear to some that these are fruitful
clues.

The comments made by Carteret about Mapian warmth,
cheerfulness, trustfulness, and open disposition are matched by
other observers. Thus Hill says:

> we hove too & they came along side without much caution or suspicion
> & many of them came on Board . . . The Chief also came on board,

he was a man about thirty years old, of very good countenance & elegant Deportment & all his behavior was marked with Propriety. These People are . . . very active, and swim as if the water was their natural element . . . They are open, free and unsuspecting, seemed lively and cheerful & even humorous, brought no weapons of war of any kind in any of their canoes that I saw but like most men in a State of Nature they were adicted to Stealing [,] Several of them having been detected in attempting to carry away small articles & when so detected seemed no way disconcerted only disappointed at not having succeeded [.] One of them succeeded in getting an Iron hook & thimble from some of the Rigging & when a Sailor requested him to deliver it he immediately jumped overboard & swam to his Canoe with it where he remained with as much unconcern as if he had done nothing wrong.[32]

A brief remark about tractability appears in the log book of the *Gypsy,* saying that the island 'used to be thickly inhabited by docile natives, who, with women used to come off the ships, and supply them with pigs and taro, etc.'.[33]

But we must not be influenced by stereotypes. Despite exceptions, the older literature of travel and exploration, especially when interpreted by philosophers and laymen, is fairly consistent in describing Micronesians as tractable but thievish; Polynesians as warm-blooded and noble; Melanesians as hostile and aggressive; and Indonesians as sophisticated but fanatical. Polynesia, and to a lesser extent Micronesia, happen to have caught the fancy of romantic idealists in the Rousseau tradition; the others did not.

On the other hand, something that can legitimately concern us about the people of Mapia is their physical appearance. Aside from Carteret's characterization, 'well made and featured', there are other general but obviously value-laden descriptions, such as Barclay's observation:

The natives of these islands are particularly well proportioned and robust; their features are regular and manly; some of them so symmetrical that I was astonished, having never seen any equal to them in either Asia, Africa, or America. There is not the least resemblance between them and the Malays, or the inhabitants of New Guinea; nor can I form the smallest conjecture from whence these islands could have been first inhabited.[34]

Evidently, Barclay had not been to Micronesia; otherwise, he might have made some comparison with its inhabitants, too.

Captain Hill of the *Ophelia* is another of those who makes a personal judgement regarding overall appearance, saying that 'they are the best looking men I have ever seen in the Pacific Ocean or South Sea, being exceeding well Shaped and Proportioned',[35] adding that a certain young man in particular 'was the best featured, as well as shaped in other respects of any Indian I have ever seen in the Islands of the South Sea or Pacific Ocean'.[36]

Opinions such as these might have some value if we knew for sure what aesthetic and racial standards were held by Carteret, Barclay, and Hill, all of them Englishmen. But we do not.

We are on safer ground when we deal with specific traits, such as the copper coloured skin mentioned by Carteret, who it will be recalled also mentioned 'fine long black hair' and 'little beards . . . pull[ed] out by the roots'. Visitors subsequent to Carteret tend to support these specific somatological observations. Writes Samuel Hill, captain of the *Ophelia*:

> These people are of a light copper color exceedingly well limbed with Small close Joints, small hands & not large feet. About the middle size but none very tall or Stout . . . long hair, some with Straight black coarse hair, others with brown hair and Bushy being somewhat crisped or Curled in my opinion by the intense heat of the Sun.[37]

Further on he adds that they 'Plucked up the Beard and Hair from all parts except the Head'. Although the colour of teeth is not a racial criterion, it is interesting to see that he backs up Carteret when he says that 'they had fine white teeth, used no quid or chewed or Smoaked'.

Observing the Mapians almost half a century later, Jungmichel says: 'These people have a copper colored skin, like the inhabitants of the Caroline Islands, and their head hair, which the men wear short, is not curly like that of the Papuans'.[38] Note that by now the men of Mapia were cutting their hair short, and that as far as biological affinities are concerned the writer makes a judgement in favour of Micronesia and against Melanesia. Jungmichel is the only one to refer to the nose, and he merely says that Mapians 'do not have flat noses'.[39] Probably he was simply implying that the nose was higher than that of Melanesians, and possibly Indonesians too.

Summarizing the documentary descriptions of the people of Mapia, the following physical characteristics emerge: a well proportioned and robust physique; long, coarse head hair, wavy to straight in form and dark brown to black in colour; sparse beards plucked out at the roots; medium to light brown skins, with a touch of reddishness; somewhat raised nasal bridges; and medium stature. In order to help determine the racial composition of the Mapians these physical characteristics will be compared with those of Micronesia, Melanesia, Indonesia, and Polynesia.[40]

The westernmost Carolines provide somatoscopic support for any claim regarding Mapia's possible Micronesian connections. The best data come from the island of Tobi, where as far back as 1832-34 the shipwrecked sailor, Horace Holden, observed that the natives had light, copper coloured skins, and that the men lacked beards because they pulled out their facial hair and forced him and his companions to do the same. The observations made in Tobi in 1898 by Captain Walsen of the four-masted barque, *Paul Rickmers,* have been summarized by the anthropologist Anneliese Eilers, and together with the observations by Hambruch and Hasebe they tend to show that the people of Tobi were not unlike those of Mapia with respect to hair form and colour, skin colour, and nose form. For the near-by islands of Sonsorol and Merir, the anthropological reports are similarly supportive, as they are for Ulithi, where in 1947 I gathered detailed information, much of it unpublished.

Comparison with those parts of Melanesia closest to Mapia, such as the coast of Geelvink Bay and the islands of Japen, Biak, Supiori, Padaido, and Numfor, shows that here the people generally have dark skins; black, frizzy hair; and flat but also sometimes hooked noses. They are basically Oceanic Negroids but tend to depart from this type in some places because of Indonesian admixture. These Melanesians do not resemble Mapians to the degree that the westernmost Carolinians and Ulithians do.

As for Indonesia, although the Mongoloid-looking type with straight black hair, light brown skin colour, short stature, and light build is found among the formerly piratical inhabitants of the Galela and Tobelo districts of northern Halmahera, it is not ubiquitous. The Moluccan islands closest to New Guinea often manifest so-called Papuan features, this being true for parts of Halmahera, Morotai, and Ceram. In any event, none of these peoples match the Mapian characteristics.

Polynesians probably differ from Mapians in being larger in both stature and girth, with sturdier bone structure and greater fleshiness. Although the nose is not usually prominent, it is often broad and massive. Polynesian hair form and colour, however, are not very different from that of Mapians.

It is unfortunate that the extensive anthropometric and serological material collected by anthropologists and others for so much of the Pacific cannot be utilized, there being no corresponding studies of Mapians. Nevertheless, I do feel that there is a basic physical resemblance between Mapians and Carolinians, and that there is nothing to encourage the belief that the Mapians seen by early observers were Melanesian, Indonesian, or Polynesian.

Returning to Mapia, we have in the coiffure of the men another kind of lead. Hill says that in 1816 'most of the men wore their hair tied or clubbed on the top of their heads'.[41] Artists depicting various Carolinians during the early part of the last century often show the men wearing their hair knotted or clubbed at the top. In addition we have the comments of anthropological observers regarding the inhabitants of Tobi, Sonsorol, and Merir around the turn of the century, to the effect that the hair was often worn in knots at the top, back, or side of the head on those islands.

Melanesian coiffures vary greatly from place to place, but nowhere do they seem to be tied or clubbed at the top of the head as on Mapia. The hairdos of places close to Mapia show considerable local differences, but at least for Salawati, the northwestern coast of New Guinea, and various settlements along Geelvink Bay, the style is not like that of Mapia. A mop was characteristic of much of the north coast of western New Guinea, including the Waropen settlements along Geelvink Bay. For the Schouten Islands there seems to be no evidence of anything but a bushy or unstyled hairdo.

For Indonesia in general and Halmahera in particular there seems to be no evidence of the Mapian types of hairdo. Polynesian hairstyles varied a good deal from one area to another, the knot being used by Samoan men, who wore it a little to the right of the crown of the head, and also by Maori men, who wore it at the back of the head. These male hairdressing practices resembled those of some western Carolinians more than they did Mapians, but the distinction is not great.

Turning to another trait, pierced earlobes, we have Captain Hill's statement that most Mapian men had their ears perforated.[42] The piercing of earlobes is a widespread cultural trait and has been known to have been practised for centuries in the west Carolines. We have evidence of this for Ulithi, as well as Tobi, Merir, and Sonsorol.

In Melanesia the wearing of pendants and rings in the ears has been noted, among other places, for the islands of Miso'ol, Salawati, Waigeu, Numfor, Supiori, Biak, and Japen, as well as Wandamen Bay, the west and east coasts of Geelvink Bay, and the rest of the north coast of Irian Jaya (former Dutch New Guinea).

Of course perforation of the lobes has long been a common practice in much of Indonesia. But in Polynesia perforation was limited to New Zealand, the Marquesas, the Cooks, Tonga and Easter Island, with the great bulk of the islands of the culture area failing to qualify.

An important Mapian culture trait, tattooing, is mentioned by Captain Hill: 'Some few of them were Slightly Tattooed after the manner of the Owhyeans [Hawaiians]'.[43] Tattooing is a widespread and highly developed Carolinian practice. It was practised on Tobi when Holden was a prisoner there, he and his shipmates being forced to undergo the painful operation. The patterns on Tobi, Merir, and Sonsorol have been observed to be much like those of Yap and Ulithi and the neighbouring Caroline Islands.

Tattooing reached less elaborate heights in Melanesia, but it is nevertheless found on the islands of Miso'ol, Salawati, Numfor, Supiori, Biak, Japen, Abere (Kurudu), and Ro'on, as well as in scattered districts along the coast of Geelvink Bay. But its occurrence is sporadic and sometimes confined to one sex alone.

In Indonesia the spread of Islam has meant a diminution of tattooing; nevertheless, the practice existed until now or the recent past on Halmahera and from Ceram southwards to the Babar Islands.

Tattooing is an almost universal trait in Polynesia, its prevalence among the old Maoris, Samoans, Tongans, Society Islanders, Marquesans and Hawaiians being well known. Only in Polynesia does it match in elaborateness the tattooing to be found in the Carolines.

We turn now to the important matter of clothing. In addition to Carteret's account[44] a fuller description of Mapian apparel is provided by Barclay:

> Their dress consisted of a treble string of coral, stones, and shells, round the waist; a narrow piece of cloth up between the legs, made out of the fibres of cocoa nut; a bracelet of tortoise-shell round the right wrist; two square pieces of mother-o'-pearl suspended round the neck by hair, one piece hanging down the front of the body, and the other down the back; a collar round the neck, of fish teeth and black coral. This was the dress of the men; and the only difference we perceived in that of the women was, a small mat tied round the waist, which reached as low as the knee.[45]

Hill says simply that the men 'wore no garment or covering of any kind except a small covering over the Sexual Parts, which but just covered it'.[46] But in 1860, according to Jungmichel, the men were covering their genitals with a sort of tree bark, like the Alfurs of Halmahera, while the women were wearing a hip garment made of some sort of plaited grass or leaves.[47] Some discrepancy is apparent in Carteret's, Barclay's, and Jungmichel's accounts, at least as far as the male garment is concerned. All three agree that the women wore a plaited or woven mat skirt, but whereas Carteret says that the men wore a narrow piece of fine matting, Barclay and Jungmichel say that they wore something made either of coconut fibre or tree bark.

Obviously the men wore pubic girdles like those of the islanders of the west Carolines. The only discordant note is Barclay's statement that the material used on Mapia was the fibre of the coconut, whatever that may mean precisely. Probably this can be discounted, especially since we know that on Tobi, Sonsorol, and Pulo Anna the material was the fibre of a certain kind of banana plant, interwoven with hibiscus bark threads to produce a pattern. The knee-length mat skirt of the women of

Mapia described by Barclay requires special explanation. In form, it probably resembled the skirt worn throughout the western Carolines (except Palau, where both sexes went naked, and Yap and Ngulu, where the women wore voluminous 'grass' skirts made of shredded coconut leaves or strips of hibiscus bark). But Barclay says nothing of the material, nor do any of the other early visitors. Most likely it was pandanus and was plaited, as on Sonsorol and Tobi.[48] Plaited or woven, it could still be Micronesian.

Melanesia does not have the kind of clothing described by Barclay. In much of the northern coastal area of north-western New Guinea the people formerly went nude. But even where clothing was used it was never loom woven or even plaited in those parts of Melanesia of concern to us, with the exception of areas in the Takar-Saar coasts of Irian Jaya, where Micronesian influence is present.

As for Indonesia, pubic girdles made of woven mats are absent. Cotton blouses, sarongs, shirts, and trousers are used where weaving is known. But some of the more remote tribes used to manufacture bark cloth garments for both sexes, or primitive leaf and plaited fibre skirts for the women, as in Buru, Aru, and Ceram. In the Tobelo and Galela districts of Halmahera, the customary basic garment for both sexes used to be made of bark.

In Polynesia the material most used for clothing was bark cloth, except that in Samoa in addition to bast and hanging-leaf garments there were plaited belts. The true loom was found only on the Polynesian outliers of Nukuoro and Kapingamarangi located in Micronesia.

Turning to the next set of clues, ornaments, we have Barclay's statement above about a 'treble string' worn around the waist, a tortoise-shell wrist bracelet, pieces of mother-of-pearl suspended ventrally and dorsally from the neck, and a collar of fish teeth and black coral. These are described somewhat similarly by Hill who, however, 'saw none of their Females' but did see some men who 'wore necklaces & broad Plates of Shells of the Pearl Oyster or of that kind commonly called Mother of Pearl' and noted that 'they also wore rings on their fingers & large bracelets on their arms made of Tortoise Shell'.[49]

The westernmost Caroline Islands have ornaments closely matching those described for Mapia. Some were noted as far back as 1832 by Holden. There is, however, no evidence there of collars of fish teeth and black coral. For the north-western coast of New Guinea and the Geelvink Bay area there is no evidence of Mapian-like ornaments, except for some tortoise shell finger rings. No Indonesian ornaments seem to match those of Mapia, except that tortoise shell rings and bracelets are found on Halmahera. As for Polynesia, its ornaments are not of the Mapia type.

A kind of armour is mentioned by Meares, who says that he saw in Mapian canoes large mats used as coats of mail that he was told were capable of resisting the attack of a spear and could scarcely be penetrated by a ball from a pistol, so strong and close was their texture.[50] Nothing like the kind of coat of mail described by Meares seems ever to have been reported for the western Carolines. Well known, of course, are the suits of sennit made by the natives of the distant Gilbert Islands, but they were something much more than Mapia's crude mats.

In some parts of New Guinea rather stiff and heavy cuirasses made of rattan were worn for protection, and in the interior north of distant Huon Gulf a kind of cloak made of several thicknesses of bark cloth was used; but neither of these matches Meares' 'large mats'. Apparently there are no reports of armour for Halmahera and Morotai, as well as the other Moluccas. As for Polynesia, the Hawaiians, Maori, and Society Islanders had various kinds of what might be called armour, but none of these corresponds to Mapia's coat of mail.

Regarding dwellings, we are simply told by Jungmichel that the people of Mapia were living in huts on the ground that were built of tree leaves.[51] The Carolinian house is leaf-thatched and almost always built on the ground rather than on poles, and never over water. This is specifically true for the westernmost Carolines, where the gabled roofs reach almost to the ground.

In Irian Jaya permanent dwellings of importance are built on poles; only the most primitive dwellings have the earth as a floor. Various studies show that for the Vogelkop-Geelvink Bay area pile dwellings are the rule. Indonesian houses are made principally of bamboo and planks, with leaf and fibre thatch, and may be built directly on the ground or raised on piles or stone platforms. In the Moluccan area, most houses are built on poles, but on Halmahera and Morotai pole-supported houses seem to be confined to the coastal areas.

Polynesian houses, except in New Zealand, were often raised on low stone-faced platforms, but in any event were not raised on posts, except where the site of a village was prone to flooding. The materials used to build dwellings were almost always wood and thatch.

Of Mapian canoes we have valuable information of a highly diagnostic character. Even though Funnell does not describe the boats that greeted him in 1705, he refers to them as 'flying proas'[52] and thereby establishes that they were single-outriggered sail boats with twin endpieces adapted for pointing the hull in either direction when under way. Previously, Funnell had stopped at Rota in the Marianas and made a sketch of a flying proa there. Carteret is not of much help, saying simply that the canoes at Mapia were 'well & neatly made [and had] fine matts for sails'.[53] Meares is of even less help, saying only that he was visited by a great number of canoes, each holding five or six people, and that they were 'of the same construction as those of the Sandwich Islands'.[54] Hill too gives it as his opinion that the canoes to some extent resembled those of the Hawaiians, and after making mention of the outrigger he goes on to describe an unusual feature:

> The carved head Pin which seems Purely ornamental on their canoes is so fitted as to turn inward on Striking against anything Performated [sic] in the Joint and Secured with the flexible and tough Roots of some tree or Shrub. Similar to those which the Canadian & Penebscot Indians make use of for the Same Purposes.[55]

Such a canoe head is a highly discrete feature that could be significant if it could be established that it is found elsewhere in the Pacific; but apparently it is not. In a leaf inserted in his manuscript, however, Hill has left us a valuable pen-and-ink sketch of a Mapian canoe, showing that the single outrigger apparatus used two booms, and that the endpieces were not only twinned but curved inward.[56]

Micronesia and Polynesia, like Mapia, are everywhere characterized by the single outrigger, except where double canoes were used. Both these culture areas generally share Mapia's two booms. Indonesia departs from Mapia because it is the classical area of the double outrigger canoe. Most Moluccan canoes use two booms, but none is single-outriggered.

Although Melanesia generally employs the single outrigger, the area that here concerns us frequently strays from the usual pattern. The majority of the canoes of the island of Waigeu and neighbouring islands off the north-western point of New Guinea, as well as those of the adjacent mainland, are entirely Indonesian in character and are similar to a type from Weda Bay in Halmahera, which has two outriggers, each with two booms. The near-by Geelvink Bay area is, however, a mixed one, with the single outrigger predominating in the Schouten Islands, Japen, and farther within the bay along the mainland and on the Wandamen coast; but regardless of the number of outriggers, the booms generally exceed two.

It is of no use to look to the Micronesian, Melanesian and Polynesian culture areas for help in trying to exploit Carteret's statement about mat sails. Such sails are ubiquitous, except in those parts of Indonesia where cotton was used instead of pandanus or other leaves.

Mapian canoes, then, are characteristically Micronesian, except for their inwardly curved endpieces, which are Indonesian in character and are most common perhaps in the Moluccas.

The extensive drinking of coconut palm wine on Mapia was noticed in 1860 by Jungmichel.[57] The drinking of the fermented sap of the coconut palm is common in the Carolines, but it may be a late introduction in many of the atolls. In Melanesia the drinking of wine made from the sugar, nipa, or coconut palms has been noted for western New Guinea, including Geelvink Bay and the Schouten Islands. The use of palm wine is well known in Indonesia, but it is absent in Polynesia, eliminating that culture area as the source of the Mapian practice.

Another Mapian trait, nose rubbing, may be of some significance—'their mode of Salutation is by touching noses as the Owhyeans'.[58] People press noses in Sonsorol, Pulo Anna, Merir, and Tobi, as well as Ulithi and probably much of the rest of the Carolines. Of course, Polynesians rubbed noses. There seems to be no evidence of the practice in the western New Guinea area or the Moluccas, including Halmahera and Morotai.

The affinities of Mapia could be established if we knew about the language of the atoll, but all we have are impressionistic conclusions on the part of early observers. We need not take seriously Meares' statement that when the *Felice* was visited by natives he was greatly astonished that they 'spoke the language of the inhabitants of' the Sandwich Islands.[59] Barclay seems to have discounted any obvious Indonesian connection by his statement: 'The natives came off in great numbers . . . and held forth a long harangue, which neither our Malays, nor any other person on board, understood';[60] but this cannot be regarded as a conclusive judgement. Jungmichel is more positive about the language, which he observed in 1860, saying that from the sounds that the Mapians made, one must deduce that the people came from the Carolines and that their language was very different from that of the Papuans, whom they did not understand.[61]

In the absence of phonological and grammatical data regarding the pre-plantation language of Mapia, comparative linguistic information about Carolinian or other Oceanic languages cannot be introduced.

Up to this point I have looked into the early descriptions of Mapian culture and physical features, compared them with Carolinian, Melanesian, Indonesian, and Polynesian traits, and found that on this basis the weight of the evidence is clearly in favour of Micronesian affiliation, with possibly some 'Papuan' and Moluccan influences no greater than those found in the western Caroline Islands.

It now remains to be seen whether Kubary's report,[62] compiled after workers had been introduced from the Carolines, Nauru and elsewhere, reinforces my conclusion about Micronesian affini-

R

ties. Kubary's report is the only professional ethnographic account that we have, and even though it was compiled hurriedly and unevenly it far surpasses anything left us either before or after his visit. Behind it lay many years of experience in the Carolines, where he lived until his final departure and death at sea.

The first and most crucial point to be determined is whether Kubary's informants were indigenes or imported plantation workers. Despite some needless confusion on the part of some contemporary writers, there is no doubt whatsoever they were Mapians. One of the indigenes was the so-called king, Marravidi, described as 'the only surviving man who has outlived his fellow men'.[63] He was about forty-five years of age. There were only three other full-blooded Mapians, one being his first wife, Fenewaytau, aged about sixty, the others being their daughter, Borokonok, aged about twenty-one, and their son, Evaluk, aged about thirteen. There had recently been a few other Mapians, including the king's younger brother, but they had departed a few months prior to Kubary's arrival in 1885. The king had a second wife, Irogoluk, aged about thirty-six, but she was not pure-blooded, being the daughter of his first wife and a man from Suf in the Kaniet Islands near the Admiralties. There were a few other hybrid relatives but she proved to be the only one who was capable of giving Kubary certain facts about the activities of daily life that the king was unfamiliar with because of the restrictions imposed on his supposed holiness. It should be stressed that King Marravidi and his handful of kinsmen lived on the northern end of Piken Island, isolated from the imported labourers whom some have erroneously thought were the sources of Kubary's anthropological and linguistic data.

The second point that can be made about Kubary is that the traits of culture and physique he recorded were indubitably Carolinian. It is not possible here to offer step by step proof of this, but a few salient points ought to be mentioned. In physical features the four pure-blooded Mapians examined in detail by Kubary were of the same type to be seen today in all the west Carolines. Significantly, the men's clothing was woven on a true loom, and the women's garments were plaited of pandanus leaves as on relatively near Sonsorol and Merir. The numerous old graves and tombs greatly interested Kubary, who thought that they had much in common with those on Yap and Ponape. He has left us a fine sketch of a Mapian canoe and it conforms to the general appearance of the boat depicted by Captain Hill of the *Ophelia*. There is no doubt that this is a Carolinian type of vessel, except for its incurving endpieces; but I do not think it is related to the *tsukpin* of Yap, as alleged by some. The strongest evidence of Carolinian affinities is, perhaps, linguistic. This is to be seen in the general word list compiled by Kubary, as well as the names of several stars and constellations used by Mapian navigators, the months of the year, the world directions, certain fish hooks, certain cultigens, and the parts of the loom, weaving materials, and products. Kubary said that he thought that 'the language of Bunaj [Mapia] was largely Ponape derived', but perhaps a better case could be made out for an origin in the western end of the Carolines. Indeed, one can go further and suggest that the people of Mapia are mostly descended from Ulithians via Tobi and the other westernmost Carolines.

NOTES AND REFERENCES

[1] Mr Edwin H. Bryan, Jr, of the Bishop Museum in Honolulu kindly supplied me with a preliminary bibliography on Mapia. Dr Saul H. Riesenberg of the Smithsonian Institution in Washington later called my attention to all the manuscript materials that I have employed in this essay and generously provided copies of portions relevant to Mapia. In turn, some of these documentary materials were copied by him from the collections of H. E. Maude and the Australian National University. For valuable assistance with the translation of German materials I am indebted to Werner Wilbert.

[2] e.g. Krusenstern 1819:111; Meinicke 1875-76:II, 365; Galis 1953-54:I, 9; 'The O'Keefe Story Brought Up-to-Date' *P.I.M.*, January 1953:68.

[3] Galvão 1944:253 n.l.

[4] Sharp 1960:26.

[5] Funnell 1707:232-6.

[6] J. Dewar, The Journal of the *Warwick*, MS. in East India Office Library, London.

[7] Carteret 1965:I, 200-1.

[8] Heeres 1900:100; Wichmann 1900:67.

[9] In the latter part of the 19th century there was much demand for men of Tana as indentured labourers and boat crews on labour vessels.

[10] J. Ruthven Le Hunte, The statement of David Deane O'Keefe of Yap made respecting certain charges brought against him by one John McGuiness. In Her Brittanic Majesty's High Commissioner's Court for the Western Pacific. Yap 19th August 1833, MS. Using official Dutch records, Wichmann 1900:68 provides a slightly variant version of the O'Keefe enterprise, one difference being that he says O'Keefe founded a settlement on Mapia in 1875 (not 1878), and J. S. Kubary gives the same year in his report (Kubary 1895:83).

[11] The Russian anthropologist, N. von Miklouho-Maclay, stopped at Mapia in 1876 on a merchant schooner but did not report anything about his stay on the atoll (Wichmann 1900:68, col. 2, fn. 2).

[12] Carteret 1965:I, 63.

[13] Heeres 1900:98. In an English summary of Heeres' article, it was erroneously stated by Edward Tregear (1901:50) that the original population of Mapia was of 'Melanesian blood'. Some mischief seems to have been caused by this translation.

[14] Trans. from Japanese, Hasebe 1928:64.

[15] Trans. from Japanese, Hasebe 1938:1.

[16] 'Far Outpost of the O'Keefe Empire', *P.I.M.*, July 1952:69.

[17] Kubary 1895:14.

[18] 'More about Mapia, Outpost of O'Keefe's Kingdom', *P.I.M.*, September 1952:70.

[19] Meares 1790:78-9.

[20] 'The O'Keefe Story', *P.I.M. op.cit.*:68.

[21] Jungmichel 1862:155-6.

[22] e.g. Meinicke 1875-76:II, 365; Kubary 1895:114; Jung 1899:380.

23 Carteret 1965:I, 200-2.
24 Eilers 1935:204-6, 347-8; 1936:245-6.
25 Eilers 1935:205; 1936:89, 246.
26 Funnell 1707:233.
27 Meares 1790:78.
28 Journal and log of *Ophelia*, Boston-Chile-China and return, January 1815-February 28, 1817, MS. in the New York Public Library, MSS. Division.
29 Log of the *Gypsy*, kept by Dr D. Parker Wilson, ships surgeon, 23 Oct. 1839-19 Mar. 1843, copy in the Department of Pacific & Southeast Asian History, A.N.U. (M 198), original at the Royal Geographical Society, London.
30 Logbook of brig *Eleanor*, Capt. E. Woodin. Log kept by mate H. Westbrook, in State Library of Tasmania, Hobart, No. C2399.
31 Jungmichel 1862:166.
32 *Ophelia*:120-1.
33 *Gypsy*.
34 Barclay 1897:284.
35 *Ophelia*: inserted page.
36 *ibid.*:120.
37 *idem*.
38 Jungmichel 1862:155.
39 *idem*.
40 The following sources have been used for comparative material: for Micronesia—Christian 1899; Damm *et al.* 1938; Eilers 1935, 1936; Hasebe 1928a, 1928b, 1938; Holden 1836; Hunt, Jr 1950; Krämer 1937; Kubary 1895; Lessa 1966, 1975; Lessa and Lay 1953; Lütke 1835-36; von Miklouho-Maclay 1878; Riesenberg and Gayton 1952. For Melanesia—Bos 1935; de Clercq and Schmeltz 1893; Cranstone 1961; Feuilletau de Bruyn 1920; Haddon and Hornell 1936-38; Held 1957; van der Sande 1907; Suzuki 1953; Wirz 1925. For Indonesia—van Baarda 1893; Baretta 1917; de Clercq and Schmeltz 1893; de Hollander 1895-98; Kleiweg de Zwaan 1925; Martin 1894, 1903; N[ieuwenhuis] 1919; Riedel 1886. For Polynesia—Buck 1938; Te Rangi Hiroa (Buck) 1930; Howells 1973; Linton 1926.
41 *Ophelia*:120.
42 *idem*.
43 *idem*.
44 See above, p. 232.
45 Barclay 1897:284.
46 *Ophelia*.
47 Jungmichel 1862:156.
48 The thick 'grass' skirts being worn early in the 20th century by the women of Pulo Anna are recent; formerly, apron mats of pandanus leaves were used. The women of Merir, too, adopted the grass skirt, but a long time ago they wore an apron mat that apparently was plaited.
49 *Ophelia*:120.
50 Meares 1790:79.
51 Jungmichel 1862:156.
52 Funnell 1707:263.
53 Carteret 1965:I, 201.
54 Meares 1790:78.
55 *Ophelia*:120.
56 *Ophelia*: inserted page.
57 Jungmichel 1862:156.
58 *Ophelia*:120.
59 Meares 1790:78.
60 Barclay 1897:284.
61 Jungmichel 1862:155.
62 Kubary 1895.
63 According to the king, 50 or 60 years ago some Gebe islanders, who had been brought to Mapia by an unnamed captain in a schooner called the *Mackenzie* in order to catch trepang, stirred up opposition when they demanded women for themselves. There was a fight, in which the Gebe chief was killed. After having left for home the intruders returned in eight very large canoes and began a series of slaughters and kidnappings.

Conquest culture and colonial culture in the Marianas during the Spanish period

ALEXANDER SPOEHR

One of the goals of both historians and anthropologists engaged in analysing socio-cultural change in the Pacific Islands since the time of first European contact is to derive conclusions at a higher level of generalization than the description of particular sequences of discrete events. For this goal to be realized comparison is a methodological necessity. The question then arises: what is the most productive frame of reference within which comparisons are to be made? This question as it pertains to the Spanish colonial history of the Mariana Islands is the subject of this essay. My point is a simple though neglected one. It is that socio-cultural change in the Marianas during the Spanish period can be most productively analysed if the Marianas are placed in an areal framework of comparison which includes the Philippines and Spanish America. The Micronesian background of the Marianas is not thereby eliminated, but the focus of interest is on a framework of comparison which lies mainly outside the boundaries of Oceania.

Spanish expansion into the non-Western world took place in two successive stages. The first was the Spanish colonization of America. The second was the extension of Spanish influence and power into the Pacific, as Spain probed westward from its newly conquered New World territories. South of the equator Spanish exploration of the Pacific Islands was transitory and did not lead to colonization. North of the equator Spain gained control of the Philippines except for the Muslim region in the south. The Mariana Islands, that convenient stopping point on the galleon route between Acapulco and Manila, fell within the Spanish orbit as part of Spain's Pacific venture. Thereafter, for three hundred years Spanish administration and Spanish culture were the dominant external forces affecting the indigenous societies in both the American and Pacific realms of the Spanish empire.

It is Spanish colonization and the impact of Spanish culture that form the basis of a framework of historical comparison which includes the Marianas, the Philippines, and Spanish America. Before considering the Marianas in this context, I offer a brief digression on anthropology and history in the two latter areas to emphasize this point. In terms of size, scale, and historical contacts, the Philippines are most appropriately compared with Mesoamerica, to which the following remarks are limited.

The analysis of socio-cultural change seems further advanced in Spanish America, particularly Mesoamerica, than in the Philippines. One reason is simply that more historians and anthropologists have worked in Mesoamerica. Published data are fuller. The ethnography of indigenous societies at the time of contact with Spain is better known and there is a much larger corpus of archaeological knowledge illuminating their prehistory. Finally, analytical concepts applied to the temporal dimensions of change in Mesoamerica are more developed. These observations can be debated, but I believe they are valid.

Historians and anthropologists working on the Philippines have certainly not been unaware of the labours of their colleagues in Mesoamerica. However, the immediate problems and interests of students of the Philippines on the one hand, and of Mesoamerica and indeed Spanish America generally on the other, has meant that the two streams of scholarship have tended to be pursued independently of each other. The understanding of long-term socio-cultural change indeed begins with a discrete area and society. But to raise the level of generalization and to increase depth of understanding, comparisons with other societies having something in common then need to be made. Here the something in common is Spain and the influence of Spanish contact agents on two culturally dissimilar parts of the world. Thus I argue that the study of socio-cultural change in the Philippines requires a more explicit framework of comparison and that the two former Spanish realms—one in America and the other in the Pacific—are the components of such a framework. Within this framework careful comparisons between the two areas of the larger events of socio-cultural change in the indigenous societies have yet to be made.

Certain general contrasts between the Philippines and Mesoamerica are of course common knowledge. There were markedly fewer Spaniards in the Philippines as compared to Mesoamerica and except for the clergy they tended to concentrate in Manila. The Spanish language did not penetrate very far into the rural countryside or very deeply into Filipino society below the élite.[1] Although a Spanish mestizo group did arise in the Philippines, it was not of the magnitude of that in Mesoamerica, and hence the ethnic division between Indian and mestizo so pronounced in the latter area did not crystallize as a pervading and enduring feature of the larger society. By the nineteenth century local Philippine leadership was exercised by the *principalia,* in some ways analogous to the ruling group when the Spaniards first arrived. But the social history of Philippine class and ethnic structure, and changes in its demographic characteristics and in its economic base, including the specific impact of Spanish contact agents on Philippine agriculture, is still all too much a matter of conjecture.

A similar comment can be made with regard to Catholicism and religious syncretism. In Mexico the Spanish found a developed native priesthood who were the custodians of a complex pantheon, to which the Spanish adapted their conversion strategy, matching Catholic saints with the most similar native deities as the clergy moved from one locale to the next. Eventually, among certain Indian communities, the cargo system of civil-religious offices evolved, related to differences in Indian and mestizo cultural patterns, and to their differing bases of economic and political power. For the Philippines there is not yet a single, intensive, and thoroughly documented study of the nature of religious syncretism. It should be undertaken in the light of comparison and contrast with comparable events in Spanish America.

The student whose main focus of interest is on indigenous Filipino society and culture during the Spanish colonial period rather than on the Spaniards and their activities, soon becomes aware of certain deficiencies in the published record. Beyond oft-repeated statements concerning the *barangay,* or lowland local group, knowledge of Philippine society and culture at the time of contact with the Spanish invaders is still relatively fragmentary. As in the case of Mesoamerica, Spanish ecclesiastics in the Philippines produced valuable accounts of the peoples they met and worked among.[2] In the Philippines, however, there was no one equal to Sahagun, that formidable missionary ethnographer of the Valley of Mexico, or even to Landa in Yucatan.

At the upper end of the time scale, modern ethnological work began in the first decade of the twentieth century among the non-Christian peoples of the Philippines. This has continued to the present day, resulting in a corpus of knowledge of great importance for comparative studies in social structure, political organization, law, economics, and human ecology. However, only with the present generation of ethnographers did anthropology join with the other social sciences in the common goal of understanding the culture of the vast majority, the long-Christianized Filipino groups living in rural areas, towns, and cities. Today ethnology in the Philippines is well advanced with an active core of Filipino practitioners.[3] The main emphasis has been on synchronic studies of specific ethnic groups. These studies are the building blocks of ethnology. The structural models they incorporate provide concepts which can be utilized in the long-term analysis of socio-cultural change. With a few notable exceptions, however, such as the work of Keesing and particularly Eggan in northern Luzon, of Hart on the plaza complex in the lowlands, and of Jocano, Fox, and others on contact ethnography, the involvement of ethnologists in the study of the historical dimensions of change in the Philippines has only begun.[4]

In terms of colonial history the Spaniards in the Philippines were indeed chroniclers, but the best known Spanish works understandably deal mainly with Spanish concerns. This is reflected in de Morga, Murillo Velarde, Montero y Vidal, Concepción, and indeed in Blair and Robertson's massive compilation.[5] A valuable view of the larger society is provided by observers such as Zuñiga and Comyn and tantalizing glimpses of Philippine life by European visitors such as Le Gentil, Mallat, and Bowring, all contributing to that body of first-hand reports out of which history is constructed.[6] The present generation of historians of the Philippines concerned with the time-span of the Spanish period—De la Costa, Majul, Corpuz, Diaz-Trechuelo, Phelan, Wickberg, and Cushner, to name only a few of the more prominent—have now raised Philippine history to a new level. Their accomplishments have brought recognition to the field, and at the same time have posed the question of the most promising directions for future work. From an admittedly personal viewpoint, one of the great needs lies in history and ethnology merging their interests in a common concern with indigenous Philippine society, viewed diachronically through the three hundred years of the Spanish colonial period, and changing in response to the influence of impinging social, cultural, and ecological factors. Larkin's regional history of Pampanga is the first important step in this direction.[7] Yet apart from Larkin's study, one must agree with Cushner that 'the basic question, to what degree did the Spanish conquest influence Philippine society, culture, and economics has not been answered'.[8]

In summary, the point of these remarks is threefold. First, the study of socio-cultural change in the Philippines during the Spanish colonial period requires a clearer focus on the indigenous society. Second, in this pursuit a closer rapprochement between history and ethnology is desirable. Third, the comparative framework in which the effects of Spanish influence and of the direct impact of Spanish contact agents on indigenous Philippine society should include comparable events in Spanish America, particularly Mesoamerica, to which the Philippines were linked by political, economic, and ecclesiastical ties.

Ancient Chamorro culture was Oceanic, and more specifically Micronesian. It is this Oceanic frame of reference that guides the archaeologist and the ethnohistorian in their attempts to delineate pre-contact culture in the Marianas. On the other hand, historic

Chamorro culture to the end of the nineteenth century falls into that Philippine-Mesoamerican (or Spanish American) framework of Spanish-dominated culture change just described. The two periods—prehistoric and historic—involve different though related perspectives. These will be briefly commented upon.

Documentary knowledge of Chamorro culture at the time of European contact is derived from one principal source, the Jesuit letters, supplemented by the fragmentary observations of earlier explorers. The first relevant compilation of Jesuit letters was published in 1683 by Francisco Garcia as a tribute to and as a biography of Sanvitores, the leader of the first Jesuit company sent to the Marianas.[9] Garcia's book was followed by a second compilation, that of Le Gobien, based largely on the first.[10] The ethnographic information in these sources is indeed valuable but nevertheless very sketchy. More has been inferred about Chamorro social organization—the presence of matrilineal descent groups, for instance—than the documentation actually supports. However, although it seems unlikely that new material will allow a reconstruction of Chamorro culture as complete as Oliver's monumental *Ancient Tahitian Society,* Hezel's report on early Jesuit sources on the Marianas invites a new and thorough archival review of the ethnographic information they contain.[11]

Contemporary archaeological work in the Marianas, much of it as yet unpublished, will also contribute an equally important body of knowledge on the Chamorros at the time of European contact.[12] This is particularly true of settlement patterns, technology, and adaptation to the island environment. And the preceding period of prehistoric occupation, which I believe will be shown to cover some 3,000 years, will also link the human settlement of the Marianas to islands to the south and eventually to a Southeast Asian homeland. Thus both historical documents and the archaeological record should provide a more definitive picture of the ancient Chamorros, against which the historic changes in their culture can be more accurately assessed. But this lies in the future.

Let us turn to the historic period in the Marianas. In geographic size and indigenous population, these islands are minuscule compared to Mesoamerica or the Philippines. The Marianas lacked those two resources, natural wealth and abundant labour, which the Spaniards exploited so effectively in the New World. Despite their convenience as a provisioning point on the long voyage across the Pacific, the Marianas attracted the Spanish primarily for missionary, not for economic, reasons. Through the accident of their location, the Chamorros became the largely unwilling subjects of the King of Spain and in the end devout Christians.

Previous writers have pointed out that the Marianas are exceptional in Oceania in that they were colonized and their inhabitants thoroughly acculturated at a much earlier date than the other islands of Micronesia, Polynesia, and Melanesia.[13] They were also different in the manner in which this colonization and acculturation was carried out. Whereas in other Pacific Islands the historic figures of trader, planter, missionary, and administrator followed their special interests, often with singular intensity, they also were often at odds among and between themselves. In the Marianas, although differences did develop occasionally between representatives of church and state, the Spanish pattern of conquest visualized the ecclesiastical and secular as but two aspects of a single effort—the programmed extension of Spanish civilization through directed culture change. This characteristic of Spanish organization makes possible conceptualizing the impact of Spanish contact agents on the Chamorros in terms of what Foster has called the 'culture of conquest' in his studies of Spain and Mexico.[14]

To paraphrase Foster, the culture of sixteenth-century Spain was not transplanted in all its regional and interclass variety to the New World at the time of the Spanish conquest. Rather there was a screening process whereby the elements of the Spanish donor culture were stripped down, or subjected to a reduction process. This selection was both 'formal' and 'informal'. The formal selection was effected through governmental and church decisions. Foster states:

> Both State and Church believed that not all Spanish traits . . . were good or desirable as parts of a civilizing mission, so by administrative decisions many elements of culture were withheld and new elements were devised to take their place. Formal processes, for example, produced standardized municipal organizations, as contrasted to the variety of local Iberian forms, and it produced the grid-plan town in place of the loosely planned or completely unplanned Spanish community of the sixteenth century. Formal processes likewise congregated Indians in villages, governed commerce and trade, and introduced an ideal or theologically purified Catholic dogma and ritual to America.[15]

The informal selection process Foster notes is less understood and harder to pin down. It applies to:

> all those unplanned mechanisms whereby the personal habits of emigrants, their food preferences, superstitions, popular medicine, folklore, music, attitudes, beliefs, hopes, and aspirations are selected and maintained in the new country . . . In informal processes, we are dealing with a multitude of personal decisions, in which each individual, through his pattern of living, is a channel of cultural transmission to the contact area.[16]

These two processes shaped Spanish conquest culture in America. With the passage of time, however, the conquest culture was itself subject to selective adoption, modification, and combination with indigenous cultural elements so that a colonial culture—to be distinguished from the conquest culture—crystallized in the contact situation and within the social system of Spanish America.

Spanish conquest culture was officially implanted in the Marianas in 1668 with the arrival on Guam of the first small group of Jesuits, supported by a handful of secular assistants and soldiers.[17] Chamorro antagonism to missionary effort then led to the strengthening of the secular arm with the appointment of the first governor in 1676 and augmentation of the military garrison. Thereafter the outlines of the conquest culture took familiar form. The Jesuits pursued Chamorro conversion to Christianity, stressing those observances basic to the ritual calendar of the Catholic Church and to the celebration of Catholic crisis rites, without a transfer of popular European religious customs extraneous to the church's central ritual and dogma. They introduced new economic plants, domestic animals, agricultural technology, a variety of previously unknown crafts, and 'hot-cold' concepts of humoral pathology. It is important to note that the conquest culture of the Marianas included elements derived from Mexico, not just from Europe, particularly the important complex of native American food plants, methods of food preparation, and associated cuisine. The state imposed its own Spanish or Spanish-Philippine plan of administration and government, with Chamorros holding the lower civil offices. This was facilitated after the end of thirty years of hostilities by the removal of the Chamorros from the northern islands and their concentration on Guam, except for the handful remaining on Rota. Both church and state programmes led to the transformation of Agaña from a village into the first town to exist in the Oceanic islands, complete with its colonial appurtenances of church, convent, Jesuit college, government house, barracks, and plaza, with the houses of the inhabitants neatly laid out in their constituent barrios. In due course, Agaña became the home of the indigenous élite.

The next stage in the culture history of the Marianas was the crystallization of what Foster has called colonial culture. I have previously designated this Hispanicized Chamorro culture, but the term lacks precision. It does not conceptually separate the conquest culture, whose point of reference is the donor society, from colonial culture, whose point of reference is the recipient society.[18] Nor does the term encapsulate the influence through informal processes of contact agents such as the Filipinos, who were not at the top of either the ecclesiastical or government hierarchies, but who settled on Guam under the Spanish umbrella. In any case, the colonial culture was a syncretic configuration vastly different from the pre-contact Chamorro culture which preceded it. It can aptly be termed Guamanian culture, for it was on Guam that it was formed.[19]

An important question is the relation of post-contact culture history to the population history of the Marianas. The latter has been known in outline,[20] but has only recently been carefully analysed by Underwood from the point of view of demography and population genetics.[21] Underwood divides the population history of the Marianas into four periods: 1521-1668, an initial period of intermittent contacts with Europeans but with population stability; 1668-1786, from the arrival of the Spanish colonizers to the low point in the drastic decimation of the Chamorro population through war and disease; 1786-1898, a period which witnessed in Underwood's terms the reintegration of 'Neo-Chamorro' culture and population recovery; and 1899-1950, a final colonial period characterized by rapid population growth and expansion. It is the second and third periods that concern us here.

The impact of Spanish conquest culture was certainly dominant in the second period, 1668-1786. The Jesuits, who were the principal carriers of the conquest culture, were expelled in 1769 while the population was still in decline. The small number of Chamorros of itself must have facilitated their acculturation. The Augustinians, who followed the Jesuits, never devoted more than minimal personnel and resources to the Marianas mission. It is reasonable to infer that the major imprint of conquest culture took place during the Jesuit régime.

The crystallization of colonial or Guamanian culture in relation to population history is more difficult to determine. In 1786 there were reported to be only 3,169 inhabitants of the islands, of whom 1,318 were Chamorros with the balance composed of a few Spaniards, American Indians, Filipinos and a sizeable mestizo group, the offspring of mixed unions.[22] During the subsequent period the population became thoroughly hybrid. Any immigration from Mexico must have virtually ceased after 1817, but this was not true of the Philippines which periodically sent new migrants. In the nineteenth century Carolinians migrated to the Marianas, but to judge from contemporary times, my impression is that rather pronounced ethnic boundaries were maintained between the Carolinian community and the remainder of the population and that the former had little effect on Guamanian culture. Although documentary sources are far from definitive, I suggest that Guamanian colonial culture was well on the way to crystallization by the time of Crozet's visit in 1772 and certainly by the arrival of von Kotzebue in 1817 and Freycinet in 1819.

The survival of the Chamorro language is a significant factor in the continuity of Guamanian culture to the present day. Although incorporating many Spanish loan words, which in some semantic domains such as weights and measures and most of the kinship terminology supplanted the Chamorro lexicon, nevertheless Chamorro grammar retained its integral characteristics and structure, as Topping's analysis, the first by a competent linguist, clearly demonstrates.[23] The persistence of Chamorro suggests parallels with the Philippines. There were never enough Spaniards in the Marianas to effect the replacement of Chamorro by Spanish. The Spaniards, including those born in Mexico, were in positions of authority but so far as can be told probably never exceeded one per cent of the population. The priests no doubt learned Chamorro and used it in communication with their parishioners, even as they do today, and as was the case in the Philippines. The earliest Chamorro grammar was written in 1688 by Sanvitores himself.[24] The extent of bilingualism during the Spanish colonial period is difficult to estimate, but Fischer has proposed that the high borrowing rate of Chamorro is an indicator of widespread bilingualism.[25] Presumably it was a characteristic of the Agaña upper class as of the Philippine upper class. Migrants to Guam must have learned Chamorro as part of their cultural adaptation; for Filipinos settling in the Marianas this would not have posed great difficulty. Chamorro is a Philippine rather than a Micronesian language, which Topping feels is probably most closely related to either Tagalog or Ilokano.[26]

If it is difficult to discern in the historical record when Guamanian culture crystallized, it is even more difficult to determine subsequent culture change during the balance of the Spanish régime. No culture is completely static and some change must have occurred. However, Guam was relatively isolated and lived on a low-level, mainly subsistence agricultural economy with minimal support from the colonial government. A few governors conscientiously attempted to stimulate economic growth, but during the latter part of the eighteenth and through the nineteenth century, formal sustained programmes of directed culture change were conspicuous by their absence. On the other hand, a question here, and indeed from the beginning of the Spanish period, is the nature and significance of those informal processes of change stemming from individual choice and action, and mediated neither by priests nor governors, but by persons of humbler status who found a home on Guam. Although figures are hard to come by, Guam did receive throughout its Spanish colonial history Filipino soldiers, civil servants, assistants in the church organization, exiles, and deportees. Some were returned but many stayed. These were Christianized carriers of lowland Philippine colonial culture.

Especially after relations with Mexico were terminated in the early nineteenth century, the Philippines were the principal source of external contact. Cultural elements as disparate as cock-fighting, machetes shaped like *bolos*, fish corrals, and dress styles diffused from the Philippines to Guam through the informal channels instituted in large degree by Filipino migrants. Abella has proposed that they were the agents responsible for aspects of Filipino culture becoming a part of Guamanian life-ways.[27] He goes so far as to ask the question: are Guamanians and Filipinos the same people?

Only a detailed analysis of Guamanian culture through time would suffice to answer the question Abella posed. Apart from the inadequacies of documentation, this is beyond the scope of this essay. However, a brief examination of a single aspect of Guamanian society and culture—family and kinship—may serve to illuminate the question.

Pre-contact Chamorro family and kinship organization are virtually unknown. The Spanish eliminated the important institution of the men's house, and any unilineal descent groups which may have existed disappeared long ago. The description which follows is drawn from twentieth century ethnography extrapolated backward in time, supported by nineteenth century sources.[28]

Whatever may have preceded it, the nuclear family became the most important kin group in Guamanian social organization. It was the familial residence unit and the primary production and consumption unit as well. A complex of church-sanctioned institutions, revolving mainly around crisis rites, supported its inviolability. Of these crisis rites, marriage was particularly important. Although one wonders about Augustinian times when often very few priests were in residence in the Marianas, nevertheless the necessity for church-sanctioned marriage became fully accepted, first no doubt by the Chamorro élite of Agaña, and eventually by all. Marriage was also an indissoluble bond. Furthermore, marriage became the symbol of social adulthood. Prior to marriage individuals regardless of chronological age were under the authority and control of their parents. After marriage the partners were recognized as adults. They were also inseparably joined as a social unit, granted their differing responsibilities. In linguistic usage a married person was referred to by linking his or her given name to that of the spouse. In speaking directly to either on any subject that might involve them both, one always used the second person plural form.

A bride price, consisting of food, clothes and jewellery for the bride, and if possible money, was a necessary part of marriage arrangements and was given by the groom's family to that of the bride. The size of the bride price reflected on the status of both families. So far as can be told, the institution of bride price was derived from the pre-contact culture, its components having been modified by acculturation.

The baptism of the first child signalized the establishment of a full family unit. More important, baptism was the foundation of ritual kinship or *compadrazgo*. Godparents at baptism served at the marriage of their godchildren, thereby relating baptism, marriage, *compadrazgo,* and the nuclear family. However, beyond a second set of godparents at confirmation, *compadrazgo* did not undergo proliferation as in the colonial societies of Mesoamerica and the Philippines. Godparents were often close relatives of the parents and there is no evidence that ritual kinship was used systematically and in major degree to extend the range of personal relationships beyond the network of true kin. In the Marianas the institution appears similar to Spanish practice, not to that of Mesoamerica or the Philippines. The reason is probably economic. In Spanish colonial times Guam never seems to have developed much of an internal marketing system and, although new crafts were introduced, full-time specialization was inhibited. The economic base for the proliferation of *compadrazgo* did not exist.

The church was further related to the nuclear family through the rites of death and through family novenas. The former were universal for all families, the latter were optional. The family novena was an event held annually by a couple in honour of a saint and usually in thanksgiving for deliverance from illness or physical harm. The novena could be passed on to a son or daughter or cease with the death of a couple.

In kinship terminology Spanish terms superseded Chamorro terms, except for those used for son, daughter, child, sibling, and spouse. The terminology was extended bilaterally, theoretically as far as third cousins. This marked the limit of exogamy, in conformity with Catholic marriage regulations. Behaviour patterns emphasized respect of young to old; of children to parents, grandparents, and older relatives, and at least before marriage of younger to older siblings. Respect for parental authority was stressed.

An important aspect of family organization was the network of reciprocal obligations which each nuclear family entered into throughout its developmental cycle. In large part these obligations revolved around the secular celebration of crisis rites and took the form of gifts *(chenchuli* or *ika)* and services *(ajudo).* Thus at the secular celebration of a marriage each nuclear family related to the groom's parents contributed as a social unit tangibles and services to help defray the cost of the occasion, with closeness of the genealogical relationship determining the amount given. A similar practice prevailed on the bride's side. These gifts were then reciprocated when the donor families held their own rites. The kinship network was thereby activated by a never-ending flow of reciprocal gifts and services among nuclear family units. The occasions themselves became important bases of family prestige.

A word should be said on the kindred. Functionally, the kindred existed if one substitutes a husband-wife pair for the hypothetical ego at the centre of the kindred. Individuals were not socially adult until marriage and hence participated in inter-family reciprocity only as representatives of their parents, not in their own right as individuals. In effect, a husband and wife merged their kindreds at marriage.

In the light of these remarks, I would propose that the structural form of Guamanian family and kinship organization was primarily the product of Spanish conquest culture. The Catholic, church-introduced celebration of crisis rites served as the instrument to give a new emphasis to the nuclear family, which the clergy themselves believed to be divinely sanctioned. Any possible competing institution, such as the men's house, was destroyed. The introduction of Spanish terms into the system of kin terminology and their bilateral extension simply reflected the significance of the nuclear family as the primary kin group. Sufficient studies of terminological change in kinship systems have now been made so that kinship terminological classification can be considered essentially an epiphenomenon, responding to changes in the structure and function of kin groups and kin relationships.

In one respect Guamanian family structure does not clearly reflect the imprint of Spanish conquest culture. There is no real evidence that the pronounced inter-family reciprocity noted above was a result of direct Spanish contact. It could have been a reworking of forms of reciprocity found in the pre-contact society or could have in part been introduced through informal channels. Counterparts are found in the Philippines.

If the structural form of Guamanian family and kinship organization is in large measure the product of conquest culture, its cultural pattern is only partly so. By cultural pattern I refer to all those items of custom that enter into what is idealogically considered proper behaviour—the preferred cuisine appropriate to a secular celebration, the order of serving guests, the dress of participants, how respect is accorded the elderly, or the social value accorded the accoutrements of a well-kept house. Here the Guamanians drew on many sources—their pre-contact culture, colonial Spain, Indian Mexico, and the Philippines—to syncretize a multiplicity of elements into their familial culture pattern. Many of these elements formed symbolic complexes giving meaning to personal relationships. It is my belief that it is in this domain of culture pattern that the informal processes of change mediated by individual migrants to Guam played a major role. It is also in this area that documentary sources are weakest, but similarities to Filipino patterns are often striking. One example is the keeping of the family *chenchuli* record. In modern times, at each celebration of a crisis rite, the family keeps a careful record of each money gift (*chenchuli*) and the name of the nuclear family who gave it. The record keeper, generally a female relative of husband or wife, sits at the door of the house, receives the gift, and records the donor's name. The record is maintained as long as the nuclear family is in existence. It is a record not just of gifts but of obligations to the donors which subsequently must be met. The identical custom is found in the Philippines. I have observed it even among the Muslim Tausug of Sulu.

There are indeed cultural differences between the Marianas and the Philippines, as within the Philippines as a whole, but Guamanian family and kinship organization is more similar to that of the lowland Philippines than to any Oceanic society. The absence of corporate descent groups, the commonalities in family structure, the type of kinship terminology, bride price, and formalized reciprocity reflect variations on a common theme. To some degree these similarities may stem from pre-contact times. In major degree they are the product of formal processes of change imposed by Spanish conquest culture. And through informal processes of change Filipino elements were incorporated into Guamanian cultural patterns.

I return to the question posed at the beginning of this essay: what are the most productive frameworks for the comparative study of socio-cultural change? For the Spanish colonial period in the Marianas, a first-level frame of reference includes the Marianas with the Philippines. A second-level framework of comparison includes the Philippines and Marianas on one hand and Spanish America, particularly Mesoamerica, on the other, both having been subjected to Spanish conquest culture and both having evolved their own versions of colonial culture. These frameworks of camparison have not yet been exploited by students of socio-cultural change and invite their attention.

Frameworks of comparison are simply devices to facilitate understanding, however, and must change with the events of change. Granted the continuity of Guamanian culture, the Marianas particularly since the Second World War have been swept by new influences shaping the future of the Pacific Islands. Urbanization, tourism, environmental degradation, and continuing economic and political dependency have all created both problems and forces of change which the larger island groups share.[29] In the study of contemporary change it is more logical to compare

S

Guam with Tahiti than with the Philippines.[30] Thus the very forces which impel change provide new comparative frameworks for its fuller understanding.

NOTES AND REFERENCES

[1] A related phenomenon was the development of a Philippine Creole Spanish termed *Chabacano* in Zamboanga and in the Manila Bay area. See Frake 1971.

[2] Among the most informative are Francisco Ignacio Alciña, Pedro de Chirino, Francisco Colín, Francisco Combés, and Juan de Plasencia. For bibliographic sources see Saito 1972. Philippine ethnography at the time of Spanish contact is summarized by Fox 1966, and by Jocano 1967. See also Eggan, Hester, and Ginsberg 1956.

[3] Saito, *op.cit.;* Zamora 1972.

[4] Keesing 1962; Eggan 1941, 1954, 1963; Hart 1955; Fox, *op.cit.;* Jocano, *op.cit.;* Eggan, Hester, and Ginsberg, *op.cit.*

[5] de Morga 1909; Murillo Velarde 1749; Montero y Vidal 1887-1895; Juan de la Concepción 1788-1792; Blair and Robertson 1903-1909.

[6] de Zúñiga 1973; de Comyn 1820; Le Gentil de la Galaisière 1779-1781; Mallat de Bassilan 1846; Bowring 1859.

[7] Larkin 1972.

[8] Cushner 1975:572.

[9] Garcia 1683.

[10] Le Gobien 1700.

[11] Hezel 1970.

[12] Reinman 1968.

[13] Keesing 1945; Oliver 1961; Maude 1971.

[14] Foster 1960.

[15] *ibid.*:14.

[16] *ibid.*:12

[17] The Jesuit priests were not all Spaniards, but they conformed to Spanish practices.

[18] Foster 1960:227-34.

[19] For histories of Guam see Carano and Sanchez 1964; Beardsley 1964. For Spanish histories see de la Corte y Ruano Calderón 1875; Olive y García 1887.

[20] Thompson 1947; Carano and Sanchez 1964.

[21] Underwood 1973.

[22] *ibid.*:19-22.

[23] Topping 1973.

[24] Burrus 1954.

[25] Fischer 1961.

[26] Topping 1973:3.

[27] Abella 1973.

[28] Principal 20th century sources are Fritz 1904; Safford 1902, 1905; Thompson 1947; Spoehr 1954. Principal 19th century sources are the accounts of Arago, Dumont D'Urville, Freycinet, Haswell, Kotzebue, and Sanchez y Zayas.

[29] For a recent symposium see Force and Bishop 1975.

[30] Fages and McGrath 1975.

The role of the beachcomber in the Carolines

FRANCIS X. HEZEL

Beachcombers are a much reviled class of men. Contemptuously dismissed as 'reprobates' or 'abandoned and degenerate characters', they have time and again been charged with infecting the islanders with whom they lived with a moral pestilence ultimately more destructive than the epidemics of smallpox and influenza that ravaged these populations. Yet as H. E. Maude has pointed out in his masterful survey of beachcombers,[1] that motley array of deserters, escaped convicts, castaways and wanderers that gathered on many a Pacific island must be credited with more positive contributions as well—not the least of which was their interpretation of Western culture to the native populations that served to prepare them for changes still to come. Aside from such important general roles as cultural mediator, beachcombers have served more specific functions that have varied with time and place, as Professor Maude clearly shows. In this essay, I propose to explore the uses to which beachcombers were put on those few islands of the Caroline group where they were found in any numbers during the nineteenth century: Palau, Kusaie and Ponape. The prominence of beachcombers and the roles they assumed differed considerably even among these three islands, as will be seen.

The classical era of beachcombing in the Carolines began in 1783 with the wreck of the East India packet *Antelope* at Palau and the involuntary three-month residence of its crew. Not that this was the first time whites had ever lived ashore in the Caroline Islands; there is an account of seven white men landing on Ulithi in 1684, most likely the survivors of a shipwreck,[2] and there were presumably others of whom no historical record remains. But these were isolated instances of a few whites living ashore over the span of more than three centuries. The founding of beach communities awaited the opening of regular ship routes through Micronesian waters, and that occurred only in the late eighteenth century.

The castaways from the *Antelope* received generous treatment at the hands of the friendly Palauans, we are told. But even after a romanticized account of their stay appeared in the form of a book, George Keate's *An Account of the Pelew Islands*, Palau never attracted a great number of whites.[3] The majority of foreigners who took up residence there for a time were, with a few notable exceptions, the victims of shipwrecks: the *Antelope* in 1783, the *Mentor* in 1832,[4] the *Dash* in 1834,[5] and the *Renown* in 1870;[6] and most of these remained for only a few months. The castaways were invariably well treated by the Palauans, it would appear. Even the survivors of the *Mentor,* whose tribulations were publicized in Horace Holden's *Narrative of a Shipwreck,* received considerate treatment and help in building the makeshift boat with which they intended to sail to the Indies; their misfortune, according to Holden, was to fall into the hands of the inhabitants of Tobi, an island some two hundred miles to the south-west of Palau. Despite the friendliness of their hosts to the castaways on Palau, only two of them elected to remain permanently on the island. They, together with a handful of other foreigners who were left by visiting ships, made up the small contingent of beach-combers who lived on Palau for any length of time before the 1870s. Evidently something more than assurance of adequate food resources and good treatment by the islanders was necessary to turn an island into a haven for discontented whites.

But if Palau could claim few white residents throughout most of the nineteenth century, the other islands in the western Carolines had virtually none. The three seamen from the *Duff* who were put ashore at their own request on Satawal and Lamotrek in 1797 are about the only whites hardy enough to have made their home on any of the tiny, poorly endowed coral atolls in the region, and they were not heard of again.[7] The high island of Yap proved just as inhospitable to potential beachcombers, if for altogether different reasons. Yapese, a strong tradition asserts, discouraged early visitors even to the point of massacring ships' crews whenever possible. The itinerant trading captains Andrew Cheyne and Alfred Tetens, the first foreigners known to have visited that island regularly, were both attacked there and did not feel that it was safe to leave a party ashore in their absence until 1866.[8]

Madan Blanchard, one of the crew of the *Antelope,* was the first white who can be said to have chosen a beachcomber's life on Palau, electing as he did to remain there as his companions put to sea one November day in 1783. Like John McCluer who gave up his command aboard the *Panther* ten years later to become the second voluntary white resident on Palau, Blanchard was adopted by Ibedul (one of the two paramount chiefs), liberally provided with native wives and property, granted chiefly status, and otherwise absorbed into the social system of the island.[9] To a much greater extent than did beachcombers on Ponape and Kusaie, Blanchard and those who followed him took on the ways of the islanders with whom they lived. Blanchard himself soon discarded his European clothes and was tattooed.[10] John Davy, who survived the wreck of the *Dash* in 1834 and chose to live out his years on Palau, must have done the same, for an officer aboard the u.s.s. *Vincennes* two years later writes with evident astonishment of finding him 'running as naked as his countrymen' (who, by all accounts, were quite naked indeed!).[11] Charles Washington, a deserter from the English man-of-war *Lyon* who had spent thirty-five years on the island by the time of the *Vincennes'* visit, was said to have become 'as thoroughly savage as any of the savages'.[12] Deprived almost completely of the companionship of other whites, the handful of beachcombers on Palau would have lacked what we might now call alternative role models. In this respect they differed greatly from whites living ashore in the eastern Carolines who were usually part of a good-sized beach community.

Apart from shipwrecked seamen and an occasional deserter, there were a few foreigners who came to Palau as members of bêche-de-mer curing parties in the 1840s and 1850s, but their residence too was ordinarily limited to a few months. The whites who stayed for longer than a year or two could not have numbered more than ten throughout the entire ninety-year period that spanned the arrival of the *Antelope* in 1783 and the establishment of the first company trade station by Hernsheim in 1874. This sprinkling of beachcombers cannot be said to have clothed the natives or anything else of the sort; in this regard, as we have just seen, they were more changed themselves than agents of change. Neither did they seem to have triggered a technological revolution among the islanders. In 1788 Palauans already carried 'iron adzes of European manufacture';[13] by 1875 they still had steel adzes and very little more. The beachcombers' main contribution was not their impact upon the material culture of Palau, but their effect on the continuing power struggle between the two competing alliances or federations of Palau. The role of the beachcomber in Palau, then, must be situated in the political context of an on-going rivalry that has survived, although not in its bloodier forms, up to the present day.

Foreigners who took up residence in Palau immediately became the personal 'property' of either the Ibedul or the Reklai, paramount chiefs of the federations of Koror and Ngetelngal (or Melekeiok) respectively. Most wound up in the court of the Ibedul for the simple reason that the harbour of Koror provided better anchorage and so was more frequented by foreign ships, but a few—Washington, Woodin, and even the great naturalist Kubary —found themselves in the opposite camp. It was dangerous for any white to attempt to play both sides for his own profit, as Cheyne's murder at the hands of the Ibedul vividly demonstrated.

The office that beachcombers performed has been loosely described as 'interpreter to the chief', a title that poorly defines their actual function. Chiefs in Palau seldom, it seems, had to fetch their white retainers to carry on normal barter with a passing ship, but almost always did so when the matter under discussion was a punitive expedition against traditional enemies. The main role of the beachcomber, one concludes from the literature, was to intercede on his chief's behalf for military aid against the rival federation and thereby enable the chief to extend his power base. The success of this diplomatic mission depended in good part upon whether the 'interpreter' could persuade the man-of-war or merchant vessel that the opposing faction were rebels who originally owed allegiance to the kindly chief who was so generously furnishing provisions for the ship, or that his enemies had acted or were preparing to act against the interests of the foreigners themselves. The use of beachcombers in this way was, of course, no novelty in the Pacific. But in Palau, unlike Tahiti and Hawaii, consolidation into a single empire never took place, the result being that beachcombers continued to serve the same political-military function until the visit of the British warship *Espiègle* in 1883 when a peace treaty between the two federations was at last signed.[14]

For nineteenth-century Palauans, as for us today, military aid meant both an arsenal of modern weapons and trained troops from abroad. The *Antelope*'s crew supplied both for Ibedul when, armed with their muskets, they joined a band of warriors from Koror in battle against the 'enemies of the king'.[15] Blanchard became the ordnance man for the chief and was entrusted with the care of the weapons left him after the *Duff*'s departure, much as Stanford was charged with the same duty by Cheyne in 1843.[16] Not all whites were trained ship's gunners like these two, but the unskilled could be used in other ways to procure weapons for one or the other federation. Two American seamen from the *Mentor* who fell into the hands of Reklai were held prisoner for four years pending the delivery of a ransom price of two hundred muskets and several kegs of powder. In the negotiations prior to the release of the two captives to an American warship in 1836 each confederation was represented by a white interpreter-diplomat: Washington speaking for Reklai and Davy taking the part of Ibedul.[17] The most desirable form of military aid, of course, was the service of a foreign man-of-war in what might legally pass as a punitive expedition against the other side. Perhaps the most prominent beachcomber to live on Palau, a West Indian by the name of James Gibbons who deserted from a whaleship around 1860, seems to have been exceptionally skilful in winning the sympathy of naval officers for Ibedul and was so employed on a number of occasions. There is good reason to believe that he was instrumental in persuading the British commanders of the *Lily* and *Comus* in 1882 to execute a raid against Melekeiok when the people there failed to make full reparation for plundering a ship that had gone aground two years earlier.[18]

We may presume that the paramount chiefs in Palau enlisted the services of their beachcomber subjects in other ways as well. No doubt some of the foreigners practised trades and instructed the islanders in them, as whites did all over the Pacific. But their importance in procuring and maintaining firearms and in enlisting military support for their chief from foreign ships appears to have eclipsed all other contributions they may have made.

Beachcombers made their first appearance in the eastern Carolines somewhat later than in Palau—not on Ponape or Kusaie, as one might expect, but in the Truk area. Two English seamen left Duperrey's *Coquille* in 1824 to live on one of the islands in the Truk lagoon,[19] and another Englishman, William Floyd, was landed by a whaleship on the near-by island of Murilo in 1827.[20] None of the three remained for very long, however; the two sailors from the *Coquille* made their way to Guam within a year and Floyd was picked up by Lutké eighteen months after his arrival. By late 1828 the short beachcombing venture in Truk had come to an end and, except for the castaways of the *Norna* who spent a few months there before they were picked up by the British warship *Sphinx* in 1862, no foreigners were known to have lived in the Truk area until the first traders were landed in the 1870s.[21]

Ponape and Kusaie, by contrast, attracted a sizable throng of white residents during the early 1830s, most of them escaped convicts or deserters from Sydney ships. It was on these two islands, alone of all the Carolines, that what may be properly called beach communities sprang up. James O'Connell, the earliest and best-known beachcomber by reason of his book, *A Residence of Eleven Years in New Holland and the Caroline Islands,* appears to have been living on Ponape by 1830—just two years after the island was rediscovered by Lutké.[22] In 1833 Captain Knights of the *Spy* found a small colony of ex-convicts living on the island, several of whom had arrived as stowaways aboard a trading vessel from Botany Bay.[23] Others may have come off the Sydney whalers *Albion* and *Nimrod* that touched at Ponape in 1832, or from any of the other British whalers that were beginning to call at the islands. Two such ships, we know, left a good number of their former hands on Kusaie at about this time: the *John Bull* reported ten desertions there in late 1830, and the *Australian* recorded about as many in 1832.[24] By 1835 there were said to be thirty Englishmen living on Ponape, and there were probably almost the same number on Kusaie.[25]

These early beach communities were far from models of harmony and good fellowship, if we believe contemporary accounts. Cheyne, who lived on Ponape for five months in 1843, tells a sorry tale of seemingly endless murders and intrigues among the whites residing there. The surgeon of the *Gypsy* in 1841 writes of one white shooting another after a quarrel, then hacking his body to pieces with a sword. 'What', he asks, 'can be expected of runaway felons from Sydney or deserters from whaling ships? The very scum and dregs of society!'[26] The Sydney press, meanwhile, grew indignant at the excesses being perpetrated by former members of its colony and demanded that a man-of-war take immediate action.[27] A warship was, in fact, given orders to visit Ponape and Kusaie for this purpose—not a British vessel, but the U.S. expeditionary ship *Peacock* cruising the area in 1841—but lack of time forced the commander to abandon his plans to 'break up the nest of rogues' in those places.[28]

What, we might ask, was the reaction of the islanders to the roguery of their foreign guests? On Kusaie, to judge from the evidence, it was the swift and brutal massacre of all the whites living on the island—not for their 'base and unprincipled conduct', but because of a wholly different kind of threat they posed to the native population. In 1835 two American vessels, the brig *Waverly* and the schooner *Honduras,* were attacked at Kusaie, possibly with the complicity of the beach community. One of the few survivors aboard the *Honduras* later reported that large guns were fired from the shore with remarkable accuracy and concluded that beachcombers had a large hand in the attempt to take the ship.[29] Even if the whites there did not take an active part in either of these incidents, they could not have been ignorant of what happened then and in 1842 when the British whaler *Harriett* was cut off and its crew murdered. A ship that lay at anchor for nine weeks in early 1843 found no whites on Kusaie and the captain presumed that they had all been killed to prevent disclosure of the natives' misdeeds.[30] Within a year there were beachcombers again established on Kusaie, but upon the visit of a British ship in February 1844 most of these new arrivals requested passage to Ponape out of fear for their lives if it ever became generally known that they were familiar with the circumstances of the *Harriett*'s loss.[31] The lot of a beachcomber on Kusaie at this time was clearly a risky one. Desertions continued as whaling traffic grew heavier and many seamen must have spent a short time on the island after taking leave of their ship, but the number of whites on the island at any single time thereafter remained small. The beach community on Kusaie never again approached its former size during the 1830s.

On Ponape there are stories of two early attempts by islanders to exterminate the white residents, both of them unsuccessful. In 1835 the island chiefs, angered at the refusal of a group of white castaways to comply with island etiquette and surrender their boat to their Ponapean benefactors, had all but decided to wipe out every white on the island. The plan was aborted, however, when the spokesman for one of the most influential chiefs refused to abide by the decision and declared that he would protect the whites in his own territory.[32] A year later an impetuous young chief from Metalanim, smarting from an insult he had received at the hands of the captain of the whaleship *Falcon,* led a party of Ponapeans in an attack on the ship's crew, killing the captain along with five others and announcing his intention to do away with every foreigner on the island. But he and his followers were soon hunted down by a combined force of whites living ashore, crew members of visiting whaleships, and four hundred Ponapean warriors; and the chief was ceremoniously hanged from the yard-arm of a British cutter. At his death some followers who remained implacable in their hatred of whites went into voluntary exile on a tiny island just off the north-eastern coast of Ponape where they were later joined by three black American deserters.[33]

It appears that on Ponape, in contrast to Kusaie, it was all but impossible for the natives to take concerted action against the beachcombers. Kusaie had a single paramount chief with jurisdiction over the entire island, while Ponape was divided into five autonomous chiefdoms. The rivalry among the five paramount chiefs of Ponape who ruled over different sections of the island virtually guaranteed that the whites would be able to find protection somewhere in situations of extremity. But it seldom came to that. Individual chiefs customarily adopted foreigners into their household, provided spouses and property, and furnished whatever else was necessary for a reasonably comfortable life. The chief was generally anxious to avoid alienating his foreign 'subject' whom he came to regard as not only a prized possession but also as something of a son.[34]

With the influx of deserters from an increasing number of whaleships during the 1840s, the population of resident whites on Ponape grew steadily—from about fifty in 1840 to one hundred and fifty ten years later. Occasionally the greater part of the ship's crew remained behind: the *Eliza* in 1836 had sixteen desert; the *Offley* in 1841 lost so many men that it could not make sail; the *Sharon* in 1842 left eleven ashore; and the *Fortune* in 1843 lost seven hands, leaving only four men before the mast.[35] Whites living ashore often furnished liberal assistance to seamen in making good their escape, although few were prepared to go quite as far as Thomas Boyd when, after reportedly inciting several of the

Maguet's crew to desert, he held two of its boat crews at gunpoint until the deserters' clothes were put ashore.[36] The establishment of a bounty of between ten and twenty dollars for the return of deserters proved to be only partially effective as a counter-measure. A boat from the *Martha* in 1856 that went ashore laden with a keg of tobacco and a barrel of beef as a reward for the capture of four of its men returned to the ship empty-handed.[37] As desertions continued, the composition of the beach community on Ponape changed to become predominantly American, with a good number of Portuguese and some Englishmen added.

Beachcombers on Ponape earned their living in a number of ways. Some practised their trades as carpenters, smiths and coopers as need for their services arose. From the very beginning there were some who served as harbour pilots aboard visiting ships, for which the customary fee was twenty dollars. In time the island was divided into several 'beats' which were assigned to particular individuals, one anchorage becoming known as 'Hadley's Harbour' after the white pilot who had worked this area for twenty years. Above all, white residents also played a major role in trade with foreign ships. For a good many years the Ponape chiefs seem to have entrusted to whites most of the responsibility for organizing and conducting trading operations, making of them middlemen of sorts. It was the whites who established the price of yams, taro and bananas, and set fees for supplying wood and water with the help of island labour. The sale of pigs and fowl was almost exclusively the prerogative of the whites until the supply was all but depleted in the 1850s.[38] For all practical purposes, the foreigners on Ponape held a corner in the island's most important market commodities, at least prior to the middle of the century. According to one early report, the payment for island produce went directly to the foreigner, who then distributed to the chief a quantity of trade goods: muskets, axes, adzes, cloth, powder and tobacco. The chief presumably used a part of this to compensate the commoners who had supplied the produce or labour; the beachcomber himself gave them nothing except for 'occasional small payments of tobacco'.[39]

White domination over the trade with whaling vessels was soon extended from Ponape to its satellite islands as well. When whites from Ponape settled on the neighbouring island of Ngatik after the infamous massacre of its male population in 1837, and later on the atolls of Mokil and Pingelap, they rapidly developed a flourishing trade in local produce. Within a short time they were breeding swine, fowl and ducks to sell to the whaleships that were laying over at these islands with greater frequency. By 1852 the *Eugenie* could report of the two Americans living on Mokil that their earnings reached as high as forty dollars a month and their wives were nicely outfitted in pretty cotton blouses.[40]

In time the islanders came to acquire greater control over their own trade. The A.B.C.F.M. mission that began on Ponape in 1852 worked actively to break the trade monopoly held by whites and provided instruction for the islanders to this end. In 1857 a pastor wrote that their efforts had already achieved a certain measure of success: the people in two of the five municipalities were able to trade directly with ships.[41] Eventually the elimination of the white middleman was complete, but not before 1870 or so; and by that time many of the fifty whites who remained on Ponape had taken positions with the companies that were already establishing outlets there.

The beachcomber on Kusaie seems to have been far less indispensable than his opposite number on Ponape. His role in trade with ships was a minor one, we might infer from the logs of visiting ships; negotiations were usually carried on directly with the chief rather than with an intermediary. The chief himself, not the beachcombers, raised livestock and poultry for barter with ships, even supplying cattle for them on occasion. Indeed, one of the reasons for Kusaie's growing popularity as a port of call for whaleships seems to have been its relative freedom from meddlesome white traders.[42] Beachcombers were not ordinarily called upon to act as interpreters, for Kusaiens were reported—as early as 1844—to possess a 'very extensive knowledge of the English language'.[43] An education in their mother tongue, we may assume, was the legacy of the early British beachcombers on the island—along with a craving for rum. Some of the *habituées* of whaleships could carry on good conversations that ranged over a surprising variety of topics, as one seaman aboard the *Cavalier* learned while listening to a young Kusaien woman chat on the subject of ice and snow.[44] Whites did not even serve as harbour pilots; 'kanakas' normally performed this duty, as many of the ships' logs show.

The relative insignificance of the beachcomber on Kusaie is reflected in the number of whites living ashore there in 1850—only four, compared with one hundred and fifty on Ponape.[45] Among other reasons for the small size of the beach community, the paramount chief of Kusaie apparently felt free to evict whomever he regarded as undesirable. As the sole ruler of the island, he had no need to accumulate a large retinue of beachcombers to be used for the political purposes of enhancing his own authority or undercutting that of rivals. Moreover, the beachcomber was not nearly as economically vital to Kusaie as he was to Ponape. Kusaie's chief could afford to be discriminating in allowing whites to settle on the island—and he was! In 1850 one beachcomber was dismissed from the island for reasons that are not stated.[46] A former whaling master, on the other hand, was encouraged to take up residence on Kusaie and made notable material improvements there before his departure two years later.[47] At the visit of the missionary brig *Morning Star* in 1857, the chief was engaged in a military campaign against two whites and a group of Rotuma natives, the purpose being to make life so unpleasant for them that they would leave the island voluntarily. It was only through the intercession of the missionaries that the chief was persuaded to allow the expatriates to remain on the island, and even then on the condition that they were not to wander out of their compound.[48] Whether the strong control exerted by the chief was responsible for keeping down the number of whites or not, the fact is that Kusaie did not have the large and rowdy beach community that Ponape had, and in 1870 there was but a single white living on Kusaie.[49]

It is not easy to single out the precise effects that the beach community had in the eastern Carolines, even on the material cultures. A few things, however, may be ascribed with certainty to beachcombers: the introduction of coconut toddy to Ponape and Kusaie, the construction of the first alcohol distillery on Ngatik, and the building of nine-pin alleys on Ponape and Kusaie.[50] Their achievements were not all of this order, it must be added; one of their number built a chapel and pulpit on Mokil so that he could instruct the natives in Christianity. Visitors to that island long afterwards testified to the 'order and decency' that were so evident among the islanders.[51]

Not all the whites living on these islands were villains and knaves, of course, and even the more disreputable beachcombers appear to have changed in the course of time. Several settled down to what might be judged by any standards a respectable life. A few—such as Louis Corgat, James Striker, and Henry Worth—even became known for their religious zeal and provided invaluable assistance to later missionaries. Others may have retained their several wives and their fondness for the bottle, but even they 'turned respectable' in that they found steady employment and ceased their homicidal quarrels.

By 1870 or so the era of the beachcomber was over in the Caroline Islands. The decline of whaling traffic, the drastic reduction in the native population, the mounting influence of missionaries, and the growing sophistication of the islanders all contributed to the demise of the beach community. But the real death blow was the arrival of the company trader who tended his well-stocked post, provisioned regularly by a company schooner. It was not long before the beachcomber was replaced by a 'more decent, clean-living type', as one visitor to Ponape chose to put it.[52] With very few exceptions, those foreigners who lived on any of the islands after this could claim that they were there on business.

Even during the years prior to 1870—a period that could rightly be called the age of the beachcomber—we have seen that the size of the beach community, its peak years, and the role of beachcombers varied widely in Palau, Kusaie and Ponape. Palau had a constant trickle of whites throughout most of the nineteenth century, with seldom more than two or three living there at one time. Beachcombers there were immediately adopted by one of the two paramount chiefs and were used to help the chief secure a political advantage over his rival, either by actually bringing his firearms into battle or by persuading European vessels to do so in his role as foreign diplomat.

On Ponape, an island that also had more than one paramount chiefdom, beachcombers did not play any great military role in island rivalries. Instead, the large beach community organized and regulated commerce with visiting ships. Even as Ponapeans gradually began to assume control of their own trade in the two decades after 1850, the beach community continued to flourish although the number of whites dropped to fifty. On Kusaie the beach community must have reached its greatest size in 1840. After that the island seems to have been less a home than a way station for deserters who were bound elsewhere. Long before 1870 the number of whites living ashore shrank to just one or two. The role of the white on Kusaie was not well defined and clearly of less importance than that of the beachcomber on Ponape.

If there is anything to be learned from all of this, it may simply be that beachcombers generally did what a particular society needed them to do.

NOTES AND REFERENCES

1 'Beachcombers and Castaways' in Maude 1968:134-47. I am indebted to Professor Maude not just for the ideas presented in his classic survey of beachcombing, but also for the generous assistance he offered in helping me locate many of the sources cited in this contribution.
2 Lessa 1962:337.
3 Keate's volume, 'composed from the journals and communications of Captain Henry Wilson', was first printed in London in 1788 and came out in four subsequent editions before 1803.
4 Holden 1836.
5 Ward 1967:V, 152-8.
6 *N.M.* 39 (1870):386-7.
7 Wilson 1799:298-305.
8 Cheyne 1971:245-78; Tetens 1958:4-26, 64-5.
9 Hockin 1803:*passim.*
10 *ibid.*:8-9.
11 Notes on the South Sea Islands by R. L. Browning, Lt. U.S.N., on board the U.S. Ship *Vincennes* circumnavigating in 1835-6, J. H. Aulick Commander, in Browning Family Papers, Library of Congress, Washington, Box 141, 405A-012, 4:224.

12 *ibid.*:262-3.
13 Phillip 1789:210.
14 There are cultural reasons to suggest that neither of the paramount chiefs ever wanted to bring the other federation completely under his own power. Palau is a society that is organized around binary divisions on every level: intra-village, village, municipal and federational. The people seem to thrive on the competition that is so deliberately built into its entire social structure.
15 Keate 1788:73.
16 Cheyne 1971:238-41.
17 Notes on the South Sea Islands, *op.cit.*:266-83.
18 Report of the Cruise by H.M.S. *Espiègle*, 10 October 1883, M.L.
19 Journal d'un voyage autour du monde, entrepris sur la corvette de S. M. la Coquille sous les ordres de M. Duperrey, Lieutenant de vaisseau, par J. Dumont d'Urville, M.L. B1300.
20 Lutké 1835-36:II, 289-91.
21 Sir Edward Hobart Seymour, Papers relating to the search for the barque *Norna*, lost in the Pacific, 1861-1862, M.L., MSS. 557.
22 O'Connell 1972.
23 Knights 1925:199-206.
24 Logbooks of *John Bull* and barque *Australian*, Capt. Edward Cattlin, Journals 1827-1836, M.L., MS. 1800.
25 *Sydney Gazette*, 2 August 1836.
26 Log of the Gypsy, *op.cit.*, Department of Pacific and Southeast Asian History, A.N.U., M 198.
27 *Sydney Gazette*, 2 August 1836.
28 Wilkes 1845:V, 109.
29 Ward 1967:III, 541-6; *Sydney Gazette*, 13 April 1837.
30 Ward 1967:III, 559-60, 568-72.
31 *ibid.*:574-7.
32 Ward 1967:VI, 135-6.
33 *N.M.*, 16 (1847):127-31, and 39 (1870):248; *H.R.A.*, Ser. 1:XX, 654-73.
34 The paternal loyalty shown to the beachcomber by his chief could itself serve to check the 'bad propensities of some of the renegade European characters', as one visitor to Ponape shrewdly noted, *N.M.* 39 (1870):247-8.
35 Ward 1967:VI, 123; Log of *Gypsy*, entry for 18 April 1841; Ward *op.cit.*: 141-3; Log of Bark *Fortune* of New Bedford, David E. Hathaway, Master, Nicholson Whaling Collection, Providence Public Library, Providence, R.I.
36 Cheyne 1971:160-1.
37 Log of Whaleship *Martha* of Fairhaven, Old Dartmouth Historical Society and Whaling Museum, New Bedford; copy Pacific Manuscripts Bureau, mf. 264:ff.333-6.
38 *Sydney Herald*, 15 May 1844.
39 *N.M.* 39 (1870):247-8; *H.R.A.*, Ser. 1:XX, 667-8.
40 Andersson 1854:283-5.
41 Letter of Rev. L. H. Gulick quoted in *The Friend*, Honolulu, 3 March 1858:17.
42 Cheyne 1971:158-9, 192-3.
43 Ward 1967:III, 574-7.
44 Journal of bark *Cavalier*, 1848-50, kept by William Wilson, G. White Blount Library, Mystic, Conn., Log No. 18.
45 Ward 1967:III, 578.
46 Journal of *Cavalier, op.cit.*
47 This was Captain Isaac Hussey of the *Planter* who came to live on Kusaie in December 1850 after he shot a seaman while suppressing a mutiny aboard his ship. Hussey signed on the *William Penn* in July 1852 as its master, but a short time later he was killed when another mutiny broke out. Jones 1861:136-7, 250, 261-2.
48 Report of the First Voyage of the Missionary Packet 'Morning Star' by Capt. S. G. Moore, *N.M.* 27 (1858):451-3.
49 W. T. Wawn's Journal, Wellington, Alexander Turnbull Library, M1971/294.
50 *N.M.* 14 (1845):505-7; Ward 1967:VI, 165; Jones 1861:146-53.
51 Ward 1967:VI, 166-7; *N.M.* 33 (1864):433.
52 Wood 1875:161.

'And, behold, the plague was begun among the people'[1]

NORMA McARTHUR

'They are agreed, that all their mortal diseases are from the ships, but they are not agreed what ships brought particular diseases', wrote the British missionaries about the Tahitians in 1804.[2] It was then only thirty-seven years since Tahiti was discovered and, naïve though the Tahitians' beliefs might have seemed to the missionaries, the people of Tahiti had experienced at least three epidemics which they could associate directly with the visits of foreign vessels. Each visit of the Spanish frigate *Aguila* in 1772 and 1774 was accompanied by 'a pestilence . . . which was neither more or less than a severe chill'[3] or alternatively, 'an epidemic of catarral fevers';[4] and after more than a decade with no European visitors—from the end of September 1777 when Cook left Tahiti[5] until July 1788[6]—there was an outbreak of dysentery following Vancouver's visit in January 1792.[7] In each of these epidemics 'many' people died, and for those Tahitians who survived all of them, or even the last, it was both natural and logical to blame the European visitors for all of their diseases. Whether it was true or not is another question.

In describing the diseases from which the islanders suffered, the missionaries and most other visitors to the Pacific in the eighteenth and nineteenth centuries could draw only on their own experience (however indirect) of the diseases then prevalent in their home countries. That there should necessarily be any parallels between the background patterns of disease and mortality in such different societies and climates strains credibility no less than does the assumption that, before the advent of Europeans into the Pacific, its people suffered no fatal diseases other than those arising from 'errors of hygiene associated with child rearing and the usual degenerative diseases'.[8] Whatever the endemic diseases may have been, and high though the mortality from some of them may have been in some years,[9] the diseases which provoked the greatest resentment, and the greatest publicity, were invariably the acute infectious diseases which assumed epidemic form.

Mostly they were diseases common to European populations and their nineteenth-century offshoots in the countries bordering the Pacific, and so they were easily identified even though nothing was known then about the micro-organisms responsible, or the mode of transmission from person to person. With the hindsight of twentieth-century medical research, especially in microbiology, the epidemic-producing diseases were principally either what are loosely described as 'droplet infections' because of the way in which the pathogens are disseminated, or those due to the contamination of food or water by bacteria. The distinction between the methods of transmission is important because the one requires relatively prolonged or close contact between individuals[10] whereas no such direct personal contact is needed for the other—food may be contaminated by flies as well as by human hands.[11]

The first group includes diseases such as measles, influenza, whooping cough and diphtheria in which the infective agent (pathogen) is contained in the droplets of saliva which are emitted when one coughs or sneezes, sings or speaks loudly. In a confined space and a moisture-laden atmosphere, the smaller droplets remain suspended in the air to be inhaled by other people present; the larger ones may fall to the ground, but if water from them evaporates, the 'droplet nuclei' might become small enough to be inhaled.[12] The micro-organisms contained in droplet nuclei might be either viruses or bacteria, and in the list given above the first two are virus diseases, the second two bacterial.

The experimental results on the effects of atmospheric conditions on the survival of micro-organisms spread in this way suggest that the infectivity of many of them, especially the smaller viruses, is prolonged by high humidity, provided it is not too extreme. Increases in temperature, on the other hand, may increase their rate of decay and, for the measles virus at least, ultra-violet radiation reduces its transmissibility.[13]

Even under the atmospheric conditions most favourable to them, none of these pathogens could cause a widespread epidemic throughout a population unless a high proportion of that population was susceptible to the infection. This susceptibility depends on each individual's previous experience of each particular infection and the duration of the immunity conferred by one attack. For virus diseases such as measles, smallpox, chickenpox or rubella a single attack may confer a lifelong immunity to those who survive it, as may the first attacks by the bacilli of diphtheria and whooping cough. On the other hand, the immunity against subsequent attacks of colds and influenza, both caused by viruses, is of much shorter duration, even when the same virus is involved.[14]

Of all the epidemics for which European shipping could be blamed, outbreaks of measles are commonly rated as the most devastating, although not all were equally fatal even when the whole population might be presumed to have been susceptible. Fiji's epidemic of 1875 is probably the most widely known, and accounts of it and others in Polynesia have been given elsewhere.[15] It is probably not coincidence that the epidemics which caused the fewest deaths occurred in the relatively dry and sunny months—April and May in Tahiti in 1854, September and October in Samoa and Tonga in 1893—whereas the epidemic in Fiji started in January, when the humidity could be expected to be high and the skies clouded. This was also the season when measles was first introduced to Aneityum, the southernmost island of the New Hebrides, in 1861.

In both Fiji and Aneityum there were also exceptional social circumstances which favoured the spread of the disease throughout the population. In Fiji it was the 'great native meeting' of the chiefs at Levuka to welcome Cakobau back from a visit to New South Wales and sign the Deed of Cession;[16] in Aneityum, the social organization imposed by the Presbyterian missionaries on the newly-converted Aneityumese, whose fate is the theme of this essay.

When John Geddie elected to begin his mission on Aneityum in July 1848 he settled at Anelgauhat, the harbour on the south-western corner of the island where James Paddon already had his sandalwood and trading station. The island is small—less than fifty kilometres in circumference—with twin peaks more than eight hundred metres high in the middle of the western half of the island, and the rim of an extinct volcano, its highest peak also about eight hundred metres, dominating the eastern half. The people lived mainly in the lower reaches of the river valleys and on the narrow coastal plain, but there were a few inland settlements near the headwaters of the rivers or the streams that fed into them.

The island was divided into six major political districts 'of very unequal sizes'.[17] Wars between districts, either singly or in combinations, were alleged to be frequent.[18] So too were the customary ceremonial food exchanges—much deplored by the thrifty Scots—between 'divisions' of the island,[19] but at the same time 'the people of one village seldom ha[d] familiar intercourse with the people of another'.[20] The existence of villages as such was denied by John Inglis,[21] who arrived in July 1852 to establish a second mission station at Aname on the north coast, about twenty-two kilometres distant by sea from Anelgauhat. He likened the Aneityumese pattern of settlement to 'a system of cottage farming',[22] and chose to describe the 'huts and gardens, solitary or in groups'[23] as 'settlements', even though one of the largest (and most obdurate) contained, on his reckoning, one hundred people.[24]

The sandalwood station at Anelgauhat was already being 'broken up' when Inglis arrived,[25] and it was effectively abandoned by October 1852.[26] Early in 1853 Geddie began 'taking the census of different villages'[27] and when his 'lists' were combined with

T

Inglis's in October 1854 they contained in all 3,800 names. Because the population was 'much scattered' and neither missionary had yet visited some of the inland settlements, they believed that this total was an under-estimate.[28] Later Inglis revised the number downwards to 'about 3,500' after 'repeatedly taking the census'.[29] In the original lists 2,200 people were reported as Christians, which meant that most of them gathered each weekday morning in small grass schoolhouses for an hour or more at sunrise,[30] being taught by native 'teachers' to read from 'an elementary school book', a 'catechism of truth' or the 'select portions of scripture' which Geddie had translated and printed.[31]

Probably most of the 'listing' for the census was done by the missionaries themselves, because at this time (and later) the teachers were selected as much for 'character' as for 'scholarship'. Geddie acknowledged that 'it often happens that the best men are not the best scholars',[32] and Inglis confirmed that 'at first our teachers were often persons of very slender attainment in scholarship; . . . we chose, as far as possible, men of character and influence, to whom the people would look up'.[33] Their educational duties were subsidiary to their evangelical responsibilities, but they were required to attend one of the two main stations regularly each week for further instruction and prayer. Their schools were also visited from time to time by one or the other missionary accompanied by a party which 'sometimes increase[d] to 50 or 100 persons'.[34]

By the end of 1860 the whole population was nominally Christian, and almost all of them congregated for an hour at sunrise each weekday morning in the nearest schoolhouse, by then 'beautiful lime houses, plastered and white-washed'.[35] There were large churches at both mission stations—Inglis's a wooden building measuring 70 feet by 31 with a four-foot veranda all round,[36] and Geddie's built of stone and 101 feet long and 41 feet wide[37]—in each of which 'about 500 persons' congregated once or twice each Sunday.[38] There were also two large schools that had been started more modestly to train Aneityumese for the extension of the mission northwards; on the north coast was Inglis's 'Normal Institution' which had 'upwards of one hundred pupils of both sexes', and on the south Mrs Geddie's 'select School' with 'about seventy scholars, chiefly . . . young men and women'.[39] The teachers who were stationed on Aneityum were still required to attend weekly prayer meetings at the main stations, and those at the 'more distant outstations' were assisted in their Sunday services by elders and deacons from the two churches.[40]

There were also two sandalwood stations, and in January 1861 a schooner attached to one of them returned to Aneityum with some of her crew infected with measles.

The disease soon spread over the *whole* island notwithstanding the
efforts made to check its progress. The population at large were laid
prostrate, and I do not believe there are half a dozen of persons on
the island, who did not take the sickness . . . Many died of the disease
itself, and many also from inattention and want of the common neces-
saries of life, as there were few able to help their neighbours. About
one-third of the population were in the short space of three or four
months swept into the grave.[41]

It is impossible to discover from the various accounts precisely where the epidemic started, or at what stage efforts were
made to check its progress throughout the population. The in-
cubation period for measles is twelve to fourteen days,[42] yet Mrs
Geddie's 'select School' continued until some time in February,
and possibly even late February.[43] Hence, if the infection was
introduced 'about the beginning of the year',[44] it seems likely that
at least five or six weeks elapsed before the normal routine of the
mission was curtailed except by sickness. On 15 March the eye
of a 'fearful' hurricane passed over the northern half of the island.
Whipped up by the wind, the sea rose either nine[45] or seven feet
above high-water mark at Inglis's station[46] and even higher farther
west, so gardens as well as houses and schoolhouses were destroyed.
In the more mountainous southern half houses and gardens were
damaged, but less severely.

By the end of March 1861 'several hundreds of the natives' were
dead, including seven of the twenty-one young people who had
been living on the mission premises at Anelgauhat 'at the time
when the disease broke out'. Although 'about the same proportion'
of those who lived around the harbour had died, elsewhere the
mortality had been 'in some instances less, and others more', but
everywhere it was 'greatest among persons in the prime of life,
while many of the old and young have been spared'.[47] The epidemic petered out some time after 1 May[48] and when 'the statis-
tics' were 'made up' in April or May the following year, the death
toll ascribed to measles and the accompanying dysentery was 'about
1200'.[49] Included in this number were the deaths of some who survived the epidemic 'in an enfeebled state' so that 'a proportion
larger than usual s[a]nk under even the ordinary diseases of the
island'.[50]

It is only for the members of Geddie's church that there is any
direct evidence as to the magnitude of the variability in the death
rates. To Geddie, then forty-six years old with his eighth child just
born, these were probably the 'persons in the prime of life' amongst
whom the death rate had been especially high. In October 1860
there were 179 church members in his district,[51] some of whom
were teachers on other islands. Because his senior school had been
operating longer than Inglis's (which opened in April 1857),

probably more than half of the seventeen teachers and their wives who were then absent from Aneityum were from Geddie's district, but assuming an even division, the deaths of sixty-eight—two elders, eight teachers and fifty-eight church members[52]—represent a mortality rate of forty-two per cent for this segment of the population.

Whether this rate applied equally to males and females, or as Inglis later contended 'the female portion of the population suffered more severely, in proportion, than the male',[53] a death rate of forty-two per cent among mature adults implies a rate perhaps as low as twenty per cent among children if one-third of Aneityum's population died in the epidemic. It is impossible to be more precise because the 3,800 names listed seven years previously were not divided into children and adults, and only Mrs Inglis, herself childless, commented on 'the comparatively small number of children'[54] then in the northern half of the island.

Both this scarcity (if scarcity there was by any but mid-Victorian standards) and the preponderance of males in the population—2,200 males and 1,600 females—were attributed primarily to infanticide.[55] 'The mothers did not murder their children . . . They left them, especially the female children, in the bush to die, or within the tide-mark to be drowned, or they nursed them carelessly and they died.'[56] Presumably much of the deliberate infanticide had stopped by 1861, but not even the strictest missionary surveillance could have prevented the careless nursing of infants while their mothers worked in their plantations. Theirs was the 'drudgery and hard labour' that produced much of the food, especially taro which was the main staple in many parts of the island.[57] They also planted and collected food for the pigs which were an essential part of any feast, and were 'as particular in baking it for them, as if it were for themselves'.[58] Traditionally only fishing and the cultivation of yams were the men's responsibility.[59]

As there was no doctrinal discrimination against women for church membership, the distorted sex ratio of the population as a whole might not have been repeated in the sample of church members cited above. If there were approximately equal numbers of men and women, and the women fared worse than the men in the epidemic, their respective death rates would have been symmetric about the rate for the group as a whole. This would not be the case if there were fewer women than men, as in the population itself, and the margin between the death rate for the women and the average for both sexes would have been greater than the difference between this average and the rate for the men.

Assuming that the death rate for males was forty per cent and that for females forty-five, and that the chances of infection and subsequent death for husbands and wives were independent of each other, only one-third of all marriages would have survived the epidemic and almost half of the people married before the epidemic would have been widowed by its end. Had the mortality rates been thirty-five and fifty per cent, almost as many marriages would have survived, but one-half of all husbands who survived would have become widowers as against forty-five per cent with the lower death rates. The higher the death rate among women —a relatively scarce commodity even before the epidemic—the less chance there was for the widowers to remarry. With a death rate of only forty-five per cent among the women, widowers had a five to four chance of quick remarriage; if the rate was fifty per cent, the widowers' chances fell to about fifteen to eight.

These estimates concern the population as a whole and ignore its division into separate communities or even the groups of communities which constituted the 'tribes' or 'districts' within which, to Inglis's despair as late as 1876, 'old notions, customs, and traditions, all of heathen origin, but still possessing much vitality, . . . rigidly' restricted the marriages of young women.[60] But the effects of the epidemic within communities of different sizes, both in terms of the numbers of people who died, the numbers of children left orphaned or motherless, and all the other social consequences of purely random variations in the mortality rates, could have been so great that even what were initially quite large groups of people might have deserted their own lands, seeing in this devastation all the wrath of God for their past wickedness and the necessity therefore to be nearer the missionary.

This last is the reason given nowadays for the long abandonment of the site of Anumej, which Geddie described as 'the largest village on the island' or alternatively, as 'our largest inland settlement'.[61] Encircled by the rim of the extinct volcano, the Anumej area is cut by the numerous creeks and rivulets which are the headwaters of the river that flows south through a steep-sided valley to the coast. The Umej people who lived at the river's mouth, about eight kilometres east of the main harbour, were early converts, as were those living at Anekra in the middle reaches of the river south of Anumej. Only the three groups lived by the river and Anumej is still remembered as by far the largest of them, quite different in size from all other settlements on the island. Geddie visited it first in January 1854, and he then reckoned it contained 'nearly 300 souls'.

By now it is impossible to gauge how isolated its people were before Geddie stationed two of his 'best' teachers among them.[62] He himself was convinced that all the inland people were 'subdued and dispised' and afraid to venture 'to the shore', but this is denied by present-day informants, grandsons of Aneityumese of 'the days of heathenism'.[63] Nothing now remains of the first school-house at Anumej, but the second was built in 1856 on a different site. It had a floor pavement of river stones and plastered walls for which the coral lime and sand were carried in from the coast.[64] The walls were blown flat in a storm about forty or more years ago, and the southern wall still covers much of the stone floor which measures about nine metres by five inside, with an extra metre of pavement outside the walls, which was probably sheltered by the thatched roof.[65]

It seems too small a building to have housed nearly three hundred people for the hour after sunrise each weekday, but if both schoolhouses were used equally, about half this number might have squeezed in, with three people sharing each square metre. At Anekra, about two kilometres downstream and a much smaller settlement than Anumej, there are still two floor pave-ments, the larger measuring twelve metres by six inside and the smaller ('where the books were kept') seven and a half by four and a half metres. Both have pavements about one metre wide outside the walls, and close to the smaller of the two pavements is the grave of Matau-ahileth, one of the 'high chiefs' so much esteemed by Geddie that he delegated his pastoral duties in this area to him shortly before 1860.[66] The larger building probably served as a chapel as well as a schoolhouse, and it may have been attended on Sundays by people from Anumej, thus providing an-other avenue for the transmission of measles into the community at Anumej.

Matau-ahileth survived the measles epidemic, but he died shortly before September 1863,[67] and it may not have been until after his death that the survivors from Anumej moved down to the coast at Umej to be nearer the missionary. By now measles ('misili' in pidgin) is only an afterthought in the oral tradition of the 'big sickness' that led to the virtual abandonment of Anumej, and the prime cause was, as elsewhere, the dysentery associated with it. Whether this was true dysentery, or merely the diarrhoea which seems to be concomitant of measles in adults, but not necessarily in children, cannot now be resolved. In the Aneityumese language there is only the one word for both.[68]

Although dysentery may be caused by so many different bacteria that any immunity acquired in one attack may afford little or no protection against subsequent infections,[69] if this was true dysentery there is still the possibility that the people of Anumej were more susceptible than many others because of their remoteness from the main harbour and the sandalwood stations. It is also possible that they were less accustomed to running very high temperatures than the coastal people who, from early child-hood on, periodically suffered 'intermittent fevers' which were probably malaria. Almost all the land at Anumej is more than one hundred metres above sea level, and in the winter of 1973 there were neither mosquitoes nor flies there.

But Anumej was almost certainly one of the areas in which the mortality rate exceeded one-third.[70] If this was so, then the death rates among the adults must have been higher than the average rate of perhaps forty-two per cent, and perhaps higher still if the children of Anumej suffered no more severely than those elsewhere. Higher adult mortality rates would have increased the social disruption consequent on the epidemic, and as well, reduced the number of survivors sufficiently for them to be welcome elsewhere in what was essentially a subsistence economy, largely dependent on agriculture and therefore land. Strangely, this fusion of Umej and Anumej was not reported by Geddie or his successors, but there is little reason to doubt the present-day informants because, where any of their stories could be checked against facts as stated by Geddie, the information was invariably accurate, and none of Geddie's writings is known to the Aneityumese.

It is idle to speculate what the mortality rate might have been had there been no Presbyterian mission on the island when measles was introduced. With the population divided between six districts sporadically at war with one another, and the people afraid to cross district boundaries unless perchance there was an alliance between their district and the other,[71] there was little chance of a droplet infection spreading far beyond the point or points of entry. Within a district the population was scattered and even if, as Geddie once asserted, the men of each small community gathered each evening in their *intiptang* (meeting house),[72] the various communities rarely came together. At the ceremonial food exchanges which presumably involved groups of communities, those giving the 'feast' gathered on one side of the piles of food, the recipients on the other, and after ritual ceremonies the food was apportioned to the recipients who carried it off to their own houses.[73]

With their conversion to Christianity all of this changed. Whatever their traditional district people could move freely about the island, and there were networks of communication between the two mission stations and even the most remote settlements. Each village or settlement had its own schoolhouse which was attended by most of its members five mornings a week for instruction by their teacher who, after the Friday morning school, repaired to the mission station with his wife for a prayer meeting and further instruction. On Sundays, people living within the radius of an hour's walk of either mission station attended church there; those living farther away attended their nearest chapel, at the main churches.[74] And Geddie's station was at the main harbour.

His stone church was approximately twice as big as Inglis's. Each of the five hundred or so Aneityumese who attended Geddie's church regularly would have had about three-quarters of a square metre of floor space, while in Inglis's church there would have been about two and a half persons per square metre inside. Traces still remain of schoolhouses other than those of Anumej and Anekra, but the coral lime floors of those near the coast have deteriorated so much that none except the penultimate chapel-cum-schoolhouse at Umej was measurable. However, the traces that remain in the thick bush now covering them indicate that generally they were very small. The largest of those seen was perhaps twenty square metres, and this probably catered for about one hundred people before the epidemic.[75] So it was not only at Anumej that the people were squeezed close together for their morning school, reading aloud and reciting the catechism, perhaps singing hymns.

It is hard to imagine conditions more favourable to the spread of droplet infections throughout a wholly susceptible population. For a time after the 1861 epidemic, the people who survived it became more assiduous in their school and church attendance. Then in May 1866 about three hundred of the 'strong and vigorous'[76] died in an epidemic of diptheria, and in June the following year there was an epidemic of whooping cough in which more than one hundred 'young children' and 'half grown boys and girls' died.[77] By this time the population was reduced to about 1,750, about half the number that had been there before their conversion. By the end of the century there were fewer than five hundred people on the island[78] and the chief cause of this continued diminution was probably tuberculosis, another droplet infection.

If the missionaries were the agents of the Lord, then indeed it may be said that the epidemics on Aneityum were the expression of His wrath.

NOTES AND REFERENCES

1 *Numbers* xvi:47.
2 J. Elder and C. Wilson, Journal Round Eimeo, 26 Jan.-21 Feb. 1804, L.M.S. South Seas Journals.
3 Rodríguez 1919:30.
4 Gayangos 1915:141.
5 Cook 1967:III, 1, 221.
6 Watts 1790:242.
7 Lee 1920:99.
8 Pirie 1972:191.
9 See, e.g., J. Geddie 22 Aug. 1856 *M.R. 1857*:97; 28 Sept. 1857, *M.R. 1858*:273; 25 Dec. 1858 [*sic*], *M.R. 1858*:321. All letters are from Aneityum.

10 Tyrrell 1967:287.

11 Burnet 1953:158.

12 Druett 1967:166.

13 Anderson and Cox 1967:210-11; Tyrrell 1967:303-4, 297.

14 Burnet 1953:98.

15 McArthur 1967:8-11, 76, 109-10, 256-7, 350-2.

16 Corney, Stewart and Thomson 1896:36.

17 Inglis 1887:24.

18 Geddie. 'The inhabitants of Aneityum', M.R. 1852:21.

19 ibid.:9.

20 Geddie, 3 Oct. 1850, M.R. 1851:101.

21 Inglis, 15 Dec. 1852, R.P.M. 1853:224. All references to R.P.M. are by courtesy of R. Adams.

22 Inglis, 'New Hebrides—Aneityum', R.P.M. 1855:275.

23 J. MacGillivray, Voyage of H.M.S. 'Herald' under the command of Capt. H. Mangles Denham, R.N. being private journal kept by John MacGillivray, Naturalist, 1852-5:95, MS. 23 Admiralty Library, London, mf. G746, N.L.

24 Inglis, 12 Dec. 1854, R.P.M. 1855:173.

25 Inglis, 12 Jul. 1852, R.P.M. 1852:790.

26 Geddie, 17 Sept. 1852, M.R. 1853:66.

27 Geddie, 1 March 1853, MS. Journal, in possession of Mrs Loraine Tompson, Melbourne.

28 Geddie, 3 Oct. 1854, M.R. 1855:125.

29 Inglis, 'State and prospects of the Bible cause in Aneityum', M.R. 1859:151.

30 Inglis, 16 Feb. 1853, R.P.M. 1853:358.

31 Geddie, 23 Sept. 1858, M.R. 1859:89.

32 Geddie, 27 Jul. 1855, M.R. 1856:180.

33 Inglis 1887:78.

34 Geddie, 29 Nov. 1854, M.R. 1855:139.

35 Inglis 1887:81.

36 Inglis, 4 April 1854, M.R. 1855:57.

37 Geddie, 4 Jun. 1860. H & F.R. 1861:40.

38 Geddie, Annual Report from Aneityum, 8 Oct. 1860, H. & F.R. 1861:129.

39 Geddie, 23 Sept. 1858, M.R. 1859:35.

40 Geddie, Annual Report, H. & F.R. 1861:129.

41 Geddie, Annual Report, 20 Aug. 1861, H. & F.R. 1862:38.

42 Burnet 1953:18.

43 Mrs C. L. Geddie, 26 Aug. 1861, H. & F.R. 1862:76.

44 Geddie, Annual Report, H. & F.R. 1862:38.

45 Inglis, 29 Jan. 1873, H. & F.R. 1873:186.

46 Inglis, 9 Oct. 1861 (from Scotland), H. & F.R. 1861:327.

47 Geddie, 3 Apr. 1861, H. & F.R. 1861:247.

48 J. Copeland, 1 May 1861, H. & F.R. 1861:272.

49 Geddie, 23 May 1862, H. & F.R. 1862:292.

50 Geddie, 12 Dec. 1861, H. & F.R. 1862:159.

51 Geddie, Annual Report, H. & F.R. 1861:129-30.

52 Geddie, Annual Report, 16 Dec. 1862, H. & F.R. 1863:38.

53 Inglis 1887:342.

54 Mrs Inglis, 13 Sept. 1854, M.R. 1855:184.

55 Geddie, 3 Oct. 1854, M.R. 1855:125.

56 Mrs Inglis, op.cit.

57 Geddie, 'The inhabitants of Aneityum', M.R. 1852:20.

58 Mrs Geddie, 8 Apr. 1850, M.R. 1850:186.

59 Anon., History of the Paciffic, n.p., n.d.:15, MS. by courtesy of D. Shineberg.

60 Inglis 1887:342.

61 Geddie, 23 Jan. 1854, MS. Journal, op.cit.; 3 Oct. 1854, M.R. 1855:124.

62 Geddie, 3 Oct. 1854, loc.cit.

63 For biographical details of the informants see McArthur 1974:6-8.

64 Patterson 1882:401-2.

65 All the floor pavements were measured with Winifred Mumford's assistance in 1973.

66 Geddie, Annual Report, H. & F.R. 1863:125.

67 Geddie, 15 Sept. 1863, H. & F.R. 1864:41-2.

[68] Daniel Kauyapae, a former Medical Orderly, pers. comm.
[69] Burnet 1953:158.
[70] Geddie, Annual Report, *H. & F.R. 1862*:38.
[71] Geddie, 3 Oct. 1850, *M.R. 1851*:102.
[72] *ibid.*:100-1.
[73] Geddie, 'The inhabitants of Aneityum', *M.R. 1852*:9.
[74] Inglis 1887:68, 113.
[75] Inglis, 12 Dec. 1854, *R.P.M. 1855*:173.
[76] Geddie, 26 Nov. 1866, *H. & F.R. 1867*:126; Inglis, 19 Jul. 1867, *H. & F.R. 1868*:16.
[77] Inglis, *loc.cit.*
[78] Buxton 1926:442.

'He can but die...': missionary medicine in pre-Christian Tonga

DOROTHY SHINEBERG

The early Wesleyan missionaries to Tonga were surprised to find that their help to cure the sick was solicited shortly after they arrived. They soon realized the large possibilities for influence that the practice of medicine could create among heathen people who were indifferent to their preaching. The missionaries themselves took for granted that 'English' medicine, like the rest of their cultural baggage, was immeasurably superior to the local variety; moreover, as Tongan medicine was intimately connected with Tongan religion, it was regarded as the devil's work.[1] But although a charitable attitude to the sick was part and parcel of the Christian religion, they hesitated to respond to appeals for treatment. Their doubts lay only in their own competence in the healing art. Peter Turner lamented that he had not taken a few lessons in medicine before he left home. 'The missionary who has the most knowledge of medicine is sure to be very popular among the chiefs and people, and will often gain access to the heathen when others would be refused', he said. 'This has often made us wish we had received a few lessons on the art of healing before we left home, as we should have been more successful among the heathen.'[2] John Thomas, who arrived in 1826, was at first diffident about attempting to cure the sick, fearing that his lack of skill might be counter-productive to the Christian cause.

> If we could cure the bodies of the people of their various diseases, It would be a great recommendation for us to the attentions of the people . . . but we have neither Skill nor means for this, and therefore in most cases, can not undertake any thing of the kind; least we should do harm to the cause of Christ, by raising the expectations of the people, when we cannot satisfy them. we are obliged therefore to tell them, that we did not come to cure their bodies but their souls, and God saves not from pain and bodily afflictions but Sin and hell, but as this latter subject is new to them, and most of them care nothing about it, but wish to be made well here, they are prevailed upon to cling to their own Otuas [gods] and follow the Tonga ways.[3]

He probably also feared revenge at the hands of Tongans should his ministrations be followed by the death of the patient. The mission had as yet made no headway, and the fate of the earlier

London Missionary Society party was close to his thoughts.[4] Nathaniel Turner had similar fears at first.[5]

Nevertheless, both Nathaniel Turner and John Thomas became busy medical practitioners in Tonga, and found the number of their clients steadily growing. A few months after expressing doubts as to the wisdom of trying to cure the sick Thomas gave medicine to a sick child upon the entreaties of his father who said he would worship the new God if his child were cured; but Thomas was careful to hedge his bets.

> I told him I was not a Doctor, I did not come to cure their bodies, but to teach them to know and worship the true God, which was to prepare their souls to live with God for ever, which was a very different thing. He accknowledged the truth of this, but thinking it possible that some simple medicines may be of service to the child, I promised to call with which he was much pleased.[6]

He gave the man some magnesia for his child, with what effect we do not know. He repeated his conviction about the usefulness of medical knowledge to a missionary: 'I feel persuaded if we had the Skill and the means of helping these people in their afflictions of body, It would open a door to much good to their Souls, where we are not allowed to go now, through predijuice to our worship'.[7] But in another year Thomas, a blacksmith by trade, was nonchalantly writing in his journal 'after the Service I went to see the sick, I bled three persons';[8] and, '[I] bled him, Bro Cross prayed and we then visited several others two of whom I bled'.[9] Sick visiting had become part of his daily routine; he was confidently diagnosing diseases and prescribing medicines, and complaining that his medical work was taking up too much of his time. For his part, Nathaniel Turner at Nuku'alofa was inundated by the sick from all over Tonga. Doubts fled; their ministrations had clearly been blessed by the Lord to advance His cause.

In spite of themselves the missionaries had been forced to yield to the pressure of Tongans demanding medical treatment, although they refused to treat those who had become ill as a result of the sin of night dancing.[10] Thomas was influenced by his horror of the Tongan method of curing the sick which involved taking the patient to a god-house for priestly incantations —'praying to the devil', in his view. This objection implicated him in offering an alternative. Naturally he advocated praying to the one true God, as he said to one woman, 'not so much to have her body cured, but least she should go to Hell fire'[11] but it became difficult not to supplement this advice by trying something out of his own medicine chest.

Moreover, it appears that the missionaries lost their fear of

vengeance for the possible death of their patients: it became clear
that the Tongans viewed the situation much more reasonably than
they had expected. Since missionaries were generally asked to
treat a patient only when all the local rituals and remedies proved
impotent, the Tongans apparently believed there was nothing to
lose. Where death was expected, missionaries were not blamed
for failure.[12]

The first resounding medical success of the missionaries in
Tonga occurred at Nuku'alofa, soon after Nathaniel Turner's
arrival there late in 1827. Turner was approached by a young
man of high rank called Tupoutotai (Tupou the Sailor), one of
the growing band of Tongans with experience abroad who were
to play such a large part in their country's history. Tupoutotai
and his brother Lolohea, called 'nephews of the King [Alea-
motu'a]',[13] suffered from what Turner described vaguely as 'a very
painful Scrophulous Gangrenas disease called by the Natives
"Ae Bala" [*pala*]'.[14] Death was the expected outcome.

> It attacked them in any part of the Body, but always in the form of
> a Boil or Ulcer. This suppurating could not be healed by any out-
> ward appli[n] whatever—but continued to spread, eating the flesh etc
> until the Sufferer ultimately pined away and died.[15]

Lolohea was already approaching death. Tupoutotai had a large
wound covering the calf of his leg and 'eaten into the bone'.[16]
In broken English he said to the missionary, 'Mr Turner, you got
any Mercury? Mercury very good for my Bala'. He explained that
he had heard from a friend who had just returned from Tahiti
that the missionaries there cured the *pala* with mercury, and
described the treatment. Turner replied that he had mercury in
his medicine chest, but was 'not skilled in the use of it'. He refused
to administer it on the grounds that, should the young man die
'his friends would lay his death to my charge, and as he was a
Chief they would kill me as a totongi, a payment'; but Tupoutotai
returned with 'his Uncle the King [Aleamotu'a] to plead his cause
with me'. Turner made the same objections to which Aleamotu'a
replied: 'His brother Lolohea is dying of this disease, and he
[Tupoutotai] will die unless you can by this medicine prevent.
If you give it him he can but die, and in that case I will take care
that no evil comes to you in consequence.'[17] Turner agreed to
administer the mercury on this condition. He consulted the medical
books he had with him and gave the patient what he decided was
the proper dose. It proved to be far too much, however, and poor
Turner believed that Aleamotu'a's promise was about to be put
to the test. An excited messenger aroused him early one morning
and took him to Tupoutotai whom he found in a 'truly frightful
state. Head Swollen, Jaws extended and Tongue standing out,

fourfold larger than usual filling the entire Cavity. I was alarmed and said to myself. This is a gone Case'.[18] It was a good description of some of the symptoms of mercury poisoning. With no real hope of reversing the situation Turner went back to his medical books and prepared an antidote which he administered. No one was more astonished than Turner to find not only that the alarming facial distortions disappeared, but also that the frightful leg sore soon looked much healthier and had diminished 'to the size of a Crown piece'. Frightened to try the mercury again, he attempted to heal the small sore with external applications but without response. He therefore administered further doses of mercury, now 'more gently', and finally effected what he called 'a thorough cure', meaning, presumably, that the sores disappeared.[19] Whether the *pala* had a later manifestation or was replaced by kidney disease due to mercury poisoning we do not know, as neither Turner nor his flock had any notion of, or interest in, the long-term effects either of the disease or the drastic medication.

The news of this event spread and *pala* cases flocked to Nuku'alofa. Turner and the other missionaries now confidently dosed them all with mercury, reporting that only two cases, already far gone, did not yield to the medication. Their success was certainly instrumental in advancing the Christian cause. As Turner put it, 'it gain'd for us a great reputation with regard to the healing Art: and was the means of bringing many Spiritual Lepers to fall at the feet of Jesus saying "Lord if thou wilt thou canst make me whole" '.[20]

At Hihifo, Tongatapu, and later in the Ha'apai group, Thomas also soon had a demanding practice. His vague and doubtful diagnoses mattered little, since the treatment was almost always the same. He usually bled first, often followed this with a purge, and always with a prayer. He bled for 'palpitations of the heart', a swollen breast, sunstroke, 'a bad arm', 'a liver complaint', 'pain in the loins' and 'fever',[21] and also bled patients described simply as 'unwell' or 'poorly'. The purge he gave was generally calomel, again a mercury compound much in vogue in the nineteenth century, though sometimes he gave rhubarb or Epsom salts. 'I bled him and gave a pill with a few grains of Calomel' is the remedy described most often in his journal. In July 1830 he described an epidemic of illness in Ha'apai: 'The complaint seems to be one, the people are taken with fever. pain in Side and shoulder with great disorder of the Stomach'. His remedy follows: 'I have bled many, and found that bleeding and opening medicine is very useful to them. I have visited five or six a day and sometimes more, so that my time is very much taken up in these things, oh that the Lord may bless his people'.[22]

On a famous occasion Thomas prescribed for Tāufa'āhau, the future King George of Tonga, who was then in the process of testing the power of his own gods against that of Jehovah. The chief had become 'very ill', according to Thomas, whose opinion was that he had taken cold from not wearing enough clothes when he was already 'low' with a 'bad arm'.[23] A later account of the same incident by the Tongan teacher Peter Vī is a good deal more dramatic. His version reports that Tāufa'āhau had been poisoned by his enemies,[24] but this theory was not mentioned by Thomas, to whom it would have been appealing, and his more mundane report made on the same day must have more credence. Thomas did, however, share Peter Vī's belief that the chief's illness was a critical point in the history of the *lotu*, as it came after Tāufa'āhau had been testing the Tongan gods by abusing them and humiliating their priests and priestesses; consequently when he fell ill 'the enimies of the Lord begin to think that the evil of his Doings in casting aside the Tonga gods is now falling upon him'.[25] Towards the evening, the chief became very ill, and there ensued a battle for the 'cure' of Tāufa'āhau which Christians and heathen alike saw as a conflict between the power of Jehovah and the Tongan gods. Thomas tried to persuade the chief to take the medicine he offered, while the heathen 'talked of removing him to their gods if he did not get better, as they took it for granted that his afflictions were on account of his sins against them'.[26] Tāufa'āhau finally took his medicine, in this case an emetic. When it made him vomit he became very angry and thought he was about to die. Fortunately for the Christians the chief was very much better in the morning and much ashamed of his conduct the previous evening. He now thanked God for his recovery;

> he eat and drank freely, and joy and delight beamed from evry countenance, those who were cast down and sorrowful, now rejoiced in the Lord and the expectations of the opposer of the Lord are cut off, to God be all the praise.[27]

Tāufa'āhau appears never to have again wavered in his loyalty to the Christians. The conversion and baptism of this intelligent and ambitious man was a large factor in the enormous success of Wesleyan Christianity in Tonga, and was later to greatly affect the history of Fiji.

Thomas occasionally departed from the bleeding and medicine routine in favour of more dramatic methods. In the case of a very sick woman who had been bitten on the hand by a fish he diagnosed tetanus and described his treatment thus: 'I talked and then prayed. afterwards got two buckets of water and poured upon her, she appeared better'. He applied some opodeldoc (a mixture of camphorated oil and soap) to her hand, and left word that 'in case the tetanus returned with violence, they should repeat the waters upon her body'.[28] The next day he reported that the patient was quite well and attending class.

> I was agreeable surprised to see the young woman, who lay as in the agonies of death last eving at the School, she seemed quite easy, her hand was covered with clotted blood. I could not have thought she would have been so well, but nothing is to hard for the Lord, Oh that many may see and fear and turn to him.[29]

Missionary medicine in Tonga had celebrated failures as well as successes. At Hihifo, the first Wesleyan mission station, the chief Ata made his own test of Tongan gods when his son Mataele was ill with what Thomas diagnosed as 'palpitations of the heart'. The Tongans were praying for his recovery to their god Lātū-fakahau, causing Thomas to intervene, requesting them 'not to pray to those who cannot help'. Asked for his alternative, he prayed to *his* God for Mataele, and also bled him and gave him opening medicine. But Mataele did not recover, and was taken away from Thomas to another god-house.[30] When Thomas objected, Ata declared that if Mataele died, it would prove that the Tongan gods were false, and he (Ata) would *lotu*.[31] Ata was a great chief. Thomas knew that his conversion was the key to success at Hihifo after three long years of failure there, and he anxiously reported on the condition of Mataele. In five days, however, Mataele was up and about and well on the way to recovery. Thomas said that he was glad to see Mataele getting better, adding somewhat wistfully 'but he has a cough which will perhaps bring on a consumption'.[32] Mataele lived and heathenism triumphed in this small corner of the world. From that day Ata was confirmed in his beliefs and remained a heathen until his death in 1833, and Hihifo did not yield to Christianity until conquered by Tāufa'āhau in 1837.

Thomas had a similar experience in Lifuka, Ha'apai, when Ate, a young man of rank, became sick soon after attending Christian worship. His illness (which Thomas described as 'apparently dropsical') defied the missionary's prayers and medications, and Ate and his family reverted to heathenism in the belief that the Tongan gods were angry with him for his infidelity.[33]

In his influential book on home medicine called *Primitive Physick,* John Wesley urged his readers not to forget 'that old unfashionable Medicine, Prayer'.[34] Wesley's followers in Tonga did not forget. Prayer invariably accompanied their bleeding and purging. Sometimes they also 'sang a few verses of an hymn'.[35] They prayed, of course, for the soul, whatever the outcome to the body, but they also believed that no physical recovery was possible without prayer for the help of God. When one of his patients, the wife of Fīnau 'Ulukālala, the high chief of Vava'u, took her medicine but refused to pray to the Christian God, John Thomas was 'astonished', as he said, 'as I had no hope of being useful to her except I prayed'.[36] But she recovered, and Thomas explained to Fīnau that it was 'not for me to make people well but it was the Lord, that although his wife would not pray, yet I prayed for her to the Lord our God'.[37] Once called to the bedside, Thomas also took the opportunity of pointing out to the sick the evil of their ways, and the connection between sin and disease, regardless of the condition of the patient.[38]

It is undeniable that the practice of medicine by the missionaries advanced the Wesleyan cause in Tonga. The readiest explanation for this is that European medical therapy was demonstrably superior to local practice, and it is the explanation either stated or tacitly assumed by writers who mention the connection.[39] It seems to me that this explanation is untrue, if one or two very specific treatments be excepted.

There is no cause to belittle the European medical science of the age of the early missionaries. Enormous strides had been taken since the seventeenth century in anatomy and physiology; surgery, while still dangerous and agonizing from the want of asepsis and anaesthesia had reached high levels of skill by the early nineteenth century; there was now a knowledge of the connection between filth and contagion, though it was based on a false theory, and this led to more attention to hygiene. There was, however, very little relationship between the state of medical knowledge and the state of medical therapy. Apart from surgery and attentive nursing there was almost nothing of any benefit that could be done for people once they had become ill, and this remained true for long after this period.

Like the physicians and home practitioners of Europe the missionaries had access to drugs known to be able to purge, cause to vomit, stimulate and sedate. These clearly had their uses, but the same functions were often performed by the herbal medicines of the islands.[40] Moreover these drugs were usually prescribed in a general way (by physicians as well as missionaries), rather than for the relief of the appropriate symptom. A few useful specifics were known, such as the selective poisoning properties of quinine and mercury, and we have seen that the disease called *pala* responded specifically to mercury treatment, at least in the short term. For the rest it is very doubtful whether the drugs given by the missionaries could have had much physical effect one way or the other, any more than they did in Europe in the same period. The physical procedures of bleeding and blistering were the stock-in-trade of European physicians as they were of the mis-

U

sionaries. They are not known to have any therapeutic effects. Fortunately, surgery was not attempted by the missionaries in Tonga but, along with bone-setting, it was an art widely practised with skill in Polynesia and Fiji.[41] The missionaries' lack of medical training does not seem very material, contrary to their own belief. About ten years later a medical missionary, George Miller, was employed in Tonga: his diary shows exactly the same repertoire of remedies as the earlier missionaries, except that he might have been an even more enthusiastic bleeder. A few extracts may demonstrate that his treatment shows no notable advance on that of John Thomas the blacksmith.

> Thursday 21 [Dec. 1843] . . . Bled three individuals, all very ill with the influenza.
>
> Saturday 10 Feby [1844] . . . Visited and bled an elderly woman who is consumptive.
>
> Sunday September 1st [1844] . . . Bled Enoch a young man taken dangerously ill.
>
> Saturday Sept[r] 7 [1844] . . . Read the burial Service over the remains of Enoch . . .
>
> Wednesday 5 [March 1845] . . . Dispensed Medicine. Visited some of the sick—bled 3 Men.[42]

He also bled himself for a variety of afflictions. Ships' surgeons visiting the various islands did little but commend the work of the missionaries and add their own dose of salts or laudanum. At Raiatea, one was impressed by John Williams's treatment of elephantiasis by blood-letting, and imitated the method.[43]

With 'care, prayer and practice', to borrow Peter Turner's phrase,[44] the limited range of early nineteenth-century therapeutics was within the grasp of the untrained missionaries. Armed with their books on home medicine, their lancet and cupping instruments and their medicine chests, they purged, bled and blistered with the best of them. Their diffidence was possibly even an advantage to the patient. Unsure of their skill and conscious of personal danger if they too obviously hastened death, it seems likely that they were more moderate in their treatments than some of the physicians at home. A missionary in Fiji ten years later expressed this hesitation very well. When he treated the Fijian chief Namosimalua of Viwa he said: 'I bled and purged him as much as I dare and I think as much as I ought'.[45]

Some of the missionaries' patients recovered and some did not. Since a very high proportion of illness ends in spontaneous recovery the number of missionary 'cures' was not remarkable. The connection between their sick visiting and Christian conversion came as a surprise to the missionaries themselves, but they had their own explanation. Peter Turner said:

It has often surprised us to witness the wonderful effects which have followed the administration of the simplest medicines in the fear of God and believing prayer. Hundreds, if not thousands, have been brought over to Christianity, in the first instance, from hearing and seeing the cures produced upon themselves and others by our medicine. In this was manifested the goodness of God in condscending to bless the feeble efforts of his servants made in his name to win men to Christ. The work is his; and he shall have the praise.[46]

It seems clear that the reputation of the Christians as healers relates far more to the irrational behaviour of sick human beings than to the relative real worth of European to indigenous medicine. No one likes to be sick. Nothing is so precious as one's health. The desire of the sick to be well can ultimately overturn their normal habits and values. The priorities are drastically changed: mean people will give all they have to buy a cure; critical people become the gullible victims of outrageous charlatanry; conservative people will experiment with outlandish cures; xenophobes will admit foreigners to their bedside to administer exotic treatments. Indeed it has often been observed that, by contrast with the norm, strangeness, expense and even painfulness can be attractive in a prospective cure.[47]

The willingness of the sick and their relatives to put aside their cultural prejudices in the hope of recovery is amply demonstrated by the islanders' appeals to Europeans for medical aid at a time when there had been no appreciable inroads into their system of beliefs.[48] It was more drastic than appeals for material goods because the origin of sickness was more intimately connected with the supernatural, and constituted an admission of the impotence of their own gods in the matter. The European visitors presented a hope to the hopeless, an alternative medicine to their own rituals and remedies. In the case of pre-Christian Tonga, it is clear that the missionaries' medical help was generally solicited after all the Tongan remedies had been tried, although sometimes European and Tongan remedies were tried concurrently.[49] This circumstance proved to be favourable to the medical reputation of the missionaries. If they failed, they proved themselves no wiser than the Tongan experts, but no more foolish either. The result was a draw. However, if they succeeded, they had disproportionate credit for curing cases which had defied orthodox remedies.

European medicine was not the only alternative available to the Tongans. In the eclectic fashion of the desperately ill, they experimented also with Fijian and Hawaiian remedies.[50] Particularly popular was the Fijian operation of *coka losi*—an exquisitely painful operation in which a thin stick or reed with an attached thread of fine sinnet was inserted through the male urethra and an incision made down to it in the perinaeum so that it might be drawn out again, after which the thread was pulled backward and forward in a see-sawing motion to induce a flow of blood.[51] It was done for 'tetanus' in the cases Will Mariner witnessed, although in Fiji it was performed for a variety of complaints, and remained in high repute there well into the colonial period.[52] While painful, the operation itself apparently produced no harmful effects, but could not conceivably have physically affected the course of a disease like tetanus, or any other, for that matter. Nonetheless, Mariner said that both the operations he witnessed cured the 'tetanus', and from the hearsay of others he reckoned the 'cure' rate as three or four out of ten. It is then perhaps a matter of no surprise that Thomas's water cure worked in the instance he recorded.

The Fijians, however, indicated that, unlike other of their operations, *coka losi* was a purely medical operation, without supernatural content.[53] The case was no doubt the same with treatments offered by lay Europeans, but it was quite otherwise with the missionary practitioners. As they themselves believed and vehemently stated that the source of their cure was really their God's power, a belief with which the Tongans found themselves entirely comfortable, it was a short step from cure to conversion.

There is a factor left out of the above discussion. It has so far been assumed that the 'cures' performed by European and Fijian remedies where Tongan remedies had failed were in most cases due to chance. Since Tongan remedies also 'cured' where European remedies failed that would seem a reasonable inference. But there remains the question of whether the very strangeness of treatments can actually assist recovery by raising the hope and faith and therefore the will-power of the patient. So far as I know, the relationship between faith and healing is unknown, although it is widely admitted that there is one. The missionaries in Tonga believed that of all the medicines they used, faith was the most effective, and the writer is inclined to agree with them.

NOTES AND REFERENCES

1 John Thomas, Journal, 15 May 1830, 14 June 1830, mf. N.L. Not all missionaries thought local medicine hopelessly inferior. David Cargill in Fiji some years later showed a good deal of respect for the indigenous pharmacopaeia (more extensive than the Tongan) and for local surgical skill. See Henderson 1931:128.
2 Peter Turner, Missionary Papers, 1831-38:109-11. MS. in M.L.
3 Thomas, Journal, 31 Jan. 1829.
4 The London Missionary Society had left ten missionaries on Tongatapu in April 1797, of whom three were killed in 1799 and the rest—except for one who had already deserted the mission—fled to New South Wales. Thomas was reading an account of the affair six months after his arrival at Tongatapu—Thomas, Journal, 8 Jan. 1827.
5 Nathaniel Turner, Personal Narrative:I, 231. MS. in M.L.

6 Thomas, Journal, 25 May 1829.
7 *idem.*
8 Thomas, Journal, 28 July 1830.
9 *ibid.,* 12 July 1830.
10 Thomas told one such that he was 'glad because he was a little unwell and I hoped he would 'learn better by what he was suffering. I refused to give any thing to a woman who applied to me but was made ill in the same way.' —Thomas, Journal, 12 July 1830. When asked by the patient's father Nathaniel Turner did treat one young man suffering from sciatica said to have been caused by his night dancing. Turner blistered his thigh, 'curing' the sciatica, but of course causing local burning which he thought 'an Antidote for his love for Night Dancing'.—Nathaniel Turner, Personal Narrative:I, 226-7.
11 Thomas, Journal, 14 June 1830.
12 The writer has found no case in Tonga in which missionary medical treatment resulting in death provoked local vengeance. It appears that there was one in Fiji, when the Christian mission was expelled from Rewa in 1855, after the death from dysentery of the chief who had been treated by a missionary.
13 Aleamotu'a, powerful chief of the Tu'i Kanokupolu family at Nuku'alofa, later Tu'i Kanokupolu, and in January 1830 baptized as Siosaia (Josiah). The two young men were also the stepsons of Ata, the sons of his high-born wife Papa.
14 N. Turner, Personal Narrative:I, 230. *Pala* literally means only 'festering sores' (the 'ae' is an article). It is difficult to identify the disease from this description. It does not seem to be common yaws, which is distinguished by the Tongans by the name *tona* and not regarded so seriously, but perhaps was yaws at a tertiary stage. 'Palla' was also noted by Mariner in the early years of the 19th century and distinguished by him from yaws ('tona'), 'scrofulous indurations' ('cahi') and 'lues venera'.—Martin 1827:11, Appendix 11, cv-cvii. Cook described a disease he saw on Nomuka in 1774 as 'leprous' and 'scrofulous', eating away the flesh—Cook 1961:450.
15 N. Turner, Personal Narrative:I, 230.
16 *ibid.*:233.
17 *ibid.*:231-2.
18 *ibid.*:232.
19 *ibid.*:233.
20 *ibid.*:234.
21 Thomas, Journal, 29 May 1829, 11 May 1829, 21 June 1830, 14 May 1830, 14 July 1830, 23 Feb. 1830, 3 Feb. 1830 and 31 July 1830 respectively.
22 *ibid.,* 31 July 1830.
23 *ibid.,* 29 July 1830.
24 As quoted in West 1865:367-8.
25 Thomas, Journal, 29 July 1830.
26 *idem.*
27 *ibid.,* 30 July 1830.
28 *ibid.,* 4 Feb. 1830. John Wesley recommended 'cold-bathing' for children suffering from tetanus and other 'nervous' and paralytic disorders (*Primitive Physick,* London, 1792, pp. 117-18), and perhaps this was the inspiration for Thomas's treatment.
29 *ibid.,* 5 Feb. 1830.
30 *ibid.,* 29 May 1829.
31 *ibid.,* 10 June 1829.
32 *ibid.,* 16 June 1829.
33 *ibid.,* 13 May 1830, 14 May 1830, 20 May 1830, 27 May 1830, 7 June 1830, 11 Sept. 1830.
34 J. Wesley, *op.cit.*:xi.
35 Thomas, Journal, 7 July 1830.
36 *ibid.,* 13 July 1830.
37 *ibid.,* 14 July 1830.
38 Thomas even lectured a woman as she regained consciousness and still could not speak—*ibid.,* 10 March 1830.
39 Henderson 1931 (chapter IX *passim*) allows that some missionaries could have accomplished little or nothing more than local healers, but believes

that all depended on the degree of medical training of the missionary. He does not question the great superiority of European medical therapy as such.

40 There was much variation in the degree of knowledge of herbal medicine in Polynesia and Fiji. The Tongan pharmacopaeia appears to have been very limited, but the Tongans borrowed freely from the Fijian, which was extensive, and held in high regard. The Hawaiians seem to have had a high reputation for knowledge of herbal remedies. The author is engaged on a general work on introduced medicine in the islands, in which it is hoped to do comparative studies of the level of European and island medicine in the early contact period.

41 In Tonga, according to Mariner, nearly everyone was skilled in bone-setting and the adjustment of dislocations (and this was very generally observed all over the Pacific). For surgery, however, the Tongans again deferred to the Fijians, preferring those surgeons who had learnt their art in Fiji—Martin 1827:II, Appendix 11, xciv-cii.

42 George Miller, Diary, 2 vols, mf. M.L. Original MS. in Alexander Turnbull Library, Wellington.

43 Waldegrave 1834:195-6.

44 Peter Turner, Missionary Papers:194.

45 John Hunt, Journal, 2 vols:II, 168-9. TS. in M.L.

46 Peter Turner, Missionary Papers:111.

47 See Haggard 1939:322-44; Camp 1974: *passim*.

48 This is true also in other areas so far touched by the writer. Kamehameha took himself to untrained Europeans for medical attention, when Hawaiian remedies failed, and he never showed any interest in Christianity to his death. Pomare of Tahiti tried European medicine long before European religion. The same was true in Samoa, Fiji and New Zealand.

49 See, e.g., Thomas, Journal, 25 May 1829, 15 May 1830, 14 June 1830, 1 July 1830, 13 May 1830 (both cures together).

50 Martin 1827:II, Appendix 11, xciv-cii.

51 Described by Mariner (Martin *op.cit.*:c-ci); by Rev. R. B. Lyth, Sundry Reminiscences:21 in Scrapbook, M.L.; by Corney 1890:646-9, 651-3.

52 Corney 1890:647.

53 *ibid.*:647-8.

'All the horrors of the half known life':[1] some notes on the writing of biography in the Pacific

GAVAN DAWS

Historians of the Pacific have not produced much in the way of biography. And when the published lives are read, it becomes clear that among the biographers there has been next to no interest in trying to account in psychological terms[2] for the ways in which their subjects lived their lives in the Pacific.

This is not really surprising. In the history profession at large, even among biographers, even in the mid-1970s, those who would argue that psychohistorical writing is worth attempting at all are in a tiny minority; it would be statistically odd to find a cluster of them in the numerically small world of Pacific historians.

As for these historians of the Pacific, until relatively recently they approached their subject as one version of European expansion, to be dealt with in conventional politico-economic imperial-colonial terms. The writing of biography, if it was done at all, was set in that sort of frame; individual life histories were looked at as particular embodiments or exemplifications of a large concrete general interest to be served.

The situation has not changed much, as far as biography is concerned, since it became usual to think of the writing of Pacific history as (desirably) 'island-centred' rather than 'Europe-centred'. Along with this re-orientation[3]—which incidentally included tacit permission for historians to write the lives of islanders as well as the lives of white men in the islands—went the general assumptions that interdisciplinary work would be useful. There is an excellent case for this approach. Even so, it has not been markedly common to see serious interdisciplinary work initiated by historians, and whatever has been projected along interdisciplinary lines has involved disciplines other than psychology.[4]

The upshot has been that the more recent Pacific biographers are like their predecessors in at least this respect: whether their subjects are island-born or European-born, they have contented themselves—when they have gone in at all for psychological discussion of their subjects—with commonsense remarks of an informal sort. This is not disparagement, just description; in all times and places the best as well as the worst biographers have been guided

by 'psychological' hunches about their subjects. The question now
is simply whether things might usefully be pushed further,
whether in fact biography written as psychohistory might not be
a responsible as well as an interesting way of approaching Pacific
history in some of its aspects.

There are of course methodological problems. Any attempt to
link psychodynamics with the processes of history is fraught with
difficulties. Psychoanalysis and the writing of history share dis-
abilities concerning verification; and both must concede that whatever explanations they purport to offer emerge from the patterns
that can be assembled from available data rather than being drawn
from any great covering law. This might seem to argue against
attempting either psychoanalysis or history-writing at large with
any expectation of arriving at usable truths—and especially against
attempting both at once. But if the attempt is to be made, it seems
reasonable enough to make it in biography. Conceding that the
data available to both psychoanalyst and biographer are (however
copious) essentially fragmentary and subject to various kinds of
distortions in their presentation, the enterprises do show potentially useful and mutually reinforcing affinities: both constitute
time-structured attempts to recover a personal history, to make
patterned sense out of a single life.

The obvious danger, of course, is diagnostic reductionism—too
much easy psychoanalytic generalization, not enough hard historical work and thought. However, one psychoanalytic methodology at least, Eriksonian ego-psychology, does invite the historian's interest and involvement by making its own insistences
on the historical content of the developmental processes of individuals. Erikson argues that human beings grow stage by stage
into the world; that the world for better and for worse prepares
an individual for an outer reality made up of human traditions
and institutions which utilize and thus nourish his developing
capacities, attract and modulate his drives, respond to and de-
limit his fears and fantasies, and assign to him a position in life
appropriate to his psychosocial powers. 'We cannot even begin to
encompass a human being without indicating for each of the
stages of his life cycle the framework of social influences and of
traditional institutions which determine his perspectives on his
more infantile past and on his more adult future'.[5] So for Erikson,
'meaning' in a life is to be sought in the fourfold complementarity
of an individual's developmental history (psychosexual and psychosocial), his stage and state of life, the state of the communities in
which he finds himself, and the history of those communities.[6]

The historian Cushing Strout (who has done biographical research in collaboration with a psychiatrist) goes on to say that
working out the implications of the Eriksonian framework for a

particular case is not a matter of fixing labels but of 'thinking one's way into the specific situation of such a person, so far as the evidence can support it, in order to see how in detail his thoughts, feelings, and actions can be understood as a process over time of an unconscious effort—*in conjunction with conscious aims*'—to achieve his own identity. 'In this light "symptoms" are not disease entities, like foreign bodies, but dramatic expressions of the ego's difficulties in finding its way to autonomy, and their interpretation calls for incorporation of psychoanalytic thinking into the historian's mind by way of his ability to see psychic disorder, distress, and disability as a language which, because of repression, cannot be put into words'. Strout observes that repression of a particular kind may in fact, as Freud found, be a widespread cultural trait. Thus the biographer needs a balanced awareness of social and intellectual factors together with an awareness of the psychic strengths and weaknesses of his subject. 'This work demands a heightened sensitivity to the *intersections* of the development of family-centred difficulties with social and cultural history, for they interact and resonate with each other. Such analysis can be convincingly presented, in large part, only in the form of a story, not in the abstraction of a kernel of generalization from a mere husk of detail.'[7] This offers an attractive enough working basis for attempting biography as psycho-history.

Let us look at a narrative from the Pacific, keeping in mind those Eriksonian intersections. The story comes from the reminiscences of Thomson MacCallum,[8] who ran away to sea as a young man and in his old age wrote a book about his life. In Samoa MacCallum worked for a trading firm, and one of his fellow-employees there told him the story of *his* life. This was a man nicknamed 'His Lordship'; he carried himself aristocratically and wore a monocle. In his own version of things he was of high but unfortunate birth. His father was titled, but his mother was only a barmaid. This unsuitable union was the result of manipulation by his father's wicked father, and when as a young man 'His Lordship' learned of it—learned that in effect his life had been ruined from the moment of conception—he set out to take revenge on the evil old grandfather. He tracked him down and, presenting himself as a gentleman, worked his way into the affections of the old man's ward, a young duchess, seduced her and impregnated her. He had revenged himself. But, ironically, in the process he fell in love with his innocent victim. There was no question of marriage—he was under false colours and in any case the duchess was promised to a prince. So she went off to bear her seducer's child in the care of a husband who was not the father. The seducer felt himself accursed and left England to wander the world. After trials and tribulations he fetched up in Samoa, and there he tortured himself with feelings of unworthiness. Much as he wanted to have a wife and children, he could not think of marriage to any decent girl. Then a girl was offered to him—the adopted daughter of an old, dying trader. He felt constrained to refuse, and explained why. Amazingly, the girl proved to be his daughter by the duchess. Her mother had confessed to her husband the prince; the prince had refused to have anything to do with the little girl who was not his, and sent her away to be raised by distant relatives. Then the foster-mother had died, leaving the child with her mourning husband. He had taken her with him in grief to the South Seas, become a trader, and now, at the point of death, was the instrument of reunion between real father and real daughter. The two returned to England, found the prince dead and the duchess still alive, after all these years still in love with the man who had taken her virtue and got her with child. So they married and lived happily ever after.

This is a very elaborate story, and many things might be said about it (one of them being that MacCallum presents it seriously), but for immediate purposes the main interest lies in the aristocratic birth of the hero and the blight of his life that led him to the islands. The story was allegedly told to MacCallum late in the nineteenth century, but there is nothing specific to the period about that sort of tale. The same general thing could be heard in the Pacific much earlier than that, and continued to be heard into the twentieth century. Indeed there is nothing special to the Pacific about it. It is in fact a version of something lying deep in the European psyche, noted by Freud, and going by the name of 'family romance'.[9] Briefly, this involves a fantasy in which the child replaces his dull, ordinary parents by parents of more interest, elegance, and power: typically aristocrats of one sort or another. Often enough the fantasy takes the form of the child having been separated from these powerful parents at birth and brought up by common folk, after which his life turns into a quest for his real identity, along with which goes a reward of some sort—an inheritance. Most children fantasize in this way, and the situation of younger children who find their access to parents' attention and affection impeded by the existence of older brothers and sisters may predispose them to family romance. The interest here is in those who carry the fantasy into adulthood.

It could readily be imagined that the fantasy would be found in the Pacific as in other non-European places, anywhere white men have been. The point is that here we are at an Eriksonian intersection of significance. It concerns the interaction of the primogeniture system with the imperial-colonial history of Britain. As a matter of historical fact, primogeniture meant that very often younger sons unable to inherit family estates had to go into the world to fend for themselves, and that world was a broad one, extending overseas.[10] As a matter of fantasy, men heavily involved in the working out of family romance would find non-Europe particularly congenial to the maintenance of the fantasy, because there their stories might well escape severe reality-testing. Thus all manner of men might turn up on the edges of empire and beyond, claiming noble antecedents and blocked inheritances. The stories of some might be referable to sociological fact, the stories of others to individual though widely-indulged fantasy. Here we have, as Strout says, a situation in which family-centred difficulties interact and resonate with social and cultural history. Elaborated versions of lives in fact or in fantasy might include as the disinheriting agent failure, crime or illegitimate birth. In the colony of New South Wales, for example, as K. S. Inglis writes, 'there were some younger sons of aristocrats, not all of them black sheep. There were perhaps, but nobody could be sure, a few royal bastards endowed with common names and sent to the farthest parts of the empire with or without parental patronage. Was William Augustus Miles, superintendent of police in Sydney, a son of King William IV? Was the merchant Prosper de Mestre a half-brother of Queen Victoria? Was Colonel Gibbes, collector of customs and father-in-law of Terence Murray of Yarralumla, a son of Mrs Fitzherbert and King George IV?'[11] From there the range extends through remittance men, to claimants whose stories exhibit varying degrees of calculation and controlled or uncontrolled imposture, to men obsessed, driven mad by fantasies unrealized and unrealizable, to the happy few who managed to turn their fantasy into fact—classically by marrying the chief's daughter or the equivalent, acquiring an estate and founding a dynasty of their own.

The remittance man is everywhere in Pacific fact and fiction; he hardly needs substantiation here. As for claimants, the most remarkable one in the Pacific hemisphere was the man who called himself Roger Tichborne, the Tichborne Claimant, allegedly the heir to a baronetcy and enormous estates in England, who pushed his claim all the way from a butcher's shop in Wagga Wagga, New South Wales, to the law courts of London, and whose case for years fascinated English-speaking people of all classes, themselves living with realities and romances determined and elicited by life in a hierarchically-arranged society in which some might inherit and others never could. (It is perhaps worth remarking here that the Claimant's legal counsel had a father who claimed descent from monarchs, heroes, saints and conquerors, and a mother who claimed descent from Charlemagne and Edward III, and who himself fathered a bastard son, invented a doctorate

of laws for himself, and proposed to found a new religion super-
seding all others, with himself for messiah.)[12] As an example of
the man driven by his fantasies, Frederick O'Brien records meeting in Tahiti a cockney pretending to be a nobleman, with a
'commission' from his 'guardian', Baron Airedale, to go around
the world fitting himself for a diplomatic career; on his return
home he would be given £500,000.[13] Robert Louis Stevenson and
his family were visited at Vailima, their home in Samoa, by a
drunk and disagreeable young man who asserted that he was third
in succession to the titles of Duke of Clarence and Avondale.[14]
On the beach in Apia about the same time was another man who
was sure he was rightfully the Duke of York.[15] And as a case of
a man destroyed by his fantasies, there is the trading captain
Charles Bishop, who after a career sailing the Pacific turned up
at Sydney early in the nineteenth century and went mad there,
claiming that he had discovered gold, that he was the governor
of the colony, and that he was the third son of King George,
'Tho' afflicted, and most unhappy in that Title . . .'.[16]

Family romance may be energizing as well as disabling, though
in the nature of things it rarely yields solid dividends of satisfaction. A case in point here is that of Peter Dillon. He was a
man of considerable drive who believed himself capable of great
things and entitled to great rewards. Born the son of an Irish
immigrant to Martinique, he was in relation to British and
French society an heir to specially powerful colonial-colonized
feelings of debarment from inheritance. He claimed connection
with an aristocratic family of Martinique, and through them by
marriage with the Empress Josephine. Dillon venerated Napoleon
(the apotheosis of the lowly boy who becomes king), and considered himself as likewise a man who would wield great powers.
The high point of his career was his solving of the mystery of the
disappearance of La Pérouse's expedition. This success he was
able to capitalize on, to the extent of an audience with the king
of France, a state pension, and a title, Chevalier de l'Ordre Royal
de la Légion d'Honneur. But this was not enough for Dillon—
nothing is ever enough for a claimant. He spent the rest of his
life trying to improve the terms of his pension, command the
respect and attention of the rich and influential, get appointments
to consular posts in the Pacific, organize emigration schemes (one
of them in connection with the Baron de Thierry), and convince
Britain to annex New Zealand (and install there as governor Sir
Augustus d'Este, the son of the Duke of Sussex by a morganatic
marriage). All his life Dillon was, as his biographer says, 'sensitive
to the honorific'; he announced himself variously as the Chevalier
Dillon, the Chevalier Sir Peter Dillon, Don Pedro Dillon, and
Count Dillon; and eventually he took to signing himself C. P.

Dillon—incorporating 'Chevalier' in his personal name and his identity.[17]

Dillon's life represents a partial politicization of family romance. Islands, of course, as small polities, offer excellent opportunities for this (consider the case of Prospero, deposed, disinherited by a brother, becoming ruler of an island). Joshua Hill's career on Pitcairn Island may be looked at in this light. For a brief period in the 1830s Hill virtually controlled Pitcairn by the force of his personality, and as his own utterances indicate, what he wanted from life was powerfully conditioned by family romance.

> I observe, *in limine,* that I have visited the four quarters of the globe, and it has ever been my desire to maintain, as far as lay in my power, the standing of an English gentleman. I have lived a considerable while in a palace, and had my dinner parties with a princess on my right, and a General's lady upon my left . . . I have (at her request) visited Madame Bonaparte, at the Tuileries, St. Cloud, and Malmaison . . . I have had the honour of being in company, *i.e.* at the same parties, with both his late Majesty George IV. then Prince Regent, and his present Majesty William IV. then H.R.H. Duke of Clarence, as well with their royal brothers. I have ridden in a royal Duke's carriage . . . I have visited and dined with some of our first families, and have been visited by a Duke . . . I have written to the Prime Minister of England . . . I was at Napoleon's coronation . . . [18]

And on and on. Hill was mad, but it took some time for this to become apparent to the Pitcairners.

It might be argued that cases such as these, however much they are elaborated, represent nothing but froth and bubble in the history of the Pacific. Perhaps so, if history is limited by definition to the concrete realities of politics and economics. Yet even there it can be shown without difficulty that two of the most influential nineteenth-century white politicians in Polynesia were acting out all their lives the most powerful of family-romance impulses. Surely this gives another kind of consequentiality to the idea of Eriksonian intersections.

Walter Murray Gibson was the Premier of Hawaii from 1882 to 1887, critical years. He involved the Hawaiian kingdom in the tangle of Pacific diplomacy by trying to create a Polynesian confederacy which would guarantee independence to island polities faced with control or annexation by the great powers. In 1887 Gibson was forced from office in a bloodless revolution mounted by white Americans at Honolulu, bringing Hawaii within a few years of annexation by the United States. Gibson is as important as any figure in Hawaiian history after James Cook. Now, Gibson was a complicated man. He rarely told the same story about his life twice, but in his various self-revelations certain themes recur, and they are the themes of family romance. Gibson was, provably, born in Northumberland,[19] the son of a small farmer. But his own elaborate version of his origins was that, as he told Nathaniel Hawthorne in 1854, he was born at sea, on a Spanish ship off Gibraltar.

> Owing to some circumstances, he has been in doubt whether he was really the child of his reputed parents; they have not seemed to love him, and though both [are] still living, it is many years since he has seen or lived with them. Since he has been in England, he has been led to inquire into the subject, and finds that there were *two* births on board the Spanish vessel, nearly simultaneous; and the supposition is, that he himself was assigned to the wrong mother.

Gibson had been investigating his background in England, and had seen in an aristocrat's picture-gallery a portrait 'bearing a striking resemblance to himself'.[20] Gibson spent his adult life chasing shadowy inheritances, attempting by whatever means to enter into his kingdom. He was involved in trying to run guns to Central America in the filibustering period; he told stories of a fabulously wealthy uncle whose heir he was to be, and other stories of buried treasure he was about to discover; he had ideas of setting himself up in Sumatra as another version of James Brooke, the White Rajah of Sarawak; he established a community of Hawaiian Mormons on the island of Lanai and ruled them as 'prince' and 'father'; and eventually, after ten years in elective politics in Hawaii, was offered the premiership, which at last gave him a real kingdom to administer. It is clear from Gibson's career that along with powerful impulses to rule and reign there went powerful impulses to self-destruction: he managed, for example, to get himself almost hanged twice, once in Sumatra as a young man and again as an old man in Hawaii—both times in political rather than criminal circumstances. He would attempt extravagant things and fail, putting himself in a disastrous position. This can be related to a particular version of family romance associated with the absence of a strong acknowledged father-figure; it is observable among illegitimates, the fatherless, or those markedly deprived of parental affection.[21]

As influential as Gibson in the later nineteenth-century politics of Polynesia, perhaps more so, was Shirley Waldemar Baker, the Premier of Tonga for many years. Baker claimed for a father a highly respected London educator with his own school, an uncle who was a physician at Buckingham Palace, another relative who was Crown Protector of Aborigines in Victoria, and a mentor who was an outstanding lawyer. Baker's wife claimed gentility of birth, saying she had been brought up in Barnard Castle. Now, the palace doctor was really in general practice in Pimlico, the connection with the Crown Protector of Aborigines was illusory, and Baker's father did not exist as a school headmaster, indeed cannot be traced at all. As for Barnard Castle, that was the name of the town where Mrs Baker's parents were in trade. The point here is that Baker's shame about obscure origins was counterbalanced by strong drives to aristocratic status, prestige and power, and he mediated all this through family romance, and maintained the fantasy all his life, as a Wesleyan missionary and later as adviser to the King of Tonga. (After he was deposed, he lived in semi-retirement in New Zealand, where he awarded himself a doctorate from the University of Chicago.)[22]

The Baker story is even more interesting when some of the others in the cast of characters are considered. Baker's great enemy on the ground in Tonga was the Wesleyan missionary J. E. Moulton, who was entitled by birth to the consolations of gentility that Baker could only hunger after endlessly. Moulton came from a distinguished enough family of churchmen and scholars, and was himself a man notably learned for the islands (by contrast with Baker, who struck visitors as being ignorant as well as common). But Moulton of Tonga was the 'colonial' Moulton, which is to say that in his family he ranked not at the top but at the bottom, and along with his talents went a disabling speech impediment, clearly of neurotic origin.[23] The man who got rid of Baker from Tonga was High Commissioner for the Western Pacific Sir John Bates Thurston, Governor of Fiji; and Thurston, as his biographer indicates, was conspicuously a self-made man, indeed partly self-invented: he embroidered his family history to make himself something of a gentleman, probably inventing along the way one relative who was duped of a lot of money and another who made off with the trust property of a landed grandfather.[24] And the man who was sent by Thurston to Tonga to tidy up after Baker, Basil Thomson, indisputably a gentleman, son of a bishop, was in family terms in the same situation as Moulton—the son who did not 'inherit' at home, who indeed even had a brother who was ahead of him in distinguishing himself in the colonies.

> I felt that I was a disappointment to my father. My eldest brother had been a success both at Eton and at New College; my second had won mathematical prizes and passed high into Woolwich; he had just won distinction as a gunner subaltern in the Zulu campaign, where he had shared a tent with the Prince Imperial. He had been selected through the influence of Lord Grimthorpe, Chancellor of the York Diocese, as one of the astronomers for the Transit of Venus and was actually in Barbados on his mission, and here was I, at the age when careers are embarked upon, with no qualifications except facility in learning languages and no prospective career.

If Thomson had ambitions, he said, 'they were to carve out fortune in the forgotten back-waters of the world'.[25] And so to the Pacific.

It is not necessary to stop with political figures to find evidence of psychosexual and psychosocially-expressed family romance among figures significant in the Pacific. Paul Gauguin, for example, bolstered his ideas about the natural aristocracy of art by reference to his romanticized descent (marked by illegitimacy) from Borgias, viceroys of Peru, and Inca rulers.[26] Herman Melville's bourgeois father was a family romancer of sorts; Melville himself, as one of his biographers remarks, displays the psychology of the decayed patrician;[27] and one of the great themes of his work is the search for the reassuringly aristocratic father-figure.[28]

As Cushing Strout observes, the 'historical value of such unusually articulate and conflict-ridden people is the power they have of bringing issues of general significance to a more vivid, intense, and clarifying focus. We not only see into them; they enable us to see into some of the profound issues of their time'.[29] Looking into their lives also leads us to Eriksonian intersections, and might lead us to go on from there to reconsider the desiderata for writing biography in the Pacific.[30]

NOTES AND REFERENCES

1 Herman Melville, *Moby Dick*, ch. 58.
2 I am referring here to psychoanalytic psychology. See the summary article by Mazlish 1974:1034-45. See also the useful cautionary article by McGlone 1975.
3 Davidson 1966.
4 Maude 1971. On the matter of writing psychoanalytically-oriented biography of islanders—this raises its own set of methodological problems, and the present paper confines itself to discussing an approach to writing biographies of white men in the islands.
5 Erikson 1972:18.
6 Kakar 1970:188.
7 Strout 1968:284-5.
8 MacCallum 1934. The story is told in 'instalments' throughout the book.
9 Freud 1959:V, 74-8.
10 Reader 1966:73; Thompson 1963:22; Perkin 1969:60. See also Rosenberg 1954:*passim*. As a 20th-century illustration of the pains inflicted by the primogeniture system and the responses it generates among 'colonials', consider this passage from George Johnston, *My brother Jack* (London 1967):21-2. The scene takes place on a Greek island, between the Australian narrator and 'a tall, youngish Englishman, a failed aristocrat who had been sent down from Oxford some years before, rather disgracefully, and who had come to this island with the evident intention of drinking himself into a conditon of irreparable decay . . . He had been telling us of some of the more lamentable interludes of his life. After he had completed the sorry account he stared broodingly into his wine glass, then shook his head sadly, and said: "None of you, of course, will ever know what it was like to be the younger son of a younger son". "No", I replied with sudden sharpness. "And you will never know what it was like to be the younger son of a tram driver!" '

11 Inglis 1974:19.
12 Roe 1974:*passim*.
13 O'Brien 1921:244-6.
14 Stevenson 1955:169.
15 Osbourne 1924:128.
16 Bishop 1967:liii.
17 Davidson 1975:*passim*.
18 Brodie 1851:211-14.
19 Adler and Barrett 1973:ix. Jacob Adler is at work on a life of Gibson.
20 Hawthorne 1941:93.
21 Choisy 1950; Iremonger 1970:16-25.
22 Rutherford 1971:*passim*.
23 Moulton 1921:*passim*.
24 Scarr 1973:2-3.
25 Thomson 1937:12-13.
26 Gauguin 1923:2; Gattey 1970:*passim*.
27 Arvin 1950:21.
28 *ibid.:passim;* Haberstroh 1971:*passim*.
29 Strout 1968:289.
30 And not only in the Pacific. A model of psychoanalytically-informed biography, about an unusually articulate, conflict-ridden man heavily involved with non-Europe in terms of dispossession and inheritance is Fawn M. Brodie, *The devil drives: a life of Sir Richard Burton* (New York 1967). Southeast Asia offers possibilities for research along these lines, beginning with James Brooke and the various Brooke surrogates. See the discussion of Charles David De Mayréna in A. Reid, 'The French in Sumatra and the Malay world, 1760-1890', *Bijdragen tot de Taal-, Land- en Volkenkunde*, 129:2/3 (1973), 234ff.; and the reference to Alexander Hare of Bandjermasin in Graham Irwin, *Nineteenth-Century Borneo: a study in diplomatic rivalry* ('s-Gravenhage 1955), 17-21.

V

Hawaiian historians and the first Pacific history seminar

BEN R. FINNEY, RUBY K. JOHNSON,
MALCOLM N. CHUN and EDITH K. McKINZIE

Academic imperialism is the charge, and promotion of indigenous scholarship is an oft proffered response. The idea that Pacific Islanders should write their own histories, or ethnographies, and not be fated to having their lives chronicled solely by outsiders, and that historians and social scientists from metropolitan countries should facilitate the growth of indigenous scholarship through training and collaborative efforts, has gained some credence in recent years. However, this very reasonable idea is perhaps not as novel as some of its promoters, and detractors as well, might think. Almost a century and a half ago an effort was made to have young Hawaiians participate in the production of their own history. Although the immediate product in question, a volume entitled *Mooolelo Hawaii,* which may be translated 'Hawaiian History', was not all that exemplary, the indirect effect of this attempt to involve Hawaiians in historical and ethnographical research, that of stimulating indigenous scholarship, was significant and bears some examination.

An American missionary, Sheldon Dibble, and an American missionary institution, the Lahainaluna Seminary, were crucial to this effort. Dibble was born in 1809 in Skeneatles, New York, and educated at Hamilton College, where he received his bachelor's and master's degrees, and the Auburn Theological Seminary, all located in New York State. He arrived in Honolulu in 1831 as part of the 'fourth company' of missionaries sent out to Hawaii by the American Board of Commissioners for Foreign Missions. After three years of service in humid Hilo, where he became proficient in Hawaiian, Dibble requested transfer to Lahaina in hopes that a lung condition, and the health of his daughters, would improve in the drier climate there. Except for a short trip back to the United States, Dibble remained at Lahaina as a teacher at the Lahainaluna Seminary until his death in 1845, presumably from tuberculosis.[1] As a scholar Dibble is perhaps best known for his *A History of the Sandwich Islands,* first published in 1843 at the Lahainaluna Seminary Press, a work that dwells heavily on the history of the missionaries and the changes wrought in Hawaii under their tutelage or influence. We, however, regard his early efforts to involve Hawaiians in a more total examination of Hawaiian history to be his most significant scholarly work.

The Lahainaluna Mission Seminary was founded in 1831 to train Hawaiian schoolteachers. In the short time they had been in Hawaii the missionaries apparently had been extremely successful in stimulating school interest among the Hawaiians, but there were nowhere near enough missionaries to go around to staff all the newly founded 'schools', which in 1831 totalled 961 and enrolled over 50,000 pupils. Lahainaluna was conceived to fill the gap by training young Hawaiians to become pious teaching assistants for the missionaries. The Seminary, which was first called a 'High School', was an ambitious undertaking, coming only a few years after the establishment of the first high schools and teacher training institutions in the United States. It played a major role in the inauguration of formal education in Hawaii and survives today as a secular school.[2] For our purposes here, however, a unique educational experiment conducted under Dibble's direction during the first years of the Seminary's existence is of primary import.

Dibble started teaching at Lahainaluna in 1834, assigned to classes in biblical studies, religious instruction and ecclesiastical and civil history. While teaching history Dibble was struck by an absurdity common to education in the colonial context. He tells us in his preface to *A History of the Sandwich Islands* that:

> It occurred to me as quite objectionable that the scholars, whilst they are becoming acquainted with other nations, should remain to a great degree in ignorance of their own. Accordingly, in 1836, I made some effort to collect the main facts of Hawaiian History. There were but few records and those recent. Most important events were afloat in the memories of the people and fast passing into oblivion. If they were to be preserved it was time they were collected.[3]

His remedy for this lack of Hawaiian historical materials was not only to set out to collect them, but also to involve his Hawaiian students in the process. He first made out a list of questions, arranged in roughly chronological order, designed to elicit the needed information. Then, Dibble relates that he 'selected ten of the best scholars of the Seminary, and formed them into a class of inquiry'. The class, or seminar as we might call it today, met at regular intervals. At the first meeting Dibble presented the first question, which was then fully discussed so that there might be agreement as to what information was being sought. Dibble then requested that the scholars:

> go individually and separately to the oldest and most knowing of the chiefs and people, gain all the information they could on the question

given out, commit each his information to writing and be ready to read it on a day and hour appointed. At the time of meeting each scholar read what he had written—discrepancies were reconciled and corrections made by each other and then all the compositions were handed to me, out of which I endeavored to make one true and connected account. Thus we proceeded from one question to another till a volume was prepared and printed in the Hawaiian language.[4]

In the preface to *Mooolelo Hawaii* itself, Dibble also says that in addition to gathering traditions and recollections from informants, the older students were charged with searching their own memories for recollections of the major events in Hawaiian history that occurred in their lifetimes.

Mooolelo Hawaii was published at Lahainaluna in 1838. It is but a sketchy start at constructing an account of ancient Hawaiian society and of the changes wrought during the first years of European contact. Its pages contain a mixture of ethnographical and historical information. There are sections on chiefly genealogies, on the Hawaiian calendar, on the character of ancient Hawaiians, on war practices and on the *kapu* system, as well as on the events during the reign of Kamehameha and Liholiho, on the succession of foreign visitors from Cook to Vancouver, on the development of the sandalwood trade, on growing depopulation and on the abolition of the *kapu* system and the arrival of the missionaries. Almost a century after its publication, John F. G. Stokes bitterly denounced Dibble for introducing a Christian bias into its pages, and particularly for, allegedly, editing or adding to the accounts of the Hawaiian informants so as to show Cook to be a man who allowed the introduction of venereal disease, allowed himself to be worshipped as a god, and so on.[5] Stokes, an Australian, was especially incensed because *Mooolelo Hawaii* was evidently intended for use as a textbook at Lahainaluna, and hence, to his mind, was instrumental in creating a strong prejudice against Captain Cook and his accomplishments among the Lahainaluna scholars who, in turn, were in a position to pass these lessons on to their pupils once they launched their teaching careers. Stokes, in fact, traces the prejudice against Cook so marked among Hawaiians in the latter half of the nineteenth century and the first part of this century to the passages about Cook in *Mooolelo Hawaii*.

At the bottom of many of the pages of *Mooolelo Hawaii* are found questions relating to the text above. These questions range from the very general to the specific, as a sample of them given below indicates: How many races does Hawaii, Tahiti, the Marquesas and all the other islands of the ocean have? What about the genealogies of the chiefs? What is the history of Kamehameha's first war of his régime? At what period did Captain Cook, namely

Lono, first stop at these islands? What did they do with the corpse of Lono? What did Vancouver give Kamehameha? Although at first glance it might appear that these questions could be the very ones Dibble's students used to elicit information from their informants, a more likely explanation is that they were intended for use, catechism-like, in drilling the students on the contents of the text.

Unfortunately, Dibble did not include in *Mooolelo Hawaii*, or in any of his other published and unpublished writings that we have been able to consult, a list of the ten Lahainaluna scholars who worked with him in producing the volume—the participants in what might be called the first Pacific history seminar. This oversight mars this, and many other works dealing with Pacific island topics wherein the author or compiler fails to indicate the indigenous collaborators or informants who provided the data on which the works were based and in some cases helped write them. In fairness to Dibble, however, it must be noted that he did not put his name on the title page of *Mooolelo Hawaii* or claim more than being a compiler or editor. The sub-title of the volume reads simply: 'written by some students of the high school [Lahainaluna], and corrected by a teacher of the school'. And, in the preface Dibble writes that 'most of the facts reported in this book were written by pupils of the high school', and that their notes from their interviews with informants 'were given to a teacher of the school who collated and revised them for printing, adding to them some words of his own'.[6] We know, however, of three of the seminar participants, David Malo and Moku, members of the first class enrolled at Lahainaluna, and Samuel Manaiakalani Kamakau, a member of the second class. It is in the careers of Malo and Kamakau, men who subsequently became renowned Hawaiian scholars, not in the pages of *Mooolelo Hawaii*, that we find the most significant impact of Dibble's effort to develop Hawaiian historical materials.

Malo is generally regarded as the leading Hawaiian scholar of his day. Jules Remy, who translated *Mooolelo Hawaii* into French as *Histoire de l'Archipel Havaiien*,[7] credits Malo with being the 'principal author' of the work. However, according to research by Malcolm Chun currently in progress it would appear that Malo's work could well have been in part based on the writings of Moku, Malo's classmate who also participated in Dibble's seminar, and one Kipela. The identity of Kipela is a mystery. Although he is not listed as ever having been enrolled at Lahainaluna, he apparently was at the school during the period in question and was active in writing on Hawaiian subjects. It may be that Kipela was a Hawaiian who had received some education under missionary sponsorship in the United States, and who was then brought back to help the Lahainaluna staff in their teaching and research.

Malo also undertook biographical research on the lives of two Hawaiian chiefs, Umi a Liloa, the great chief of fifteenth-century Hawaii, and Kamehameha. He apparently undertook field work on Hawaii in researching the life of Kamehameha, but unfortunately the finished manuscript, 'History of Kamehameha', has since disappeared.[8] Malo's greatest work, however, was his own *Moolelo Hawaii*.[9] This was written over the course of several years at the request of Lorrin Andrews, the principal of Lahainaluna, and was completed in 1839 or 1840.[10] It was written in Hawaiian, and although J. F. Pogue apparently used it in 1858 to enlarge and publish another version of Dibble's *Mooolelo Hawaii*,[11] the work was not published until 1903 when an English translation by Nathaniel B. Emerson, entitled *Hawaiian Antiquities*, appeared.

Malo's *Moolelo Hawaii* was apparently the standard reference work, and reference point, for other scholars working on Hawaiian traditions in the last century. It apparently circulated in manuscript copies, some of which survive today. According to Dorothy Barrère, who has edited the translated works of Kamakau and I'i, Malo's work was the 'skeleton upon which Kamakau and I'i put clothes'[12] by adding material left out or only briefly outlined by Malo. Although *mo'olelo* may be translated as 'traditions' or 'history', the use of the gloss 'antiquities' in the English title is perhaps more fitting as Malo is more concerned with describing the nature of ancient Hawaiian society than he is with developing a narrative history from oral traditions. As such the book is more of an ethnology than a history. Indeed, the recent printing of an inexpensive paperback edition of *Hawaiian Antiquities* has allowed it to be used as the principal text in the basic anthropology course on ancient Hawaiian society now taught at the University of Hawaii.[13]

Malo's leading position in Hawaiian studies may stem in part from the fact that Malo was the first-born among the prominent nineteenth-century Hawaiian scholars, and thus perhaps had a better chance to observe changing customs and discuss them with persons whose experience extended well back into the eighteenth century. Malo was born in Keauhou, Hawaii Island, in 1793. His father was attached to the court and army of Kamehameha, and Malo had an opportunity, while growing up, to be associated with high chief Kuakini (Governor Adams), the brother of Queen Ka'ahumanu, and with Auwai, one of Kamehameha's favourite chiefs, a man who was well versed in Hawaiian traditions. Emerson credits this association with learned and well-placed men, plus what he calls Malo's 'shrewd and inquiring mind as well as a tenacious memory', with being crucial to the quality of Malo's work.[14]

Several years after the arrival of the missionaries Malo moved from Hawaii Island to Lahaina where he came under the sway of the missionary William Richards, was converted and baptized David. As David Malo he became an ardent Christian, sought to learn English but failed, and enrolled at Lahainaluna School in 1831 at the age of thirty-eight as one of its first pupils. Malo was held over after completing his course to become a teaching assistant, as well as a researcher. Although Malo served as the first Superintendent of Schools for the Hawaiian Kingdom from 1841-45, he apparently spent most of his time after leaving Lahainaluna and before his death in 1853 serving as a Christian minister on Maui.[15] Malo can easily be charged, as Emerson has done,[16] with displaying the bias of a zealous Christian convert in his writings, by either criticizing or omitting mention of past beliefs and practices at variance with Christian doctrine. What is more outstanding, however, is that Malo was able to undertake the amount of research and writing that he did when, as a Christian convert, student and then minister, he was actively involved in rejecting major facets of his natal culture. In fact Stokes,[17] Dibble's arch-critic, compliments Malo for his integrity and maturity in not passing on in his writings the strident criticism of traditional religious practices and the anti-Cook bias which Stokes attributes to his mentor.[18]

Kamakau was born at Mokuleia in the Waialua section of Oahu in 1815, and entered Lahainaluna in 1833 as a member of the second class enrolled there. He remained at Lahainaluna until 1846, serving as a tutor and teaching assistant in history, writing, mathematics and geography, and helping Lorrin Andrews compile his *Dictionary of the Hawaiian Language,* which was published in Honolulu in 1865.[19] Kamakau, like Malo, was apparently inspired to research Hawaiian traditions and history through participation in Dibble's seminar, although his scholarly career diverged somewhat from that of Malo.

From the time he left Lahainaluna up until his death in 1876 Kamakau was in and out of government service. He served in various minor posts on Maui, and had a brief tenure as District Judge of Wailuku—only to be removed from office for malfeasance. He was elected to the legislature in 1851, representing Hana, Maui, and represented over the next two decades various other districts in Maui and on Oahu. Kamakau was also a member of the Board of Commissioners to Quiet Land Titles, and the Royal Hawaiian Agricultural Society as well.

Kamakau was indefatigable in research and a voluminous writer. Abraham Fornander apparently depended heavily on

Kamakau's field work to gather the legends and traditions upon which much of his two major works, *An Account of the Polynesian Race* and *Collection of Hawaiian Antiquities and Folk-lore*,[20] is based. He is most famous, however, for the numerous newspaper articles that he published from 1865 until 1871 in two Hawaiian language newspapers, *Ku'oko'a* and *Ke Au 'Oko'a*. Many of these have since been translated and recently published in a series of three monographs. Of these, *Ruling Chiefs of Hawaii* qualifies Kamakau as a leading Hawaiian historian. It deals with the lives of the great chiefs of ancient Hawaii up to the time of Cook, and then gives a narrative of Cook's visit and the subsequent development of the monarchy up until 1852. The other two, *The People of Old* and *The Works of the People of Old*, deal primarily with ancient Hawaiian society and culture, and hence qualify Kamakau as an ethnologist as well.[21]

Kamakau is more vulnerable to criticism than is Malo. Although this contrast may be at least partially a function of the sheer volume of Kamakau's published material compared to Malo's one book, several writers have criticized Kamakau's judgement. While Stokes lauds Malo for not aping Dibble's biases, he notes that a young and impressionable Kamakau apparently was influenced to a point where he amplified in his newspaper writings the derogatory and allegedly unfair account of Cook given in *Mooolelo Hawaii*.[22] Thrum, Kamakau's only biographer, considers him to be unstable on the basis of his political record, his abrupt change from Protestantism to Catholicism and his jumping from one newspaper staff to the other.[23] A third writer, Dorothy Barrère who has edited Kamakau's newspaper stories for monograph publication, is more specific in her criticism.[24] She considers that both Kamakau and Kepelino (Kahoali'ikumaieiwakamoku), another Hawaiian historian of the day, are responsible for altering or creating Hawaiian legends designed to reconcile Hawaiian traditions with Christianity, and to account for the discovery and settlement of Hawaii. These Kumuhonua Legends, as she terms them, are to be found in the writings of Kamakau and Kepelino, and in the pages of *An Account of the Polynesian Race*, by Abraham Fornander who apparently employed Kamakau to gather and furnish him with Hawaiian traditions. While the evidence for falsification seems strong, one is tempted to suggest that both Kamakau and Kepelino may have been engaging in some Polynesian leg-pulling for the benefit of *Haole* scholars intent on collecting Hawaiian creation and origin explanations.[25]

Rather than dwell on these points of criticism, we would prefer to close this discussion by highlighting one of Kamakau's more judicious statements. In 1841 the Royal Hawaiian Historical Society was formed at Lahainaluna by King Kamehameha and several of his officials, Dibble and other missionaries and several Lahainaluna scholars, including Malo, and Kamakau who was elected treasurer of the organization. Tasks of research and writing were divided among members. Kamakau was assigned the history of Kihapi'ilani, a famous Maui chief; Malo, the history of Umi a Liloa; Timothy Ha'alilo (the King's secretary) the history of Kamahameha, and Keoni Ana (John Young II) the history of the first foreigners in Hawaii. Work proceeded for three years, but the Society lapsed in 1845 upon the death of Dibble, who may well have inspired the whole project, and upon the removal of the King and court to Honolulu. Lamenting the passing of the Society, and with it an opportunity to undertake research on an organized scale, Kamakau noted that it might then be too late to do work of this kind as there were few knowledgeable informants left:

> Now, when a chief is asked concerning his place he excuses his ignorance by pleading that he is a *malihini* [newcomer], and so on; the reason for this is that the old chiefs are dead. There are no more people conversant with old history; those who are left try to make out that they are beacon lights on historical subjects, when in fact their knowledge on these subjects is only limited. Still others are those foreigners who claim to know so much about our land and people, but whose knowledge is only superficial.[26]

NOTES AND REFERENCES

1 Ephraim W. Clark, 'Brief Notice of the Life and Labors of Rev. Sheldon Dibble', *The Friend*, Honolulu, 1 March 1845:33-6; n.a., 'Sheldon Dibble', *Hawaiian Mission Childrens Society Annual Report* 1931:10-11.
2 Lecker 1938.
3 Dibble 1843:iii.
4 *ibid.*:iii-iv.
5 Stokes 1931:68-104.
6 This is our literal translation. Reuben Tinker, a missionary colleague, elaborates what was meant by 'some words' when he renders the last part of the phrase: '(adding dates) and occasionally sentences and paragraphs of his own'. (Reuben Tinker, [Translation of]) *Mooolelo Hawaii, Hawaiian Spectator*, Honolulu 1839, II:59. If Stokes' critique of Dibble were fully accepted, it could be argued that Dibble could have deliberately played down his role in writing *Mooolelo Hawaii* in order to make his 'thoughts' appear to originate from the Hawaiian scholars and their informants.
7 Remy 1862. An incomplete translation into English of *Mooolelo Hawaii* by Reuben Tinker appeared in the *Hawaiian Spectator*, II:58-71; 211-31; 334-41; 438-47 (Honolulu, 1839) and was continued but not completed in *The Polynesian* 28 July, 1, 8, 15, 22 August 1840.
8 Emerson 1951:xii.
9 *Mo'o-'ōlelo* comes from two morphs, *mo'o*, 'succession of', and *'ōlelo*, 'speech (*lelo*, tongue). *Mo'olelo* is a contraction of the compound *mo'o-'ōlelo*.
10 Emerson 1951:xv; Alexander 1951:xviii.
11 Emerson 1951:xii.
12 Barrère, pers. comm., 23 Sept. 1971.
13 The course is perhaps unique among anthropology courses in that all the assigned texts normally used over the last five years as it has been taught

by Ben Finney have been either wholly written (Malo 1951; I'i 1959; and Kamakau 1964 and 1961), or co-authored (Handy and Pukui 1972) by persons indigenous to the culture being studied.

14 Emerson 1951:vii.

15 Lecker 1938:209; Kuykendall 1932:35-6.

16 Emerson 1951:viii.

17 Stokes 1931:98.

18 Young Hawaiian radical students at the University of Hawaii are wont to dismiss Malo for his description of the great power of Hawaiian chiefs over land, production and the lives of commoners, apparently because his picture is at variance with their own conception of a pre-capitalist Polynesian society. However, a close reading of Malo reveals that he also details the duties and obligations of the chiefs, and shows the limits of their powers. Compared with the accounts of Dibble and other foreign observers of the time, Malo is in fact a most sensitive political analyst, particularly when it comes to the relationship of chiefs and commoners.

19 Thrum 1918:40-61; Lecker 1938:182-4.

20 Fornander 1878-85 and 1916-1920.

21 Kamakau 1961, 1964 and 1975. A fourth volume, *Mo'olelo a Ka Po'e Kahiko* (*Traditions of the People of Old*), is in preparation. All these have been translated by Mary Kawena Pukui, the leading contemporary Hawaiian scholar, and edited by Dorothy Barrère.

22 Stokes 1931:98.

23 Thrum 1918:46-7.

24 Barrère 1969.

25 cf. Lātūkefu 1968 and France 1966.

26 Thrum 1918:41-3.

Bibliography of works cited

Abella, Domingo 1973, 'Guamanians and Filipinos: are they the same people? An introduction to the study of Philippines-Marianas relations', *Guam Recorder* (Agana, Guam), 3:12, 9-12.

Adler, Jacob and Gwyn Barrett (eds) 1973, *The diaries of Walter Murray Gibson 1886, 1887* (Honolulu).

Alexander, W. D. 1951, 'Introduction' *in* Malo 1951, xvii-xviii.

Althusser, Louis and Étienne Balibar (eds) 1970, *Reading Capital,* abridged trans. of *Lire le Capital* by B. Brewster (London; 1st pub. Paris 1968).

Ambrose, W. R. and R. C. Green 1972, 'First millenium [*sic*] BC transport of obsidian from New Britain to the Solomon Islands', *Nature* (London), 237:5349, 31.

Anderson, J. D. and C. S. Cox 1967, 'Microbial survival' *in* Gregory and Monteith 1967, 203-26.

Anderson, Nils J. 1854, *Eine Weltumseglung mit der schwedischen Kriegsfregatte "Eugenie" 1851/1853* (Leipzig; Swedish ed., Christiania 1854).

Aoyagi, Machiko 1966, 'Kinship organisation and behaviour in a contemporary Tongan village', *J.P.S.*, 75:2, 141-76.

Arieti, Silvano (ed.) 1974, *American handbook of psychiatry,* 2nd ed.; 3 vols (New York).

Arvin, Newton 1950, *Herman Melville,* American Men of Letters ser. (New York and Toronto; R:1957, 1966).

Baarda, M. J. M. van 1893, 'Île de Halmaheira, départment Galèla, Indes Néerlandaises (Moluques)', *Bulletins de la Société d'Anthropologie de Paris,* 4, 4th ser., 533-68.

Balibar, Étienne 1970, 'On the basic concepts of historical materialism', *in* Althusser and Balibar 1970, 201-8.

Banks, Joseph 1962, *The Endeavour journal of Joseph Banks 1768-1771,* 2 vols, ed. by J. C. Beaglehole (Sydney; R:1963).

Barclay, Andrew 1807, 'Description of St. David's Islands, in the passage to China', *Naval Chronicle* (London), 18, 283-5.

Baretta, J. M. 1917, *Halmahera en Morotai. Bewerkt naar de memorie van den kapitein van den generalen staf* (Batavia).

Barnard, Noel (ed.), with Douglas Fraser 1972, *Early Chinese art and its possible influence in the Pacific basin: a symposium . . .,* 3 vols; vol. III (New York).

Barnett, R. D. 1958, 'Early shipping in the Near East', *Antiquity* (Gloucester, Eng.), 32:128, 220-30.

Barrère, Dorothy B. 1969, *The Kumuhonua legends, a study of late 19th century Hawaiian stories of creation and origins,* Pacific Anthropological Records, no. 3 (Honolulu).

Bass, George F. (ed.) 1972, *A history of seafaring based on underwater archaeology* (London).

Beardsley, Charles 1964, *Guam past and present* (Rutland and Tokyo).

Beckwith, Martha (trans. and ed.) 1951, *The Kumulipo: a Hawaiian creation chant* (Chicago; R:Honolulu, 1972).

Bellwood, Peter 1975, 'The prehistory of Oceania', *Current Anthropology* (Chicago), 16:1, 9-28.

Berndt, Ronald M. and Peter Lawrence (eds) 1971, *Politics in New Guinea: traditional and in the context of change. Some anthropological perspectives* (Nedlands, W.A.).

Bishop, Charles 1967, *The journal and letters of Captain Charles Bishop on the north-west coast of America, in the Pacific and in New South Wales 1794-1798*, ed. by Michael Roe; Hakluyt Society 2nd Series no. 131 (Cambridge).

Biskup, Peter 1968, 'Hermann Detzner: New Guinea's first coast watcher', *Journal of the Papua & New Guinea Society* (Port Moresby), 2:1, 4-21.

Blair, Emma H. and James A. Robertson (trans. and eds) 1903-09, *The Philippine Islands, 1493-1898* . . ., with hist. intro. and additional notes by Edward G. Bourne; 55 vols (Cleveland; R:Taiwan 1962).

Bos, Hendrik C. 1935, *Bijdrage tot de anthropologie van de bevolking der Schouten-eilanden (Nederlandsch Nieuw-Guinea)* (Rotterdam).

Bowring, John 1859, *The Philippine Islands* (London).

Brady, Ivan A. 1975, 'Christians, pagans, and government men: culture change in the Ellice Islands' *in* Brady and Isaac 1975, II, 111-45.

———— and Barry L. Isaac (eds) 1975, *A reader in culture change,* 2 vols; vol. II (Cambridge, Mass. and New York).

Brodie, Walter 1851, *Pitcairn's Island, and the islanders, in 1850* (London).

Brøgger, A. W. and Haakon Shetelig 1951, *The Viking ships, their ancestry and evolution,* trans. by Katherine John (Oslo).

Brosses, Charles de 1756, *Histoire des navigations aux terres australes,* 2 vols (Paris).

Brown, Paula 1963, 'From anarchy to satrapy', *A.A.,* 65, 1-15.

Buck, Peter H. (Te Rangi Hiroa) 1930, *Samoan material culture,* B. P. Bishop Museum Bulletin 75 (Honolulu).

———— 1938, *Vikings of the sunrise* (New York; R:Chicago 1959 as *Vikings of the Pacific*).

———— 1950, *Material culture of Kapingamarangi,* B. P. Bishop Museum Bulletin 200 (Honolulu).

Burnet, Macfarlane 1953, *Natural history of infectious disease,* 2nd ed. (Cambridge; 1st pub. 1940 as *Biological aspects of infectious disease.* R:1972).

Burrow, J. W. 1966, *Evolution and society: a study in Victorian social theory* (Cambridge).

Burrus, E. J. 1954, 'Sanvitores' grammar and catechism in the Mariana (or Chamorro) language (1668)', *Anthropos* (St Augustin, Germ.), 49, 934-60.

Buxton, Patrick A. 1925/26, 'The depopulation of the New Hebrides and other parts of Melanesia', *Transactions of the Royal Society of Tropical Medicine and Hygiene* (London), 19, 420-54.

Camp, John 1974, *Magic, myth and medicine* (London).

Carano, Paul and Pedro C. Sanchez 1964, *A complete history of Guam* (Rutland and Tokyo).

Carroll, Vern (ed.) 1970, *Adoption in eastern Oceania,* Association for Social Anthropology in Oceania Monograph no. 1 (Honolulu).

———— (ed.) 1975, *Pacific atoll populations,* Association for Social Anthropology in Oceania Monograph no. 3 (Honolulu).

Carteret, Philip 1965, *Carteret's voyage around the world 1766-1769*, 2 vols, ed. by Helen Wallis; Hakluyt Society 2nd Series nos 124-5 (Cambridge).

Case, Humphrey 1969, 'Neolithic explanations', *Antiquity*, 43:171, 176-86.

Chalmers, James 1886/87, New Guinea—past, present, and future', *Proceedings of the Royal Colonial Institute* (London), 18, 89-122.

Champion, Ivan F. 1932, *Across New Guinea from the Fly to the Sepik* (London).

Chaunu, Huguette and Pierre, et al. 1955-59, *Séville et l'Atlantique (1504-1650)*, 8 vols in 13. École Pratique des Hautes Études, VI° section, Centre de Recherches Historiques: Ports-routes-trafics, 6 (Paris).

Cheshire, Geoffrey C. 1972, *Cheshire's modern law of real property*, 11th ed., ed. by E. H. Burn (London).

Cheyne, Andrew 1971, *The trading voyages of Andrew Cheyne 1841-1844*, ed. by Dorothy Shineberg; Pacific History Series no. 3 (Canberra).

Choisy, Maryse 1950, 'Le complexe de Phaéton', *Psyché* (Paris), 5, 715-31.

Chowning, Ann 1972, 'Ceremonies, shell money and culture among the Kove', *Expedition* (Philadelphia), 15:1, 2-8.

———— 1973, 'Milke's "New Guinea cluster": the evidence from northwest New Britain', *Oceanic Linguistics* (Honolulu), 12, 189-243.

———— and Ward H. Goodenough 1971, 'Lakalai political organization' *in* Berndt and Lawrence 1971, 113-74.

Christian, F. W. 1899, *The Caroline Islands; travel in a sea of little lands* (London and New York).

Churchward, C. Maxwell 1959, *Tongan dictionary* (London).

Clercq, F. S. A. de and J. D. E. Schmeltz 1893, *Ethnographische beschrijving van de west- en noord-kust van Nederlandsch Nieuw-Guinea* (Leiden).

Comyn, Tomás de 1820, *Estado de las islas Filipinas en 1810* (Madrid; R:Eng. trans., Manila 1969).

Cook, James 1955-67, *The journals of Captain James Cook on his voyages of discovery*, 3 vols in 4; vol. I(R:1968), II(1961), pts 1 and 2 (1967) ed. by J. C. Beaglehole; Hakluyt Society Extra Series nos 34-36 (Cambridge).

Corney, Bolton G. 1890, 'On certain mutilations practised by natives of the Viti Islands', *Report of . . . the Australasian Association for the Advancement of Science* (Sydney), 2, 646-9, 651-3.

———— (trans. and comp.) 1913-19, *The quest and occupation of Tahiti by the emissaries of Spain during the years 1772-1776 . . .*, 3 vols; Hakluyt Society 2nd Series nos 32, 36, 43 (Cambridge).

————, J. Stewart and B. H. Thomson 1896, *Report of the Commission appointed to inquire into the decrease of the native population: 1893* (Suva).

Corte y Ruano Calderón, Felipe M. de la 1875, *Memoria descriptiva e histórica de las islas Marianas . . .* (Madrid).

Cortesão, A. and A. Teixeira da Mota (eds) 1960, *Portugaliae monumento cartographica*, 6 vols (Lisbon).

Counts, David and Dorothy 1970, 'The *vula* of Kaliai: a primitive ceremony with commercial use', *Oceania* (Sydney), 41:2, 90-105.

Cowell, Reid 1951, *The structure of Gilbertese* (Beru, Gilbert Is).

Cranstone, B. A. L. 1961, *Melanesia: a short ethnography* (London).

Crocombe, Ron (ed.) 1971, *Land tenure in the Pacific* (Melbourne).

Cumberland, Kenneth B. 1954, *Southwest Pacific: a geography of Australia, New Zealand and their Pacific island neighbours* (Christchurch; R:rev.ed. New York 1968).

Cushner, Nicholas P. 1975, Review of J. N. de Zuñiga, *Status of the Philippines in 1800, Journal of Asian Studies* (Ann Arbor, Mich.), 34:2, 571-2.

Dahlgren, E. W. 1916, *Were the Hawaiian Islands visited by the Spaniards before their discovery by Captain Cook in 1778? A contribution to the geographical history of the north Pacific Ocean . . .,* Kungl. Svenska Vetenskapsakademiens Handlingar. Band 57, no. 4 (Stockholm).

Damm, Hans *et al.* 1938, 'Zentralkarolinen. II. Halbband: Aurepik-Faraulip-Sorol-Mogemog' *in* Thilenius 1938, vol. 10 (II, B, 10).

Dark, Philip J. C. 1974, *Kilenge life and art: a look at a New Guinea people* (London).

Dart, Raymond A. 1957, 'The earlier stages of Indian trans-oceanic traffic', *Nada* (Salisbury, Rhodesia), 34, 95-115.

————— 1960, 'Africa's place in the emergence of civilisation', Van Riebeeck Lectures, South African Broadcasting Corporation (Johannesburg).

[Davenport, H. C.] 1952, 'Far outpost of the O'Keefe empire'; 'More about Mapia, outpost of O'Keefe's kingdom', *P.I.M.*, 22:12 (July), 69; 23:2 (Sept.), 68-70.

Davidson, J. W. 1966, 'Problems of Pacific history', *J.P.H.*, 1, 5-21.

————— 1975, *Peter Dillon of Vanikoro: chevalier of the South Seas,* ed. by O. H. K. Spate (Melbourne).

Decktor Korn, Shulamit R. 1974, 'Tongan kin groups: the noble and the common view', *J.P.S.*, 83:1, 5-13.

DeVries, Keith, with Michael L. Katzev 1972, 'Greek, Etruscan and Phoenician ships and shipping' and 'The Kyrenia ship', *in* Bass 1972, 37-64.

Dibble, Sheldon 1843, *History of the Sandwich Islands* (Lahainaluna, Hawaii).

Dick, H. W. 1975, Prahu shipping in Indonesia: the institutional framework (Canberra; unpub. seminar paper, Dept of Economics, Research School of Pacific Studies, A.N.U.).

Doran, Edwin Jr 1971, 'The sailing raft as a great tradition', *in* Riley 1971, 115-38.

————— 1972, '*Wa, vinta* and trimaran', *J.P.S.*, 81:2, 144-59.

————— 1974, 'Outrigger ages', *J.P.S.*, 83:12, 130-40.

Druett, H. A. 1967, 'The inhalation and retention of particles in the human respiratory system' *in* Gregory and Monteith 1967, 165-202.

Dunn, F. L. 1970, 'Cultural evolution in the late Pleistocene and Holocene of Southeast Asia', *A.A.*, 72:5, 1041-54.

Edwards, Clinton R. 1965, *Aboriginal watercraft on the Pacific coast of South America,* Ibero-Americana, 47 (Berkeley and Los Angeles).

————— 1972, 'New world perspectives on pre-European voyaging in the Pacific', *in* Barnard 1972, III, 843-87.

Eggan, Fred 1941, 'Some aspects of culture change in the northern Philippines', *A.A.*, 43, 11-18.

————— 1954, 'Some social institutions in the Mountain Province and their significance for historical and comparative studies', *Journal of East Asiatic Studies* (Manila), 3:3, 329-35.

————— 1963, 'Cultural drift and social change', *Current Anthropology*, 4:4, 347-55.

—————, Evett D. Hester and Norton S. Ginsberg (supervisors) 1956, *Area handbook on the Philippines*, 4 vols; Human Relations Area Files: Philippine Studies Program (Chicago).

Eilers, Anneliese 1935, 'Westkarolinen. I. Halbband: Songosor, Pur, Merir', *in* Thilenius 1935, vol. 9, pt 1 (II, B, 9, i).

————— 1936, 'Westkarolinen. II. Halbband: Tobi und Ngulu' *in* Thilenius 1936, vol. 9, pt 2 (II, B, 9, ii).

[Ellis, Fred] 1953, 'The O'Keefe story brought up to date', *P.I.M.*, 23:6 (Jan.), 68-9.

Ember, Melvin 1962, 'Political authority and the structure of kinship in aboriginal Samoa', *A.A.*, 64, 964-71.

Emerson, N. B. 1951, 'Biographical sketch of David Malo', *in* Malo 1951, vii-xv.

Emory, Kenneth P. 1965, *Kapingamarangi: social and religious life of a Polynesian atoll*, B. P. Bishop Museum Bulletin 228 (Honolulu).

————— 1975, *Material culture of the Tuamotu archipelago*, B. P. Bishop Museum Pacific Anthropological Records, no. 22 (Honolulu).

Erikson, Erik N. 1972, *Young man Luther: a study in psychoanalysis and history* (London; 1st pub. New York 1958).

Fages, J., F. Ravault, C. Ringon and Cl. Robineau 1970, *Tahiti et Moorea: études sur la société, l'économie et l'utilisation de l'espace*, Travaux et Documents de l'O.R.S.T.O.M. (Paris).

Fages, Jean and Thomas B. McGrath 1975, 'Tourism development in Guam and Tahiti: a comparison', *in* Force and Bishop 1975, 27-32.

Fallers, Lloyd A. 1965, *Bantu bureaucracy: a century of political evolution among the Basoga of Uganda* (Chicago and London; 1st pub. 1956).

Feuilletau de Bruyn, Willem K. H. 1920, *Schouten- en Padaido-eilanden* (Batavia).

Finney, Ben R. 1964, Polynesian peasants and proletarians: socio-economic change in the Society Islands (Cambridge, Mass.:Ph.D. thesis, Harvard University; pub. Cambridge, Mass., 1973, rev. & updated).

Firth, Raymond 1940, 'An analysis of *mana*: an empirical approach', *J.P.S.*, 49:196, 483-510 (reprinted *in* Firth 1967, 174-94).

————— 1967, *Tikopia ritual and belief* (Boston, London).

Fischer, J. L. 1961, 'The retention rate of Chamorro basic vocabulary', *Lingua* (Amsterdam), 10, 255-66.

Force, Roland W. and Brenda Bishop (eds) 1975, *The impact of urban centers in the Pacific: papers from . . . the second Inter-Congress of the Pacific Science Association . . . 1973* (Honolulu).

Fornander, Abraham 1878-85, *An account of the Polynesian race: its origin and migrations and the ancient history of the Hawaiian people . . .*, 3 vols (London; R:Vermont and Tokyo 1969).

————— 1916-20, *Fornander collection of Hawaiian antiquities and folk-lore*, ed. by Thomas G. Thrum; Memoirs of the B. P. Bishop Museum, vols IV, V (pts 1 and 2), VI (Honolulu).

Foster, George M. 1960, *Culture and conquest: America's Spanish heritage*, Viking Fund Publications in Anthropology no. 27 (New York).

Fox, Robert B. 1966, 'Ancient Filipino communities', *in* Jocano 1966, pages n.a.

Frake, Charles O. 1971, 'Lexical origins and semantic structure in Philippine Creole Spanish', *in* Hymes 1971, 223-42.

France, Peter 1966, 'The Kaunitoni migration: notes on the genesis of a Fijian tradition', *J.P.H.*, 1, 107-13.

Frazer, James G. 1925-30, *The golden bough: a study in magic and religion*, 3rd ed., 12 vols; vols I and III (London; orig. pub. 1911).

Freud, Sigmund 1959, *Collected papers*, auth. trans. under supervision of Joan Riviere, 5 vols; vol. V, ed. by James Strachey. International Psycho-Analytical Library no. 37 (New York).

Frézier, A. F. 1716-17, *Relation du voyage de la mer du sud aux côtes du Chily et du Perou, fait pendant les années 1712, 1713 & 1714* (Paris; Eng. ed. London 1717).

Friis, Herman R. (ed.) 1967, *The Pacific basin: a history of its geographical exploration*, American Geographical Society Special Pub. no. 38 (New York).

Fritz, G. 1904, 'Die Chamorro. Eine Geschichte und Ethnographie der Marianen', *Ethnologisches Notizblatt* (Berlin), 3:3, 25-110.

Funnell, William 1707, *A voyage round the world. Containing an account of Captain Dampier's expedition into the South Seas in the ship St George, in the years 1703 and 1704* (London; R:Amsterdam and New York 1969).

Gage, Thomas 1928, *The English-American: a new survey of the West Indies . . .*, ed. by A. P. Newton; Broadway Travellers ser. (London; 1st pub. 1648).

Galis, R. W. 1953, 'Geschiedenis' *in* Klein 1953-54, I, 1-65.

Galvão, Antonio 1944, *Tratado dos descobrimentos*, 3rd ed; Biblioteca Histórica de Portugal e Brasil, Série Ultramarina no. 1 (Pôrto; first pub. 1563).

García, Francisco 1683, *Vida, y martyrio de el venerable padre Diego Luis de Sanvitores de la Compania de Jésus, primer apostól de las islas Marianas, y sucesos de estas islas . . .* (Madrid; trans. by M. Higgins, *Guam Recorder*, 1938-39).

Gattey, Charles N. 1970, *Gauguin's astonishing grandmother: a biography of Flora Tristan* (London).

Gauguin, Paul 1923, *Avant et après* (Paris).

Gayangos, Don Thomas 1915, 'Journal of the *Aguila's* second expedition to Tahiti, by Lieut.-Commander Don Thomas Gayangos', *in* Corney 1913-19, II, 103-86.

Gennep, Arnold van 1960, *The rites of passage*, trans. of *Les rites de passage* by M. B. Vizedom and G. L. Caffee (London; 1st pub. Paris 1909).

Gessler, Clifford 1937, *Road my body goes* (New York; Eng. ed., *The dangerous islands*, London).

Gladwin, Thomas 1970, *East is a big bird: navigation and logic on Puluwat atoll* (Cambridge, Mass.).

Gluckman, Max 1963, *Order and rebellion in tribal Africa: collected essays with an autobiographical introduction* (London).

———— 1963, 'Succession and civil war among the Bemba—an exercise in anthropological theory', *in* his *Order and rebellion in tribal Africa*, 84-109.

———— 1965, *Politics, law and ritual in tribal society* (Chicago, Oxford).

Godelier, Maurice 1972, *Rationality and irrationality in economics*, trans. of *Rationalité et irrationalité en économie* by B. Pearce (London; 1st pub. Paris 1966).

Goldman, Irving 1970, *Ancient Polynesian society* (Chicago).

Golson, Jack 1972a, 'The Pacific Islands and their prehistoric inhabitants' *in* Ward 1972, 5-33.

———— 1972b, 'The remarkable history of Indo-Pacific man: missing chapters from every world prehistory', *J.P.H.*, 7, 5-25.

Goodenough, Ward H. 1953, *Native astronomy in the central Carolines*, University of Pennsylvania Museum Monographs (Philadelphia).

Goody, Jack 1966, 'Introduction' *in* Goody 1966, 1-56.

———— (ed.) 1966, *Succession to high office*, Cambridge Papers in Social Anthropology 4 (Cambridge).

Green, R. C. 1973, 'The conquest of the conquistadors', *World Archaeology* (London), 5:1, 14-31.

———— and M. Kelly (eds) 1970-71, *Studies in oceanic culture history*, 2 vols. Papers presented at Wenner-Gren Symposium on Oceanic Culture History, Sigatoka, Fiji, August 1969; Pacific Anthropological Records, nos 11 and 12 (Honolulu).

Gregory, Herbert E. 1930-31, *Report of the Director for 1929-30*, B. P. Bishop Museum Bulletins 78, 82 (Honolulu).

———— 1935, *Report of the Director for 1934*, B. P. Bishop Museum Bulletin 133 (Honolulu).

Gregory, P. H. and J. L. Monteith (eds) 1967, *Airborne microbes: seventeenth symposium of the Society for General Microbiology . . .* (Cambridge).

Grimble, Arthur 1921, 'From birth to death in the Gilbert Islands', *Journal of the Royal Anthropological Institute* (London), 51, 25-54.

Groube, L. M. 1971, 'Tonga, Lapita pottery and Polynesian origins', *J.P.S.*, 80:3, 278-316.

Guthrie, W. K. C. 1950, *The Greeks and their gods* (London).

Haberstroh, Charles J. Jr 1971, Melville's fathers: a study of the father substitute in Melville's fiction (Philadelphia; unpub. Ph.D. thesis, University of Pennsylvania).

Haddon, A. C. 1920, 'The outriggers of Indonesian canoes', *Journal of the Royal Anthropological Institute*, 50, 69-134.

———— 1937, 'The canoes of Melanesia, Queensland, and New Guinea' *in Canoes of Oceania*, vol. 2; B. P. Bishop Museum Special Pub. 28.

———— and James Hornell 1936-38, *Canoes of Oceania*, 3 vols; B. P. Bishop Museum Special Pubs 27-29 (Honolulu).

———— and James Hornell 1938, 'Definitions of terms, general survey, and conclusions', *in Canoes of Oceania*, vol. 3; B. P. Bishop Museum Special Pub. 29.

Haggard, Howard W. 1939, *Devils, drugs and doctors: the story of the science of healing from medicine-man to doctor* (London; 1st pub. 1929).

Hale, Horatio 1846, *United States Exploring Expedition. During the years 1838, 1839, 1840, 1841, 1842. Under the command of Charles Wilkes, U.S.N.* Vol. VI:*Ethnography and Philology* (Philadelphia).

Hammer-Purgstall, Joseph von 1834-39, 'Extracts from the *Mohi't* [i.e. Muhīt], that is the Ocean, a Turkish work on navigation in the Indian seas' [comp. by Admiral Sīdī Alī (Alī Reis ibn Husain), 1553 (1554?)], *Journal of the Asiatic Society of Bengal* (Calcutta), 3:35 (1834), 545-53; 5:56 (1836), 441-68; 6/2:70 (1837), 805-12; 7/2:81 (1838), 767-74; 8:94 (1839), 823-30.

Handy, E.S.C. and M.K. Pukui 1972, *The Polynesian family system in Ka'u, Hawaii* (Rutland and Tokyo; 1st pub. Wellington 1958).

Harding, Thomas G. 1967, *Voyagers of the Vitiaz Strait: a study of a New Guinea trade system* (Seattle).

————— and Ben H. Wallace (eds) 1970, *Cultures of the Pacific: selected readings* (New York and London).

Hart, Donn V. 1955, *The Philippine Plaza complex: a focal point in cultural change,* Yale University Southeast Asia Studies, Cultural Report Series 3 (New Haven).

Hasebe, Kotondo 1928a, 'On the islanders of Togobei (Nevil's Island)' (in Japanese), *Jinruigaku Zasshi* (Tokyo), 43, 63-9.

————— 1928b, 'The tattooing of the Micronesians' (in Japanese), *Jinruigaku Zasshi,* 43, 120-48.

————— 1938, 'The natives of the South Sea archipelago' (in Japanese), *Jinruigaku Senshigaku Kōza* (Tokyo), 1, 1-35.

Hawthorne, Nathaniel 1941, *The English notebooks,* ed. by Randall Stewart (London and New York; R:New York 1962).

Heeres, J. E. 1900, 'De Mapia-eilanden', *Tijdschrift van het Koninklijk Nederlandsch Aardrijkskundig Genootschap* (Leiden), 17, 97-105.

Held, G. J. 1957, *The Papuas of Waropen,* Koninklijk Instituut voor Taal-, Land- en Volkenkunde, Trans. ser. 2 (The Hague; 1st pub. as *Papoea's van Waropen,* 1947).

Henderson, G. C. 1931, *Fiji and the Fijians 1835-1856* (Sydney).

Hernández de Oviedo y Valdés, Gonzalo 1851-55, *Historia general y natural de las Indias, islas y tierra firme del mar Océano,* ed. by J. A. de los Ríos, 3 pts in 4 vols (Madrid; 1st 20 books orig. pub. Seville and Salamanca 1535-37).

Hezel, Francis X. 1970, 'Catholic missions in the Caroline and Marshall Islands: a survey of historical materials', *J.P.H.,* 5, 213-27.

Hides, Jack 1935, *Through wildest Papua* (Glasgow).

————— 1936, *Papuan wonderland* (London; R:Sydney 1973).

Hockin, John Pearce 1803, *A supplement to the account of the Pelew Islands* [by George Keate] . . . *from the journals of the Panther and Endeavour, two vessels sent by the Honourable East India Company to those islands in the year 1790; and from the oral communications of Captain H. Wilson* (London). N. B. Bound with Keate 1803, *q.v.*

Holden, Horace 1836, *A narrative of the shipwreck, captivity, and sufferings of Horace Holden and Benj. H. Nute; who were cast away . . . on the Pelew Islands in the year 1832 . . .* (Boston).

Hollander, J. J. de 1895-98, *Handleiding bij de beoefening der land- en volkenkunde van Nederlandsche Oost-Indië*, 2 vols; 5th ed. (Breda; 1st pub. 1861).

Hooper, Antony B. 1966, Marriage and household in two Tahitian communities (Cambridge, Mass.:unpub. Ph.D. thesis, Harvard University).

Hornell, James 1936, 'The canoes of Polynesia, Fiji, and Micronesia', *in Canoes of Oceania*, vol. 1; B. P. Bishop Museum Special Pub. 27.

————— 1943, 'The fishing and coastal craft of Ceylon', *The Mariner's Mirror* (London), 29:1, 40-53.

————— 1946a, 'The role of birds in early navigation', *Antiquity*, 20:79, 142-9.

————— 1946b, *Water transport: origins & early evolution* (Cambridge).

Howells, William 1973, *The Pacific Islanders* (London and New York).

Humboldt, Alexander von 1851-64, *Cosmos: a sketch of a physical description of the universe*, trans, from German by E. C. Otté [*et al.*]; 5 vols, vol. II (1864); Bohn Scientific Library (London; 1st pub. Stuttgart 1845-58).

Hunt, Edward E. Jr 1950, 'A view of somatology and serology in Micronesia', *American Journal of Physical Anthropology* (Philadelphia), n.s. 8:2, 157-84.

Hymes, Dell (ed.) 1971, *Pidginization and creolization of languages: proceedings of a conference at the University of the West Indies . . . 1968* (Cambridge).

Ii, John Papa 1959, *Fragments of Hawaiian history as recorded by John Papa Ii*, trans, by Mary K. Pukui, ed. by Dorothy B. Barrère (Honolulu).

Inglis, John 1887, *In the New Hebrides: reminiscences of missionary life and work, especially on the island of Aneityum, from 1850 till 1877* (London).

Inglis, K. S. 1974, *The Australian colonists: an exploration of social history 1788-1870* (Melbourne).

Iremonger, Lucille 1970, *The fiery chariot: a study of British prime ministers and the search for love* (London).

Jack-Hinton, Colin 1969, *The search for the islands of Solomon 1567-1838* (Oxford).

Jocano, F. Landa (ed.) 1966, *Filipino cultural heritage* (Manila).

————— 1967, 'Philippines at Spanish contact: an essay in ethnohistory', *in* Manuud 1967, 49-89.

[Jones, John D.] 1861, *Life and adventure in the South Pacific. By a roving printer* (New York).

Joyce, R. B. 1971, *Sir William MacGregor* (Melbourne).

Juan de la Concepción [Fr] 1788-92, *Historia general de Philipinas . . .*, 14 vols (Manila).

Jung, Emil 1899, 'Die Insel Mapia', *Deutsche Kolonialzeitung* (Berlin), 16:40, 380.

Jungmichel [J. A.] 1862, 'De St. Davids- of Mapia-eilanden, benoorden Nieuw-Guinea', *Tijdschrift voor Indische Taal-, Land- en Volkenkunde* (Batavia), 11:3rd ser. 2, 155-6.

Kaeppler, Adrienne L. 1971, 'Rank in Tonga', *Ethnology*, 10:2, 174-93.

Kakar, Sudhir 1970, 'The logic of psychohistory', review article of Erik H. Erikson: *Gandhi's truth: on the origins of militant non-violence,*

Journal of Interdisciplinary History (Cambridge, Mass.), 1:1, 187-94.

Kamakau, Samuel M. 1961, *Ruling chiefs of Hawaii* (Honolulu).

———— 1964, *Ka Po'e Kahiko: the people of old*, trans. by Mary K. Pukui, ed. by Dorothy B. Barrère; B. P. Bishop Museum Special Pub. 51 (Honolulu).

———— 1975, *Na Hana a Ka Po'e Kahiko: traditions of the people of old*, trans. by Mary K. Pukui, ed. by Dorothy B. Barrère; B. P. Bishop Museum Special Pub. 61 (Honolulu).

Keate, George, 1788/1803, *An account of the Pelew Islands, situated in the western part of the Pacific Ocean. Composed from the journals and communications of Captain Henry Wilson, and some of his officers, who, in August 1783, were there shipwrecked, in the Antelope . . .*, 1st ed.; 5th ed. 1803 (London).

Keesing, Felix M. 1945, *The South Seas in the modern world* (New York; R:rev. ed. 1972).

———— 1962, *The ethnohistory of northern Luzon* (Stanford).

Klein, W. C. (ed.) 1953-54, *Nieuw Guinea: de ontwikkeling op economisch, sociaal en cultureel gebied, in Nederlands en Australisch Nieuw Guinea*, 3 vols ('s-Gravenhage).

Kleiweg de Zwan, J. P. 1925, *De rassen van den Indischen Archipel, Ons Mooi Indië* ser. (Amsterdam).

Knights, John B. 1925, 'A journal of a voyage in the brig "Spy", of Salem, (1832-1834), John B. Knights, master', *in* Marine Research Society 1925, 168-207.

Koch, Gerd 1965, *Materielle Kultur der Gilbert-Inseln. Nonouti, Tabiteuea. Onotoa*, Veröffentlichungen des Museums für Völkerkunde, Berlin, n.F.6, Abteilung Südsee III (Berlin).

———— 1971, *Materielle Kultur de Santa Cruz-Inseln, unter besonderer Berücksichtigung der Riff-Inseln*, Veröffentlichungen des Museums für Völkerkunde, Berlin, n.F.21, Abteilung Südsee IX (Berlin).

Krämer, Augustin 1906, *Hawaii, Ostmikronesien und Samoa: meine zweite Südseereise (1897-1899) zum Studium der Atolle und ihrer Bewohner* (Stuttgart).

———— 1937, 'Zentralkarolinen.I. Halbband:Lamotrek—Gruppe—Oleai —Feis', *in* Thilenius, 1937, vol. 10, pt 1 (II, B, 10, i).

Krusenstern, I. F. von (Kruzenshtern, Ivan Fedorovich) 1819, *Beyträge zur Hydrographie der Grössern Ozeane als Erläuterungen zu einer Charte des ganzen Erdkreises nach Mercator's projection* (Leipzig).

Kubary, J. S. 1895, *Ethnographische Beiträge zur Kenntnis des Karolinen Archipels* (Leiden; orig. issued in 3 pts, 1889-95).

———— 1895, 'Notizen ueber einen Ausflug nach den westlichen Karolinen', *in* his *Ethnographische Beiträge*, 79-114.

Kuykendall, Ralph S. 1932, 'David Malo, the first superintendent of schools of the Hawaiian Kingdom', *Fortieth Annual Report of the Hawaiian Historical Society for the Year 1931* (Honolulu), 35-6.

Lach, Donald F. 1965/70, *Asia in the making of Europe*, 2 vols; vol. I bks 1 and 2 (Chicago and London).

Lambert, Bernd 1966, 'The economic activities of a Gilbertese chief' *in* Swartz, Turner and Tuden 1966, 155-72.

———— 1971, 'The Gilbert Islands: micro-individualism', *in* Crocombe 1971, 146-71.

———— 1975, 'Makin and the outside world', *in* Carroll 1975, 212-85.

Langdon, Robert A. 1969, European castaways in the Pacific before Captain Cook (Canberra; unpub. seminar paper, Dept Pacific Hist., Research School of Pacific Studies, A.N.U.).

Larkin, John A. 1972, *The Pampangans: colonial society in a Philippine province* (Berkeley).

Lātūkefu, Sione 1974, *Church and state in Tonga: the Wesleyan Methodist missionaries and political development, 1822-1875* (Canberra).

Laufer, Carl 1951, 'Erstgeburtsfeiern auf dem westlichen Neubritannien', *Anthropos*, 46, 200-8.

Lawrence, P. and M. J. Meggitt (eds) 1965, *Gods ghosts and men in Melanesia: some religions of Australian New Guinea and the New Hebrides* (Melbourne).

Leach, Edmund R. 1954, *Political systems of highland Burma: a study of Kachin social structure* (Cambridge, Mass.).

Leahy, Michael J. and Maurice Crain 1937, *The land that time forgot: adventures and discoveries in New Guinea* (New York and London).

Lebedev, Dimitri M. and Vadim I. Grekov 1967, 'Geographical exploration by the Russians' *in* Friis 1967, 170-200.

Lecker, George T. 1938, Lahainaluna 1813-1877, a study of the history of Hawaii's pioneer educational institution (Honolulu:unpub. M.A. thesis, University of Hawaii).

Lee, Ida 1920, *Captain Bligh's second voyage to the South Sea* (London and New York).

Le Gentil de la Galaisière, G. J. H. 1779-81, *Voyage dans les mers de l'Inde . . . à l'occasion du passage de Vénus . . . 1761, & . . . 1769*, 2 vols (Paris; R:Manila 1964, trans. as *A Voyage to the Indian Seas*).

Legge, J. D. 1958, *Britain in Fiji 1858-1880* (London).

Le Gobien, Charles 1700, *Histoire des isles Marianes, nouvellement converties à la religion Chrétienne; & de la mort glorieuse des premiers missionnaires qui y ont prêché la foy* (Paris).

Lessa, William A. 1962, 'An evaluation of early descriptions of Carolinian culture', *Ethnohistory* (Bloomington, Ind.), 9:4, 313-403.

———— 1966, *Ulithi: a Micronesian design for living* (New York).

———— 1975, *Drake's Island of Thieves: ethnological sleuthing* (Honolulu).

———— and Tracy Lay 1953, 'The sociology of Ulithi atoll', *American Journal of Physical Anthropology*, n.s.11, 405-12.

Levison, Michael, R. Gerard Ward and John H. Webb 1973, *The settlement of Polynesia: a computer simulation* (Canberra and Minneapolis).

Lewis, David 1972, *We the navigators: the ancient art of landfinding in the Pacific* (Canberra).

———— 1974, 'Voyaging stars: aspects of Polynesian and Micronesian astronomy', *Philosophical Transactions of the Royal Society* (London), Ser. A, 276, 113-48.

Lewthwaite, Gordon R. 1967, 'Geographical knowledge of the Pacific peoples', *in* Friis 1967, 57-86.

Lieber, Michael D. (ed.) 1977, *Exiles and migrants in Oceania*, Association for Social Anthropology in Oceania Monograph (Honolulu).

Ling, Shun-Sheng 1956, 'Formosan sea-going raft and its origin in ancient China' (in Chinese), *Bulletin of the Institute of Ethnology Academia Sinica* (Taipei), 1, 1-23; Eng. trans. 25-54.

———— 1968, 'Outrigger canoes in ancient China and the Indo-Pacific Ocean' (in Chinese), *Bulletin of the Institute of Ethnology Academia Sinica*, 26, 1-25; Eng. summary 26-8.

———— 1969, 'The double canoe and deck[ed] canoe in ancient China and Oceania' (in Chinese), *Bulletin of the Institute of Ethnology Academia Sinica*, 28, 233-61; Eng. summary 262-72.

Linton, Ralph 1926, *Ethnology of Polynesia and Micronesia*, Field Museum of Natural History Guide, Pt 6 (Chicago).

Loeb, Edwin M. 1926, *History and traditions of Niue*, B. P. Bishop Museum Bulletin 32 (Honolulu; R:New York 1971).

Lundsgaarde, Henry P. 1968, 'Some transformations in Gilbertese law, 1892-1966', *J.P.H.*, 3, 117-30.

———— 1970, 'Law and politics on Nonouti Island' *in* Harding and Wallace 1970, 240-64.

———— and Martin G. Silverman 1972, 'Category and group in Gilbertese kinship: an updating of Goodenough's analysis', *Ethnology* (Pittsburgh), 11:2, 95-110.

Lutké, Frédéric (Litke, Fedor Petrovich, also Lütke) 1835-36, *Voyage autour du monde exécuté par ordre de Sa Majesté l'Empereur Nicolas 1er, sur la corvette le Séniavine dans les années 1826, 1827, 1828 et 1829*, 4 vols (Paris).

McArthur, Norma 1967, *Island populations of the Pacific* (Canberra).

———— 1974, Population and prehistory: the late phase on Aneityum (Canberra: unpub. Ph.D. thesis, A.N.U.).

MacCallum, Thomson Murray 1934, *Adrift in the South Seas: including adventures with Robert Louis Stevenson* (Los Angeles).

Macdonald, Barrie 1971, Policy and practice in an atoll territory: British rule in the Gilbert and Ellice Islands, 1892-1970 (Canberra: unpub. Ph.D. thesis, A.N.U.).

McGlone, Robert E. 1975, 'The new orthodoxy in psychohistory', *Group for the Use of Psychology in History Newsletter* (Stony Brook, N.Y.), 4:2, 4-9.

Mackie, J. D. 1964, *A history of Scotland* (Baltimore, Md; Harmondsworth, Middlesex).

Malinowski, Bronislaw 1944, *A scientific theory of culture, and other essays* . . . (Chapel Hill, N.C.).

Mallat de Bassilan, Jean Baptiste 1846, *Les Philippines: histoire, géographie, moeurs, agriculture, industrie et commerce des colonies espagnoles dans l'Océanie*, 2 vols (Paris).

Malo, David 1951, *Hawaiian antiquities (Moolelo Hawaii)*, B. P. Bishop Museum Special Pub. 2, 2nd ed.; trans. from Hawaiian by N. B. Emerson, 1898 (Honolulu).

Manuud, Antonio G. (ed.) 1967, *Brown heritage: essays on Philippine cultural tradition and literature* (Quezon City).

Marine Research Society 1925, *The sea, the ship and the sailor: tales of adventure from log books and original narratives*, Pubs of the Marine Research Society, VIII (Salem, Mass.).

Marsden, Peter 1972, 'Ships of the Roman period and after in Britain', *in* Bass 1972, 113-32.

Marstrander, Sverre 1963, *Østfolds jordbruksristninger: Skjeberg*, 2 vols; Instituttet for Sammenlignende Kulturforskning. Serie B: Skrifter, 53 (Oslo).

Martin, John 1827, *An account of the natives of the Tonga Islands . . . from the extensive communications of Mr William Mariner*, 2 vols (Edinburgh; 1st pub. London 1817).

Martin, K. 1894, *Reisen in den Molukken, in Ambon, den Uliassern, Seran (Ceram) und Buru: eine Schilderung von Land und Leuten* [*Geologischer Theil*, 1903] (Leiden).

Martínez de Zúñiga, Joaquín 1973, *Status of the Philippines in 1800* (Manila; trans. of *Estadismo de las Islas Filipinas*, 1st pub. Madrid 1893).

Marx, Karl 1967, *Capital: a critique of political theory*, ed. by Frederick Engels; 3 vols (New York:1st pub. Hamburg 1867-94 as *Das Kapital. Kritik der politischen Oekonomie*).

Mathews, R. H. 1908, 'Aboriginal navigation', *Queensland Geographical Journal* (Brisbane), n.s., 23:9, 66-81.

Maude, H. C. and H. E. 1932, 'The social organization of Banaba or Ocean Island, Central Pacific', *J.P.S.*, 41:4, 262-301; reprinted *in* Silverman 1971.

Maude, H. E. 1963, *The evolution of the Gilbertese Boti: an ethno-historical interpretation*, Memoirs of the Polynesian Society, no. 35 (Wellington).

———— 1964, 'Beachcombers and castaways', *J.P.S.*, 73:3, 254-93; also *in* Maude 1968.

———— 1967, 'The swords of Gabriel: a study in participant history', *J.P.H.*, 2, 113-36.

———— 1968, *Of islands and men: studies in Pacific history* (Melbourne).

———— 1971, 'Pacific history—past, present and future', *J.P.H.*, 6, 3-24.

———— and Ida Leeson 1965, 'The coconut oil trade of the Gilbert Islands', *J.P.S.*, 74:4, 396-437.

Mauss, Marcel 1970, *The gift: forms and functions of exchange in archaic societies*, trans. of *Essai sur le don, forme archaïque de l'échange* by I. Cunnison (London; 1st pub. Paris 1925).

Mazlish, Bruce 1974, 'Psychiatry and history', *in* Arieti 1974, I, 1034-45.

Meares, John 1790, *Voyages made in the years 1788 and 1789, from China to the north west coast of America . . .* (London; R:Amsterdam and New York 1967).

Medina, J. T. 1914, *El descubrimiento del Océano Pacífico: Vasco Núñez de Balboa, Hernando de Magallanes y sus compañeros*, 3 vols; vol. I, *Núñez de Balboa* (Santiago de Chile).

Meinicke, Carl E. 1875-76, *Die Inseln des stillen Oceans, eine geographische Monographie*, 2 vols (Leipzig; R:Amsterdam, 1969).

Miklouho-Maclay, N. von 1878, 'Die Insel Wuap', *Globus* (Hildburghausen, Germ.), 33:3, 40-5. (Original article cites author as 'Miklucho-Maclay.')

Montero y Vidal, D. José 1887-95, *Historia general de Filipinas: desde el descubrimiento de dichas islas hasta nuestro dias*, 3 vols (Madrid).

Morga, Antonio de 1909, *Sucesos de las islas Filipinas* (Madrid; 1st pub. 1609; R:Cambridge (trans.), 1868, 1971).

Moulton, J. Egan and W. F. 1921, *Moulton of Tonga* (London).

Murillo Velarde, Pedro 1749, *Historia de la provincia de Philipinas de la Compañia de Jesús* (Manila).

Needham, Joseph, with Wang Ling 1959, *Science and civilisation in China*, vol. 3: *Mathematics and the sciences of the heaven and the earth* (Cambridge: R:1970).

————, with Wang Ling and Lu Gwei-Djen 1971, *Science and civilisation in China*, vol. 4, pt III: *Civil engineering and nautics* (Cambridge).

Neuhaus, Karl 1962, *Beiträge zur Ethnographie der Pala, Mittel-Neu-Irland*, Kölner Ethnologische Mitteilungen, 2 (Köln).

Newbury, Colin 1956, The administration of French Oceania 1842-1906 (Canberra: unpub. Ph.D. thesis, A.N.U.).

N[ieuwenhuis, A. W.] 1919, 'De Alfoeren van Halmaheira', *Indië* (Haarlem), 3:14, 227.

Nilles, John 1953, 'The Kuman people: a study of cultural change in a primitive society in the Central Highlands of New Guinea', pts 1 and 2, *Oceania*, 24:1 and 2, 1-27 and 119-31.

Nooteboom, C. 1932, *De boomstamkano in Indonesie* (Leiden).

Nowell, Charles E. (ed.) 1962, *Magellan's voyage around the world: three contemporary accounts* (Evanston, Ill.).

O'Brien, Frederick 1921, *Mystic isles of the South Seas* (New York).

O'Connell, James F. 1972, *A residence of eleven years in New Holland and the Caroline Islands*, ed. by Saul H. Riesenberg; Pacific History Series no. 4 (Canberra).

Olive y García, Francisco 1887, *Islas Marianas . . .* (Manila).

Oliver, Douglas L. 1961, *The Pacific Islands*, rev. ed. (New York; 1st pub. Cambridge, Mass. 1951).

———— 1974, *Ancient Tahitian society*, 3 vols; vol. II (Honolulu; Canberra 1975).

Ollman, Bertell 1971, *Alienation: Marx's conception of man in capitalist society*, Cambridge Studies in the History and Theory of Politics (Cambridge).

Osbourne, Lloyd 1924, *An intimate portrait of R.L.S.* (New York).

Palm, C. H. M. 1962, 'Vaartuigen en visvangst van Anjor Lor, Bantam, West-Java', *Bijdragen tot de Taal-, Land- en Volkenkunde* (The Hague), 118:2, 217-70.

Pambrun, Henri 1958, *Le régime foncier dans les territoires d'outre mer et en Polynésie française* (Papeete).

Panoff, Michel 1964, *Les structures agraires en Polynésie française: rapport d'une mission effectuée dans le cadre de la Recherche Scientifique et Technique d'Outre Mer 1961-1963*, École Pratique des Hautes Études, V° et VI° Sections, Centre Documentaire pour l'Océanie, Rapports et Documents 1 (Paris).

———— 1970, *La terre et l'organisation sociale en Polynésie*, Bibliothèque Scientifique: Collection Science de l'Homme (Paris).

Patterson, George 1882, *Missionary life among the cannibals: being the life of the Rev. John Geddie, D.D., first missionary to the New Hebrides . . .* (Toronto).

Pawley, Andrew 1967, 'The relationships of Polynesian outlier languages', *J.P.S.*, 76:3, 259-96.

———— and Kaye Green 1971, 'Lexical evidence for the proto-Polynesian homeland', *Te Reo: Proceedings of the Linguistic Society of New Zealand* (Auckland), 14, 1-35.

Perkin, Harold 1969, *The origins of modern English society 1780-1880* (London and Toronto).

Phillip, Arthur 1789, 1790, *The voyage of Governor Phillip to Botany Bay; with an account of the establishment of the colonies of Port Jackson & Norfolk Island . . . to which are added the journals of Lieuts. Shortland, Watts, Ball, & Capt. Marshall . . .;* 1st ed., 1789; 2nd ed. 1790 (London).

Pigafetta, Antonio 1962, 'First voyage around the world' *in* Nowell 1962, 85-268.

Pike, Kenneth L. 1971, *Language in relation to a unified theory of the structure of human behavior,* 2nd rev. ed.; Janua Linguarum, Series Major, no. 551 (The Hague and Paris; 1st pub. 1954-60).

Pirie, Peter 1972, 'Population growth in the Pacific islands: the example of Western Samoa', *in* Ward 1972, 189-218.

Prinsep, James 1836, 'Note on the nautical instruments of the Arabs', *Journal of the Asiatic Society of Bengal*, 5:60, 784-94.

———— 1838, 'Note . . .' [on 'Extracts from the *Mohi't*', trans. by Joseph von Hammer-Purgstall], *Journal of the Asiatic Society of Bengal*, 7/2:81, 774-80.

Radford, Robin 1972, 'Missionaries, miners and administrators in the Eastern Highlands', *Journal of the Papua & New Guinea Society*, 6:2, 85-106.

Read, K. E. 1955, 'Morality and the concept of the person among the Gahuku-Gama', *Oceania*, 25:4, 233-82.

Reader, W. J. 1966, *Professional men: the rise of the professional classes in nineteenth-century England* (London).

Reay, Marie 1964, 'Present-day politics in the New Guinea Highlands', *A.A.*, 66 (spec. issue), 240.

Reinman, Fred M. 1968, 'Guam prehistory: a preliminary field report' *in* Yawata and Sinoto 1968, 41-50.

Remy, Jules 1862, *Ka mooolelo Hawaii: histoire de l'Archipel Havaiien (Iles Sandwich): texte et traduction* [of *Mooolelo Hawaii (Histoire Havaiienne)*] *précédés d'une introduction sur l'état physique, moral et politique du pays . . .* (Paris and Leipzig).

Riedel, Johan G. F. 1886, *De sluik- en kroesharige rassen tusschen Selebes en Papua* ('s-Gravenhage).

Riesenberg, Saul H. and A. H. Gayton 1952, 'Caroline Island belt weaving', *Southwestern Journal of Anthropology* (Albuquerque, N.M.), 8:3, 342-75.

Riesenfeld, Alphonse 1950, *The megalithic culture of Melanesia*, 2 vols (Leiden).

Riley, Carrol L. *et al.* (eds) 1971, *Man across the sea: problems of pre-Columbian contacts* (Austin and London).

Rodríguez, Máximo 1919, 'The diary of Máximo Rodríguez', *in* Corney 1913-19, III, 1-210.

Roe, Michael 1974, *Kenealy and the Tichborne cause: a study in mid-Victorian populism* (Melbourne).

Rosenberg, Sidney 1954, Black sheep and golden fleece: a study of nineteenth century English attitudes toward Australian colonials (New York: unpub. Ph.D. thesis, Columbia University).

Ross, W. A. 1969, 'The Catholic mission in the western Highlands', *in The History of Melanesia: papers delivered at a seminar sponsored jointly by the University of Papua New Guinea, the Australia National University, the Administrative College of Papua and New Guinea, and the Council of New Guinea Affairs* . . . (Canberra and Port Moresby), 319-27.

Rutherford, Noel 1971, *Shirley Baker and the King of Tonga* (Melbourne).

Sabatier, Ernest 1939, *Sous l'équateur du Pacifique: les îles Gilbert et la mission Catholique, 1888-1938* (Paris).

————— 1954, *Dictionnaire Gilbertin-Français* (Tabuiroa, Gilbert Is.; Eng. trans. 1971).

Safford, William E. 1902, 'Guam and its people', *A.A.*, 4, 707-29.

————— 1905, *The useful plants of the island of Guam, with an introductory account of the physical features and natural history of the island, of the character and history of its people, and of their agriculture*, U.S. National Museum: Bulletin:U.S. National Herbarium, Contributions, vol. IX (Washington).

Sahlins, Marshall 1972, *Stone age economics* (Chicago and New York; R:London 1974).

————— 1972, 'The spirit of the gift', *in his Stone age economics*, 149-83.

Saito, Shiro 1972, *Philippine ethnography: a critically annotated and selected bibliography* (Honolulu).

Salisbury, Richard F. 1964, 'Despotism and Australian administration in the New Guinea Highlands', *A.A.*, 66 (spec. issue), 225.

————— 1965, 'The Siane of the Eastern Highlands', *in* Lawrence and Meggitt 1965, 50-77.

Sande, G. A. J. van der 1907, *Ethnography and anthropology*. Vol. 3 of *Nova Guinea: uitkomsten der Nederlandsche Nieuw-Guinea-Expeditie in 1903 onder leiding van Dr. Arthur Wichmann* (Leiden).

Scarr, Deryck 1973, *The majesty of colour: a life of Sir John Bates Thurston*. Vol. 1: *I, the very bayonet* (Canberra).

Schaefer, Alphons 1938, 'Kavagl, "der Mann mit der Zaunpfahlkeule": ein Beitrag zur Individuenforschung', *Anthropos*, 33, 107-13.

Schneider, David M. 1968, *American kinship: a cultural account*, Anthropology of Modern Societies ser. (Englewood Cliffs, N.J.).

Sharp, Andrew 1960, *The discovery of the Pacific Islands* (Oxford).

Shaw, Joseph W. 1972, 'Greek and Roman harbourworks', *in* Bass 1972, 87-112.

Shutler, Richard Jr 1971, 'Pacific Island radiocarbon dates: an over-view' *in* Green and Kelly 1970-71, II, 13-27.

Silverman, Martin G. 1970, 'Banaban adoption', *in* Carroll 1970, 209-35.

————— 1971, *Disconcerting issue: meaning and struggle in a resettled Pacific community* (Chicago and London).

————— 1977, 'Making sense', *in* Lieber 1977, pages n.a.

Simpson, Colin 1954, *Adam in plumes* (Sydney).

Sinoto, Yosihiko H. 1970, 'An archaeologically based assessment of the Marquesas as a dispersal center in East Polynesia', *in* Green and Kelly 1970-71, I, 105-32.

Souter, Gavin 1963, *New Guinea: the last unknown* (Sydney; R:1974).

Southall, Aidan W. 1956, *Alur society: a study in processes and types of domination* (Cambridge).

Spate, O. H. K. 1965, *Let me enjoy: essays, partly geographical* (Canberra).

Speaight, George 1955, *The history of the English puppet theatre* (London).

Spoehr, Alexander 1954, *Saipan: the ethnology of a war-devastated island,* Fieldiana, vol. 14 (Chicago).

Stevenson, Fanny 1914, *The cruise of the "Janet Nichol" among the South Sea Islands; a diary by Mrs. Robert Louis Stevenson* (New York).

———— and Robert Louis 1955, *Our Samoan adventure: with a three year diary by Mrs. Stevenson now published for the first time together with rare photographs from family albums,* ed. by Charles Neider (New York; London 1956).

Stevenson, Robert Louis 1892, *A footnote to history: eight years of trouble in Samoa* (London; R:London 1967).

———— 1900, *In the South Seas: being an account of experiences and observations in the Marquesas, Paumotus and Gilbert Islands . . .* (London; 1st pub. New York 1899. R:Honolulu 1971).

Stokes, John F. G. 1931, 'Origin of the condemnation of Captain Cook in Hawaii: a study in cause and effect', *Thirty-Ninth Annual Report of the Hawaiian Historical Society for the Year 1930 . . .,* 68-104.

Strout, Cushing 1968, 'Ego psychology and the historian', *History and Theory* (The Hague), 7:3, 281-97.

Suzuki, Makoto 1953, 'On the constitution of aborigines in Geelvink Bay, West New Guinea', *Proceedings of the Seventh Pacific Science Congress* (Auckland and Christchurch 1949), vol. 7 (Christchurch).

Swartz, Marc J., Victor W. Turner and Arthur Tuden (eds) 1966, *Political anthropology* (Chicago).

Taylor, E. G. R. 1971, *The haven-finding art: a history of navigation from Odysseus to Captain Cook* (London; 1st pub. 1956).

Tetens, Alfred 1958, *Among the savages of the South Seas: memoirs of Micronesia, 1862-1868,* trans. from German by Florence M. Spoehr (Stanford, Calif.).

Thilenius, G. (ed.) 1935-38, *Ergebnisse der Südsee—Expedition 1908-1910,* vols 9-10 (Hamburg).

Thompson, F. M. L. 1963, *English landed society in the nineteenth century* (London and Toronto).

Thompson, Laura 1947, *Guam and its people* (Princeton; R:Westport, Conn. 1969).

Thomson, Basil 1902, *Savage Island: an account of a sojourn in Niué and Tonga* (London).

———— 1937, *The scene changes* (New York; London 1939).

Throckmorton, Peter 1972, 'Romans on the sea' *in* Bass 1972, 65-86.

Thrum, Thomas G. 1918, 'Brief sketch of the life and labors of S. M.

Kamakau, Hawaiian historian', *Twenty-sixth Annual Report of the Hawaiian Historical Society for the Year 1917* . . ., 40-61.

Topping, Douglas M., with B. C. Dungca 1973, *Chamorro reference grammar* (Honolulu).

Toynbee, Arnold J. 1934, *A study of history*, vols 1-3; vol. I (London).

Tregear, Edward 1901, 'The Mapia Islands', *J.P.S.*, 10:37, 50 (Eng. summary of Heeres 1900).

Turner, George 1861, *Nineteen years in Polynesia: missionary life, travels, and researches in the islands of the Pacific* (London).

———— 1884, *Samoa: a hundred years ago and long before* . . . (London).

Tyrrell, D. A. J. 1967, 'The spread of viruses of the respiratory tract by the airborne route', *in* Gregory and Monteith 1967, 286-306.

Underwood, Jane H. 1973, 'Population history of Guam; context of microevolution', *Micronesica* (Agana, Guam), 9:1, 11-44.

Waldegrave, W. 1833, 'Extracts from a private journal kept on board H.M.S. *Seringapatam* in the Pacific 1830', *Journal of the Royal Geographic Society*, 3, 168-96.

Ward, R. Gerard (ed.) 1967, *American activities in the Central Pacific 1790-1870* . . ., 8 vols; vols III, V, VI, (Ridgewood, N.J.).

———— (ed.) 1972, *Man in the Pacific Islands: essays on geographical change in the Pacific Islands* (Oxford).

Watts, [John] 1790, 'Lieutenant Watts's narrative of the return of the Lady Penrhyn transport, containing an account of the death of Omai, and other interesting particulars at Otaheite', Chap. XXI *in* Phillip 1790, 233-56.

Werbner, Richard P. 1967, 'Federal administration, rank, and civil strife among Bemba royals and nobles', *Africa* (London), 37:1, 22-49.

West, F. J. 1956, 'Colonial development in Central New Guinea', *Pacific Affairs* (Vancouver), 29:2, 161-73.

———— 1958, 'Indigenous labour in Papua-New Guinea', *International Labour Review* (Geneva), 77, 89-112.

———— 1968, *Hubert Murray: the Australian pro-consul* (Melbourne).

———— 1972, 'Papua New Guinea: Australian policy reviewed', *Current Affairs Bulletin* (Sydney), 49:1, 2-14.

West, Thomas 1865, *Ten years in South-Central Polynesia: being reminiscences of a personal mission to the Friendly Islands and their dependencies* (London).

White, Carmel 1967, 'Early stone axes in Arnhem Land', *Antiquity*, 41:162, 149-52.

Wichmann, Arthur 1900, 'Die Mapia- oder Bunai-Inseln', *Petermanns Mitteilungen aus Justus Perthes' Geographischer Anstalt* (Gotha, Germ.), 46, 66-9.

Wilkes, Charles 1845, *Narrative of the United States Exploring Expedition. During the years 1838, 1839, 1840, 1841, 1842*, 5 vols (Philadelphia; 1st pub. 1844).

Willis, I. 1969, 'Who was first? The first white man into the New Guinea Highlands', *Journal of the Papua & New Guinea Society*, 3:1, 32-45.

Wilson, James *et al.* 1799, *A missionary voyage to the Southern Pacific Ocean performed in the years 1796, 1797, 1798 in the Duff, commanded by Captain J. Wilson. Compiled from the journals of the officers and the missionaries* . . . (London).

Wirz, P. 1925, 'Zur Anthropologie der Biaker, Nuforesen und der Bewohner des Hinterlandes der Doreh-Bai', *Archiv für Anthropologie* (Brunswick, Germ.), n.s. 20, H2/4, 185-215.

Wood, C. F. 1875, *A yachting cruise in the South Seas* (London).

Yawata, I. and Y. H. Sinoto (eds) 1968, *Prehistoric culture in Oceania: a symposium*, Eleventh Pacific Science Congress, Tokyo 1966 (Honolulu).

Zamora, Mario D. and José Y. Arcellana (eds) 1971, *A bibliography of Philippine anthropology*, Supp. Series I of *Verge*, vol. 3 pt 2 (Baguio' City, Philippines).

Zúñiga, Joaquín Martínez de, see Martínez de Zúñiga, Joaquín.

Contributors

ANN CHOWNING, Professor of Anthropology, The University of Papua New Guinea

MALCOLM CHUN, Student in Hawaiian studies, University of Hawaii

GAVAN DAWS, Professor of Pacific History, The Australian National University

GREG DENING, Professor of History, University of Melbourne

KENNETH P. EMORY, Senior Anthropologist, Bernice P. Bishop Museum, Honolulu

BEN R. FINNEY, Associate Professor of Anthropology, University of Hawaii

NORAH FORSTER, Senior Research Assistant in Pacific History, The Australian National University

DEREK FREEMAN, Professor of Anthropology, Pacific Studies, The Australian National University

NIEL GUNSON, Fellow in Pacific History, The Australian National University

FRANCIS X. HEZEL, Director of the Micronesian Seminar, Truk

RUBY JOHNSON, Assistant Professor of Hawaiian, University of Hawaii

ADRIENNE L. KAEPPLER, Anthropologist, Bernice P. Bishop Museum, Honolulu

BERND LAMBERT, Associate Professor of Anthropology, Cornell University

ROBERT LANGDON, Executive Officer, Pacific Manuscripts Bureau, The Australian National University

WILLIAM A. LESSA, Professor Emeritus of Anthropology, University of California

DAVID LEWIS, Senior Research Fellow, East West Center, Honolulu

HENRY P. LUNDSGAARDE, Professor of Anthropology, The University of Kansas

KATHARINE LUOMALA, Professor Emeritus of Anthropology, University of Hawaii

NORMA McARTHUR, Senior Research Fellow in The Research School of Pacific Studies, The Australian National University

EDITH McKINZIE, Student in Hawaiian studies, University of Hawaii

DOUGLAS OLIVER, Professor of Anthropology, University of Hawaii

DOROTHY SHINEBERG, Reader in History, Faculty of Arts, The Australian National University

MARTIN G. SILVERMAN, Associate Professor of Anthropology, The University of Western Ontario

O. H. K. SPATE, Professor in The Research School of Pacific Studies, The Australian National University

ALEXANDER SPOEHR, Professor of Anthropology, Faculty of Arts, University of Pittsburgh

FRANCIS WEST, Dean of Social Sciences and Professor of History and Government, Deakin University, Geelong

Index of Personal Names and Titles

Titles and honorifics are in italics. Prefixes are incorporated in surnames where usage permits as in Anglicized European names and some French surnames.

Subject Index

Numbers in bold characters refer to detailed references.

343

Subject Index

349

pahi, 50
Palau, 47, 230, 240, 261-5, 271-2
Pampanga, 250
Pangai, 181, 183, 186-7, 189, 201
Papua, 4, 58, 215, 220-2
Papuans, 231, 233-4, 236-7, 243
patuiki, 155-6
Pearl Harbor, 12-13
Pegun, 228
Pentecost Island, 58-9
Peru, 37, 53
Peruvian slave trade, 137, 163n
Philippines, 34, 37, 46-7, 50, 52-3, 247-51, 254-60
Phoenix Islands, 1-2, 8-10, 14, 16
phosphate industry, 4-5, 12, 32, 94, 104-6
physical appearance of Islanders, 231-2, 235-8, 244
Pidgin English, 203-4
Piken Island, 244
Pikina, 135
Pilolevu College, Ha'apai, 191
Pingelap, 268
Pitcairn Island, 10-13, 36, 39, 303
planters, 252; *see also* crops
Pleasant Island, *see* Nauru
polygamy, 223
Polynesia, 17, 42, 46-63, 81-2, 110, 128-30, 144-5, 147, 150, 152-4, 157, 159, 188, 199, 228, 231-2, 235-43, 252, 274, 292, 296, 303-4
Ponape, 244-5, 261-2, 265-72
pongipongi, 179, 187-90
population figures, Aneityum, 276, 278, 282; Buariki village, 69-70; Butaritari, 82; Guam, 254; Mapia, 230, 234; Napuka, 128; Puamau, 139; beachcombers on Kusaie, 269-70; Ponape, 267
Port Moresby, 16
Portuguese, 268
Puamau, 139
pue raatira, see raatira
Pukapuka, 13, 61
Pulo Anna, 233, 239, 243, 246
Puluwat, 62
Pumatehati, 130-1, 133
Purari, 219-20

Queen Sālote College, 180, 184

raatira, 114, 126
Rabi, 12-14, 94n, 103-4, 109
rahui, 112-13
Raiatea, 114, 121, 292
rainmaking, 155, 157-8
Rakahanga, 13
Ramu valley, 216
Rarotonga, 13
Rebiamul, 217
reciprocity, 76, 126, 199, 257-8
relationships, **94-109**; *see also* kinship

religious beliefs, traditional, 61, 83, 110-13, 118, 131, 134-8, 142-61, 163, 166, 181, 185, 196, 206, 222, 279, 285-6, 289-90, 293-4, 313; *see also* Christianity
remittance men, 301-2
Rennell Island, 58
retaliation, 67, 83-4, 142, 149, 155-8, 218
ritual kinship, 257
ritual system, 98-9; *see also* ceremonies, ceremonial objects
Ro'on, 239
Rota, 38, 241, 253
Rotuma, 36, 270
Royal Colonial Institute, 214
Royal Hawaiian Agricultural Society, 313
Royal Hawaiian Historical Society, 314-15

Sa'anapu, 163, 165-7, 171
Saar, 240
Sabbath observance, 75, 155
sail types, claw (Hawaiian, Marquesan, Reef Island, Mailu), 57 (fig.), 58-9, 65-6; Tahitian half-claw, 57 (fig.), 58; lateen (Indian Ocean, Indonesian boomed, Mediterranean, Polynesian), 54, 55 (fig.), 56, 58; Samoan *soatau*, 56, 57 (fig.), 58; square sail, classical Egyptian, 53-4, 55 (fig.); canted, 53-4, 55 (fig.)
St David's Islands, *see* Mapia Islands
Saipan, 38, 62-3
Salamaua, 218
Salawtai, 238-9
Samoa, 39, 47, 50, 52, 55-6, 61, 67, 71, 146, 154, **163-73**, 184, 186, 238-40, 275, 296, 299-300, 302
San Cristobal, 4, 39
sandalwood trade, 136, 275-6, 280, 310
Sandwich Islands, *see* Hawaii
sanitation, 221, 225
Santa Ana, 4
Santa Cruz Reef Islands, 47, 59, 61, 65-6
Satawal, 62-3, 262
schools, 75, 116, 126, 180, 184, 191, 213, 216, 276-8, 280-2, 309, 311, 313
Schouten Islands, 227, 233, 238, 242-3
Sepik river, 215, 221
settlers, *see* expatriate Europeans
shamans, 154-5, 158
ships: *Aguila*, 273; *Akaroa*, 10; *Albion*, 265; *America*, 136; *Antelope*, 261-4; *Australian*, 265; *Bordelais*, 136; *Bounty*, 10; *Carnatic*, 229; *Cavalier*, 269; *Comus*, 265; *Coquette*, 136; *Coquille*, 265; *Cumbrian*, 229; *Daedalus*, 135; *Dash*, 262-3; *Duff*, 262, 264; *Eleanor*, 229, 234; *Eliza*, 267; *Essex*, 136; *Espiègle*, 264; *Eugenie*,

140°
160°
20°
MARIANA IS
Guam
M I C R O N E S I
Ulithi
Yap
Ngulu
Palau
Truk
Ponape
Kusai
C A R O L I N E I S
Kapingamarangi
Mapia
0°
Manus
Jayapura (Hollandia)
New Ireland
Aitape
Rabaul
Irian Jaya
Willaumez Peninsula
Mt Hagen
NEW GUINEA
Goroka
New Britain
SOLOMON IS
Lae
Papua New Guinea
Port Moresby
Honiara
Tulagi
Rennell
M E L A N
20°
NEW CALEDONI
A U S T R A L I A
140°
160°